JUDICIAL SYSTEM IN ISLAM

WORLD OF ISLAM, VOL. - 7

JUDICIAL SYSTEM IN ISLAM

By

Dr. M.I. Navaid

D P H

DISCOVERY PUBLISHING HOUSE PVT. LTD.
NEW DELHI-110 002

First Published-2010

ISBN: 978-81-8356-534-9

Published by:
DISCOVERY PUBLISHING HOUSE PVT. LTD.
4831/24, Ansari Road, Prahlad Street
Darya Ganj, New Delhi-110002 (India)
Phone: 23279245, 43764432 • Fax: 91-11-23253475
E-mail: parul.wasan@gmail.com • dphbooks@rediffmail.com
web: www.discoverypublishinggroup.com

Printed at:
Sachin Printers
Delhi

Preface

The moment, the term 'Islam' confronts someone, a world of far-stretching frontiers starts embossing in one's imagination. Islamic culture and civilization took birth about fourteen centuries ago in the lap of the Arabian desert. A piece of land—covered out-and-out by the blanket of ignorance, cruelty and long-harboured grudges and differences with regard to caste, creed and colour—gave birth to an apostle of mercy and kindness, love and affection, at a time, when the intensity of inhuman acts – stone melting and heart-rending barbarity – reached its peak. A nation which was always at daggers drawn over petty matters, and which knew not how to bow out of pride and ignorance, is now among the loftiest and noblest people in the world – the Arabs. This overall transformation from enmity to brotherhood, cruelty to kindness and pride to passionate submission is one of those live miracles of the last Messenger and Prophet of the Almighty, Hadrat Muhammad (Pbuh) which has left whole of the world stunned. Presently, a world in itself, Islamic world comprises more than fifty countries.

Islam is not only a religion but also a complete code of conduct. As per the Quranic injunctions, Islam is the only religion which Allah, the Almighty, gifted to mankind to enable people to live a successful life, both here and hereafter. Different Prophets and Messengers (Pbut) brought Islam for their respective people as per their requirements, keeping pace with evolving growth and progress of human civilization. Thus, passing from the earliest generation of man onto the times of Prophet Muhammad (Pbuh), Islam reached the mark of completion and consummation, having the best from all its preceding versions. That's why it's incumbent upon every Muslim that he should respect, along with Islam, all earlier religions, which came before Islam and feel the same reverence in his heart for all the Prophets, regardless, when and where they came on the scene.

Since the inception of Islam, down to the present hour, men of exceptional qualities came in this world, who held high the banner of Islam and promoted the cause thereof unflinchingly, heart and soul. They left no stone unturned in teaching and convincing their people how to lead a happy and moderate life here, a prosperous one hereafter and how to make the best of the opportunities granted to them by Allah, the Almighty. It is also Islam, which gave humanity the gift of democracy for the first time. Decentralisation of wealth and property, consent-based marriage, rights of the Almighty as well as those of fellow human-beings, respect for the elders, affection for the young, promotion of peace and integrity in society and obligatory attainment of knowledge, with exclusive reference to the science of the day, etc. are a few of the injections, Islam enjoins upon every individual.

Prophet Muhammad (Pbuh) came in this world to abolish all evils from the earth. He had a heart, full of kindness; the kindness, which knew no bounds and was completely unprejudiced. Seeing his determination, divine help also descended to his succour to shore up his morale and courage. Though, all the Prophets and Messengers (Pbut) were tortured and violence was directed to them by the unbelievers of the day, yet, the kind of violence and pain, suffered by the last Prophet Hadrat Muhammad (Pbuh) was unmatched. Even then, he never cursed any one or ill-willed for the foes of Islam. He would say that he had been sent to have mercy for all. All through his life, he suffered innumerable brutalities, but in turn he wished people all the best. As a result, he succeeded in posting the colourful flags of triumph and brought about such a grand revolution in the history of mankind, which has no parallels. People, who were thirsty of blood of one another once, became so close together that each one of them felt proud in sacrificing his life for the good of others. Such was and is the bond of Islamic fraternity—stronger than that of blood.

Present modest work, an encyclopaedia, *per se,* namely, ***World of Islam*** is the fruition of tremendous toil. This work not so voluminous, virtually covers all the features, aspects and dimensions of Islam, as a faith and way of life. Hopefully, it would prove to be successful in painting the picture of Islam, with a photographic precision and let people know, what's what. Enlightening comments and wise suggestions are heartily solicited.

— Editor

Contents

1

Introduction

The causes affecting capacity are found in those factors that prevent *capacity for acquisition* and *capacity for execution* from taking full effect. The existence of these factors may result in the total absence of capacity or in deficient or incomplete capacity. For purposes of the present discussion, we may refer to all such forms as defective capacity.

The *manat* (legal basis) for the capacity for acquisition, as we have said, is being a natural person *(insaniyyah),* and it is death alone that can cause a change in this kind of capacity. We have seen, however, that under certain circumstances a corpse may have such a capacity. Reason *(aql)* and discretion *(rushd),* on the other hand, are the bases for the capacity for execution, and each factor that has the power to influence and affect the normal functioning of the human mind can become a cause for defective capacity.

It is pertinent to note that many of the causes of defective capacity mentioned here will appear to the reader to be the same as the general defences in criminal law, or as other grounds for waiver of liability in civil or ritual matters.

The jurists divide the causes of defective capacity into two kinds: natural causes *(samawiyyah)* and acquired causes *(muktasaba).* We may designate these as natural and acquired causes. Some of these causes have already been explained in the previous chapter, while discussing deficient and imperfect capacities of various persons: women, slaves, *janin* (foetus), corpse, and fictitious persons. Some of these will not be repeated here, but can be classified under natural or acquired causes.

Natural Causes of Defective Capacity: These are causes that are beyond the control of the subject *(mukallaf),* and result from an act of the Lawgiver and Creator. Under this heading, the jurists list ten causes: *sighar* (minority); *junun* (insanity); *atah* (idiocy); *nisyan* (forgetfulness); *nawm* (sleep); *ighma* (unconsciousness; fainting; epilepsy); *riqq* (slavery); *marad* (illness); *hayd* (menstruation); *nifas* (puerperium; post-natal state of woman); and *mawt* (death). We shall discuss a few of these here, the rest are either obvious or have a greater bearing on *ibadat.*

Legal Aim

A discussion of the *maqasid al-shariah* (the purposes of Islamic law) as well as the principle of *maslahah,* before discussing the rational sources, becomes necessary due to several reasons. The first is that the principle of *maslahah* has grown to envelope all the rational sources. Each rational source is today considered part of the larger doctrine of *maslahah.* The second is that this principle is considered the most important and the most comprehensive instrument of *ijtihad* for the modern times; its discussion must therefore precede that of the rational sources. A third reason is that the larger doctrine of *maslahah* must be distinguished from the narrower principle of *maslahah mursalah,* which is considered one type of rational source within the broader doctrine.

The meaning of *maslahah* is discussed first and is followed by a description of the purposes of Islamic law or the *maqasid al-shariah.*

Classification of Aims

The jurists break up the *maqasid* into three levels. This has already been pointed out. The first level is that of the necessities *(darurat),* which have been maintained by all societies and without which the social structure will collapse. These are the primary *maqasid* and the jurists focus mostly on these. They are supported by the supporting needs *(hajat).* The third level is that of complementary values and norms *(tahsinat).*

The important point made by jurists about the significance of each level is that the primary purposes are supported by the two other levels. However, if the last two levels are abolished the primary purposes will stand by themselves. This is not true for the lower levels. Thus, the existence of *hajat* and the *tahsinat* depends upon the primary purposes and they cannot be maintained on their own.

Din	Life	Family	Intellect	Wealth
Public	Public	Public	Public	Public
Private	Private	Private	Private	Private

The importance of the individual purposes within the *darurat* is reflected in the order in which they are stated. Thus, *din* has precedence over life, life has precedence over *nasl, nasl* has precedence over *aql,* and *aql* has precedence over *mal.* This is not all. Each of the primary purposes may divided into public and private purposes. The public purposes seek to preserve the interests of the community as whole, while the private purposes protect the rights of individuals. Again, the purposes are divisible into those securing the rights of Allah and those preserving or protecting the rights of the individuals. There is a fine distinction between the two kinds of divisions, though many modern scholars tend to consider them identical. The distinction lies in the fact that there are three kinds of rights to be identified rather than two. These are the right of Allah, the right of the community as whole, and the right of the individual.

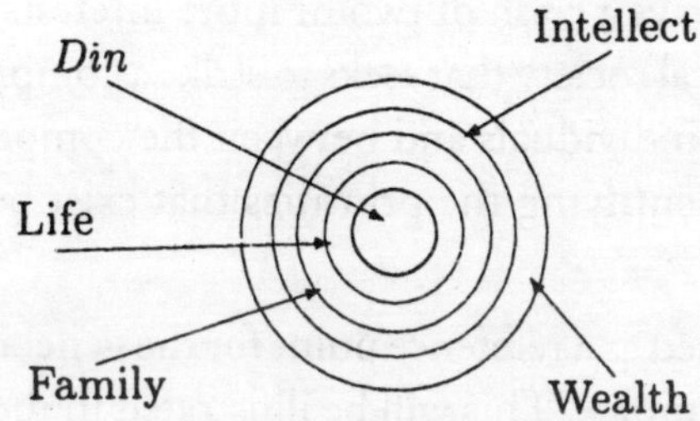

The relationship that exists between the primary purposes may be highlighted by visualising outer shells serving or protecting the inner shell or shells. Thus, the innermost shell is represented by the preservation and protection of *din*. This represents the foremost purpose of the *Shariah*. The shell surrounding it is that of life, which is itself surrounded by *nasl* and so on. The outermost shell is that of the preservation of wealth that serves all the inner shells and is subservient to them.

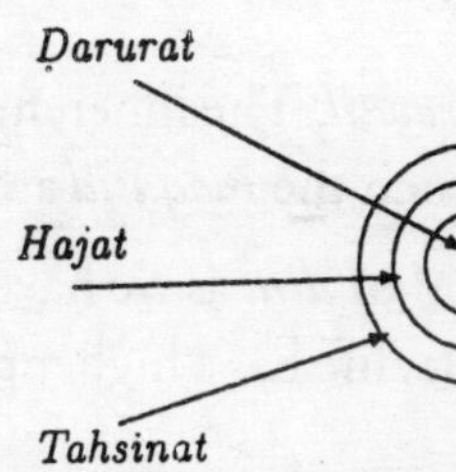

Each primary purpose considered to be a necessity has its own supporting needs and complementary norms. These are also to be viewed as shells, one inside the other. This relationship is explained by al-Shatibi through examples. Considering the example of prayer *(salat),* he says that the essential parts of the prayer are its *arkan* (elements) and *faraid* (obligations). Whatever is besides these is meant to complete and complement it. The parts of prayer are distributed among the *maqasid* in such a way that each outer shell forms a protective boundary for the inner shell. One who crosses the outer shell or boundary will soon demolish the inner shell. Thus, the person who gives up the *nafl* (supererogatory) prayers will soon give up the *sunan,* and will finally demolish the *faraid.* There are many instances in the law, he says, that correspond with the analogy of *nafl* and *faraid.* For example, even a drop of wine or a small quantity of it is prohibited, because it leads to the consumption of larger quantities, though it does not intoxicate or damage the intellect. A severe penalty is provided for stealing a thing of small value as it leads to the stealing of larger amounts and to robbery. In the same way, the ethical and moral norms hover around and protect the main and essential legal norms. The *Haji* and the *tahsini* are, therefore, to be considered the servants of the *daruri.*

Priorities within the Maqasid: The relationships described above indicate that some purposes have a higher priority than others, that is, they would be preferred in case of a clash between two interests. This fact also highlights an important point that while deciding a legal case or while attempting to understand the position of Islamic law on an issue, one cannot look at one purpose or interest alone. There is always a clash of two or more interests. This is achieved through the machinery of organised political society that seeks to strike a compromise between the conflicting wants, desires, and claims of individuals and between the competing interests. Looking at the purposes of law alone and identifying the priorities that exist between them would present a simplistic view of things.

The *maqasid* are always used as a reference point for the general principles of the law, and this makes the situation highly complex. This will be illustrated in the third part of this book under the discussion of the third mode of *ijtihad* (see page 309). Nevertheless, the *maqasid* considered alone present a fair picture of the entire system even for the layman, who is not trained in the law. If he observes a few rules, he can easily determine the answer to a question that he may have about the law. For the present purposes, we shall describe three main rules that govern the employment of the *maqasid.* Some other minor rules can be stated, but the idea is to avoid too much detail and technicalities.

Rule 1: The Stronger Interest Shall Prevail: The inherent strength of the interests secured by Islamic law is reflected in the order in which the *maqasid* are listed by the jurists.

Thus, the preservation and protection of *din,* as we have pointed out earlier, has preference over the preservation and protection of life; life has a higher priority than *nasl; nasl* is prior to *aql;* and *aql* is preferred over *mal.*

Din	Life	Family	Intellect	Wealth
First	Second	Third	Fourth	Fifth

In practice this would mean, for example, that *jihad* has priority over preservation of life, and if an individual is asked to participate in it and give up his life in the cause of Allah, there is legal justification for it. Preservation of life has a higher priority than the protection of *aql.* Therefore, if a person is facing death in a desolate place due to lack of water and the only thing available to him is wine, he is under an obligation to save his life by drinking the wine. Life has priority over *mal* too and it is permitted to take the property of another person without fear of penalty during a famine, if such taking results in the saving of life or lives.

In the same way, the *darurat* have priority over the *hajat,* which in turn have priority over the *tahsinat.*

Rule 2: The Public Interest is Prior to the Private: The different categories of the purposes can be understood in terms of public and private interests. Whenever a public interest is in conflict with a private interest, the public interest will prevail. The example used by the jurists is that of material handed over to artisans and craftsmen. The original rule of deposit *(wadiah)* required that this material being a deposit would not be compensated by the craftsmen in case it was destroyed, and the burden of proving tort *(taaddi)* or negligence would be upon the customer, the owner of the property.

This rule was changed to conform with the public interest, because the craftsmen were misusing the facility. The burden of proof was shifted to the craftsman, who had to show the absence of negligence. The Hanafis based this change on *istihsan.* The example is expected to show that the public interest requiring security of transactions and protection of property of the general public was given preference over the interest of individuals, that is, the craftsmen.

In this case, both interests, public as well as private, lie within the same category, that is, the preservation of wealth. Does the rule that the public interest prevails over the private cut across all the categories? Can a public interest in a lower category be preferred over a private interest in a category with a higher priority? Apparently it can. Yet, the matter is not that simple; it involves the discussion of the three kinds of rights mentioned above, individual rights guaranteed by the *Shariah,* and the exact meaning of public interest. We do not have space to discuss all these issues here. This discussion will be taken up in a separate study of justice and Islamic law.

Another example used by al-Ghazali upholds justification of taxation by the *imam* when the public interest is at stake. He permits a ruler in need of money to levy taxes in order to organise *jihad.* Here what we are calling public interest is actually the right of God, which may not be the same as the right of the state.

Rule 3: The Definitive Interest Prevails Over the Probable: This rule has been the cause of confusion for some jurists following al-Ghazali, and the confusion is witnessed in the works of some modern scholars too. Al-Shatibi states very clearly that all the interests preserved and protected by the *Shariah* are definitive *(qati).* He repeats this point over and over again, and it is in fact a fundamental assumption of his work.

The question, therefore, arises that if all interests are definitive, where does the probable interest come from? The answer to this issue is that the probable goals of the law belong to the area that is beyond the purposes and has been discussed above. These purposes have not been discussed by the jurists in detail. Most of the goals like building of civilization, maintenance of security, equality, freedom and others would come under this heading. From another perspective, these goals have neither been rejected by the Lawgiver nor have they been directly acknowledged.

Two cases mentioned by al-Ghazali have been mentioned under the discussion of *maslahah mursalah* in the following chapter. There are, however, other possibilities too for probable interests to exist within the structure discussed, but we would like to leave this topic for the researcher here and devote adequate space to it in a separate study mentioned in the previous section.

Concept of Maslahah

The words *maslahah* and *manfaah* are treated as synonyms. *Manfaah* means "benefit" or "utility," that is, it leads to some kind of benefit. In its literal meaning *maslahah* is denned as (*jalb al-manfaah wa-daf al-madarrah)* or the seeking of benefit and the repelling of harm. If this literal meaning is pursued further it will lead to something similar to the principle of utility expounded by Jeremy Bentham, which means securing the maximum human happiness. The seeking of human happiness in this sense may imply three things:

(i) That the happiness sought here is dependent upon human desires or reason. The pursuit of such happiness may or may not coincide with the form of benefit or *manfaah* intended by the *Shariah.*

(ii) The emphasis in this form of happiness will always be on the collective utility, that is, the happiness of the entire community and the interests of the individual may be given a back seat.

(iii) The pursuit of pure utility may ultimately lead to the economic analysis of law (as expounded by Richard Posner and the Chicago School). In other words, all legal decisions must be reduced to a cost-benefit analysis either financial or economic. This may or may not suit the goals of the *Shariah.*

Manfaah (benefit or utility), however, is not the technical meaning of *maslahah.* What Muslim jurists mean by *maslahah* is the seeking of benefit and the repelling of harm as directed by the Lawgiver. The seeking of utility in Islamic law is not dependent on human reason and pleasure. Al-Ghazali, therefore, defines *maslahah* as follows:

> As for *maslahah,* it is essentially an expression for the acquisition of *manfaah* (benefit) or the repulsion of *madarrah* (injury, harm), but that is not what we mean by it, because acquisition of *manfaah* and the repulsion of *madarrah* represent human goals, that is, the welfare of humans through the attainment of these goals. What we mean by *maslahah,* however, is the preservation of the ends of the *shar.*

Three things are Obvious from this Statement:

(i) That the pursuit of human goals and the principle of utility based on human reason is not what is meant by *maslahah.*

(ii) That *maslahah* is the securing of goals or values that the Lawgiver has determined for the *Shariah.*

(iii) That the goals determined for the *Shariah* by the Lawgiver may or may not coincide with values determined by human reason. Thus, reasoning based upon the principle of utility or on economic analysis may sometimes be acceptable to the *Shariah,* but it may be rejected at other times when there is a clash of values.

Types of Maslahah

Muslim jurists classify *maslahah* in several ways. These classifications are expected to show us how this principle covers most of the rational sources and how the discussion of the sources is linked with the purposes of Islamic law. Some of the most important classifications are provided below.

First Classification: Maslahah Acknowledged or Rejected by the Shariah: For purposes of this classification, it is important to understand that the underlying causes of the *ahkam* present a hierarchical structure of attributes. Sometimes the *Shariah* recognises a lower level attribute as the basis for the law, while at other times it accepts a higher level attribute. The level at which an attribute is acknowledged indicates the type of rational source being used. The classification that follows is based on the recognition of attributes at different levels. Four types of *maslahah* are discussed under this heading:

1. *Maslahah Acknowledged at the Level of the Lowest Category:* The first type is *maslahah* acknowledged by the Lawgiver at the level of the lowest category *(naw).* Take the case of drinking *khamr* (wine). The underlying cause at the lower level could be "intoxication," that is, losing of one's senses. A higher level cause could be the "protection of the intellect."

   Recognition of a cause at the lower level means that the rational source invoked is analogy *(qiyas).* This means that the law can be extended to other things on the basis of analogy using the rule: whatever intoxicates is prohibited. Prohibiting intoxication is, therefore, the repelling of harm or the securing of an interest protected by the law *(maslahah).* All those cases where the Lawgiver has identified underlying causes at the lowest level fall under the first type of *maslahah.* Further, this tells us that using analogy *(qiyas)* is one type of *maslahah.*

2. *Maslahah Acknowledged at the Level of the Genus:* The second type is *maslahah* that is acknowledged by the Lawgiver at the level of the genus, that is, at a level higher than the lowest category. Such a recognition takes us beyond the level of analogy into the realm of other rational sources, especially *maslahah mursalah.* This recognition of attributes can go up to the highest level of the purposes of law. The purposes of Islamic law at the highest level are five: Preservation of *din;* preservation of life; preservation of *nasl* (progeny); preservation of intellect; and preservation of wealth. The jurists illustrate the recognition of these attributes through a large number of examples. Thus, the Companions of the Prophet (peace be on him) were not sure whether the text of the Quran should be compiled, because the Prophet had not done so during his lifetime. In the interest of "preservation of *din*" they decided that it should be gathered and compiled. The texts clearly mention that a life is to be taken for a life in the case of *qisas* (retaliation). Where two or more persons participate in the murder of one person, should more than one life be taken for a single life? It was decided that in the interest of the "preservation of life"

such a law should be made. The details of this type will be explained under the discussion of *maslahah mursalah* as well as under the discussion of the third mode of *ijtihad.*

3. *Maslahah that is Rejected by the Shariah:* The third type *maslahah* is one that is not acknowledged by the *shart ah,* because it clashes with a text. The jurists have found it difficult to give examples of this type. They provide hypothetical cases. Let us assume that the *hukm* for a person indulging in sexual intercourse during fasting is the freeing of a slave. A jurist may say that this provision gives a loophole to a very rich person, because setting free a slave is nothing for him. Such a jurist may say that this option should therefore not be available to a rich man in the interest of "the preservation of *din.*" The *Shariah,* however, does not recognise such a measure and the argument is without foundation and is rejected. In other words, a provision proposed in contradiction of what the *Shariah* has already provided will not be recognised or a *maslahah* that clashes with a text of the Quran or *Sunnah* is rejected.
4. *Maslahah that is Neither Acknowledged nor Rejected:* The fourth type is a *maslahah* that is neither acknowledged by the *Shariah* nor is it rejected. This type of *maslahah* is one that is strange *(gharib)* for the *Shariah.* An example will be provided under the discussion of *maslahah mursalah* for ease of understanding.

Second Classification: Maslahah According to its Inner Strength: This classification is based upon the purposes of Islamic law and their types. The types of *maslahah* according to their inner strength are three: *darurat* (necessities); *hajat* (needs); and *tahsinat* (complementary goals).

1. *Darurat (Necessary Interests):* Necessary interests are those without the protection of which there would anarchy and chaos in society. The absence of protection for these interests would mean the loss of everything that we hold dear. These prized social interests are five in number:

   (a) Preservation and protection of religion *(hifz ala al-din).*
   (b) Preservation and protection of life *(hifz ala al-nafs).*
   (c) Preservation and protection of progeny *(hifz ala al-nasl).*
   (d) Preservation and protection of intellect *(hifz ala al-aql).*
   (e) Preservation and protection of wealth *(hifz ala al-mal).*

2. *Hajat (Supporting Needs):* The second type of interests are called *hajat* or supporting interests required by the necessary interests for their smooth operation and implementation. If these supporting interests are not protected by the law there would be hardship and loss in the performance of social functions. This means that the primary or necessary interests would not be lost, but there would be considerable friction and difficulty in their protection. The examples of these interests given by jurists pertain mostly to exemptions granted by the law. For example, the exemptions available due to illness or

journey in case of worship serve these interests, just like the contract of *salam* (advance payment) works as an exemption to facilitate transactions. The necessary interests do not depend on these exemptions or supporting needs, but their operation is facilitated.

3. *Tahsinat (Complementary Interests):* These interests provide additional rules that lead to the moral and spiritual progress of the individual and society. Examples are: voluntary *sadaqah* and many ethical and moral rules (like the command not cut trees or to kill animals during war). In reality, the *tahsinat* tell us that there is a moral shell around the necessities and supporting needs provided by the *Shariah.* Thus, morality goes hand in hand with the law and there is no separation as may be found in Western law.

This classification shows the types of purposes of the Islamic law and the relationship between them.

Third Classification: Definitive and Probable Interests: Some jurists, and some later writers, have maintained that there are interests that are definitive (*qati)* and those that are probable *(zanni).* Jurists like al-Ghazali and al-Shatibi have spent considerable time in showing that all the interests classified according to their inner strength above are definitive, because they have been constructed through a process of induction *(istiqra)* rather than deduction. Certain cases of interests that have been called strange or *gharib* may, however, be deemed to be probable. Yet, the major area of probable purposes lies in the area called *ashbah* by al-Ghazali. (See the figure below, as well as the section on what lies beyond the *maqasid.).* This issue is found in Western law as well when values are classified according to different types of rationality, with some legal philosophers, like Kelsen, maintaining that most interests or values preserved by the law do not meet the standards of rationality that can be called definitive. These, however, are values identified by human reason. We shall have something more to say about this when we discuss the third mode of *ijtihad* in the next part of this book.

Fourth Classification: Public and Private Interests: The necessary interests, the supporting needs and complementary interests can all be divided into public interests and private interests. In fact, the settlement of legal disputes always involves some kind of conflict or clash between public and private interests or between two private interests.

The problem that arises, especially in modern times, is whether public interests are based on the rights of Allah *(haqq Allah)* or on the rights of the state *(haqq al-saltanah)* or are these the same thing?

The Doctrine of Maslahah and Maslahah Mursalah: Distinction: The principle of *maslahah mursalah* was first used by Imam Malik, the founder of the Maliki school. It was elaborated and developed in the works of al-Ghazali. Out of this discussion there emerged a larger doctrine of *maslahah,* which is much wider than the principle or source of Islamic law called *maslahah mursalah.*

The larger doctrine requires that during the use or employment of rational sources to discover the law, each derived law must be checked against the purposes of Islamic law or the *maqasid al-shariah.* If there is some compatibility *(munasabah)* between the derived law and the purposes, then the law is valid, otherwise it may be rejected. In this sense, all the rational sources fall under this larger doctrine. Thus, the larger doctrine covers *qiyas, istihsan* and *maslahah mursalah.* In other words, each of these rational sources has now become or is deemed a type of this larger doctrine. It is for this reason that the meaning of *maslahah* and the nature of the purposes of law has been discussed before the description of the rational sources.

Maqasid al-shariah or the Purposes of Islamic Law: The Purposes of Law are Divided by al-Ghazali into two Types:

- *Dini* or purposes of the Hereafter.
- *Dunyawi* or purposes pertaining to this world.

Each of these is divisible into *tahsil* or securing of the interest and *ibqa* or preservation of the interest. *Tahsil* is the securing of a benefit *(manfaah)* and *ibqa* is the repelling of harm *(madarrah).* The phrase *riayat al-maqasid* (preservation of the *maqasid)* is used to indicate both *tahsil* and *ibqa.*

The worldly purposes *(dunyawi)* are further divided into four types: the preservation of *nafs* (life), the preservation of *nasl* (progeny), the preservation of *aql* (intellect), and the preservation of *mal* (wealth). Each worldly purpose is meant to serve the single *dini* purpose. When all types are taken together, we have five ultimate purposes of the law:

- *Din* (religion),
- Life,
- Progeny (may be called the preservation of the Family),
- Intellect, and
- Wealth.

The Purposes of Islamic Law

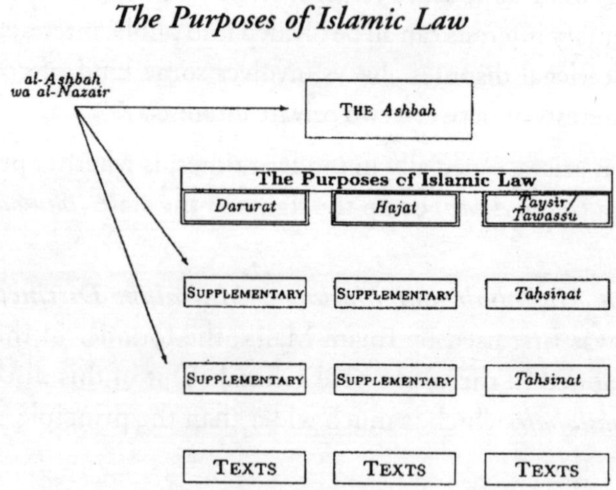

These five purposes are designated as *darurat* (necessities) and are the primary purposes of the law. These are followed by the *hajat* (needs), which are additional purposes required by the primary purposes, even though the primary purposes would not be lost without them. The third category is that of purposes that seek to establish ease and facility *(tawassu* and *taysir)* in the law; these are called the *tahsinat* (complementary values).

The relationship of the purposes of Islamic law may be seen in the figure:

What is Beyond the Purposes?: If we move beyond the ultimate values recognised as the purposes of the law, we reach the area of weaker attributes, which are also used by the jurists for extending the law. This is the area of the *ashbah* (probable values). These too are organised in the form of the particular and the general. This is the area of the probable or *zanni maqasid.*

Thus, the purpose beyond these purposes could be the building of civilization, security, the maintenance of equality, freedom, and many other values that are preserved and protected by each society and they are expressed as the aims of justice in Western law. The Muslim jurists did not deal with such values, because they are probable and do not fall in the area of certain rationality. An attribute depicting such values is called *wasf baid* or a distant value; it is distant in comparison with the *darurat,* each of which is a *wasf qarib* or near value.

Maqasid al-shariah and the Texts: The purposes of Islamic law have been determined from the texts through a process of induction *(istiqra)* rather than through deduction. This is the reason why the *maqasid* are considered definitive *(qati),* and can be relied upon without a doubt, and the same pattern is to be found in the other details of the *Shariah.* He quotes a large number of verses of the Quran to show how the ultimate purposes are indicated by the texts.

The Nature and Structure of the Purposes of the Shariah: The structure of the *maqasid* is understood by appreciating the relationship of the primary purposes among themselves, and their relationship with the secondary and supporting purposes. As the *maqasid* are designed to ultimately serve the interests of the Hereafter, it is this relationship that may be examined first.

Primary Purposes in the Service of the Hereafter: The first purpose of the *Shariah* is to secure the interest of Man that pertains to the Hereafter. It is for this reason that the purposes are divided into *dini* or purposes of the Hereafter and *dunyawi* or purposes restricted to this world. The worldly purposes, in combination, seek to preserve and protect the interest of *din.*

Al-Ghazali says that the second purpose, which is the preservation and protection of life, may be considered by some to have a higher priority than *din,* because without life there would be no religion. This argument takes collective life into consideration, and in this sense it would also hold true for the intellect too, because the existence of *aql* is considered by jurists to be a condition of *taklif* (legal obligation). He points out, however, that some provisions of the law clearly support the superiority of the interest of *din.* For example, the interest of *din* is preferred when the subject is asked to give up his life in the way of Allah, that is, for *jihad.* The relationship of the necessities or the primary purposes is seen through the following figure:

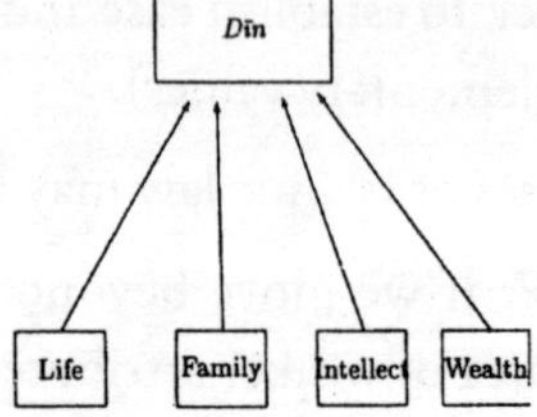

Al-Shatibi devotes three of the thirteen rules, in which he discusses the relationship among the purposes, to the discussion of the Hereafter. The most important point he makes in this context is that the identification of the interests of Man has not been left to the whims and fancies of human beings, that is, to human reason, because all the purposes seek to establish and maintain life in this world to serve the interests of the Hereafter.

He also discusses the concept of utility and points out that benefits and harms are relative; they may vary from individual to individual, and from one situation to the other. If harm and benefit cannot be established directly from the texts, then, it is to be linked to what is usually considered beneficial or harmful. The general rule that he derives is that since the *maqasid* serve the interests of the Hereafter the determination of what is beneficial and what is harmful cannot be left to human reason. He seeks support from a number of Quranic verses. One of these is:

> And if the Truth had followed their desires, verily the heavens and the earth and whosoever is therein had been corrupted. [Quran 23 : 71]

In his view, the role of human reason begins after the *Shariah* has laid down the essential principles. The first of the thirteen rules he expounds is devoted to this point.

The primary purpose of the *Shariah,* then, as indicated already, is to free Man from the grip of his own whim and fancy, so that he may become the servant of Allah by choice, just as he is one without it. The preservation and protection of *din* is intended by the Lawgiver to achieve this.

The two Faces of the Maqasid: Perhaps the most important feature of the *maqasid* is their dual thrust. Al-Ghazali discusses this dual nature in detail in his book called *Jawahir al-Quran.* This point has been ignored by almost all the later jurists, except for al-Shatibi.

The dual feature of the *maqasid* is evident in the use of the terms *ibqa* and *hifz,* which we may call preservation and protection. Al-Shatibi considers these the two aspects of *hifz.* The first he says is "what affirms its elements and establishes its foundations." The second is "what repels actual or expected disharmony." The focus of later jurists, and hence that of modern scholars, has been on the aspect of protection alone.

Each purpose, however, has a positive or aggressive aspect and a negative or defensive aspect. From the positive aspect, the interest is secured by establishing what is required by the *Shariah* through each of its *maqasid.* Thus, the interest of *din* is secured by the creation of conditions that facilitate worship and establish the other essential pillars of Islam. The interest of life is secured by creating conditions for the existence of life.

The interest of progeny is supported by facilitating and establishing family life. The interest of intellect is secured by promoting the means for the growth of the intellect. The interest of wealth is secured by creating proper conditions for the growth of wealth.

Din	Life	Family	Intellect	Wealth
+ve Establish	Establish	Establish	Establish	Establish
-ve Defend	Defend	Defend	Defend	Defend

From the defensive or the protective aspect, interests are secured by preventing the destruction or corruption of the positive aspect. Thus, *jihad* is prescribed for defending *din,* while prayer, fasting, pilgrimage, and *zakah* help establish it. It is the duty of the *imam* to ensure proper conditions for both, while it is binding upon each subject to fulfil these duties, individually and collectively. Life is preserved through the provision of sustenance and the maintenance of good health, while it is protected or defended through the provision of penalties for those who destroy life without legal justification.

Nasl is promoted through the maintenance of healthy family life and the institution of marriage, while penalties are provided for those who would corrupt it and destroy its values. The preservation of *aql* is achieved through the provision of education and healthy conditions for its growth, while penalties are provided for the consumption of substances that destroy the intellect. Preservation of wealth is achieved by encouraging its growth, while theft or misappropriation of wealth is punished through penalties.

Rulings for Minority

It is the state or condition of a human being after birth and before puberty. This, in fact, is not a cause of defective capacity or even an obstacle in its way, but a necessary stage in the growth of the human being. It is considered as a cause for noting its effect upon capacity or *ahliyyah.*

- Minority does not affect capacity for acquisition or *ahliyyat al-wujub.* All rights and obligations are acquired as their establishment requires merely a *dhimma* and the *manat* (being a natural person), which is the basis for the capacity for acquisition. Minority does not oppose this *manat.* The jurists, therefore, maintain that the minor is liable for compensation of property destroyed by him, for goods and services bought, for maintenance of relatives, and also for *zakat* according to some.

- Capacity for execution or *ahliyyat al-ada* requires *aql* (reason) for its fulfillment, and this the non-discriminating minor *(sabi ghayr mumayyiz)* lacks, because he does not understand the *khitab*. He is, therefore, not liable for the *ibadat,* for financial transactions, or for punishments. The Hanafis make an exception in the case of the *sabi mumayyiz* or one who has attained some discretion. The *ibadat* of such a minor are rewarded in the Hereafter, and it is a matter of controversy whether the *khitab* of *targhib* or recommendation is addressed to him. He is not liable for punishments, but financial transactions undertaken by him are valid in certain cases. Transactions that are purely harmful for such a minor, like donating his property, have no legal effect. Transactions that are purely beneficial or those that are evenly balanced between profit and loss are allowed, with the prior permission of the guardian or his subsequent ratification. The position of the *sabi mumayyiz* may be compared with the contract for necessaries by a minor under sections 11 and 68 of the Pakistan Contract Act. The freedom allowed to the *sabi mumayyiz* by the Hanafis is much wider than that under the law. In other countries, the contracts of a minor may be considered valid with an option for the minor to rescind the contract and return the property.

Rulings for Insanity

Junun has no effect on *ahliyyat al-wujub,* because rights and obligations are established for and against an insane person, who is deemed liable for *itlaf* (destruction of property), payment of *diyah,* and the like. The *manat* of such a capacity is *insaniyyah,* and the *majnun* is a human being. *Junun,* however, completely negates the *ahliyyat al-ada,* because of lack of *aql.* The insane person, therefore, has no liability for *ibadat* or punishments, and all his transactions are void. While the *fuqaha* consider insanity as effective in negating the capacity for performance they do not describe the meaning of insanity in detail. In Pakistan, section 84 of the Pakistan Penal Code appears to follow what are called the M Naghten Rules for insanity in England.

These rules have been criticised by lawyers as well as doctors as being inadequate. A number of other tests have also been devised, like the "irresistible impulse test," the "Durham test," and the "American Law Institute or Model Penal Code test." It is suggested here that Muslim scholars need to explore these issues in some depth. They may either accept the tests devised in different countries or devise some new tests. The same holds true for idiocy and death illness. Such questions must be answered on the basis of empirical evidence.

Rulings for Jest

When a person uses words without intending to convey either their primary or their secondary meanings, that is, their denotations or their connotations, he is said to speak in jest *(hazl).* Such a person may, for instance, use words employed for the contract of marriage, but does not intend the *hukm* (effect) of such a contract.

Speaking in jest has no effect on the capacity for acquisition; rights as well as obligations will, therefore, be acquired. The basis of *insaniyyah* required for this kind of capacity is not altered by jokes.

Hazl or jest cannot negate the capacity for execution either, because such a person has not lost his intellect or discretion. Contracts, on the other hand, require consent and willingness to give rise to legal effects. The person speaking in jest does bring about the apparent form *(sighah)* of the contract, but has not given his consent in reality. The Hanafis, therefore, consider the transactions of such a person as invalid, except transactions like marriage, divorce, manumission, *ruju* (retraction), and the like. This is based on the tradition that says, "Three things intended seriously are taken seriously, and if intended in jest are also taken seriously: marriage, divorce, and the freeing of a slave." Some jurists do not maintain this exemption, and treat all statements made in jest as being ineffective. The Shafiis maintain that statements made in jest are to be considered valid at all times, because the person has brought about the cause—the *sighah* (form)—and must, therefore, bear the consequences. This is based on the objective theory of contracts that is followed in Islamic law by most schools.

Rulings for Indiscretion

This defect concerns financial transactions, that is, transactions undertaken carelessly and in a manner that a prudent person is likely to avoid. The result is foolish waste and squandering of property.

The tendency in a person to waste his property affects neither his capacity for acquisition nor his capacity for execution. The effect of *safah* is that a person, who has attained puberty, is subjected to interdiction *(hajr)* till such time that he mends his ways. This view is upheld by the majority. It is based upon the necessity *(darurah)* of preserving his wealth, because preservation of wealth is an acknowledged purpose of the law. Abu Hanifah maintains that interdiction can last only till the age of twenty-five, after which the property of the individual is to be delivered to him, because at this age the individual is to be preferred over property.

Rulings for Coercion

Ikrah is a situation in which one is forced to do something without his willingness. It has no effect either on the capacity for acquisition or the capacity for execution, because this state does not affect life or reason and discretion. It does, however, negate free consent and willingness.

Effect on Free Will: The jurists disagree about the extent to which *ikrah* can affect free will. The views of these jurists may be classified into two opinions:

1. The first opinion maintains that *ikrah* is an obstacle in the way of *taklif* (creation of an obligation). Thus, the *khitab* is not directed towards a person under coercion or under duress, because this person is prevented from understanding the *khitab*. Among those

who hold this opinion are Shafii jurists, who maintain that free will is a condition of *taklif. Ikrah,* according to the Shafiis, arises under a threat of death, hurt, perpetual confinement, and the like. It does not arise for causes of a lesser gravity, like a threat to property. *Ikrah* defined this way is, in their view, divided into two kinds:

a. *Justified Coercion:* This is like the order of a *qadi* directing a debtor to pay his debts to his creditors, or his command to a man to divorce his wife after the passage of the period of *ila,* as required by Shafii law. This kind of *ikrah* does not affect the free will of a person, as the duty is imposed by the Lawgiver. Thus, any transaction in property undertaken under coercion for paying off creditors shall not be declared void.

b. *Unjustified Coercion:* Coercion without justification is again of two types. The first type is where acts committed are legally permissible under coercion. Such acts, if committed through words or deeds, have no legal effect and are considered void. If these acts can be attributed to a third person, then, they are attributed to the person coercing or threatening another. For example, compensation for property destroyed through coercion shall be paid by the person who coerces the other. The second type are acts that are legally prohibited, like murder and rape. In such cases the person coerced shall be fully liable along with the person who coerced him.

2. The second opinion is held by the Hanafis, who divide *ikrah* into three types:

   a. First is coercion that negates free will or choice. This is coercion under threat of death or loss of limb.

   b. The second type is coercion that negates consent, but makes free will irregular or *fasid.* This is brought about by confinement for a long period or by beating and torture that does not lead to loss of life or limb.

   c. The third type is *ikrah* that does not negate consent nor does it make free will *fasid.* The example is confinement of close relatives. Some Hanafi jurists do not accept this third category, and link it with one of the categories above, depending upon the nature of the threat to dear ones.

Effect of Coercion on Legal Capacity: The Hanafis maintain that the condition of *taklif* is the existence of the right to choose and not its validity *(sihhah).* Irregular or *fasid* free will, they say, is sufficient for the existence of *taklif.* In all the above cases of *ikrah,* free will is not invalid *(Batil)* though it may be irregular. *Taklif,* therefore, may accompany *ikrah.*

To Facilitate the Understanding of the act, for which Coercion is Taking Place, the Hanafis Divide it into Three Types:

1. *Transactions:* These are divided into two kinds, on the basis of the effect of *ikrah:*

   a. First are transactions that do not accept rescission, and do not depend upon consent, for example, divorce, manumission, marriage, retraction of divorce, *zihar, ila, afw* (forgiveness) in intentional murder, and oath *(yamin.)* All these transactions are valid under coercion, because they amount to a termination (*isqat)* or relinquishment of a right, and relinquishment cannot be reverted, because these transactions are not dependent on consent.

b. *Second are Transactions that accept Rescission or Revocation and Depend upon Consent:* These are like sale, mortgage, hire, and other commutative contracts. These contracts accept rescission and depend upon the existence of free consent. The *hukm* of such contracts concluded under coercion is that they are irregular *(fasid.)* They can be ratified by the coerced party, after coercion has ceased to exist, in which case they are declared as valid *(sahih).*

2. *Admissions and Confessions:* All admissions and confessions, in order to be valid, must be accompanied by free will.

3. *Acts in General:* Acts, for this purpose, are divided into two kinds by the Hanafi jurists.

a. First is the case when the coerced is a mere instrument in the hands of another, like a person picking up another and throwing him upon another thereby causing death, or hurt, or causing damage to property. If A causes B to fire at a bush knowing that C is hiding behind it, thus, causing the death of C, then, A shall be guilty of murder, while B will be an instrument in his hand. Other cases can be imagined. In such cases the act is attributed not to the instrument, but to one who caused him to move.

b. Second is the case when the coerced cannot become an instrument in the hands of another, for example, in the commission of *zina* or eating of food. In such a case, the person coerced is fully aware of his actions. Here the person coerced is guilty of *zina* or for compensating property consumed. In the case of drinking of *khamr,* however, *hadd* is waived on grounds of *shubhah.*

Mistake and Ignorance (Khata, Shubhah, and Jahl): The topics of *jahl* and *khata* are usually discussed separately, while the topic of *shubhat* is not discussed under defective legal capacity. All three are interrelated and deal with concepts that are similar to what in Western law are called mistake of law and mistake of fact.

The word *shubhah* is usually translated as doubt. The most important evidence in this respect is the tradition of the Prophet (peace be on him) in which it has been said that the *hudud* penalties are to be waived in case of *shubhah.* This is usually taken to mean "benefit of doubt" given to the accused. While this meaning may be covered by the tradition it is not its primary concern. The rule of giving benefit of doubt to the accused is generally accepted as a rule of evidence in Islamic law. Further, this rule deals with the doubt in the mind of the judge as to whether an offence has been proved beyond doubt. The tradition, according to the jurists, deals with doubts in the mind of the subject at the time of commission or omission of an act. These are of several types: *shubhah fi al-dalil* (mistake of law); *shubah fi al-milk* (mistake as to ownership); *shubhah fi al-fil* (mistake in the commission of the act); and *shubhah fi al-aqd* (mistake as to the governing law in the contract).

For example, assuming that in the early days there was a person who was under the impression that temporary marriage is permitted, that is, he may not be aware of the abrogating evidence. If he entered into a temporary marriage under this impression, the marriage contract was declared void, but the law would waive the *hadd* penalty in such a case (this does not mean that *tazir* was also waived). There could have been a possibility of the occurrence of such a case in the early days when people were not aware of the law. Today it is unlikely to happen. In any case, it is an example of *shubhah ji al-dalil* as well as *shubhah ji al-aqd.* If some of the heirs pardon the murderer, but some of the other heirs, who have not pardoned him, execute him, they will not be subjected to retaliation due to *shubhah ji al-dalil* (mistake of law). They may be awarded *tazir.* Today, these heirs are not permitted to take the law into their own hands. It should be obvious that exemptions for mistakes of law are given where the issue is subject to *ijtihad.* Where the matter is not subject to *ijtihad,* and is clearly known, or is supposed to be known to Muslims by necessity, there can be no exemption.

In the early days, when slavery was permitted, a husband may be under the impression that his wife's slave girl is also within his ownership. Under this wrong impression if he were to consider her *milk yamin* and act upon it he would be under *shubhah ji al-milk.* The *hadd* penalty would be waived in such a case (though not *tazir).* If a man aiming at an animal were to hit a human being, he would be guilty of manslaughter *(qatl khata)* and not murder. This is an example of *shubhah ji al-fil.*

The law gives some exemption in such cases and lays down principles that may be applied to new cases. It can be seen with ease, however, that ignorance or mistake does not affect the capacity of acquisition at all. It does not affect the capacity for execution either, the basis for which is understanding or *aql.* The only problem here is that the understanding of the subject is hampered somewhat, but the law takes notice even of this. This shows that ignorance and mistake are not causes of defective capacity at all, but statutory grounds of defence or exemptions.

Jahl (ignorance) may, thus, be that of law or of fact. In general, ignorance of law is no excuse for a subject present within the *dar al-Islam.* This, however, should not be confused with the acts of a Muslim residing in the *dar al-harb.* The Hanafis make an exemption for some of the unlawful acts of such an individual, because he is not enjoying the protection of the Islamic state during his stay abroad. Submission to the Islamic state and being subject to its jurisdiction is also stated as a condition of *Taklif* by some jurists. The issue of jurisdiction of the Muslim state is expressed as a principle by the Hanafi jurist al-Dabusi:

> The principle according to our jurists is that the world is divided into two *dars: dar al-Islam* and *dar al-harb.* According to Imam al-Shafii the entire world is a single *dar.*

In other words, al-Shafii does not grant the same exemptions to an individual residing in enemy territory.

Rulings for Death-illness

This is a condition in which the mind of a sick person is dominated by the fact that he will die because of his illness. It is of no consequence whether the person actually dies from this illness or from something else and whether the illness is in fact a terminal illness. Two conditions must be met before an illness may be declared a death-illness:

- The deceased person must be convinced that he is approaching death, irrespective of the nature of the disease. Diseases like common colds and headaches, however, are not taken into account for such purposes. Some jurists associate other circumstances with this state, like a person on a ship that is caught in a storm, or like a person facing a death sentence.
- Death should follow such a conviction, even if it is not caused by the feared illness.
- Some jurists stipulate a third condition here by saying that death must occur within one year of the commencement of illness, because any period above this would mean that the person is accustomed to his illness and that the fear of death is remote.

Marad al-mawt (death-illness) has no effect on the capacity for acquisition or on the capacity for execution, and it is in fact a condition of *taklif,* because it is the capacity to perform an act that is affected here and not the capacity to understand it.

A person suffering from such an illness is prohibited from entering into transactions that are in excess of one-third of his wealth. In other words, it takes the *hukm* of *wasiyyah.* This condition is stipulated to protect the rights of the heirs. The reason assigned is that the rights of the heirs get linked to the estate as soon as *marad al-mawt* takes hold. The Lawgiver has laid down that such rights are to come into play after the death of the person, but to protect the rights of the heirs and creditors it is assumed that death has already occurred. The justification provided is that the transactions of such a person are not those of one who wishes to live, but of one who is ready to depart.

The Following Rights are Attached to the Estate of the Person Suffering from *Marad al-mawt:*

- *Rights of Creditors:* The creditors have a right prior to all, even if the debts consume all the estate.
- *Rights of Beneficiaries:* The rights of beneficiaries restrict the transactions to one-third of the estate, however, amounts in excess of one-third will be valid if permitted by the heirs.
- *Rights of the Heirs:* These rights are linked to the estate from the time of the commencement of illness, and any transactions undertaken by the sick person will be assigned *ahkam* as follows:

1. *Transactions with a Counter-value:* If the person suffering from death-illness concludes a contract of sale with no apparent loss in it, that is, at the market value, then the creditors or the heirs cannot have it set aside. It is to be assumed that such a sale was

undertaken to fulfil his genuine needs and not with the intention to deprive his creditors or heirs. Abu Hanifah maintains that if such a sale is made to one of the heirs, it is to be declared as void even if it is at market value. The two disciples maintain that the sale is valid. The difference of opinion is due to the question whether the right of the heirs is linked to the *ayn* (substance) of the thing or to its value.

2. *Transactions without a Counter-value:* If the transaction is a *hibah, waqf, sadaqah,* or a sale at less than the market value, or a purchase at more than the market value, then such a transaction will be restricted to one-third of the value of the estate, after the creditors have been satisfied.

Three Conditions must be fulfilled before the Rights of the Creditors can Come into Play:

(a) That the transaction was without a counter-value or without adequate counter-value. This would cover transactions like gift, charity, *waqf,* sale at a discount, or purchase at a premium.

(b) That the transaction involves the transfer of a thing *(ayn)* itself and not its use, provided that the benefit conferred through use will terminate upon the death of the owner. Some Hanafis do not consider the benefits arising from the use of a thing as *mal.* The use of land, or of a house, or of an animal are examples that explain this case. The majority *(jumhur),* however, consider the use of benefits as *mal.*

(c) That the transaction must be in *ayan* (substance of things) and not in the revenue or profit derived from them. Any assignment of profits arising from a *sharikah* or *mudarabah* will not be affected by this condition.

Besides transactions, any admission or acknowledgement of debts by the person suffering from *marad al-mawt* may also invoke the rights of creditors and heirs. Al-Shafii is of the opinion that acknowledgement by a person suffering from death-illness is valid and is not affected by the rights of the creditors or the heirs. The reason he assigns is that a person approaching death would normally tell the truth, even if he is a habitual liar. The Hanafis, on the other hand, make a distinction between two cases:

(a) Acknowledgement of debt in favour of an heir: An acknowledgement in favour of an heir can have legal effects if the rest of the heirs permit it. This is due to the apprehension that one heir may have been preferred over the others.

(b) Acknowledgement of debt in favour of a stranger: An acknowledgement favouring a stranger is valid. These debts are called *duyun al-marad* and are to be paid after all other debts, called debts of health, have been satisfied.

The Malikis distinguish between cases where an allegation of a "bond of affection" can be made, that is, where a possibility of undue influence is likely. For example in the case of a wife, close relative, or friend. The basis is the bond existing between them and not the blood relationship.

Acquired Causes of Defective Capacity: Acquired causes are those that are created by Man or in which human will and choice are the basic factors. Muslim jurists list seven such causes: ignorance *(jahl),* intoxication *(sukr),* jest *(hazl),* indiscretion *(safah),* journey *(safar),* mistake *(khata, shubhah),* and coercion *(ikrah).* We will discuss some of the important causes, noting their effects on the capacity for acquisition and on the capacity for execution.

Rulings for Intoxication

Drunkenness is a state caused in a human being due to the use of an intoxicant, which temporarily suspends the proper functioning of the mental faculty.

Intoxication does not cause a change in the capacity for acquisition, as its basis is the attribute of being a human. Thus, a drunken person possesses a *dhimma* (legal personality) with a complete capacity for acquisition, and he is held liable for destruction of life and property, and also for all obligations, for maintenance, and even for *zakat.* All these duties and obligations require the existence of the capacity for acquisition alone, and intoxication does not negate it.

The basis for the capacity for execution, on the other hand, is *aql* (reason) and *rushd* (discretion); these are negated in the case of the drunken person by the state of drunkenness. The *khitab* is not addressed to the drunken person, because he does not comprehend it. The state of such a person is worse than that of one who is asleep, for the latter can be awakened; it is worse than that of an idiot, who may understand parts of the speech addressed to him.

The jurists agree unanimously that the *khitab* is not directed towards the intoxicated person if such intoxication has been caused by the legal use of intoxicants. For example, the person who has consumed liquor without knowing what it is or when he has done so under coercion or under duress to save his life. In such cases, the *hukm* for this person will be the same as that of the person under a spell of fainting.

Muslim jurists disagree about the person who is intoxicated when such intoxication is caused by prohibited means. The Hanafis and some other jurists do not consider such a cause to have any effect on the capacity for execution and on the understanding of the *khitab.* Thus, the *ibadat* are established against such a person and he will be held liable for delayed performance *(qada),* along with the accompanying sin. Any transaction or acknowledgement he makes is valid and enforceable against him. He acquires criminal liability for acts committed in such a state, though he can retract his confession made in this state regarding a case of *hudud,* as these are pure rights of Allah.

The argument provided by the Hanafis is that intoxication is a crime and as such cannot be an excuse for waiving punishments. Further, one reason why intoxication has been prohibited is that it leads to other *khabaith.* Moreover, if the acts of the drunken person are to be exempted from liability, it will become a means for the commission of offences, and for evading liability. Relying on the verse, "O ye believers, approach not prayer when you are intoxicated, until you know what you say," [Quran 4 : 43] they maintain that it is obvious that the *khitab* is addressed to the drunken person and he is expected to understand the meaning and import of the verse even when he is intoxicated. If this is not the interpretation, it would amount to saying to a person under a spell of madness, "Do not commit such an act when you are insane." It is for this reason that the drunken person is held liable for his acts.

Some jurists are of the opinion that an intoxicated person has no capacity for execution, because his *aql* (reason) is completely impaired by the state of intoxication. They maintain that the Lawgiver has already provided a penalty for the offence of intoxication and holding him liable for his transactions as well, that is, those undertaken in such a state, would amount to punishing him twice for the same offence, a kind of double jeopardy. They argue that the verse about avoiding prayers in an intoxicated state is actually addressed to a sober person telling him to avoid becoming intoxicated before the time of prayer, an act over which he has control, as compared to the person subject to fits of madness over which he has no control.

Modern jurists try to prefer the second opinion as it may be closer to some forms of Western law. It must be noted, however, that consuming liquor is an offence in Islamic law and it may not be so in the law.

Rulings for Idiocy

It is a state in which a person at times speaks like a sane and normal person, while at others he is like a madman. It is also described as a state in which a grown-up has the mind of a child. The capacity of an idiot is deemed equivalent to that of a *sabi mumayyiz,* who can be permitted by his guardian to undertake some transactions.

Sleep and Fits of Fainting (Nawm, Ighma): Sleep and fits of fainting have relevance for purposes of *ibadat,* as well as for crimes and torts. They do not affect *ahliyyat al-wujub,* because the attribute of *insaniyyah* is intact. Persons in such a condition, however, do not understand the *khitab.* Their capacity to understand things is temporarily affected and prevented from normal functioning. The liability for missed *ibadat* lingers against such a person and these have to be performed as *qada* (delayed performance). There is no liability for punishments and transactions. If a person, while sleeping, falls on a child during sleep and kills it, there is no liability for punishment, but compensation is another matter for which there may be strict liability.

Rulings for Forgetfulness

This is a state in which a person is not very careful about things though he has full knowledge of them, as distinguished from sleep and fits of fainting in which such knowledge is lacking. Forgetfulness does not affect *ahliyyat al-wujub* nor does it affect the capacity for execution. The *khitab,* however, becomes operative as soon as the person remembers. Transactions undertaken by such a person are valid and enforceable against him.

2

Legal Application

We have already examined the theoretical bases of society as they are outlined in the Quran and the Traditions, and we have looked briefly at Muslim society as it evolved in the course of history. It now remains for us to ask: Is it possible today to renew something similar to that form of Islamic life for the present and for the future?

It is not sufficient that Islam should have been a living force in the past; it is not enough that it has produced a sound and well-constructed society in the time of the Prophet and in the age of the Caliphate.

Since that distant time, there have been immense changes in life—mental, economic, political, and social. There have even been material changes on the Earth, and in its powers relative to man. All these things must be carefully considered before an answer can be given to our question.

There is also the further consideration which cannot be overlooked in any discussion which is directed to a practical and particular end, rather than to a theoretical and general; we must discover why it was that the spread of the Islamic spirit came to a halt in matters of political and economic theory only a short time after the era of the Prophet. Was this the longest possible span of life which the inner spirit and resources of Islam could command? Before dealing with these two considerations, we must emphasise the following truths:

> "That Islamic society today is not Islamic in any true sense." We have already quoted a verse from the Quran which can not in any way be honestly applied today:
> "Whoever does not judge by what Allah has revealed is an unbeliever."

In our modern society, we do not judge by what Allah has revealed; the basis of our economic life is usury; our laws permit rather than punish oppression; the poor-tax is not obligatory, and is not spent in the requisite ways. We permit the extravagance and the luxury which Islam prohibits; we allow the starvation and the destitution of which the Messenger once said:

> "Whatever people anywhere allow a man to go hungry, they are outside the protection of Allah, the Blessed and the Exalted."

The Imam Ibn-Hazm also delivered a fatwa on the same subject, to the effect that if a man dies in starvation in any town, the people of that town are regarded as having killed him, and the blood-money may be demanded of them. We permit this and similar things which have long been the subject of vain protest. Yet, the Quranic text is undeniably applicable to such things.

It refers to the existence in our modern society of such laws as those which permit usury, adultery, and refusal to pay the poor-tax, which thereby prove themselves to be in opposition to the divine laws laid down in the Quran. So long as Muslim society adhered to Islam, it manifested no weakness and no tendency to abdicate its control of life. It was when it fell away from Islam that these things took place. Emphasis on this fact will compensate for the idle aspersions which Western scholars have cast on our faith, and which they have evidenced from history.

These aspersions have been taken up by some in the East who were either gullible or mercenary, and have been the cause of the sullying of hundreds of pages by such men, under the claim of being liberal thinkers and accurate scholars. This is nonsense, and can only serve as a pretext for the false, the gullible, or the mercenary mind. We may now return to treat the two considerations whose discussion we deferred until we had noted the above points. We may start by answering the second question, why did the spread of the Islamic spirit come to a halt a short space after the time of the Prophet? Here again, we must emphasise two historical facts:

> "This halt was only partial, never complete. It took place only in a limited sphere, that of politics."

The tolerant Caliphate became a tyrannical monarchy:

> "The public funds were made accessible to the monarch, his relatives, his courtiers, and his flatterers, while they became inaccessible to those who had a true claim on them by the laws of Allah and His Messenger. But the remainder of the teachings of Islam remained in force; the charity and benevolence, the mutual help and responsibility tolerance and freedom of conscience and human equality, the payment of the poor-tax and the alms, and all the other positive and negative ordinances of Islam—all these continued in force to a greater or a lesser extent in many Muslim communities. "The Shariah even continued in force as the system of civil law until the nineteenth century, when we introduced French law, thus giving the coup de grace to another tie which bound us to the beliefs of Islam.

The change which overtook the system and the development of politics—a partial change, as we have just said—was the product of an unfortunate mischance, as we have already contended.

The mischance was that the control should fall into the hands of the Umayyads, first in an indirect way in the reign of Uthman, and later quite openly in the reign of Muawiyya. If we are to be fair to Islam we cannot hold it responsible for the Umayyads; for it was injured far more by this clan of the Quraish than by the fiercest of its enemies.

It is certain that, if the life of Umar had lasted several years longer, or if Ali had been the third Caliph, or even if Uthman had become Caliph when he was twenty years younger, then the course of Islamic history would have been very considerably changed. For the policy which Umar enunciated was:

(a) to take excessive wealth from the rich and give it to the poor;

(b) to equalise the stipends assigned to the people, as had been the practice under Abu-Bakr.

If Umar had done this, there could have been no opposition to a policy so consistent with Islam. Umar's conscience was above all question, as was his zeal for the faith; the reverence in which he was held for his fidelity to the faith was similarly above the attacks of jealousy and doubt.

If this programme had been carried out by Umar, it would have restored economic and social equity to the Islamic world, and the civil war would have been averted at its very beginning, or, at the least, would have been postponed for a long time. Or if Ali had succeeded Umar, he would have guided the people in Umar's policy, whatever might have been the position of the Quraiship, who had more self-confidence in dealing with Ali than they had in dealing with Umar.

In this case, the matter would not then have come to the stage of rebellion or civil war. The Umayyads would not have later aspired to power; for their nobles had no high standing in Islam because of their early conversion or their renown in the early wars; they were only among the "forced" converts who embraced Islam at the conquest of Mecca, when the success of the new faith was already assured. Under such circumstances they could have held office in the army or in provinces, but with no special reason for holding or being kept out of office, such as they gained in thirteen years under the reign of Uthman.

But it will be asked: How were the Umayyads able to effect such a speedy revolution during a period of turmoil in Islam? Does this not indicate that the Islamic system is unsteady by nature, or at least unsuited to permanency? Does it not indicate that by nature Islam provides no adequate safeguards against such revolution? We must here take account of the conditions of the Islamic state in that age, and we must reckon not only with factors of external power, but also with those of internal agitation.

The truth is that, at that stage Islam was in a ferment, and the really strange thing is that the Umayyads did with it only as much as they could. For "the fact is that the astonishing speed of the conquests, to which history can produce no parallel, added to Islamic society a huge territory, teeming with various races and skills, intellects and languages, systems, traditions, and heritages.

However strong the spirit of Islam may have been, and however powerful in suppressing all these heritages, an element of time was essential before all this new material could be homogenised, before a change could be wrought in the old moral ideas, the rooted traditions, the cherished social systems and customs. Thus, the Umayyad attack on the spirit of Islam just at this juncture took place at a unique point of time; if it had been stayed for a space, it could never have accomplished all that it did.

We have seen that the bulk of Muawiyya's support lay in Syria, a conquered country, rather than in Arabia itself. Those of his supporters who did hail from the Peninsula, such as Amar ibn al-As, were of a nature akin to Muawiyya himself, men who trampled down the moral element in their reckonings, who justified the means by the end, and who justified the end simply on the grounds that they desired it.

As for the suggestion that the Islamic system does not provide by nature adequate safeguards against revolution, for one thing we must bear in mind that this system was assailed by revolution before it had properly struck roots; and for another thing we must remember that in practice no system has any such real safeguards. Where, for example, are the safeguards of democracy in Europe? This is a strongly entrenched system, which has achieved a definite form, and which has had time to establish itself and to spread its influence over a long period into every quarter of life.

Yet, where were its safeguards at the time of the Nazi revolution, or the Fascist, or the Spanish? Or again take the institution of free speech in the United States, whose people fled from Europe to form a free society—where are its safeguards? Today a few newspaper and radio companies can hold a monopoly of both information and opinion, and can forbid any contrary opinions to find their way to the eyes, the ears, or the thoughts of the people.

The truth is that any suspicion that the Islamic system does not afford safeguards against revolution is due to ignorance of what is practically feasible in any system. It betrays also an ignorance of the true facts of Islamic history; we have the evidence of the minor rebellion in the Hejaz, and of the great rebellion against Uthman; we have the evidence of the Qarmatian rebellion and of many others, all of which were directed against exploitation, arbitrary power, and class distinctions. The spirit of Islam has continually and successfully resisted all such things, in spite of the grievous injuries which it has suffered at their hands throughout thirteen hundred years.

The spread of the spirit of Islam, then, was not halted because that spirit was unable to establish itself, nor because it was found inadequate to cope with the demands of the life. As we shall shortly see, this spirit has been continuously operative in many of the aspects of life and society. The halt in its spread was the product of an unfortunate mischance at a unique point of time. And it was when that mischance brought to Islam a Caliph who retained something of the true spirit of the caliphate in the person of Umar II, that the spread of Islam became again apparent, and the government again truly Islamic. But then the times were not propitious for such a truly Muslim Caliph to restore what had been destroyed, or to establish the roots of Islamic traditions in the political system.

But, nonetheless the attempt of Umar II does give us a clear indication that the inner power of Islam was really strong and capable of application in very different times. For his attempt followed the oppressive and evil age of the Umayyads, and it indicated clearly that a renaissance of Islamic government was possible, and not out of question.

We must repeat our contention that even when the spread of the Islamic spirit came to a halt in the realm of politics—though even here it was only a partial halt—it still continued to operate in other aspects of both social and individual life. It continued to realise many of its ideals, and to achieve many of its aims; indeed even to the present day it is still effective in such spheres as are not strongly under the influence of politics. As the Frenchman, Gouilly, says in Islam and the Great Powers:

> "The number of Muslims in Madagascar is not less than three quarters of a million. Most European authorities explain the spread of Islam in the native villages by the fact that it is a unifying religion which ensures for the negro an equality and justice for which he longs; it emancipates him finally from the bondage of priesthood and superstition, and even from the nightmare of evil spirits."

H.A.R., Gibb writes in Whither Islam?:

> "Islam still has it in its power to render a conspicuous service to mankind. There is no other society which can show such a record of having united various races in one unity based on equality. The great Islamic community in China, and the still smaller community in Japan, all show that Islam has still the power completely to reconcile such divergent elements as those of race and class. If ever the opposition of the great states of the East and West is to be replaced by understanding, this can only be done through the medium of Islam."

Muslim's Conduct during Crusades: The conduct of the Muslims during the Crusades showed the full inspiration of the strong spirit of Islam, as it rose superior to worldly considerations, treachery and ruthlessness. It showed a belief in the unity of mankind and the relationship of humanity beyond all differences of faith, and above all temporal and ephemeral enmities. Salahuddin was not the only one whom the history of the Crusades has recorded as being of the true and lofty Islamic spirit; rather would this description apply to all the Muslim armies which took part in these long and bitter wars. And this remained true despite the foul deeds of the Crusaders. These may be exemplified in the fall of Jerusalem on the fifteenth of July, 1099 A.D. (492 A. H.), during the first Crusade.

The Muslims sought refuge and sanctuary in the Aqsa Mosque, but the Crusaders followed them inside and dispatched them with their swords, so that blood flowed through the sacred precincts in a flood. In this act, the Crusaders violated a solemn treaty which their leader had made with some of the Arabs. This was only one example of the barbarity of the Crusaders, involving as it did a violation of their honour, punishment of the living, and retaliation on the infirm and the children.

Even after that, when fate turned against the barbarians, their treatment at the hands of the Muslims was imbued with the Islamic spirit, which was strong enough to check the desire for vengeance in Muslim hearts, and to keep them within the bounds of humanity and religion.

Again, within our own times, the recent war against the Jewish settlers in Palestine had revealed the penetration of the Islamic spirit. Even after the long interval during which Muslims have been divorced from the spirit and traditions of their faith, these have proved effective in keeping the Arab forces from taking vengeance for the most horrible and inhuman crimes committed by the Zionists in the Holy Land. They have been effective in keeping Muslim armies tune to the lofty tradition which their religion has maintained for fourteen centuries, and that in the midst of a constant record of inhumanity.

While we are discussing the inner vitality of Islam, we must not overlook the succession of disasters and calamities, both internal and external, to which Islam has been subjected throughout its long history. Yet, it is still a powerful element in human history, and commands the attention even of some occidentals as a means of saving humanity from it present dilemma, as we have already seen in the quotations from Gouilly and Gibb.

Despite the fact that such men are unable fully, to comprehend the Islamic spirit, but confine themselves rather to a review of its practical profit as it now exists, than to an appreciation of its profound spiritual content. For it is difficult for occidentals who have been brought up in the shadow of a deeply rooted materialistic civilization—and such we shall later see that it is to appreciate this subtle spiritual element.

We have already indicated that the first internal disaster which overtook Islam, namely its subjugation by the Umayyads. This was an interlude which neither permanently affected the practical traditions of Islam nor altered its spiritual exhortations and laws. It did not produce any permanent social principles, any accepted practical traditions, or any rooted practices.

We must now examine quickly the more important developments which befell Islam, and mark their influence through the following centuries. The first of these is to be found in the rise of the Abbasid state, with its reliance on racial elements newly converted to Islam. The attitude of these people to their new religion was never whole-hearted, because of the national loyalties whose roots remained strong within them.

But as time passed on, the Abbasid state deserted these elements on which it had been founded, and which were now beginning to acquire a tincture of Islam, for others whose nucleus was a body of Turks, Circassians, Dailamites and such like. So, this dynasty continued to find its support in elements which were opposed to the spirit of Islam, and to which it gave a favoured position because it relied on them. There was nothing to withstand these racial elements—and hence to withstand the power of the dynasty—except the spirit of Islam, with all the inner force and vitality which it could muster.

Then followed the destructive raids of the Tartars, bursting with savage ferocity on the Islamic world. Without delay Islam turned aside the force of the onslaught, swallowed it up, and assimilated it. Yet, this was not accomplished without causing in the spirit of Islam itself a profound upheaval in which the practices and traditions of this religion were forcibly modified.

Nonetheless in spite of the humiliation of the state by the Tartar onslaught, the Islamic community continued powerful and loyal to its ideals, and constant in the fundamentals of its religion, no matter how far it may have wandered from them in a few purely official aspects.

We must also bear in mind here that the Roman Empire, the building and growth of which had occupied almost a thousand years, was cut off and fell into pieces in a single century, as a result of the incursions of the Huns and Goths; nothing was left of it except a few scattered traces.

However, the Islamic state remained in occupation of a wide territory, although its building had occupied little more than half a century, and though it had to contend with a number of internal struggles between ruling families, as well as the external attacks of the Tartars, and others. Such factors demonstrate the intense vitality of Islam, in that it was able to meet these circumstances.

As we trace the development further, in the West we find the war in Spain, and in the East the disaster of the Crusades. In the first of these Islam was worsted, in the second it was victorious. But from that time to this it has had to contend with ferocious enemies of the same spirit as the Crusaders, enemies both open and hidden.

But the final overthrow of Islam took place only in the present age, when Europe conquered the world, and when the dark shadow of colonisation spread over the whole Islamic world. East and West alike. Europe mustered all its forces to extinguish the spirit of Islam, it revived the inheritance of the Crusaders'-hatred, and it employed all the materialistic and intellectual powers at its disposal. With these it sought to break down the internal resistance of the Islamic community and to divorce it gradually over a long period from the teachings and the heritage of its religious faith.

When we speak of the hatred of Islam, born of the Crusading spirit, which is latent in the European mind, we must not let ourselves be deceived by appearances, nor can we let their hypocrisy blind us to the fact that they deny to us any freedom of religion. They say, indeed, that Europe is not as unshakably Christian today as it was at the time of the Crusades and that there is nothing today to warrant hostility to Islam, as there was in those days. This is entirely false and inaccurate. General Alien by was no more than typical of the mind of all Europe, when, entering Jerusalem during the First World War, he said:

"Only now have the Crusades come to an end."

Similarly, the Governor of Sudan was no more than typical of the European mind when he placed all governmental power at the disposal of missionaries in the Southern Sudan, while forbidding any Muslim trader even to enter the country. It happened once that a certain official was stationed for a rather long time in South, and so asked for a transfer to the North; it was not granted. He then bethought himself to try lifting up his voice in the Muslim call to prayer; that single act sufficed to ensure his transfer the following day. And England is, of all the European countries, the most tolerant and patient and skilful in reconciling questions of religion.

People sometimes wonder how this obstinate spirit of resistance to Islam can persist so strongly and to such a pitch in a Europe which has discarded Christianity, and where the exhortations of preacher and monk no longer fill European ears as they did in the age of the Crusades. But this fact ceases to be surprising when we take into account two facts:

> "The enmity which the Crusaders stirred up was not confined to the clangour of arms, but was, before all else and above everything, an intellectual enmity. The European mind was poisoned by the slurs which the Crusaders' leaders cast on Islam as they spoke of it to their ignorant Western compatriots. It was in that age that there grew up in Europe the ridiculous idea that Islam was a religion of unbridled passion and violent sensuality, that it consisted merely of formal observances, and that it had no teaching of purity or of regeneration of heart. And this idea had remained as it started.

"This loathing spread space. The ignorant mass of Crusaders had dependents in many places throughout Europe; and the process was hastened by the Spanish Christians in their war to deliver their country from 'the yoke of the idolaters".

But the downfall of Muslim Spain was to require many centuries before it was completed; when this protracted struggle and the constraint which it involved grew too great, a hostility to Islam started to take root in Europe, and ultimately became permanent.

Finally, it took the form of a complete extirpation of Islam throughout Spain after a conflict which reached a pitch of ferocity and bitterness hitherto unknown. The cries of joy which all over Europe greeted this event were unfortunately uttered in ignorance of the consequences which would arise; for the result was that science and learning were blotted out, and in their place came the ignorance and the barbarity of the Middle Ages.

But before the echoes of these happenings in Spain had died away, there took place a third event of immense significance, which was to hasten the breaking of the ties between the Western world and Islam. This was the fall of Constantinople to the Turks. Europe had always looked to Byzantium as a relic of the glory of ancient Greece and Rome, and had regarded it as the fortress of Europe against Asiatic barbarism. In the centuries which followed, and which were filled with wars, the hostility of Europe to Islam was no longer a question of merely academic importance; it was now a question of political import also. And this fact further increased the violence of that hostility.

In addition to all this, Europe derived great profit from this cleavage. The Renaissance or rebirth of European arts and sciences in the widest sense arose particularly from an Islamic and Arab source; in most cases it can be traced back to material contacts between the East and the West. Europe profited more than did the Muslim world, but it did not acknowledge the gift, because it was blinded by its loathing of Islam. Or, more correctly, the reverse is true, that loathing increased with the passage of time, until it was second nature.

At this point, loathing swamped all understanding whenever the word 'Muslim' was mentioned; it entered into all their thoughts until it came to form a permanent part of the thinking of every European, man or woman. And still stranger than this is the fact that this feeling continued to flourish even after all the movements of intellectual exchange. Then followed the age of the Reformation, during which Europe was divided into various sects, each continually employed in arming itself against every other; yet hostility to Islam was the common feature of all of them.

This in turn was followed by an age when religious feeling started to subside, but the hostility to Islam continued unabated. One of the clearest proofs of this is that French philosopher and poet, Voltaire, was one of the bitterest critics of Christianity and of the Church in the eighteenth century; yet, he was at the same time violently hostile to Islam and to its Messenger. A few score years later came the age in which Western scholars commenced to study foreign learning and to regard it with a measure of sympathy.

All matters connected with Islam the traditional dislike began to creep in under a form of partisan spirit which was not conducive to academic study. Thus, the gulf which history had dug between Europe and the Islamic world remained still unbridged. Dislike of Islam thus became a fundamental part of European thinking; and the fact that the first Orientalists of the modern age were Christian missionaries who were working in Muslim territory meant that the picture which they formed of the teachings and the history of Islam was distorted; for it was founded on an axiomatic conception that Europeans were superior to 'idolaters'.

Despite the fact that Oriental studies have now been liberated from missionary influence, this intellectual bias had persisted, although any mistaken view can no longer claim the excuse of ill-informed religious zeal. Hence, the attacks made by Orientalists upon Islam betray an inherited characteristic, and a peculiarity of nature; they are based on an impression created by the Crusades, and shaped by all the mental influences of these on the early Europeans. But it will immediately be asked:

> How does it happen that an ancient antipathy such as this, which was originally religious in its basis, and which in the period of its birth owed its inception to the spiritual mastery of the Christian Church, can persist in Europe in an age when religious convictions are no more than a matter of antiquarian interest?

There is never anything surprising in such a situation; for it is well known to psychology that men may lose all the religious beliefs which they held in their youth, and at the same time retain some of their personal idiosyncrasies, even those which formerly centered upon the very religious beliefs which they have now discarded. It is these idiosyncrasies which provide the intellectual motivation for every act of such men. This is the state which obtains in Europe regarding Islam.

Despite the fact that the religious convictions which gave rise to European hostility to Islam have now lost their power and been replaced by a more materialistic form of life, yet the ancient antipathy itself still remains as a vital element to pour a secret poison into the European mind. So far as the strength of this antipathy is concerned, it undoubtedly varies from one individual to another, but that it exists is indisputable. The spirit of the Crusades, though perhaps in a milder form, still hangs over Europe: and that civilization in its dealings with the Islamic world still occupies a position which bears clear traces of the early Crusader spirit."

European imperial interests can never forget that the spirit of Islam is firmly opposed to the spread of imperialism. Such an opposition must either be crushed or at least diverted. No weight need be attached to the contention of gullible or mercenary writers that religion is of no concern to Europeans, that the source of European power is not religious, and that the only thing about the Muslim world which Europe fears is its material power. Fundamentally, religion is a spiritual power which is always effective for the provision of material powers.

Islam is essentially different from Christianity; it encourages the fostering of material powers, it enjoins self-defence and defensive war, and it warns the weaklings who tamely submit that theirs will be an evil fate in this world and in the next.

"Prepare for them as much as you can in the way offerees and cavalry, with which you may overcome Allah's enemies and your own."

"Do not take unbelievers for your friends in preference to Believers."

"So let those fight in the way of Allah who would exchange the life of this world for that of the next."

"Do not grow weary or grieve now that you have the upper hand, if you are true Believers..., etc."

Spiritual and Material Powers: Islam is at once a spiritual power and an incentive to material power; it is at once a form of opposition in itself, and an incentive to a still more forcible opposition. Therefore, European imperialism cannot but be hostile to such a religion. The only difference lies in the fact that the form of that hostility varies according to the imperialistic methods of each nation, and according to local conditions. Thus, for example, France declared open war on Islam in the Western Arab world, under the name of "Protecting the Barbars," or some such phrase. But England took a more devious and tortuous road to the same end in Egypt, that of education.

Its aim was to encourage the growth of a general frame of mind which would despise the bases of Islamic life, and even of Eastern life. When this was accomplished there would be a generation educated into this frame of mind, ready to go out into the schools and educational offices to imbue the coming generations with the same ideas.

These would set a fashion in manners and customs which would ultimately lead to the permanent establishment of the desired frame of mind, and would emphasise the difference between the basic elements of Islamic education and the policies of the Education Ministry. Thus, England could dispense with open hostilities as a means of opposition to religious convictions. And this objective was actually ascribed by a large and influential party to a desire to establish a pan-Egyptian mentality. In the Southern Sudan, again, there was no call for such guile; the position there was simply that which we have already described in speaking of the Christian missionaries and the Muslim merchants.

Thus, each imperialist state has proceeded by one means or another to oppose and to throttle Islam since the last century, and even before that. And that they still proceed to do essentially the same thing in concert is obvious from the position taken up by the United Nations on the question of Indonesia and Holland, on that of Kashmir, India and Pakistan, and on that of Hyderabad, India and the Nizam. Finally the same thing is supremely evident in the position of the United Nations on Palestine.

There are those who hold that it is the financial influence of the Jews in the United States and elsewhere which has governed the policy of the West. There are those who say that it is English ambition and Anglo-Saxon guile which are responsible for the present position. And there are those who believe that it is the antipathy between East and West which is responsible. All these opinions overlook one vital element in the question, to which all other elements are subordinate, the Crusader spirit which runs in the blood of all occidentals.

It is this which colours all their thinking, which is responsible for their imperialistic fear of the spirit of Islam, and for their efforts to crush Arab strength. For the instincts and the interests of all occidentals are bound up together in the crushing of that strength. This is the common factor which links together Communist Russia and Plutocratic America.

The truly remarkable thing is that the spirit of Islam has survived all these attacks which have been launched against it from the earliest period of its life right up to the present. It has persisted, in spite of sudden assaults and the effect which these have had on its life; it had lasted out, in spite of the modern conquest by Western civilization with its material and educational weapons, from which some Muslims have borrowed the means of breaking down and destroying Islam at the direction of imperialistic powers.

Despite all these things, the spirit of Islam has remained essentially sound, and its inner force had left clear imprints on the course of human life in the broadest sense. Islam has left its marks on the forms and objectives of civil government throughout fourteenth centuries to the present day. There is no political or military institution in the world that owes something to Islam; and this has been true even in those ages when the Muslim world has been weak and divided, when it has seen its spiritual, social, and economic life disturbed.

But the period of obscurity and weakness is now at an end, and the tide of Islam has commenced to rise. In East and West alike the Arab world is gaining unity, and two great Islamic blocs have made an appearance in Pakistan and Indonesia. These are portents which cannot be overlooked, significant of the underlying vitality of Islam. They are significant also of the massive resources of Islam, sufficient to bring about a complete renewal of Islamic life. Such a renewal need not be based merely on wishful thinking or on good fortune; rather it may be based on actual concrete facts which are apparent to the sight.

I personally, quite apart from the religious faith, have an absolute belief in the possibility of a renewal of Islamic life within the Muslim world. I believe in the soundness of Islam as a worldwide, rather than a local, system for the future. I have no desire to take refuge in vain speculation, but I do believe this to be not only possible, but even easy.

Not that there will not be various and vast difficulties; there will also be great tasks which must be accomplished before the complete renewal of Islamic life can take place with any facility within Muslim society. The assessment of these vast obstacles, and the inspiration to undertake the tasks involved is something which is necessitated by any true understanding of the immensity of the goal at which we are aiming, and of the weight of responsibility awaiting any man who aims at that goal. It is something which is necessitated also by an understanding of the importance of public opinion in such vast undertakings.

But, it is not enough for any one man to issue a ringing call for hope to become actuality, and expectation reality. The results and the consequences must be assessed, and the man who exhorts others must equally offer to them the same vast effort which he demands of them.

In the very nature of the case, the wide divergence between existing political theory and the spirit of Islam, which has arisen over a long period and has hence become deep-seated, will make it a matter of some difficulty to return to a theory which is truly based on that spirit. For the machinery of the state and of society, the foundations of life in all its aspects, the spiritual and intellectual background are all so built up on specific bases that they are difficult to change without the application of vast energy over a long time. And the longer the time, the greater the difficulty, and the greater the need for yet vaster and longer enduring effort.

The time factor is linked up with another consideration in the present age. We do not live only in this world, but we cannot live in isolation from it. Thus, our interests and our needs are interwoven. The with this present world, which is governed by a certain form of civilization, involving an outlook completely contradictory to that of Islam. This we shall see later. In one respect, this fact will slow down our progress along the path of renewing the true Islamic form of life, and in another respect, it will lay additional responsibilities upon us.

The importance of this last consideration is enhanced by the fact that this Western world with which our interests are interwoven is at the present moment stronger than we; we do not have today the control over it, or the strength equal to its strength, that we had in the first age of Islam. At the same time, it is hostile to us, and in particular hostile to our religion. Therefore, it will not permit us to produce a new Islamic system, or to renew a truly Islamic form of life, however great the effort we put forth. This result we could hope for only if we had control of the Western world, if our strength were comparable to its, or if it were honest with us and with our religion to which we seek to return.

But all this does not mean that return to the Islamic system is impossible. All that it means is that this is a great and difficult task, requiring unremitting effort. Above all it demands courage to believe in it, boldness to face the inevitable results, patience to endure the hard work demanded, and faith to believe that this is necessary for Islamic society and for mankind as a whole. It demands the fostering of a new mentality, whose task will not be simply to elevate the existing state of things, but rather to produce a new and perfect state.

This is our task. We have already seen the foundations on which the system must be built; thus, we can now balance the profits which we shall enjoy if we return to it against the labours and sacrifices which we must make in order to realise it. When our faith in these profits reaches the point at which they outweigh the sacrifices, then let us settle the matter, make up our kinds, and leave the result with Allah.

Perhaps one valuable aspect of the present situation might be pointed out here. The great Western civilization has led the world into two global wars within a quarter of a century; after the second of these it has led it to a complete division into two blocs, an eastern and a western, and to the constant threat of a third war.

It has brought about a state of hostility in every quarter, it has produced starvation and destitution and adversity throughout three parts of the world. It should be pointed out also that the social fabric of the whole world today is in that state of insecurity and instability where it must look for new foundations and search for some spiritual means of restoring to man his faith in the principles of humanity.

We must not, however, read more than is legitimate into this readiness of the Western world to accept the foundations of our Islamic civilization; this is another matter. Although it may be, it noted that such a man as Bernard Shaw says that the West had already started to turn in this direction, and even prophesied that it well come to it eventually, in these words:

> "I forecast that the religion of Muhammad will be accepted in Europe in the near future, for it has already started to gain some acceptance. The priests of the Middle Ages insisted on portraying Islam in the darkest colours, either out of ignorance, or from criminal bigotry; but they were led to excess by their hatred of Muhammad and his religion; indeed they held him to be the anti-Christ. For myself I find it preferable to call Muhammad the saviour of mankind, and I believe that if such a man were given authority over the modern world, he would succeed in solving its problems and giving it peace and happiness. And how great is the world's need of these things."

Western Perspective: There were some impartial thinkers in the nineteenth century who discovered how much value there is in the religion of Muhammad. Among them were Carlyle, Goethe, and Gibbon. From this fact, there has arisen a salutary change in the attitude of Europe towards Islam. Thus, Europe has seen a great advance in the past years of the twentieth century, and has even started to respect the faith of Muhammad.

It may be that in the century that lies ahead, Europe will make further progress, and will acknowledge the contribution of this faith towards a solution of its problems. Many among may own nation and among all European nations already belong to the religion of Muhammad, a fact which enables us to say that the conversion of Europe to Islam has already begun. But so far as we can see Shaw's prophecy is still no more than a prophecy—if, indeed, it is not intended to drug the senses of Muslims and to make them content to wait idly for Europe to embrace their faith. But, however, this may be, we must at least wait until time has proved such a statement, for two principal reasons:

1. There is this deep-seated and inherited hostility to Islam in the very European nature itself. This is at present augmented by the opposition of imperialistic interests to the very existence of our faith, as being an obstacle in their path.
2. European culture is rooted in material foundations, and the influence of intellectual and spiritual interests are very weak; such has been the case from the time of Roman civilization to the present day. This matter requires detailed consideration, and a full treatment, rather than merely a brief mention. So, we must here make an extended study of this important question: Is it possible for Islamic and Western civilizations to work together in partnership? And if so, then what are the limits of that partnership?

We have already asserted at the beginning of this book that Europe was never at any time truly Christian, because by its very nature its people had to fight over their meagre territories.

Thus, the tolerant principles of Christianity could gain no footing in such a stubborn ground. In addition to this, Christianity is essentially an asceticism, a refusal to live, or to take an interest in, a practical worldly life. To these two factors we must now add a third, to which we have already made a passing reference.

This factor was the existence of the Roman Empire, and its position to thwart the path of Christianity, together with the permanent influence of that empire on the bases of European civilization even today. And that despite the infusion of Christianity which the Roman Empire received in its last days.

We may quote here some passages from Islam at the Cross-roads, which we find completely satisfactory: The doctrine on which the Roman Empire was founded was to destroy by force, or to exploit other people for the sole benefit of the mother country. In order to indulge this privileged body the Romans saw nothing wrong in their violence and nothing humiliating in their oppression.

The famous Roman justice was a justice for Romans only. It is apparent that such a tendency as this is possible only on the basis of a materialistic ideal, which is wholly devoted to wordly life and civilization—though it may be an ideal promoted and shaped by a philosophical taste.

In any case it was far removed from any appreciation of spiritual values. The Romans did not really understand religion; their traditional Gods were only variant forms of the Greek myths which, as being mere shades, were never believed to have any connection with social affairs, and which were never permitted to interfere in any way with the real business of life. Their duty was to speak in metre through the agency of their attendant priests, when questions were asked of them; but no one ever expected them to enunciate laws for the guidance of mankind. Such was the soil in which modern Western civilization grew up, though during the period of its growth it undoubtedly came under many other influences. Thus, in the very nature of the case, it changed and thereby modified the legacy which it had received from Rome in more than one way. Nevertheless the fact remains that all that is truly great in the modern West, whether of life or nature, owes its origin to Roman civilization. Hence, since, the intellectual and social environment of ancient Rome was always secular rather than religious—and that no exhypothesis, but in actual fact—so the same environment persists in the modern West.

The European mind has neither possible argument against the complete futility of religion nor will it ever admit the need for such an argument. For modern European thinking in general leaves the absolute outside its scheme of practical considerations— although—it does tolerate religion, and even at times may assert that it is a social virtue. Western civilization does not irrevocably disown God, but it can see no place and no significance for Him in its present intellectual system. It has made a virtue out of a philosophical inability on the part of man, that is to say, out of his inability to take a comprehensive view of the whole field of life.

European, modern Europe tends to attach the greatest practical importance to the values deriving from the experimental sciences, or at least from those sciences from which may be expected some perceptible influence of human social relationships. And because the question of the existence of God does not fall into either of these categories, the European mind tends to drop the concept of God out of the sphere of practical considerations. A question emerges here:

> "How is this tendency to be reconciled with Christian thought? Is not Christianity a faith founded on the Absolute, as is Islam? And is it not ostensibly the spiritual background of Western civilization? There is no doubt that all these things are true. But there could not be any greater mistake than to imagine that Western civilization is the outcome of Christianity. The true philosophical basis of the Western system is to be sought in the ancient Roman view of life as a matter of advantage, quite independent of absolute values."

It is a view which can be summarised thus: Because we have no specific knowledge, either in the way of practical experience, or in that of proof, about the fundamentals of human life, or about its destiny after physical death; therefore, it is best for us to confine our powers to those material and mental fields which are accessible to us, rather than let ourselves to be tied down to metaphysical and moral questions arising from claims which can have no intellectual proofs.

Such an argument as this which is characteristic of modern Western civilization, will certainly not find acceptance in Christian thought, as it will not in Islam or in any other religion, simply because it is essentially religious. Thus, to try to establish a casual relationship between Christianity and modern Western civilization, is a gross historical error.

Christianity may indeed have played a very small part in the rise of intellectual materialism which today dominates modern Western civilization, but the truth is that the growth of this spirit had been the product of Europe's prolonged struggle, against the Christian Church, and against its supervision of life. In its general aspect Christianity today is a purely spiritual thing, as was the case with the Roman deities, which were neither permitted nor expected to exert any real influence on society.

No doubt there are in the West individuals who are still prepared to judge and to think on a religious basis, prepared to fight a last ditch action to reconcile their beliefs with the spirit of their civilization; but they cannot be more than isolated cases. To Europe as a whole it is a matter of indifference whether the political system is 'democratic or fascist, plutocratic or bolshevist, technical or intellectual.'

Europe knows but one necessary religion—the worship of material prosperity; the only belief that it holds is that there is but one goal in life—the making of that life easier and easier. It is, as the definition has it in significant terms, an escape from the tyranny of nature.' The shrines of such a culture are huge factories and cinemas, chemical laboratories and dance-halls and power stations. The priests of such a worship are bankers and mathematicians, cinema stars and scientists and aviators.

The inevitable result of this state of affairs is that man strives to gain power a pleasure; this brings into being quarrelsome societies, all armed to the teeth and intent on mutual destruction whenever their conflicting interests come into active opposition. On the intellectual side, the upshot has been the evolution of a humanism with a moral philosophy confined to purely scientific questions, in which the highest criterion of good or evil is whether or not any given thing represents material progress.

The sum and substance of all this is that the present-day European conscience is not ready to accept the spirit of Islam, or to seek in it a solution of human problems. But even so, it is not impossible that even this may take place after a number of other changes and developments in the West, and after the Islamic world itself has entered upon a clearly defined and independent renewal of Islamic life. In this, the West may find philosophical realities and practical truths which will attract its attention and balance its thinking. But it is my personal belief that many generations must elapse before the West will be able to appreciate the spirit of Islam in any real sense.

Again, the substance of this argument is that the mode of the Muslim doctrine that work must serve moral ends, cannot be reconciled with the mode of the modern Western doctrine that morals must serve some material advantage. We must reckon with this fact, and hence we must work to establish a sound form of Islamic life; this cannot be achieved by the importation of elements borrowed from abroad, since such elements will not fit into the texture of our native beliefs.

The Muslim world will have to admit defeat on the first occasion on which it seeks to renew its own life by borrowing Western ways of thought, life and custom. Such an experiment can only result in the suffocation of that very form of life which it seeks to revive; for from the very first step the Muslim world will be departing from its own true and natural path.

This path involves a belief based on Islam that the moral element is fundamental to the structure of life; it regards work as a means to moral ends, and it will not make material advantage the highest aim of morals. We have already seen in an earlier chapter of this book that Islam satisfies all the highest aims of life, among them the moral consciousness. We have also seen that Islam's supreme virtue is that it preserves the unity of life, and that it makes no distinction between the means and the ends. It will not lend its authority to any idea that there is an opposition between material and spiritual in the substance of life or in the nature of the universe or of mankind; rather it emphasised that the whole of life is a unity which must make an orderly progress towards the highest objectives.

Islam, then, enunciates for men a complete theory of life. This theory is always liable to growth by development or by adaptation; it is not open to change or to adulteration, either in its fundamentals or in its general aims. Therefore, in order that this complete theory may bear its full natural fruits, it is necessary to make a complete application of it. Otherwise, even the slightest change in its fundamentals or its aims will produce a disorder, because it will no longer be in conformity with the Islamic conception of life.

The continual growth of this universal theory by development or by adaptation is a natural product of the nature of Islam; it is encouraged by Islam, the institutions of which are adapted to recognise it. Analogy, interpretation, and the wide powers entrusted to the head of the state—all these are living methods of ensuring growth through development and adaptation, in order to keep pace with life and to meet its needs as they emerge. But there is one thing which must be kept in mind: these developments must not pass out with the roots of the fundamental Islamic theory, nor must they be allowed to serve any foreign aim; they must not betray the spirit of Islam or give allegiance to any other spirit in preference to it.

The criterion by which we may accept or reject any development is first to compare it with the basic theory and the general spirit of Islam. Anything that is in agreement with this theory and this spirit we may accept, and anything which is contrary to these we must reject. Thus, we may profit by all the fruits of human labour within the bounds of our basic philosophy of the universe, man and life; we need raise no barriers between ourselves and human endeavour, nor need we stand in isolation from the continuous business of living.

Above all we must be firmly convinced of the value of faith and enthusiasm; we have a scheme of life greater than any possessed by the followers of any religion or school or civilization which has yet been born. And that is to say the least of it.

No renaissance of Islamic life can be affected purely by law or statute, or by the establishment of a social system on the basis of the Islamic philosophy. Such a step is only one of the two pillars on which Islam must always stand in its construction of life. The other is the production of a state of mind imbued with the Islamic theory of life, to give permanence to external forces leading to this form of life, and to give coherence to all the social, religious and civil legislations.

Social justice is an integral part of this Islamic life. It cannot be realised unless this form of life is first realised, and it cannot have any guaranteed permanence unless this form of life is built up on solid foundations. It is similar in this to all other social systems; it must have the support of public belief and confidence in its merits. Failing this, its foundations will be purely spiritual, and its establishment will depend on the force of religious and social legislation; these are too weak to sustain it, in which case it may easily miscarry.

Hence, Islamic legislation is more akin to ecclesiastical ordinance because it depends on religious belief. Thus, we must always keep in mind the necessity for a renaissance of our religious faith; we must cleanse it of all accretions, such as alterations and interpretations and ambiguities; only thus can it be a support for the necessary social legislation which will establish a sound form of

Islamic life. This form of life will depend upon legislation and exhortation, those twin fundamental methods of Islam towards the achievement of all aims.

We must, then, establish our Islamic theory in individuals and societies, at the same time as we set up the Islamic legislation to regulate life. And the natural method of establishing that philosophy is by education.

But how can we possibly induce Islamic theory by education? For educational methods and modes of thought are essentially Western and essentially inimical to the Islamic philosophy itself; first, because they stand on a materialistic basis which is contrary to the Islamic theory of life; and second, because opposition to Islam is a fundamental part of their nature, no matter whether such opposition is manifest or concealed in various forms.

As we have already maintained, we shall advertise our defeat the first time that we adopt a Western theory of life as the means of reviving our Islamic theory. So, primarily, we must avoid the ways of Western thought; rather we must choose the ways of native Islamic thought, in order to ensure pure results.

The import of these words is not that we should adopt a position of isolationism in regard to thought, education, and science; all these are a common heritage of all the peoples of the world, in which we among the foremost have a fundamental part. We shall continue to take our rightful share in the furtherance of these things, even if it should become apparent that we are far removed from the influence which they exert. For the only true and permanent form of cooperation is that between all the nations of the Earth.

Isolation from human life, then, is not our aim; rather what we seek is to build up a characteristically Islamic theory of life, and to renew that form of life now, when it is apparent even to some of the more enlightened occidentals that the philosophy of materialistic Western civilization is a danger to the continued existence of man.

It breeds in human nature a ceaseless anxiety, a perpetual rivalry, a continual strife, and a weakening of human ties to the breaking point. And this is spite of all the triumphs of science which could have tended to human happiness and peace and content, had it not been that the bases of the Western philosophy of life were purely materialistic and hence unsuitable to men along the path to perfection.

As long as our aim is the building up of this Islamic theory along these lines, we must make a distinction between things which we may profitably accept, and those which we may profitably reject, out of Western society. Only thus may we complete the building of an Islamic society out of sound materials which will produce a structure secure against cooperation and opposition alike, against both borrowing and giving.

From another point of view we must ensure to the theory of life which we establish a safeguard in the form of a period of fostering...fostering, that is, in our own minds rather than in its own essence. For Islamic life in itself is a strong and definite thing when in does not stand in awe of any other Western form. Rather, it is we who need to be fostered and nurtured, as we are living on a strange diet hence we must be on our guard while we are engaged in the establishment of our new system.

In the case of the pure sciences and their applied results of all kinds, we must not hesitate to utilise all things in the sphere of material life; our use of them should be unhampered and unconditional, unhesitating and unimpeded.

Similarly, we must be careful to derive the fullest profit from other things also; from philosophy, which is the intellectual treatment of the universe and life; from literature which is the emotional treatment of these things; from history, which is a factual treatment, and from legislation, which is a treatment of the relationships between individuals and societies.

It will do us no harm to make use of the pure sciences in all the spheres of life; but on the other hand, it will do us harm to account these as the sum total of life; for such a view involves a philosophy which is not ours. It tends to establish a conception of the universe and of life which is at variance with the Islamic conception of those things; ultimately, it would led us along a path which is not that of Islam. It is this path which has produced the present ailments of mankind, and which is responsible for their present troubles.

It is sometimes objected that even if this be so, the pure sciences themselves cannot be held responsible, because essentially they cannot be divorced from the method of Western thought. The experimental method rests on the basis of a definite philosophy which is neither intellectual nor spiritual; if this had never established itself in favour, science would never have followed the course which lately it has taken.

In the same way, science can never remain in isolation from philosophy, nor can it be content to be influenced by philosophy without in turn influencing it. For philosophy is benefited by the experimental results of science, and is influenced by it in aim and method.

Thus, a study of pure science involves a study of philosophy, which is influenced by that science, and which in turn exerts an influence on it. All this is over and above the fact that the applied results of science must influence all material life, methods of gaining a living, and the division of wealth. All this will in due time produce new forms of society based on a new philosophy, or at least based on a theory of life which must be influenced by these developments in the course of life.

All this is very true. But what must be there is no possibility of living in isolation from science and its products, though the harm that it does may be greater than the good. There is no such thing in this life as an unmixed blessing or an unalloyed evil. Thus, Islam does not oppose science, or the utilisation of science; there is nothing contrary to the spirit of Islam in culling the fruits of science from all the sources of the world.

But while we may acknowledge the universal influences of philosophy and culture, history and law, together with all their consequences in the way of educational methods and modes of thought and logic, we must set all of this in its proper place on a spiritual Islamic foundation. We must hold to the guiding principle that all the results and material consequences of science do not essentially affect our universal philosophy of life and custom.

When we mention educational methods we might well bear in mind here that these are indivisible and inseparable from the general philosophy of the community. Thus, when we borrow Western methods of education, systems of training and curricula, we borrow also a general scheme of philosophy and a mode of thought which underlies these methods and systems and curricula, whether we like it or not.

There is a belief that these are questions of pure 'pedagogy', and therefore universal and identical throughout all countries. This is a naive and shortsighted belief, encouraged by the delusion of the psychologists, who give an undue weight to their own subject; despite the difference between psychology and philosophy, such men believe that they can master their own subject, and through it can answer the philosophical questions of education also.

That claim is one thing, but the actual fact is quite another. Psychology may perhaps be a pure science to be studied in the laboratory. But the treatment of its results and the use to which these are put, such as educational techniques and curricula—all these things are still influenced by the general philosophy of life, still accept the dictation of that philosophy, and still form an integral part of it.

Moreover, the very fact that psychology is ruled by the laboratory is one of the influences exerted by experimental philosophy, or by the experimental method. It is this same method which in later years has governed all materialistic Western thought. The only type of independence which psychology can expect from the philosophy which is its mentor is that superficial independence which cannot influence the final result.

For an example, we may look to the American curriculum, their methods of education and instruction, these are more akin to vocational training than to any system of thorough and systematic study; they have as their objective the promotion of technical skill based on theoretical principles. The reason for this tendency is to be sought in the philosophy of pragmatism, founded by Charles Pierce in 1878 which was advanced by William James and applied by John Dewey, the modern educational philosopher. This school of thought represents a reversal of the accepted terms of thought and study: bare ideas and theoretical principles are abandoned, as is the study of things according to their logical class and nature. According to Pragmatism, all study should be confined to the practical effects and result of objects.

According to Charles Pierce of Pragmatism the idea is no more than a secondary product of some act or activity; it is not in itself a reality. For example, I may have the 'idea' of the horn of an automobile passing in the street; this 'idea' gains no meaning by my study of its nature, its origin, and the method of its production. It may be a reality or it may be a figment of imagination; it may be produced by the ear and the nervous system, or it may be produced by the horn, whether, the automobile is turning right or left, and whether a path must be cleared for the vehicle and its driver. It means only:

> "I am about to change the direction of my vehicle and to proceed in a different direction. Hence, Pragmatism argues that the idea is secondary to the act, or the product of certain conditioning circumstances. This is the first step along the path of Pragmatism in which all the remaining steps must follow."

It has been the rise of this theory or this method of thought which has produced the educational techniques of America. It has been responsible for a teaching curriculum and a system which will encourage the mind to take this view of things and to rationalise life along this line. Also, it is this which has given American life its most characteristic mark, which has directed it towards technical production, and which has to a large extent diverted it from academic and theoretical education.

Accordingly, we must reckon with this general philosophy of life; if we borrow educational techniques, teaching systems, and curricula, this philosophy underlines all of them. This philosophy shapes and forms them, assisted by the results of pure psychology. Such an influence is inevitable, though this same science in its methods and in its results is itself influenced by that very philosophy.

From the theoretical point of view, then, our method of establishing an independent Islamic scheme of thought is to proceed readily but cautiously in the matter of borrowing such a philosophy along with its concomitants, such as educational techniques, teaching systems and curricula, literature, history and law. But we shall deal now with all these subjects together.

Universe and Mankind: So far as the study of philosophy is concerned, we have already indicated the universal theory of Islam on the universe, life and mankind, this is essentially different from the nature of other universal philosophies which have originated in the West from the days of the Greeks to the present. This is not the place to discuss this difference, and it will suffice to recognise merely that there does exist a radical divergence.

A petition of peculiar importance was once addressed to the Azhar University concerning a matter which was not favourably regarded in this quarter. It requested that study be directed to this universal Islamic theory of life and that a full and clear treatment of it be given in modern terms and applications; also that it be compared with other schools of philosophy. But the Azhar, instead of responding to this petition, continued to teach in its Faculty of Theology what it called the errors of Islamic philosophy, taken from the writings of Ibn-Sina and Ibn-Rushd.

This is, of course, a reversion to Greek philosophy, which has no real connection with the universal philosophy of Islam. Thus, in effect, the petition sent to the governors of the Azhar was neglected, and a spiritual and intellectual defeat was acknowledged in our primary seat of learning, a defeat for the Islamic theory of life.

If, then, we are to establish a sound Islamic theory of the universe, life and mankind, it is essential that Western philosophies and their moral corollaries should not be studied at all in our secondary schools, and that they should be studied in the university only after at least two years in the department of philosophy. And by the very nature of the case they should not be studied in the Azhar colleges until the very end of the course. In every centre of study such Western philosophies should be preceded by a course in pure Islamic thought, as distinct from the so-called "Islamic philosophy," in order to emphasise the true Islamic viewpoint.

Thus, the minds and thoughts of the students will assimilate the native bases of the spirit of Islam, together with its ideas on the universe, life and mankind, good and evil, work and reward, and all the other philosophic aspects of pure Islamic belief. This having been assured, we may in the later years of university study proceed to give some account of the other philosophies; these would include Greek philosophy and its opposition to Islamic, modern European and American philosophy; these should be compared in every case with Islamic philosophy.

In this way, we can ensure that the student's mind and conscience will not be too much influenced; we can ensure also a minimum influence on student's ideas and thoughts, because by then they will be equipped for critical appreciation. They will have the requisite knowledge to reject all that does not agree with the fundamental modes of thought of a Muslim people. Under these circumstances their new knowledge will not harm, but will rather benefit students; for it will be purely academic knowledge, largely independent of any influence on their conscience or on their conception and understanding of life and its requirements.

We have already given one example of pragmatism in its view of things. But in this example, there was no indication of the dangers inherent in that philosophy or in its method; so we must now follow out this philosophy in its further results, in order to note the dangerous influences of its intellectual system on many a nation which follows such modern of thought.

Most people believe in God. This is an idea which logically may be either false or true. Intellectual theory says:

> "If God really exists, then His existence must be logically demonstrable. Pragmatism on the other hand attacks the problem from a different angle, and lays the emphasis on a different aspect. In its view the truth of the idea of God does not depend on logical necessity; it depends solely on the profit of this idea to our well-ordered life, in our daily activity and on our experiences. If the idea tends to produce a profit in life, then it is sound and therefore true. Hence, God does exist. Apart from this test, pragmatism claims, in the first place we cannot judge this idea; and in the second place we cannot trust our own judgement."

The Islamic line of thought differs to a greater or lesser extent from that of pure intellectual theory, insofar as it does not entrust the whole question to human logic alone, but relies also upon revelation. But it is in complete opposition to pragmatism; for when we follow out its logic to a conclusion we find that the idea of God must disappear if the outward benefits of material life are not forthcoming.

The idea of God loses its existence because it cannot control its instruments and set the machinery in motion. In consequence, material profit becomes the sole criterion, not only of the acceptance or the rejection of things, but also of existence or non-existence. This implies a state of affairs in which man loses all nobility, where he is neither more nor less than an instrument.

Policies in this world cannot be divorced from such philosophies. Thus perhaps, we are not far from the truth when we say that the policy of the United States on the Palestine question and its stand in the United Nations on the question of Egypt were merely the results of its intellectual background of pragmatism— in conjunction, of course, with other factors.

The idea of right and justice had little effective place in materialistic American life; and hence it had little chance of permanent acknowledgment in international policies. This idea is perhaps the most satisfactory comment on these puzzling policies. What we do not want is to establish such an intellectual background as this, in our Islamic society. We must therefore be cautious about the study of Western philosophy until we have first established in adolescent minds a firm, strong, and clear pattern of thought which is founded on the universal Islamic theory.

Similarly, we must be cautious about borrowing educational techniques, curricula, and systems of teaching; for all of these are ruled by the general field of philosophy in their native lands; they subserve the aims which that philosophy assigns to them, whether immediate or remote.

Moral Philosophy: Literature is the emotional response to life. It issues from the same well-spring whence flow in any culture all the philosophies, the religious beliefs, the experiments and the influences. Literature is the most important factor in the establishment of a moral philosophy of life, and in the production of any specific influence on the human mind. Hence, we must exercise care in the choice of Western literature which we make available to our youth, alike in their Arabic and their foreign studies.

It is not necessary to take this as meaning that our youth are to be prohibited from reading European literature; what we have in mind here is simply a process of choice and selection. For in this literature, there are elements, the spirit of which is at one with the spirit of Islam. By this, we do not mean that such books 'encourage goodness and reprobate wickedness' for literature is no preacher to exhort and to direct. Rather, we mean that such books have a view of life which is spiritual and moral, rather than materialistic, and that they acknowledge the spiritual values of life.

This type of literature agrees in spirit with the general teachings of our Islamic theory; it can therefore do no harm to the moral consciousness of our youth, nor can it upset their emotional and mental development at a dangerous stage. This dangerous stage lasts at least until the third year of university work, if not until the time of graduation.

There is no harm, but rather great benefit, in having private reading including all types of the literatures of the world, without restraint or exception. But the prime aim of a process of choice and selection is to safeguard the period of adolescence from being debilitated and led astray.

History is a branch of literature; but it is one which has its own characteristics, and which therefore had also its peculiar dangers. For history is a presentation of the events of life, and it is necessarily influenced by the materialistic background of the West. Even if it is by intellectual theory that it is influenced, it will still ignore the spiritual powers and their effect on the course of events, together with the spiritual explanation of facts. It will give its own interpretations, designed to establish a philosophy of life independent of the spirit and unconnected with moral aims. Here, it is opposed to Islamic theory.

Beyond this, historians, who have been for the most part Europeans, have made the history of Europe the focal point of world history. In view of the nature of man this is excusable, and we have borne it with patience as a characteristically Western and European delusion. Yet, if our youth are to study history in this spirit and by this method, then they will finish with two false beliefs:

1. That spiritual factors have no influence on the course of events in time, or at least that any such influence is very weak.
2. That Europe is the mistress of historical events, and that the influence of the East and of Islam is exiguous.

Both these ideas have harmful and dangerous results; they establish a false general idea of life, of the world, and of events, and they endanger our patriotic pride and our pride in Islam, which is so necessary in face of the sweeping pride of Europe. In order to guard our youth from this evil we must take the two following steps:

1. We must begin by putting general world history, as Islam views it, in perspective, in the form of events and happenings. We must not be concerned solely with the European point of view in this present dangerous fashion. In such a history we must give Europe its rightful place and no more, and we must emphasise the part played in world history by the East in general, and by Islam in particular.
2. We must change the present curriculum of history teaching in our schools and colleges. We must start by teaching primarily the history of Islam throughout the Muslim world, and by expounding it from the Islamic point of view. It is not enough to teach our children the history of Islam as written by Western authors, or as expounded by Western philosophies. When their minds are filled with the history of their own countries, then we can give them the world history as written by ourselves, to form the next stage of study. And when they have completed that, then we can give them in successive stages the remainder of the developments of history.

The study of law is similarly influenced by the Western point of view, by Western philosophy, history, law, and society. For law is a reflection of society, or is produced by it; and society is the offspring of all these factors.

In order to build up a sound Islamic doctrine, we must teach Islamic law in a broad general way before beginning to teach any specific legal system. The teaching of Islamic law must be firmly in the control of Muslim professors, and the Western point of view must not be allowed to obtrude, except in the later stages. Similarly, the study of law in general must not be opened up till that same later stage.

It is one of the requirements of Islamic life that the religious law shall occupy a paramount position; and that very fact will make necessary such a study of Islamic law as we have indicated. The great necessity which faces our professors of Islamic law in this field is to follow the authoritative path traced out by the Imams and their students at the time of the first growth of Islamic law.

When we have disposed of this theoretical question of the objective, we are still confronted by that of the specific constitutional enactments which will ensure a sound form of Islamic life and which will guarantee social justice to all. In this question, it is not possible to take a stand purely on the form of the original Islamic life; rather we must utilise all possible and permissible means which fall within the general principles and the broad foundations of Islam. Nor must we be afraid to use also all the discoveries which man has made in the way of social legislation and systems, so long as the principles of these do not run counter to the principles of Islam, and so long as they are not opposed to its theory of life and mankind.

We must include these in our legislation so long as they conduce to the true welfare of society, or so long as they ward off any impending evil. In the two principles of 'public interest' and 'blocking of means' we have two clear Islamic principles which give wide powers to the temporal ruler to ensure the general welfare at all times and in all places. Before we go on to deal with the application of these two principles it might be well to quote a short passage in explanation of them.

Public Interest: Any welfare measure which has no specific detailed authority to support it is known as a measure of public interest. The question of whether or not it is a root of jurisprudence is a matter of dispute among the jurisconsults. Al-Qarafi has argued that all the jurisconsults have used it or have admitted it as a proof at one time or another, even though in lecturing most of them deny it the status of a root. He says in regard to this point:

> "Other people loudly deny the validity of public interest. But when the case is closely examined, they are found to refer to the word in its absolute sense. They do not trouble to take any account of the evidence offered by the reference of the term in its synonyms and contexts; they hold that it means merely convenience, and that such is the sole meaning of the phrase, public interest."

No matter whether this claim is true or false, it is certain that the validity of any measure of welfare which lacks a specific validating authority is a matter on which the *Ulama* may well disagree. And even if public interest is not one of the accepted roots of jurisprudence, at least it had the status of a custom, as Al-Qarafi indicates. The opinions of the *Ulama* in this matter can be divided into four main views, as follows:

1. The Shafites and those who share their opinions do not believe in any form of public interest whose validity is unsupported by legal evidence; for they only admit legal precedents and the treatment of these by analogy, based on the existence of a solid connection between the root and its derivatives, that is to say, between a case governed by a precedent and another analogous to it. If we follow Al-Qarafi we must admit that it is strange that they should deny public interest while they admit analogy.
2. The Hanafites and others of similar opinions maintain the principles of preference and analogy, but their interpretation of preference is sometimes almost indistinguishable from public interest. A fair estimate would say that in their system they make a greater use of interest than do the Shafites, But even so, the extent to which they do use it is negligible, and hence we cannot say that this principle is one of the roots of their system; not, at least, on any grounds of the use which they make of it in itself.
3. There are those who attach an excessive importance to public interest, even to the point of making it stronger than precedent in their dealings with cases; they regard it as a form of precedent, or rather, as a form of consensus. Thus where the *Ulama* are agreed on a point turning on precedent, but some aspect of that point runs counter to public interest, then the validity of the latter is the stronger. This applies also to specific cases, as Al-Tufi has maintained.
4. There are those who hold a middle course, which is the soundest of all. Here, validity is granted to public interest, but it is not derived from precedent, which is held to be entirely different. To this view most of the Malikite rites adhere.

Malik held that public interest was an independent root of the system of jurisprudence, but that it was a derived, rather than an original root; and that so, for the following reasons:

1. The Companions of Allah's Messenger found that questions arose after his death which had not been apparent during his lifetime. Thus, they collected the noble Quran in book form. This had not been done in the time of the Messenger, but now such a collection was in the public interest; for they feared that the Quran might be forgotten because of the deaths of those who had memorised it. Umar saw such men dying in numbers during the Wars of Apostasy, and, fearing that through their death the Quran might pass from memory, he advised Abu-Bakr to have it collected in book form to this the Companions gladly assented.

2. After the death of Allah's Messenger his Companions agreed that the punishment for wine-drinking should be eighty lashes. Their reason for this was the public interest or general inference; for they saw that drinking tended to produce lying and the slandering of chaste women because of the wild talk in which drinkers indulged.
3. The orthodox Caliphs agreed upon imposing conscription on craftsmen, although the root principle was that the exercise of their craft was a matter of good faith. But it was found that unless they were conscripted they would neglect the care of the people's belongings and wealth. There was great need of craftsmen, and therefore, it was in the public interest to conscript them, that they might perform the duties which they had. Thus Ali, when he prescribed the conscription, said: 'The people's interests cannot be served otherwise.'
4. Umar ibn-al-Khattab used to claim half of the wealth of those governor whom he suspected of having increased their resources by extortion. This also was a form of public interest, because to his mind it was in the interests of the governors to prevent them capitalizing on their power to amass money and heap up illegal plunder.
5. It is told of Ali that he poured out on the ground milk which had been adulterated with water, as a lesson to the man who had done it. This act also was akin to public interest, to show that people were not to adulterate goods.
6. There is tradition that Umar put a whole community to death for the murder of one man, for which they had been jointly responsible. This he did because the public interest demanded it. There was no precedent for the case, but the public interest demanded that the case be considered as one of premeditated murder of a sacrosanct individual. To let the murder pass unavenged would have been to deny the root principle of 'an eye for an eye', while to choose one out of the many who had a hand in the business would have made the whole matter ridiculous. For the man chosen would know that in his case it was not a case of retaliation. Or if it were said that this was an anonymous murder, a killing without a killer, on the grounds that every single individual could not be said to be the murderer, then the guilty party was the community itself. The whole of a community can commit a murder in exactly the same way as an individual criminal. And murder can be charged against a community just as it can against a single person, and the members of the community stand in the same relation to the act of murder as does an individual. Hence, the community furthers the public interest when it prevents bloodshed and guards communal life."

Role of the Imams: Another general aspect of public interest is the power which is granted to the Imam to levy upon the rich whatever toll he thinks that the circumstance warrants. This he can do when the public treasury is empty, or when the army has extraordinary needs, while there are no funds to meet those needs. Toll may be levied until the treasury is replenished, or until the needs are sufficiently met.

Further, the Imam has the duty of instituting this levy at times of bountiful harvest and plentiful crops, so that the rich will not be overburdened by the fact that it is they alone who pay it. The public interest here lies in the fact that if a just Imam did not do this, his power would be in vain, and wealthy establishments would provide an incentive to civil war, and to attacks by envious persons. It is sometimes said that the Imam, instead of enforcing the provisions of the levy, borrows money for the public treasury. To this Al-Shatibi retorted that:

> "Borrowing in times of need is allowed only when the treasury has the prospect of more revenue. Otherwise, or alternatively when the revenue is too small to be sufficient, then recourse must be had to the principle of a levy."

A means is that which leads to an end, and to 'block the means' is to remove it. The sense of the phrase is that anything which conduces to a forbidden end is itself forbidden, while anything conducive to a desirable end is itself desirable. Thus, for example, adultery is forbidden, and, therefore, to admire the charms of a strange woman is also forbidden, as being a means towards adultery.

On the other side, attendance at prayers is compulsory, and therefore an effort to attend prayers is also compulsory, as is leaving one's business to make that effort. To make the pilgrimage is compulsory; therefore an effort to visit the Sacred House and to perform the other rites of pilgrimage is also compulsory.

The fundamental reason for the validity of 'blocking the means' is a realisation of the repercussions and final results of all actions. If they are conducive to those public interests which constitute the aims and objectives of the dealings of man with man, then they are as desirable as those aims themselves. But if they are not equally desirable, or if their results might be evil, then they are forbidden just as evil is forbidden, even though the means may be somewhat less objectionable.

In considering the results of actions, the matter of interest is not the purpose or the objective of the agent; rather, it is the result and outcome of his action. The individual will be rewarded or punished for his intention in the next world; but in this world, it is according to its result and outcome that an action is good or bad, desirable or undesirable. For this world must take its stand on the welfare of mankind, on judgement and justice, and these things require a scrutiny of results and outcomes rather than of estimable aims and worthy intentions. A man who out of a sincere love for the worthy intentions and for the worship of Allah reviles idols has gained the approval of Allah by the formulation of his purpose; and yet, he has forbidden such reviling in cases where it would result in the rage of the idolaters, who would then revile Allah the Great, Himself. So, His exalted words run:

> "And do not revile those who invoke deities other than Allah, lest in response they revile Allah without knowledge." In this noble prohibition, regard it had to be the actual consequences, rather than to the commendable religious aim. Hence, it appears

that in cases which tend towards crime or evil, the veto is directed not towards the aim itself, which is sincere, but towards the consequences which will arise; thus an act may be forbidden because of its consequences, even though Allah may be aware that the intention underlying it is sincere.

Sometimes also a man may seek an evil end through a legal act, in which case he is guilty in his own conscience and in the sight of Allah. But no man may take measures against him, nor may any legal penalties be invoked upon him. Such is the case of man who cuts the price of his goods in order to injure a business rival. This is undoubtedly a legal act; yet, it is a means towards a crime, that on injuring another.

This crime is the man's object, but in spite of that his action cannot be punished by the power of the law, nor does it fall under any penalty which the law of the land can impose. His action, from the point of view of intention, is a means to evil, but externally it is a means to public and private benefit. Undoubtedly the seller benefits by selling, by the circulation of his goods, and by the goodwill which he gains; equally certainly the public benefits by the cut in price, by which a general lowering of prices is encouraged.

The principle of blocking the means had regard not only to individual aims and intentions, as we have seen, but also to the encouragement of public welfare and to the prevention of public evil. Thus, it must take account of the consequences along with the intention, or even of the consequences alone.

The principle of 'means' is firmly established in the Quran and the Sunna. In the former, there is the verse: "And do not revile those who invoke Gods other than Allah, lest in response they revile Allah without knowledge." Of this it is related that the idolaters said that they were content to have their Gods reviled if they in turn could revile Muhammad's God. Thus again: "O you who believe, do not say Raina; say Unzurna and hearken. This was because the Muslims used the former word with good intention, but the Jews took it as implying a derogatory sense to the Prophet."

In the Sunna there are many stories of the Prophet and many decisions of his Companions. Among them is that of his refusal to kill the hypocrites, lest the unbelievers should have a pretext for saying that Muhammad killed his Companions.

There is also the story that the Prophet forbade a man who had loaned money to accept a gift from the debtor, unless the gift was counted as part repayment of the loan. The reason was simply that the gift was a means of postponing payment, and was therefore a form of interest. For the lender would get his money back and extra also in the form of the gift. We have also the account of the Prophet's having forbidden that men's hands should be cut off in time of war; the purpose was to stop this practice leading to an illegal treatment of fighting men which would inevitably ensue.

Similarly, laws should not be intermitted in times of war, lest freedom become licence; the two are closely related. And there is the account of the earliest Believers, both Emigrants and Helpers, having on their death-beds appointed their divorced wives as their heirs; this they did because there was a suspicion of a plot to debar such wives from inheriting. It was not even certain that such a plot existed, but divorce was a 'means' which might have produced injustices.

Again, the Prophet forbade monopolies, saying: 'Only sinners hold monopolies.' For a monopoly is a means to oppress the people in all things which are considered to be essential. But there is no law against a monopoly in any article which cannot injure the people by being withheld, such as cosmetics and the life; for these things do not come under the heading of necessities.

The Prophet also forbade any man who had given alms to buy them back, even though, he might see them displayed for sale in the market. Thus, he sought to check the means to recover what had been given to Allah, even by purchase. Thus, anyone who gives alms is forbidden to repossess them by purchase, and is yet more stringently forbidden to repossess them by other means. To permit repossession by purchase might be a means of cheating the poor; the rich out of his wealth would give alms to the poor, and might then buy them back from him at less than their value. The poor man, on the other hand, would see some profit to himself, and thus his conscience would not oppose the sale.

Thus, there are many indications of this principle, deriving from the Messenger and his Companions. Ibn-Qiyam has collected some ninety such examples from actual occurrences, in all of which the principle of blocking the means is clearly illustrated.

"Means are counted to be half of the legal principles of Islam."

These two principles, that of public interest and that of blocking the means, both run back to a common root, that of ensuring the welfare of society. They are integrally connected with the established laws of Islam and with its general purposes. It is these two principles which can guide us towards the legislation necessary to ensure a sound form of Islamic life and to include in its scope a comprehensive social justice. This principle must be our concern in a general work dealing with social justice in Islam; yet, it is desirable to mention some of the things which Islam is able to ensure in this sphere for the present and the future. We must also deal with the legislation necessary to produce these things, so that it may be used as a pattern for analogous treatment in other cases. We cannot deal with all possible developments but these may be safely left to the dictation of circumstances times and conditions.

Fruitless Efforts

After taking stock of the failure of the national constitutions and international charters in protecting the fundamental rights of man, we now come to the basic question: Why could not man so far succeed in finding out a satisfactory arrangement for the protection of his rights, and why this problem has defied thought, intellect and understanding of man so far?

The Quran furnishes a definite and decisive answer to this. It tells that there is only one cause of all this corruption. You have changed the Sovereign, and the tin-gods you have fashioned for yourself as the centre of all your obedience and loyalties have you in their clutches and are denying you your rights. The Quran says that the first covenant of man was made with his Creator and the real Ruler of this universe.

And according to this covenant recognizing God as the Sovereign every one had individually taken an oath of allegiance to Him alone and none else besides Him. Nor shall any partners be assigned to Him whether it be in His Person, attributes or authority. This oath of allegiance and bearing witness to His Sovereignty was the basis of man being made the vicegerent of God, the true Sovereign, and his being sent in His Realm with a way of life prescribed for him. Here he had to run all his individual and collective affairs according to this code of conduct as also according to the guidance received from Him through His Messengers and His Revelations from time to time.

In this covenant, which was renewed and reminded of from time to time and which was presented to mankind in its most perfect and complete form through the last Prophet, Muhammad (Salam) and for ever made immune against perversion, so that it may serve for the guidance of mankind to the end of days, the absolute rights and powers of the Sovereign. His kingdom which knows of no frontiers, the true nature of His man's relationship with Him and His servant—the position of man in the world, the goal of his life, the means of attaining this goal, the norms of success and failure, the mutual relationship between man and man, the sphere of the activities of individual and collective life, the powers of those entrusted with the collective affairs of men in this kingdom of God, the limits and conditions of obedience, accountability for each and every deed of his before the Sovereign in the Hereafter and according to the record of his conduct here in this world, the reward or punishment, every thing is given in such detail that in their light the right and straight path of life has been made quite evident.

Now whoever takes to the straightpath, also called the path of rectitude by the Quran, is successful in this life as well in the next, to be rewarded with eternal bliss; and whoever, leaving this path, takes to another path of his own liking and chalked out by himself, is doomed to failure here in this life and liable for eternal torment in the next.

The whole Quran was revealed to point out this "Straight Path" and the "Path of Rectitude", The Psalms of David, Torah and Bible were all revealed to make clear this path. Right from the first man and prophet of God, Adam, to the last Prophet Muhammad (Salam) all the prophets come only with this message: "Servants of God! Do not make the servants of God your god. You are passing your life under the only Sovereign Whose unlimited, eternal and all pervading authority and rule extends over every little particle of this universe. Other than Him you have no Lord and Cherisher, no Absolute Ruler, no Master and no Sustainer. Going through the Quran we find that all the prophets had the one and only mission —to end the sovereignty of the tyrants of their time, Pharaoh, Nimrods and others and redeeming the servants of God from abject slavery to them, bring them back to the service and obedience of the wisest of judges."

Before taking stock in some detail of the effects on human life of living up to the terms of this covenant and also of turning away from it, let us see what that first covenant was which the servants of God made with their Lord.

> When thy Lord drew forth the children of Adam—from their loins—their descendants, and made them testify concerning themselves, (saying): "Am I not your Lord (Who cherishes and sustains you)?" They said: "Yea ! We do testify!" (This) lest you should say on the Day of Judgement: "Of this we were never mindful" or lest you should say: "Our fathers before us may have taken false gods, but we are (their) descendants after them: wilt thou then destroy us for the deeds of men who were futile."
>
> (Al Quran VII: 172-173)

The Covenant: Long before commencement of the life of man on earth, was this covenant made, and has certain very prominent points for our consideration:

1. Accepting Allah as one's only Cherisher and Lord.
2. All the men from the time without beginning to the end of days taking oath of allegiance to God individually and their being witness to that oath.
3. Promise on oath to abstain from polytheism or taking any other god instead of God or ascribing partners to the one and only God.
4. Closing the door for putting forth the creed and practices of forefathers as an excuse for polytheism.
5. Accountability for each and every deed of this world in the next.

Allah also made arrangements for continual reminders and renewal of the commitment after this first ever covenant of His servants, lest digressing from the straight path of guidance, they may not fall into the abyss of lowness and disgrace by becoming the slaves of any one else other than Allah. The covenant made with men collectively, was made individually also with the prophets who were sent for the ratification and as a reminder of their first covenant, although they were among those participating in the first covenant as the progeny of Adam. But to make them realise the high position and the great responsibilities of that position, the Lord and Cherisher of the Heavens and the Earth took an oath of allegiance from them individually:

> Behold! God took the covenant of the Prophets' saying: "I give you a Book and Wisdom; then comes to you an apostle, confirming what is with you: do ye believe in him and render him help". God said: "Do ye agree and take this My covenant as binding on you?" They said: "We agree". He said: "Then bear witness, and I am with you among the witnesses." If any turn back after this, they are perverted transgressors.
>
> (Al Quran III: 82)

These covenants of the position of vicegerency and that of prophet-hood were renewed time and again. Allah renewed this covenant with every prophet and every Ummah separately:

> And remember We took from the prophets their covenant: from Nuh, Ibrahim, Moses and Jesus, the son of Mary: We took from them a solemn covenant that (God) may question the (custodians) of Truth, concerning the Truth they (were charged with): And He has prepared for the unbelievers a grievous Penalty.
>
> (Al Quran XXXIIL-7-8)

The covenants made with the prophets did not only include acceptance of Allah as the Sovereign and exclusion of others from servitude meant for Allah alone, but they were also asked to take an oath of allegiance to Allah that they would proclaim the faith of Allah over all other religions and redeem them from the rebels who have taken to the path of disobedience and rebellion, and in the realm of Allah have carved out a kingdom for themselves, and made the servants of Allah their own slaves, and depriving them of the freedom conferred on them by Allah, have tried to make them subservient to themselves. Reminding the prophets of their mission, the Quran says:

> The same religion has He established for you as that which He enjoined on Nuh—the which We have sent by inspiration to thee—and that which We enjoined on Ibrahim, Moses and Jesus: camely, that ye should remain steadfast in Religion and make no divisions therein. (Al Quran XLII: 13)

The Ummah, literally a group, a community or a nation, in Islamic terminology, a group or community organised on the basis of revelation and the teachings and preachings of an apostle or prophet of God for whose guidance the prophets had been sent, were also asked to take an oath of allegiance and were reminded of their covenants. Addressing the children of Israel it was said:

> God did aforetime take a firm covenant from the children of Israel, and We appointed twelve captains among them. And God said: "I am with you if ye (but) establish regular prayers, practise regular charity (give Zakat regularly), believe in My apostles, honour and assist them, and loan to God a beautiful loan, verily I will wipe out from you evils, and admit you to Gardens with rivers flowing beneath; but if any of you, after this, resisteth faith, he hath truly wandered from the path of rectitude.
>
> (Al Quran V: 13)

At another place the same covenant has been recalled to mind thus:

> And remember a covenant from the children of Israel (to this effect): worship none but God; treat with kindness your parents and kindred, and orphans and those in need; speak fair to people: be stead fast in prayer; and Practise regular charity (give Zakat regularly). Then did ye turn back, except a few among you, and you back-slide (even now). And remember We took your covenant (to this effect): shed no blood amongst you, nor turn out your own people from your homes: and this ye solemnly ratified, and to this ye can bear witness. (Al Quran II: 82-84)

In these verses we find not only acceptance of Allah as one's Lord and Cherisher, but the whole code of conduct for which the covenant had been made. These verses also reveal that all the prophets of Allah have been coming with the same message. These injunctions for establishing prayers and paying the Zakat is not just poor-due or alms or charity as translated by some translators of the Quran. Of the two types of worships, one involving physical effort, like prayer and fasting, and the other spending out of the God-given bounties, in His way. Zakat falls in the second category. It is just as obligatory as prayers, and not optional as the words alms or charity suggest.

A believer not paying Zakat in spite of capacity to do so, is a transgressor. But one denying its obligatory nature is no more a believer unless and until he repents and mends his mode of thought spending in the way of Allah, kind treatment to parents, kindreds, orphans and those in need, speaking only the truth, respect for human life and abstaining from making people the targets of oppression and tyranny, have not been given to the followers of Muhammad (Salam) alone but all the Ummah of the past had been given the same injunctions, and Allah has taken .he covenant of all peoples to abide by the same code of conduct for life for the establishments of human society on moral principles.

The children of Israel have also been reminded of their covenants with Allah in Quran 11: 93, 95, III: 187 and IV: 154-155.

Let us now have a look at the following remarks of the Quran about the followers of Jesus Christ:

> From those who call themselves Christians, We did take a covenant, but they forgot the part of the Message that was sent to them. (Al Quran V: 14)

After relating the account of the covenants taken from the Ummah of the past, breach of trust and its fatal consequences, the Quran addresses the Ummah of the Last Prophet thus:

> And call in remembrance the favour of God unto you, and His covenant, which He ratified with you, when ye said "We hear and we obey": and fear God, for God knoweth well the secrets of your hearts. (Al Quran V: 7)

Alongwith reminding the Ummahs separately of the responsibilities of their covenants, Allah, drawing their attention to their first ever covenant, addresses the entire mankind thus:

> Did I not enjoin on you, O ye children of Adam, that you should not worship Satan; for that he was to you an avowed enemy? and that ye should worship Me, for this was the straight path? (Al Quran XXXVI: 60-61)

The Quran, along with making mankind realise the responsibilities of their covenant, puts before them very clearly the consequences of living up to it and also those of its contravention, so that they may not remain labouring under the misapprehension, that there is going to be no accountability and punishment for their breach of trust, nor be dispirited with the erroneous idea that making good his promise was not going to benefit him. Allah, giving glad tidings of a great reward to the keepers of the trust and warning to the defaulters against a painful torment, Himself makes a covenant with His servants:

> Nay—those that keep their plighted faith and act a right,—verily God loves those who act a right. As for those who sell the faith they owe to God and their own plighted word for a small price, they shall have no portion in the Hereafter.
>
> (Al Quran III: 76-77)

> Those who break God's covenant after it is ratified, and who sunder what God has ordered to be joined, and do mischief on earth: these cause loss (only) to themselves.
>
> (Al Quran II: 27)

The same thing has been said in verse 25 of Surah Rad (XIII) in a slightly different manner. Pointing out the difference between those keeping their pledge and those breaking the vow and the reason for the different treatments meted out to them, Allah says:

> Is then one who doth know that which hath been revealed unto thee from thy Lord is the Truth, like one who is blind? It is those who are endued with understanding that receive admonition; Those who fulfil the covenant of God and fail not in their plighted word.
>
> (Al Quran XIII: 19-20)

These verses of the Quran reveal that right from Adam to the last individual of his off spring, every one of us, under the first ever covenant and then its renewal individually through every Prophet, is strongly bound in this covenant with his Greater and Master that he would not take any one else as his Lord and Cherisher and shall not bow down his head before any one in subservience other than Him. He shall not recognise any one as his absolute ruler and shall shape his individual and collective life according to the guidance and injunctions received from his Sovereign through the prophets raised by Him, received finally in their most perfect form through Muhammad, His last Prophet, made immune against all perversion and distortion. If ever a mortal among them rises to proclaim himself as their god, his claim shall be thrown back into his face; and he shall receive the treatment that rebels deserve. He himself will obey his Lord and Cherisher and call others too to it. Not in any single affair of his life he will act but in accordance with the injunction of Allah, conveyed through His prophet and obey only those in authority obeying Allah and His prophet and he will completely abstain from polytheistic practices.

After this elucidation of the First Ever covenant and its renewal let us now see what are the effects of recognising Allah as the sole Sovereign or rejecting His Sovereignty, on man's life, and how through the decision of man on one or the other side, the distance between the Truth and Falsehood goes on increasing until they are poles apart, and how man basically enjoying the status of the vicegerent of Allah and the noblest entity in this universe, next only to his Lord, losing all his high status and position falls into the abysmal depths of lowness and disgrace.

He, the Lone Sovereign: Under the covenant of Allah, taking Him alone as the Sovereign, and to stick to it as His obedient servant, the following inference automatically emerges.

1. The state has come into existence not through any social contract but as the natural corollary of the covenant between man and his Greater and Master.
2. According to this covenant, there is only one Lord and Cherisher and all the rest are His servants.

   To command is for none but God: (Al Quran XII: 54)

   It is for Him alone to create and to govern ? (Al Quran VII: 40)
3. There is no partner in His authority (Sovereignty), nor any equal.

   He has no partner in (His) dominion: (Al Quran XVII: III)

   Nor does He share His command with any person whomsoever. (Al Quran XVIIL: 26)

   Do not turn to any one except Allah for help. There is no god other than Allah. (Al Quran XXVIII: 88)
4. His authority is eternal and all pervasive. Not a single particle in the entire universe is beyond His control.

   To Him belongs what is in the heavens and on earth and all between them and all beneath the soil. (Al Quran XX: 7)

   To Him belongs every being that is in the heavens and on earth: all are subservient to Him. (Al Quran XXX: 26)
5. This world of ours and the entire universe beyond it is one kingdom or State.

   Blessed be He in Whose hands is Dominion; and He over all things hath power; (Al Quran LXVII)

   His Throne doth extend over the heavens and the earth. (Al Quran 11: 255)
6. Man is the vicegerent of Allah on earth and as such after his Creator, he is the noblest and most dignified entity in the universe.

   It is He Who hath made you (His) Vicegerent on earth. (Al Quran VI: 165)

   We have honoured the sons of Adam; provided them with transport on land and sea: given them for sustenance things good and pure; and conferred on them special favours above a great part of Our creation. (Al Quran XVIL: 70)
7. The logical result of there being one single authority (Sovereign) and one single kingdom (State) is the unity of mankind. As the citizens of a single state and the subjects of One Sovereign, all men are equal. All differences and distinctions of colour, race, language and territory are baseless.

O mankind! We created you from a single (pair) of a male and a female, and made you into nations and tribes, that ye may know each other (not that ye may despise each other). (Al Quran XLIX; 13)

8. The natural concomitant of the unity of mankind was that the whole offspring of Adam must have been given the same code of conduct for their life. The Quran says:

   The Religion before God is only Islam (Submission to His Will) (Al Quran III: 9)

Faith, from Day One: This is not the religion represented by Muhammad alone. All the prophets of Allah through the ages had been calling humanity to this faith, and they were all Muslims (Submitting to the Will of Allah).

9. A single code of conduct for life provided man the basis for the building up of the same individual and collective character. In spite of the differences of natural capacities, trends, and leanings, the different natures of the obligations and responsibilities, the unity of the goal and the similarity of basic sentiments and factors of the building of character gave man the same hue as regards his thought and action, which Allah Himself termed 'Colour from Allah.'

   (We take our) colour from Allah, and who is better than Allah at colouring. We are His worshippers. (Al Quran 11: 138)

10. This code of conduct for man's life is based on the highest moral and spiritual values. Therefore it completely ends the clashers interests, existence of classes, and antagonism and conflicts between individual and collective life and establishes among men perfect harmony of thought and a strong relationship of practical cooperation. It also strikes at the roots of snatch and grab, plunder, exploitation and greed and creates in man the spirit of mutual sympathy and sacrifice. And in this way putting an end to the possibility of grouping together of classes based on material interests, brings into existence a classless society. Morality is the spirit and foundation-stone of this code of conduct for human life. The Quran puts forth this morality as the greatest attribute of the Prophet:

    And thou (standest) on an exalted standard of character. (Al Quran LXVIll: 4)

    You have indeed in the apostle of God a beautiful pattern (of conduct) (Al Quran XXXIII: 21)

11. In this code of conduct, field for competition and vying with one another has been provided so that the spirit of striving and action and the natural desire of man to go ahead of others may help in the manifestation of his individual capabilities and the development of his personality. But this spirit of competition had been cleansed of such motives of getting material comforts and fulfilment of personal ends and aspirations in a manner which creates enmity between man and man, push him down to the lowest level of beasts. Here, there is competition but in "Taqwa" or fear of (the displeasure of) Allah

which aims at the purity of soul, the moral elevation and inculcate the quality of obedience to the commandments of Allah with all one's heart and soul and the total submission of one's personality. Here, greatness does not mean a person possessing more wealth than others, living in high and magnificent mansions and enjoying luxuries denied to millions of men like him. Rather real greatness lies in his record of good deeds and obedience to Allah which may elevate his position in the sight of Allah and he may be entitled to better reward than others.

> The most honoured of you in the sight of God is (he who is) the most righteous of you. (Al Quran XI-IX: 13)

This is the criteria of superiority established by Allah. According to this standard a person can excel others only in the field of virtue and piety. No other standard of honour and superiority carries any weight with Allah.

12. The code of conduct for man's life is not merely a lifeless collection of beautiful principles. There is a powerful sanction behind it. And it is this sanction that is its real spirit. The Sovereign says:

> Then shall any one who has done an atom's weight of good see it! And any one who has done an atom's weight of evil shall see it. (Al Quran XCIX: 7-8)

> Verily We have warned you of a Penalty near, the day when man will see (the Deeds) which his hands have sent forth. (Al Quran LXXVU1: 40)

This concept of the accountability in the Hereafter introduces an element of responsibility in his life and protects him from becoming refractory and instead of following the dictates of his own will and the strong urges of his innerself, he keeps before himself the will and pleasure of his Master: his Lord and Cherisher.

13. In this kingdom of God there is perfect rule of law. The duty of his servants is to follow this law in their own lives, and in their capacity as the vicegerents on earth it is their duty to enforce it also. None of them, not even any prophet of Allah has any right to make the slightest change in this law by way of amendment, cancellation, deletion or addition.

The way an ordinary person follows it in his life, a prophet has also to do the same. There are no privileged personages here and no body is above the law. Such a concept of the rule of law is not to be found any where except in the faith of Allah:

> We have sent down to thee the Book in truth, that thou mightest judge between men, as guided by God. (Al Quran l.V: 105)

> Say: "It is not for me, of my own accord, to change it: 1 follow naught but what is revealed unto me: if I were to disobey my Lord, I should myself fear the penalty of a Great Day (to come). (Al Quran X: 15)

14. Like the eternal, untransferable and irrevocable, sovereignty, the fundamental rights conferred on man by Him are eternal and irrevocable. No body has a right to change or curtail them. These well protected and definite rights establish a firm relationship between the individual and the state, and instead of mutual bickerings and strife, make them each other's helper and guardian.

    The Divine laws do not change every day. In those spheres (of life) in which He has given man freedom (of choice) no one has any rights to meddle with it. And where He has given definite commandments, no one has any right of legislation in that sphere.

    The word of thy Lord doth find its fulfilment in truth and in justice: None can change His words: (Al Quran VI: 115)

    No change (let there be) in the work (wrought) by God: that is the standard Religion. (Al Quran XXX: 30)

    No change will thou find in the practice approved, of God. (Al Quran XXXIIL: 62)

    There is none that can alter the word and Decrees of God. (Al Quran VI: 34)

That means, the code of conduct for life of man conferred by Allah is a permanent constitution, not an iota of which can be changed until the end of days.

Pondering over the consequences of abiding by the covenant of Allah one must invariably conclude that in taking this covenant, Allah has been most beneficent and gracious to man. This covenant is really the Magna Carta of freedom through which the sovereignty of man over man has been put to an end.

Allah abhors it that man whom. He gave such a beautiful shape (And has given you shape and made your shapes beautiful Al Quran XL:64), and created man in the best of moulds, (We have indeed created man in the best of moulds, Al Quran XCV:4), who has been endowed with the wealth of knowledge (And He taught Adam the names of all things; Al Quran 11:31) unto whose service were pressed all the objects in the universe (Seest thou not that God has made subject to you men all that is on the earth, and the ships that sail through the sea by His command—Al Quran XXIL65), and breathing into him His own spirit, made him worthy of the obeisance of the angels (Breathed into him of My spirit, fall ye down in obeisance unto him. Al Quran XV:29), he should degrade himself by serving other men like himself and fall down in obeisance to other creatures (much lower than himself), thus divesting himself of the honour and greatness conferred on him by Allah, should go down the abysmal depths of degradation and lowliness. He repeatedly brings home to man, in man's own interest that in the creed of the unity of Allah there is honour, superiority, dignity and eminence. Slightest digression from this creed ultimately leads to perdition and destruction. That is why the entire stress of the Quran is centred on two points, the unity of Allah and the position of roan as servant of Allah. It elucidates the point in different contexts and forbids him to bow down to any person or thing. He says:

1. Verily those whom ye call upon besides God are servants like unto you: (Al Quran VII: 194)
2. Such is God your Lord: to Him belongs all Dominion. And those ye invoke besides Him have not the least power. (Al Quran XXXV: 13)
3. If there were in the heavens and the earth, other gods besides God, there would have been confusion in both! (Al Quran XXI: 22)
4. Nor is there any god along with Him: (if there were many gods) behold, each god would have taken away what he had created, and some would have lorded it over others! (Al Quran XXJII: 91)
5. Say: if there had been other gods, with Him,—as they say, behold, they would have sought out a way to the Lord of the Throne! (Al Quran XVIL: 42)
6. God puts forth a Parable—a man belonging to many partners at variance with each other, and a man belonging entirely to one master: are those who equal in comparison? (Al Quran XXXIV: 29)

To clarify the position of all other claimants to the position of Lord and Cherisher and to rid man of the awe with which they seem to inspire him, the Quran has adopted a unique method to bring home the truth:

> O men! Here is a parable set forth! Listen to it! Those on whom besides God, ye call, cannot create even a fly, if they all met together for the purposes! And if the fly should snatch away anything from them, they would have no power to release it from the fly. Feeble are those who petition and those whom they petition!

Can we imagine that the servant of Allah could be enslaved by any power in the world however great? Is there any other sovereign who could bow his head before himself?

The one act of obeisance (to the Lord) which weights heavy upon thee rids man from bowing down at so many other door steps.

After having had a glimpse of the human society coming into existence as a logical result of recognising Allah as our Sovereign, let us now proceed to take stock of the effects and (evil) consequences of rejecting Him as the only Sovereign and turning away from fulfilling the demands of man's covenant with his Lord and Cherisher, which are before us in a very definite and material form.

1. When man refused to recognise the covenant of Allah immediately the problem cropped up where to seek the sanction for his own rights, the entity of the state and the authority of the rulers. Under which legal documents, the relations of the individual and the state

should be determined? This dire need made them invent an imaginary covenant under the name of social contract.

2. The real covenant had made man take an oath of allegiance to recognise his Creator and Master as his Lord and Cherisher. The hypothetical covenant compelled man to take men like himself as gods and bow down to them, and in this way started the lording of man over man.
3. In the true covenant the Sovereign was one entity. The false covenant brought into existence sovereigns without number who had to be vested with all the rights and powers of the real Sovereign, and man had to put on his own neck the yoke of the gods he had carved out for himself.
4. The unity of authority had given birth to unity of the state. Now the multiplicity of the authority (sovereignty) has divided the world into hundreds of small states and humanity has been badly scattered.
5. Allah's authority is all -pervasive and eternal. When sovereigns with transient and limited authority came into existence and they tried to make their sovereignty eternal and their powers unlimited, oppression and mischief came in their wake. These gods carved out by man himself fell out among themselves, and their quarrels and fights, greed for conquest, lasciviousness. and exploitation destroyed the peace and tranquility of mankind.
6. Man as the vicegerent on earth enjoyed the highest position of greatness and dignity in this world and was the choicest creation. He had now become the lowest of the creatures of earth in the realm of men passing as gods. He had no value as a human being. Some sovereign enjoyed the spectacle of his being torn to pieces and devoured by the carnivorous blasts, some others overeigns consigned him to the flames and yet others made him the fuel of gas chambers. Some one had him broken on the rock or had him crushed in a press; others rode on thrones borne by him, as a beast of burden, on his shoulders. Then there were those who pilloried him or put iron collar round his neck like a dog and drove him in herds like cattle to be sold in slave markets. Some sovereigns attempted his wholesale annihilation by dropping atom bombs on him and some others drowned him in oceans. And even now they are competing with one another which of them can kill how many more men per second. In short, these sovereigns, fashioned by man himself, made life miserable for him. Neither his life nor property nor his dignity and honour are safe at their hands. He has got himself entangled in the meshes of a net of torture and is finding it impossible to get out of it.
7. All men had been made equal in status as men by Allah. Now colour, race, territory, tongue and other distinctions have grouped them into various nations and then the every day growing national interests and their protection took the shape of a regular philosophy

that gave rise to the curse of nationalism which brought the small and weak nations under the yoke of the powerful ones.

It was from the womb of this nationalism that Hitler's Nazism, Mussolini's Fascism and American and British imperialism took birth as its offshoots, and first they took the rest of the world into the grip of their colonialism and then the clash of interest led to the two world wars throwing humanity into the hell of misery, destruction and death.

8. All the children of Adam had received the same code of conduct for life from Allah. Now when men decided to formulate a way of life for himself, so many strange, contradictory and disproportionate philosophies, theories and concepts emerged before him that he was bewildered. Not one of them was such as could be acceptable to the entire humanity since they bore stamps of particular interests and particular geographical and historical background, particular atmosphere and above all the stamps of limited knowledge and intellect. The multiplicity of these theories and concepts so much confused man that, with all his intellect, he totally lost sight of the Straight Path of Life.

   Plato and Hebal's Idealism, John Stuart Mill's Individualism, Benthan's Utilitarianism and from Marx's Communism down to Godwin and Kropotkins Anarchism, hundreds of ideologies with particularities of time and places, and their interpretations by thousands, bewildered man and confining him to various intellectual and political circles, not only cut off from one another but antagonised them.

9. Since the code of conduct for man's life formulated by himself was not based on a common goal and moral values, there was no possibility left of any uniformity of character. Every petty sovereign, with a view to serve his particular national interest, under a peculiar system of training, moulded the citizens into a mould of character that they may prove good citizens for their own country, but outside the boundaries of their country, for the rest of the world, they may play the role of dacoits, plunderers, murderers and goondas. It was thus that there was no basis left between man and man for universal brotherhood. All of them became enemies of one another's life and property, honour and dignity, country, race, country's resources and government and authority. The separation of the centres of beliefs and thought, aims and objectives, tendencies and leanings and obedience and loyalty , separated them all, one from the other, and converted the entire world into a place of contradictions, differences, tensions and enmity.

10. The code of conduct for man's life conferred on him by Allah was based on the highest moral teachings. Man rebelling against Allah and putting aside the morals, made the material interest the basis of his efforts. This attitude of every one looking to his own interests created enmity among men living in the same country. Instead of sacrifice and sympathy and cooperation and well-wishing among them, tendencies of selfishness and man-baiting were aroused. It was this self interest that on the one hand created aggressive

loot and pillage and on the other classes came into being for organised defence. And then the cold and hot war among these classes, made man bloodthirsty thus destroying the peace and tranquility of the world. This class war became an organised philosophy according to which cutting the throats of men belonging to the opposite group came to be a virtuous act, and to get killed in this way was regarded martyrdom.

11. According to the Divine code of conduct for man's life the real field of competition was *taqwa* or fear of (the displeasure of) Allah. But this was now replaced by the struggle for an abundance of luxury goods and satisfaction of the carnal urges and proving them further excitants. This field of competition changed every person into a slave of his cravings and created in him a craze for amassing wealth by fair means or foul. All the barrier of approved and prohibited were removed, and the criterion of greatness came to be the abundance of luxury goods. This trend of thought putting man on the path of selfishness and sensuality made him a wolf for the other individuals of the society.

12. The common frailty of all the systems or the ways of life designed by man is this that there is no sanction behind their moral principles. Firstly, they do not attach the importance to morality which it enjoys in the Divine way of life. And if at all some moral principles are decided upon for a civilized social life they prove lifeless and defunct, since there was no power to compel man to abide by them. Turning away from the belief in the life Hereafter, man became used to irresponsible attitude in life. He made the life of this world the be-all and end-all of man's destiny, and totally obvious of any accountability in connection with the deeds here in the earthly existence, he became refractory. If at all he followed some moral principles in his collective life for the "collective interests" he reserved his rights to keep the individual life totally free from the hold of these principles, and in this sphere of his life came down to the animal level.

13. In the kingdom of God there was rule of law, but in the kingdom established by man the will of the ruler became the law. The Will of the true Sovereign manifested itself in the form of a permanent and eternal constitution, whose applicability was pervasive and beyond the limits of time and space. But the will of the sovereign carved out by man himself is always wavering-now this way and the next moment some other way. Its applicability is limited to a specific period and a particular region. It is subject to amendments day in and day out, and with every change of the sovereign which are so frequent it changes too. That is why the concept of the "rule of law" in the constitution framed by man is a fraud.

14. The rights conferred on man by Allah were permanent and untransferable. But the transient nature of the constitution framed by man made the fundamental laws, under this constitution, also transient and changeable, and made them a regular subject of wrangling and struggle between the individual and the state. Now these rights have to be fought for

by the individuals before they can have them. But the single kick of a dictator smashes them like glass bangles. These are those serious and destructive consequences man has to face in this life for the crime of breaking off with the true Sovereign as His servant and making men like himself his sovereigns. He had declared his independence to escape the checks put on him by the Divine Law and to live independently in His Realm a life free from all restrictions. But did he really come by his cherished freedom and independence? Did he get a chance to live a life of his own choice? Or was it just the opposite in as much as leaving One God, he had to crown men like himself with sovereignty, bow himself down at their feet, to surrender all his freedoms, fundamental rights, and his dignity and greatness due to the highest status as the vicegerent of Allah on earth, and submit his life and property and honour, his resources and mental and physical powers to be used by them. And in his abject servility to them, he got nothing from them but the worst subjugation, degradation infamy and grief and despair.

Which of the gods carved out by man himself has not raised the slogan: "Who is superior to Us in strength?"—Al Quran XLI: 15 and "I am your Lord most High/'—Al Quran LXXIX: 24 and not tyrannised and oppressed his own and aliens and not ruined thousands of homes for an odd fancy of his?

The fact is that man was not created for sovereignty and rule. His mission in life is service to Allah and not to take upon himself the role of God. His Creator has deeply ingrained slavery, devotion and service to Allah in his nature.

> I have only created Jins and men, that they may serve Me. (Al Quran LI: 56)

Here in this verse service and devotion do not mean only prayer, fasting and praising God, but along with these forms of service, devotion also includes this that Jins and men have not been created for the worship, obedience and subservience to any one other than Allah. They are not to bow down to or obey and follow the laws of any one else; not to regard any body as one who can make or mar their destiny and not to pray or petition any one other than Allah. In all matters pertaining to life, perfect obedience to one God and to carry out His orders alone is service to Him.

Man has been endowed with all the qualities of the head and the heart and all the physical powers to meet the demands of this service. To overlook this position of his as the servant of Allah, is to rebel against himself, his nature and it invariably results in his proclamation of his own divinity or bowing down in devotion to some false god. As soon as man proceeds on this course of rebellion, tyranny and mischief also find their way in his deeds. Since Allah has created all men with the same nature some one of them becoming the ruler and others being the ruled, both are against their nature. Sovereignty, be that of a king or a dictator as individuals, of the citizens of a State or the people of the world as a whole, tyranny must raise its head, since the sovereignty of man in every individual or collective form, brings into existence a sovereign that is incapable of taking the place of the true Sovereign, which is at the root of all mischief on earth.

The cause of this mischief is that Allah due to His self-sustained entity, His immortal position, His Power of creation, His capacity as Lord and Cherisher of the worlds, and other unlimited and peerless attributes of His, is the (true) Sovereign, His authority is not borrowed or a gift from any one but a part of His entity; His authority emanates from His Own self and not from any one else; He Himself is independent of every thing and every prop. He does not take any thing from any body, but His Own bestowal and endowment extend to every tiny particle of the universe; one and all are needy and depend on His bounties for sustenance, but He is free from want and is independent. So the high position of sovereignty becomes Him alone. But whoever, other than He comes up with the claim of sovereignty, cannot boast of any one of these attributes. Considering all his powers, capabilities, his knowledge and perception, his sentiments and feelings, his necessities and urges and the natural limitations of his authority and intention, he is just like other men.

Now the question is that with all these human frailties, how he is to impress other people with his superiority and supremacy: how he is to make a show of his sovereignty and rule, and how to compel others to submit to his subjugation and obediences. There is one and only one way of doing it.

And that is, to make or at least show himself big, he should snatch and grab from those living in his sphere of authority, the power to rule, rights and privileges, wealth and property, rank and dignity, and take into his possession all the resources and means of meeting the needs of right from the protection of his own life to that of his seat of authority. And once he is in possession of these powers and resources, he is to rally and organise them and use them for grabbing more of such powers and resources. And when the limited resources of his own country do not suffice to meet his needs and ambition, he is to attack his neighbours and snatch and grab their resources and man-power. And he is to be constantly engaged in the struggle to extend his sphere of influence and meeting other rivals on the same path (of expansionism), should go on annihilating them or be himself annihilated in a clash with them.

There is no other course open to him, since he himself, according to the example furnished by the Quran, is incapable of making a fly or recover something snatched by the fly from him. All his affairs are conducted with the power and resources grabbed by him from others. And as the powers and resources, through usurpation, accumulate with him, there is a proportionate increase in his despotism, his awe-inspiring majesty and grandeur, the expanse and height of his mansions, the abundance of the articles of luxury, and the sphere of his authority, and exactly in the same (inverse) proportion, those in the clutches of his powerful authority go on getting deprived of their liberties, their rights, their means of sustenance, their liberties and their honour and dignity.

In most countries of the world this kind of rule prevails. The world strategy of the super-powers too is taking this course. Wherever and whenever man, getting loose from the service of Allah has taken up the rein of rule over the fellow man in his own hands, the result has always been tyranny and oppression-constant tyranny. There is no concept of man's sovereignty without oppression and tyranny.

This malady can neither be remedied through any constitution framed by man nor through any change in the system of government on the concept of man's sovereignty. The only way to get rid of it is that man should in all humility recognise the right of God's Sovereignty and come down to his true position of the servant of God. He should neither try to take on the role of a god, nor allow any one else to dominate over him as a god.

Applied Laws

This tax was a compulsory duty in Islam, levied on all possessions according to a sliding scale of one-tenth, one-twentieth, and one-fortieth. In all cases, it represented a very small fraction, and hence, it is but natural that the question should arise: How could such a small sum be of assistance to all the Muslim poor? To answer this question we must consider the following facts:

1. The small amount of capital on which the tax had to be paid made the greater part of the community liable to it. The exemption value for the poor-tax was fixed at six pounds, which meant that practically all the population had to pay the tax; thus the income from it was relatively great.
2. Disbursements from the tax money were confined to specifically limited classes of people. For their livelihood the great majority had to rely on work, which has always been reckoned by Islam to be the primary source of a living.
3. Most important of all, the livelihood of the very poor did not depend solely upon this source of income. There were also the vast sums acquired as booty during the war days, sums which lasted for more than half a century. In this booty all the fighting men shared, and most of them were of the poor classes. They received four-fifths of the booty, while the other fifth was turned into a charitable foundation for the benefit of all classes of necessitous persons, relatives, orphans, the destitute, and the wayfarer. And when Umar resolved not to take the booty away from the conquered countries, but to leave it for the benefit of the native peoples, he instituted the land-tax in its place, as this later on was sufficient to provide for all the poor.

Today, the last primary source of revenue is no longer available, and the poor-tax in itself is not sufficient. Therefore, we must consider alternative sources to take the place of booty and plunder, in order to provide an ample living for the generality of men.

Before we consider new sources we must first exhaust the poor-tax as a source in itself. It is a compulsory duty, and it must be paid if the community is justifiably to be described as Islamic. For the payment of the poor-tax is a spiritual duty as well as financial one. Again, we must consider the source of the poor-tax as including all types of property, some of which are not at present included because they were not familiar in the early days of Islam.

That is to say, we must bear in mind those forms of wealth which are liable to the poor-tax but which are not mentioned in the Quran except generally in the verse:

> "O you who have believed, expend of the goods which you have acquired, and of that which We have provided for you from the Earth. And do not propose any evil in thus expending it; for you got it yourselves only by connivance."

The fact that the poor-tax was prescribed as a duty only upon such types of property as were familiar in the time of the Prophet does not prevent its being prescribed today as a duty on all that is known as Property or wealth, and on all that produces an income. It may not be of difference that such things may not be the kind on which the tax was originally imposed.

Similarly, we can control the outlets for the tax money, just as Umar exercised the same control when he stopped payments designed to convert unbelievers. It must not be given in any form of money to those who are eligible for it; rather it must be given to them in the basic form of goods or services, or it must be used to buy for them some part of their basic necessities. The source of their livelihood must be fixed and unconnected with any kind of temporary or haphazard charity; for these things are not in accord with the needs of modern life.

But in any case such detailed considerations have no place in this book. The scope of our thinking here is the broad field of the promotion of social justice and equity, as the Muslim world gives its attention to a renaissance of the true Islamic life.

Mutual Responsibility of Society: The Prophet said: "Any household which suffers a man to remain hungry among them is outside the protection of Allah, the Blessed and the Exalted." In this brief sentence, he emphasised the principle of mutual responsibility in society, a principle which most of us must recognise from the precedents and the examples provided by our study of the Quran. This principle was authoritatively imposed on both the individual and the social conscience. Today the law must again enforce it as an essential root of Islam. This means that the law can enforce that which Umar intended to enforce:

> "If I had known earlier what I now know, I would have taken the excess of their wealth from the rich and given it to the poor."

Thus, the law can impose taxes, the only limit of which is the establishment of equality in the social sphere, the removal of crime and oppression from the community in general, and the ample provision of food and drink, clothing and housing, medical treatment and skill for every single individual in the country. It does not matter how much tax is placed upon capital so long as the latter is not thereby made incapable of work and of reasonable increase; this condition must be observed because the steady turning of the wheels of labour brings other benefits which cannot be overlooked.

Thus, the law can put into the hands of the poor with perfect justification a stretch of funded property which they may use without paying any basic rent, or at a nominal rent, that they may from it obtain a means of life. For this constitutes a source of livelihood and is the only means of work within their power. By this act the law will fulfil the Messenger's words:"

> "Anyone of you may permit to his brother the use of his land as gift, without exacting for it any agreed rent."

The law may also with justification fix the wage of the factory or the farm worker at a stipulated proportion of the production or of the harvest. The lowest limit of this wage must be a competence to cover food and drink and clothing, and medicine and medical care to a certain extent. The standard is to be taken as that of a moderate living, determined by the proportion of the inhabitants of the country to its general wealth.

General Taxation: Every individual in the Muslim community has the duty of taking a share in the general expenses of the state according to his ability. We have already noticed the opinion of the Imam Malik on what may be done when the treasury is empty, or when the needs of the army are increased; the law has the power according to need to levy a toll on the wealth of the rich. Similar to the needs of the army are the other needs of the state, such as improvements in public services, irrigation of waste lands, the education of the people, and the medical treatment of the sick.

All these things are communal duties which must be met and satisfied just as much as the needs of the army; they must be preserved as strongly as frontiers and defence posts must be guarded. This is particularly true today when wars make demands on all the resources and services of the belligerent nations. In modern war, everyone may be said to be in the army, and thus should be capable of taking responsibility in time of peace.

Public Resources: Monopolies on the necessities of life are forbidden by Islam. A monopoly on food is forbidden, for example, since Islam has always asserted the communal ownership of water, pasturage, and fire, as being the primary needs of life. But the needs of life are not unchangeable, varying as they do from age to age. Consequently, the preservation of this general Islamic principle demands what is known today as the nationalisation of natural resources.

It is essential not to have in the hands of private individuals or companies the resources of water, light, heat, electricity, coal and oil, or the resources of public transport and public food supplying, and other such things. For private ownership gives the power of monopoly, imposes upon the general public he will of the monopolists, and permits them to indulge in that disgraceful exploitation which we witness today.

The head of the state has the power to make all these things state-owned, and to fix prices and costs of them so that they can get it at equitable rates without excessive prices. By these means the Islamic aims for the checking of monopolies can be realised.

Public Interest and the Blocking of Means: Everything which tends to advance the public welfare or to retard oppression of the public is a duty laid upon the law, and everything which tends towards a prohibited end is itself prohibited. The application of these established principles of Islam lays on the law today following duties:

1. The taking of excessive wealth out of the hands of bloated capitalists. The fact that such excessive wealth is in their possession tends towards a number of crimes. In the first place, it tends to produce that luxury which is forbidden by Islam. Luxury is a relative matter, which can be defined only in terms of the general condition in each age and country. The permanent rule is that luxury shall not increase beyond the mean struck by the national wealth in proportion to the population. One result of luxury is the iniquitous rise in prices which springs from the fact that one section of the populace has an unlimited power to buy, while the goods available for sale are not equal to the demand. Another result is the rise of social vices, springing from the fact that some people possess more money than they need; to dispose this, they look for illegal outlets and seek sensual and corrupt pleasures; through these, their morals and their standards are degraded, and on the other hand their victims are the needy men and women who always exist in an unbalanced society.

2 The removal of extreme, poverty, because it results in the way of crime and evil. These results include a great number of social evils which can only exist in surroundings of privation and destitution, theft, infamy, and moral degradation, a general atmosphere of corruption. This is over and above the vast differences which are set between those who have and those who have not, the hatreds and the social disturbances which the law must prevent before they occur by removing their causes. If it be asked how this extreme poverty is to be removed, it is by the ample provision of work for every able-bodied man, and by the provision of an adequate wage, by social security for all who are disabled, and by speedy relief. This is the method in general outline; the specific applications are easy once the general aim is established.

3. The struggle against disease and ignorance: Because of their evil effect on the individual and the community these weaken the general strength of the community and afford a footing to its enemies. This condition is forbidden, as is any factor which leads to it. Nothing can oppose disease and ignorance successfully except a rise in living standards and in general wealth; but the laws of charity and such other things are only a palliative to soothe the sore, not to heal it. The real treatment is that every individual should be possessed of private means for medical and educational purposes. Or alternatively that medical care and education should be provided free to every individual in the country on a common basis and to a common level. The rich must not be able, by money, to get more than the poor in schools or hospitals.

Legacies: When there are present at the division of the estate relatives, orphans and poor people, give them a provision out of it and speak to them fair. Thus runs the Quranic precept. It clearly means that out of every estate there must be a share for relatives, orphans and the poor. The law has the power of disposal according to the nature of the case; it may change the beneficiaries, or it may leave them unchanged. So, Umar did in the case of paying out money to convert others to Islam. The law also has the power to apply the regulations according to the needs of the estate or according to those of the community.

We must remember that the meaning of being 'present' can legitimately be extended to cover virtual presence, 'that is to say, existence. In every community, there are orphans and poor, and there is no necessity for them to be present in person when an estate is being divided; they are already present in time and space. So by the power of the law all duties must be enforced which are not enforced by the power of conscience.

Mutual Help and Usury: Islam rooted out usury, and fought it in all its forms and appearances; hence, it is impossible for any form of Islamic life to exist on an economic basis which includes the principles of usury. We have already discussed the causes which made Islam unable to countenance usury, but they may be summed up by saying that it is the negation of the spirit of mutual help and friendliness. If usury obtains, then it is to the benefit of the capitalist who can thus increase his wealth without working and without the risk of loss.

The national economy must be set on a basis of mutual help rather than of usury. All the faults which can be alleged against the later system have been summed up to justify its rejection by Maulana Muhammad Ali in his book, *Islam and the New World Order*, from which we may quote the following passage:

> "It is objected that to forbid interest on money will hinder business and commercial transactions, and will hinder the accomplishment of important domestic projects. We may grant the truth of this, but on the other side we have the far greater advantage that to proscribe interest will prevent world wars, which can only end in misery, and which are kindled and inflamed only by loans and debts governed by interest. And if we examine the facts of the case, we shall find that from the very first, trade followed its natural course and spread over more and more widely! Wider limits were brought within the Islamic sphere. So that today the Islamic states are still among the greatest of the old-established countries of the civilized world."

This prohibition of usury cannot in any sense be reconciled with the conditions of the new world which materialistic Western civilization is bringing into being. The social system most required is that practical system which Islam today has in mind, which was successfully applied in practice by, at its inception, centuries ago. The As for the capital sums, without which business cannot be carried on, there was little difference between the gains which they made under the

Islamic system and those which they made by ordinary lending; for the Islamic system was in effect of partnership between capital and labour. Such a partnership is not impossible, for the Islamic system holds that capital and labour should share together in all profit and loss; whereas the result of paying a steady rate of interest is that, capital makes a continual profit, even when labour had to work at a loss.

It is sometimes objected that the partnership of capital and labour in both profits and losses is not practicable, because it means that regular accounts have to be kept, since this is one of the necessities of trade; and further, because trading records have to be available for the assessing of taxes which have to be paid. But all the share-issuing companies which take part in trading on a large scale have to keep accounts.

Indeed this partnership system is more to the public advantage than that of giving all the dividends to capital; for it is the latter system which produces most of the evils of capitalism, and which is the source of the oppression of the workers. And the loans which are floated by governments or companies to carry out immense projects such as railroads or canals or such things have done no more than prove this point.

But since the system of state banking depends on the principle of mutual help, which is approved by the Islamic social system, it must be of great benefit to mankind.

This is a general statement, the particular details of which are too lengthy for a book dealing with general ideas. At the same time, there can be no harm in giving an example as a guide to the general objective which we have in mind. Suppose, the state decrees the abolition of interest on funds in banks, companies, public enterprises, and private loans, what will happen then?

What will happen will be that capitalists will find themselves unable to increase their wealth except by two general methods. First, they may put it to some profitable use themselves in manufacture or trade or agriculture. Or second, they may put it to a profitable and helpful use by investing it in share-issuing companies, where the share values may rise or fall. Both these methods are sanctioned by Islam, and neither of them will work the slightest injury to economic life.

It is sometimes feared that the rich will refrain from depositing their money in the banks, which generally finance the large public projects. This is an imaginary danger which gains currency among us because we are familiar only with European methods of using money.

In Europe, the primary natural impulse is to make money increase; this can be accomplished only by using it for some means of exploitation, and so, this natural impulse is a guarantee that money will not be kept out of circulation. But when he desired to take in handsome large project to justify what is known as the great ear of production, we have the power to create legislation covering various kinds of industry; this legislation enacts that no new enterprise may be set up except on the basis of capital over such and such a sum. On that capital sums flow in to take up shares and to become liable to profit and loss on the market.

Thus, there is no more need for banks, except for the issuing of currency. If other banks wish to make a profit, then they must only with permission-in some profit seeking enterprise, where the shares are liable to fluctuation in the open market. But the system will not stop the flow of capital, either domestic or foreign; for the greater proportion of capital wealth is not deposited in banks, but is put out to profit in enterprises.

At for insurance companies, it may be that their basis is Islamic, inasmuch as the funds which are deposited with them are liable to profit and loss, to fall or rise. Funds deposited in these companies are put to work in profit-seeking enterprises, subject to fluctuation. Everytime a beneficiary receives more than he has paid in, the amount of the company's loss is deducted from the remainder of the depositors in proportion to the funds which they have invested. Thus insurance companies' members form a body united for mutual help; in effect they pay out of their own pockets to support any unfortunate one of their number, when need arises.

They have a form of security from which they can benefit in time, of hardship or need. This can be applied also to savings banks and similar institutions, all of which rest on the basis of mutual help in one way or another, and from which funds are employed in profit-seeking enterprises, always liable to fluctuation. Such institutions have no fixed rate of interest, and hence our economic system here can be free from the taint of usury; hence also all capital is compelled to work as the only method of achieving profit and increase.

Gambling: Gambling is a dishonest practice, both in act and in spirit, for it represents an effort to make money without working. In addition, it produces enmity and hatred among its adherents, and gives rise to laxity and insecurity in the fabric of society. There are many forms of gambling, of which lotteries are but one. It is not any spirit of charity which prompts people to buy lottery tickets, not is it any desire to assist works of healing and charity. It is merely the desire to gain more money without working.

This is at once practically and spiritually dishonest, as we have said; it hinders and retards the feelings of mercy. There is no need to mention the disgraceful foreign race-meetings which draw their immense crowds; this is merely the outcome of luxury, and the corrupting result of luxury loving natures with their aversion to virtue and their love of vice, with their avarice except when money is lavished on sensual pleasures and coarse enjoyment.

We must halt the practice of gambling altogether, with its green tables, its tempting lottery tickets, and its late hours. Islamic life had need of none of these things, and Islam will never admit that relations between man and man should ever stand on such a basis, or that charity should spring from such impure desires.

Prostitution: Prostitution is the product of spiritual degradation and material destitution, sometimes together and sometimes separately. Islam prohibits illegal sexual intercourse in all its forms, and the most degraded of these is prostitution. Lewdness is the poison characteristic of an unbalanced community, for the two factors which produce prostitution are excessive wealth and humiliating necessity. It was once said:

> "A well-born woman cannot feed from her own breasts because she is hungry; but she may do so if she is in danger of death."

We must not expose people on the one hand to the trials of need, and on the other to the temptations of wealth and other things, and then expect them to be models of self-control and virtue. The principle of blocking the means, demands that the law gives attention to check this thing at its root. The laws affecting prostitution must be established without delay.

Alcohol: The nature of these laws needs no discussion. Alcohol is undeniably forbidden, and the Islamic community can never countenance its use. It is closely related to prostitution in most cases, and is especially allied to it socially; similarly, it is related to luxury and to the destitution which arises from luxury. For luxury produces a spiritual weakness and a need for inhibiting thought and vital activity by means of some intoxicant. Whereas the life, the work, and the watchfulness which Islam prescribes can never be reconciled with alcohol or with any other drug.

Islam forms a plastic social system, capable of adaptation to all times and all circumstances; it is preserved by its general spiritual principles. Its duty is to ensure a form of life which will be virtuous, sound, productive, and strong; to ensure a comprehensive social justice based on all the foundations of human nature, and aiming at giving every man his due. But it must never stand in the way of fruitful individualism, nor must it permit individualism to become a harmful egotism.

The Islamic theory of life is the finest that the world has known because it brings together the material and the spiritual elements of life, making out of them a unity directed towards the highest standards and aimed at patterns which can be actually achieved. It does not envisage objectives which are woven only of the imagination.

But the perplexed and disturbed world, fearful and cautious, can only be brought to Islam and to peace, can only be given complete security and justice, when it returns to this perfect social system, under the will of Allah.

3

Enforcement of Justice

1. Societies and states do not prosper without peace and cannot survive without justice and its proper administration. All the jurists and sages are of the opinion that administration of justice is one of the fundamental functions of a state. What is administration of justice? It is enforcement of good and right; it is suppression of evil and wrong. This is why the Holy Quran says:

   Those who, if we give them power in the land, observe the prayer and pay the *Zakat* and enjoin what is good *(al-maruf)* and forbid what is evil *(al-munkar).* (XXII: 41)

2. The commission of error is inherent in human nature. This leads to commission of wrong that affects the rights of the people and sometimes causes breach of peace in society. The clash of interests creates disputes among them. It requires an authority to decide their disputes. Hence, people resort to arbitrament so that peace and prosperity may prevail. This function of administration of justice is called *qada* in the terminology of Islamic law.

3. The significance of administration of justice, being recognised by the civil societies and human reason. There is no need of stressing the point any longer. For the Muslims, it is sufficient to say that the Prophet himself decided the disputes among the litigant parties that appeared before him, awarded punishments to the defaulters and appointed deputies entrusting them with judicial powers. That is why Umar b. al-Khattab in a letter to his *qadi,* Abu Musa al-Ashari categorically remarked: Administration of justice is a firm obligation and a practice being followed and to be followed.

4. Evaluating the significance of justice, Al-Sarakhsi thinks that it is one of the foremost duties after the belief in Allah and one of the highest forms of worship. The Muslim

jurists say that judicial work is a part of the great responsibility entrusted by Allah to human beings *(al-wilayat al-Kubra)*. Hence, the position of a *qadi* is supreme. Ali b. Abi Talib is reported to have advised his governor of Egypt:

And confer upon him *(the qadi)* a high position which the nearest one to you cannot covet as it being beyond his capability. *(Nahj al-Balaghah,* XXII: 58)

According to another statement of Ali, reported by Shiite jurists, the function and position of a judge are evaluated as follows:

O Shurayh, you are occupying a seat where only a Prophet or his legatee (*Wasiyy,* nominee) sits, or one who is reprobate. (M.Sangalaji; *Qada dar Islam:* 21)

Hussain, his son, is reported to have said that in verse 38:20 the words *wa fasl al-khitab* denote science of administration of justice, referring to the merit of the prophet Daud.

5. Commenting on the necessity and significance of administration of justice, Ibn Farhan, a Malikite jurist, observed that the knowledge of *qada* stands supreme among all sciences. The office of the *qadi* holds the highest position in the society since it is an office previously held by the prophets. It aims at deciding cases relating to murder, marriage, property and lawfulness and unlawfulness of transactions.

Literal Meaning of Qada

6. Adjudicating and the act of judgment is called *qada* in the works of Islamic law *(fiqh)*. The word *qada* has several connotations. According to *Arabic English Lexicon* by William Lane, the word *qada* primarily means, he finished a thing entirely, by word or by deed. Hence, it is used for decreeing and deciding judicially.
7. According to Muhammad Sallam Madkur, it means to fulfil a desire to pay a debt, to command. This is why the *qadi* is also called *hakim* because he prohibits a transgressor from an unjust action.
8. According to Muhammad Shahir Arsalan, the word *qada* used in the Holy Quran connotes several meanings *viz;* (1) to intend; (2) to fix a limit; (3) to fulfil a desire; (4) to perform a religious duty; (5) to give an order and judgement; and (6) to kill.
9. According to Ibn Manzur (d. 7th A.H.), the author of Arabic Lexicon, *qada* means to strengthen a thing, to ratify it or to dispose it of or be relieved of it. Its primary meanings are to cut and divide in parts (partition). It also means to manufacture and measure as says Abu Dhuayb, a famous poet:

and upon both of them are neatly set forth (coats) that are made by Daud (David) or manufactured by Tubbas those who bestow liberally.

It also means exhaustion when used for tears. According to Zohri, as reported by Ibn Manzur, the word *qada* has several connotations all of them refer to dispose of a thing and to complete it. The Holy Quran says:

(And hasten not with the Quran ere its revelation hath been perfected unto thee).

In the following verse, the word *'qudiya'* has been used in the sense of completion of the term, according to al-Zohri (if we sent down an angel, then the matter would be judged, no further time would be allowed them).

Meanings of Qada

10. Because of the various connotations of this word, the *fuqaha* have used it in the sense deciding the disputes by a judge. The person who performs this work is called *qadi* by them.

11. Muhammad Sangalaji observes that the act of deciding the disputes is called *qada* because the *qadi* brings the matter to an end, disposes of the dispute and passes a final order. It is also called *hukm* (decree, because the underlying word prohibits a transgressor from an unjust action).

12. The translations of definitions of the word *qada;* as enunciated by the *fuqaha* are as follows:

   (i) In terminology of Shariah the word *qada* means to decide the disputes and dispose of the differences and conflicts; (al-Sadr al-Shahid; *Sh. Adab al-Qadi,* I., 126)

   (ii) In Shariah, the word means a binding order (decree); (Ibn al-Humam; Sh. *Fath al-Qadir,* V. 453)

   (iii) It is a binding word/order passed by the public/general authority; *(Alamgiriyyah,* V: 107)

   (iv) To inform about and determine a commandment of the *Shariah* in a binding manner; (Ibn Farhun; *Tabsirah,* I; 12)

   (v) To act as an intermediary between the Creator and the creature in order to perform and execute among them the orders and commandments of the Creator through the divine Book and the *Sunnah (Ibid);*

   (vi) It is an office of deciding the disputes between the people in order to dispose of the suits and put an end to controversies and conflicts. (Ibn Khaldun; *Muqaddimah,* 22)

   (vii) The act of *qada* in a dispute means to discover and determine what is proved and established. (M. Shahir Arsalan, *Al-Qada wal-Qudat,* 21)

13. The word *qada* has been defined by the Shiite scholars as follows:

    (i) Passing order by one who is empowered by the *Shariah* and one who is eligible and capable of issuing a *fatwa* being in possession of detailed knowledge of the laws of *Shariah,* about particular persons in order to establish the rights and execute them in favour of the rightful; (M. Sangalji; *op. cit;* 10)

    (ii) Naraqi Kashani, a Shiite scholar, says that *qada* is a power of adjudicating a specific case of a person in order to establish a wordily punishment/ penalty or a right *(Ibid).*

14. All the definitions of *qada* are approximately, equivalent to the modern definitions of judgement, that are reproduced below for the sake of comparison.

    The official and authentic decision of a court of justice upon the respective rights and claims of the parties to an action or suit therein litigated and submitted to its determination. (Black's *Law Dictionary,* S.V. judgement)

    The sentence of the law, or decision pronounced by the court, upon the matter contained in the record.

    The judgement though pronounced or awarded by the judges, is not their determination and sentence, but the determination and sentence of law. It is the conclusion that naturally and regularly follows from the premises of law. Judgment depends not on the arbitrary caprice of the judge but on the settled and invariable principle of justice.

    Judgement is the determination of a court declaring the rights to be recognised and the remedies to be awarded between parties upon facts found by the court or jury, or admitted by the parties or upon their default in the course of proceedings instituted for redress of a legal injury. (M.A. Hafeez; *Judicial Methodology,* 5)

Significance of Qadi

15. The Person who performs the onerous task of deciding the disputes and awarding or sentencing a binding order is called *qadi.* He is also called *hakam* or *hakim,* but the latter two words are seldom used for this purpose in the works of *fiqh* since *'hakam'* is generally used for an arbiter and *'hakim'* for a ruler or an executive authority.

Reality of Qada

16. It is stated in the previous pages that according to 'Umar, *qada* is a 'firm obligation', and according to al-Sarakshi, "one of the foremost obligations". The *fuqaha* are of the view that it is a collective obligation. The proper words used by them for this purpose are *'fard/ wajib kifayah'.*

    Fard or *Wajib* means an obligation and *kifayah* means that if someone from amongst the community perform the obligation it will be deemed as done and performed by all; but if none from amongst them perform the duty the whole community will be the sinner.

Eligibility for a Qadi

17. Lengthy discussions about the qualifications of a *qadi* have been made by the *fuqaha.* According to some *fuqaha,* there are as many as about thirty conditions of eligibility for the office of *qadi,* whereas some *fuqaha* have reduced them to three. The requisite qualifications of a *qadi* are not specified in a single *nass* (Quranic verse or *Hadith).* Hence, the qualifications of a *qadi* mentioned by the *fuqaha* mostly depend on inferences and deductions. The best discussions in this connection *are* made by Ibn Jarir al-Tabari, Ibn Qudamah, Ibn Farhun, al-Marghinani, Muhammad Sallam Madkur and Muhammad Sangalaji. Hence, an analysis of the arguments of these writers will serve the purpose.

18. According to al-Marghinani, a *Hanafi* jurist, the authority of a *qadi* is not valid unless he possesses the qualifications necessary for a witness, and that he should be a *mujtahid.* It means that in the opinion of al-Marghinani, the conditions of competence for the office of *qadi* are two-fold, *viz.* that the person appointed to the office of *qadi* should be eligible for becoming witness and that he should be a *mujtahid.* But to be a *mujtahid,* according to the *Hanafis* is not an essential condition for holding the office of *qadi.* Explaining this condition al-Marghinani remarks that the "more approved" *(sahih)* view is that the qualification of being *a mujtahid* is merely a preferable condition and not indispensable for a *qadi,* since the appointment of an unlettered person to the post of *qadi* is valid according to the *Hanafis.* But al-Shafii holds that it is not valid.

19. This brief discussion of the author of *al-Hidayah* lead us to the following conclusions:
    (i) That a minor who has still not attained the age of puberty cannot be a *qadi;*
    (ii) That a non-Muslim is not eligible for holding the office of *qadi;*
    (iii) That an insane person cannot be a *qadi;*
    (iv) That a person convicted of *qadhf* (slandering with commission of adultery) loses his competency for the office of *qadi;*
    (v) That a *fasiq* (profligate) is competent to become a *qadi* though the appointing authority (*sultan)* should not select a *fasiq* for the office of *qadi;*
    (vi) That a woman may be appointed as *qadi* in those cases wherein her evidence is admissible.

20. Ibn Qadamah, a *Hanbali* jurist, lays down following three conditions for the office of *qadi:*
    (i) *Kamal— perfection:* Kamal is of two kinds: (i) *Kamal al-Ahkam* and (ii) *Kamal al-Khilqah.* By *Kamal al-ahkam* Ibn Qudamah means the conditions of being eligible for performing general religious duties. These conditions are of being: (a) adult, (b) sane, (c) free and (d) male. *Kamal al-Khilqah* means not to suffer from physical deficiency, that is, the appointee should be of sound organs of speech, hearing and sight;

(ii) *Adalah-probity:* He who is *fasiq* (Profligate) is not competent for the office of *qadi;*

(iii) *Ijtihad:* It means that a person who is not fully conversant with Quran, the *Sunnah.* The *Ijma,* the different opinions of the jurists, the *qiyas* (juristic analogy) and the Arabic language is not eligible for the post of *qadi.*

21. To be fully conversant with the Quran means the knowledge of ten things, *viz* (1) words of singular meaning conveying the specific sense *(Khass);* (2) words of plural meaning conveying collective sense *(amm);* (3) absolute commandments *(mutlaq);* (4) qualified commandments *(muqayyad);* (5) verses that are decisive *(muhkam);* (6) verses that are allegorical and susceptible to different interpretations *(mutashabihat);* (7) verses that are of concise and general nature *(mujmal);* (8) verses that *are* explained *(mufassar);* (9) abrogating *(nasikh);* (10) abrogated *(mansukh).*

22. Requisite knowledge of *hadith* means the knowledge and understanding of those *ahadith* in which the law is laid down; the knowledge of those *ahadith* which are transmitted continuously by a large number of narrators *(mutawatir)* and of those which *are* transmitted by one or two narrators; the knowledge of those *ahadith* which are reported from the Prophet by a Successor *(Tabii)* without mentioning the name of the first narrator *(al-mursal),* and of those which are reported from the Prophet through a Companion as well as the knowledge of continuous chain *(musnad),* broken chain *(munqati),* knowledge of sound *ahadith,* weak *ahadith,* of those *ahadith* that are mainly accepted and of those which are disputed.

23. Requisite knowledge of *qiyas* means knowledge of the conditions of validity of analogy, kinds of *qiyas* and the method of analogical reasoning.

24. A person who is fully conversant with all these things and is well-versed in the Arabic language and literature dererves to be called a *mujtahid.*

25. Al-Tabari is of the view that making a decision of a legal point is like expressing the legal opinion *(fatwa)* in a certain case. Therefore, a person who is eligible for issuing a *fatwa* is qualified for being a *qadi.* By this analogy, a woman is eligible for the post of *qadi.*

26. According to Malikite point of view, a man is not eligible for holding the office of the administration of justice unless he is cognizant of precedents and the opinions of his predecessors, taking counsel of those who are worthy of having a say in the matter.

27. This view is based on a ruling of 'Umar b. Abd al-Aziz. Imam Malik is, however, of the view that a person to be appointed as a *qadi* must be a *faqih.* This means that only a person who is well-versed in law is competent for the post of *qadi.*

28. Ibn Farhun, a *Maliki* jurist, relying upon the view of Qadi lyad gives the following qualifications of a *qadi:*

(i) Being a Muslim;

(ii) Being sane;
(iii) Being male;
(iv) Being free;
(v) Being adult;
(vi) Being righteous;
(vii) Being knowledgeable;
(viii) Soundness of hearing;
(ix) Soundness of sight;
(x) Soundness of the faculty of speech (not being dumb).

29. The first seven are the conditions for eligibility and the last three are the conditions for competency. It means that if a *qadi,* during his tenure of office, loses the soundness of hearing or sight or speech he will be liable to dismissal from his office. According to some *Shafiite fuqaha* a blind person can be appointed as a *qadi.* The same opinion is ascribed to Malik though denied by Ibn Farhun. Muhammad Sangalaji relying upon the opinion of Shahid Awwal (Abd Allah Shams al-Din Amuli) says that *qada* is analogous to *ifta.* Hence being Mujtahid, being of pure birth and capable of writing, alongwith the above mentioned qualifications are also necessary for a *qadi.* He is also of the opinion that the condition of *ijtihad* for a *qadi* is recommended by all the *fuqaha (ijmai).* The detail of the requisite knowledge for being a *mujtahid* as given by Sangalaji is of wider dimension than that given by Ibn Qudamah.

30. In connection with the condition of *ijtihad* proposed for the office of *qadi,* al-Hilli, a Shiite jurist, vehemently upholds that there is a unanimous agreement of the jurists of Jaafari school that performance of judicial work by *muqallid* (conformist) is not permissible. He further says that this is the unanimous opinion of all the Muslims.

31. *Qada,* whether it is analogous to evidence or to *ifta,* its sole purpose is to administer justice. Hence, anyone who has this ability can be appointed as a *qadi.*

32. As far as the assignment of woman, *fasiq* and *jahil* (not well versed in *fiqh)* is concerned the history does not relate any case to show (or to prove) that the appointment of these three categories was ever in practice. The Muslim rulers, during the reign of *al-Khulfa al-Rashidin (Orthodox Righteous Caliphs)* and even after that period, elected only those male persons for the post of *qadi* who were erudite and proficient scholars. This is because the functions of *qada'* is to assist the ruler in carrying out his responsibilities. It is a point of discussion in a forthcoming chapter. If a *qadi* is incapable to administer efficient justice he creates more problems and enhances difficulties for the ruler. Hence, the discussion about the eligibility of woman, *fasiq* and *non-mujtahid* were of pure academic and legal nature with least effect upon the practical administration of *qada.*

Status of a Lady Qadi

33. The question of the appointment of a woman as a *qadi* requires our due consideration. With the developments of the modern society, women are taking active part in almost all walks of life. In the Muslim countries, a tendency of equal participation of women in the affairs of government is prevalent though not still in practice.

34. According to the discussions of the *fuqaha* as shown in the foregoing pages, there seems no absolute restriction on the appointment of a woman as *qadi* because she is capable of issuing a *fatwa* and in many cases her evidence is admissible.

35. The formula laid down by Ibn Qudamah impliedly excludes a woman from being a *qadi* as the appointee to the office of *qadi* ought to be *Kamil al-Ahkam* and *Kamil al-Khilqah*. Not only by the above-mentioned formula but also by the express arguments of Ibn Qudamah a woman cannot be a *qadi* for the following reasons.

(i) She is not *Kamil al-ahkam* whereas man is *Kamil al-ahkam;*

(ii) She is not *Kamil al-Khilqah* because she is given to forgetfulness according to the following Quranic verse:

> And if two men are not available then a man and two women, from among those whom you approve as witnesses, so that if either of the two errs, the one may remind the other.
> (II: 282)

Ibn Qudamah quotes a *hadith* which reads: A nation who entrusted their affairs to a woman will never prosper.

36. It is noteworthy that *Kamal al-Khilaqah* has no relevance with eligibility for the post of *qadi.* Only those requirements of physical fitness are necessary that have direct connection with the performance of *qada.* For example, a lame person is not disqualified for the post of *qadi,* whereas the dumb and deaf *are* not competent for the job. The only defect of womenfolk pointed out by the learned author is their forgetfulness. Now, the question is whether a strong memory is indispensable for a judge or not. It may be better determined by the judges who have been practically performing the function of judgment. The argument advanced by Ibn Qudamah, however, is not forceful and convincing.

37. Women have been prohibited from performing some duties which have no direct effect on performance of judicial work. In a certain case, if only woman is available and she is more learned and prudent than the men available, especially when no qualified man is found, there seems no reason for disqualifying a woman for the post of *qadi.* As for the *hadith* quoted by Ibn Qudamah in this connection it may be noted that the *hadith* is not relevant to the question under discussion. Al-Bukhari narrates this *hadith* as follows:

> Abu Bakrah narrates that when it reached Allah's Messenger that the people of Persia have appointed the daughter of *Kisra* their ruling queen, he said, Never will prosper a nation that has entrusted its affairs to a woman.
> (al-Sahih, K. al-Maghazi)

Ibn Qudamah himself is of the opinion that a slave is not eligible for the post of *qadi,* but the *hadith* in the context of *imarah* (rulership) says: "If a maimed slave is appointed your ruler and he leads you by the Book of Allah, listen to him obey him".

From this *hadith* one can infer, following the argument of Ibn Qudamah, that a slave is competent for the post of *qadi* whereas the inference is not acceptable to Ibn Qudamah himself.

Likewise, the former inference from the *hadith* in the context of the rulership of woman is not credible. Secondly, when a solitary tradition *(Khabar al-Wahid)* conflicts with the agreed practice of the senior Companions of the Prophet, and the derivative laws based on the Quran and Sunnah, does not ential certainty, particularly when it is an unfamiliar and disapproved one, about obligation and prohibition according to the principles of jurisprudence laid down by the Hanafites.

38. The *hadith* narrated by al-Bukhari about the rulership of woman requires detailed discussion and the following two important points are to be kept in view in this connection:

39. Abu Bukrah recalled this saying of the Prophet on the occasion of the Battle of Camel *(Waqaat al Jamal)* and before this critical juncture neither Abu Bakrah nor any other Companion narrates the *hadith* cited above.

40. According to the commentaries of *Sahih al-Bhukhari,* the Prophet spoke these words either when he heard making the daughter of *Kisra* their ruler or when he was informed that his letter was torn into pieces by the *Kisra.* This was a great incident. Had the Prophet said these words narrated by Abu Bakrah on this occasion, many other Companions would have transmitted this report, particularly on the occasion of the Battle of Camel, to save the Companions of the Prophet from fratricidal war.

41. Ibn Farhun, a *Maliki* jurist, advances another argument as to the ineligibility of a woman for the post of *qadi:*

A woman is not eligible for the post of *qadi* because of her defect and because her speech is (sometimes) an allurement and because only the (beautiful) figure of some women is an allurement. (Ibn Farhun; *Tabsirah,* 25)

42. The second part of argument leads us to permissibility of woman as a *qadi* amongst women because in this case neither her speech nor her face will prove an allurement.

43. There are, however, some external and circumstantial checks that make the performance of judicial work by a woman rather difficult. Hence it may be recommended that women should not be appointed *qadis.* They may be appointed as jurisconsults in order to give them an opportunity to play their role in the affairs of government.

44. In Ansar Barni vs. Federation of Pakistan, a petition was filed before the Federal Shariat Court of Pakistan in order to challenge the appointment of women as judges or magistrates for the following reasons:

(i) They (women) discharge their functions of Qadi without observing pardah which is clear violation of the injunctions of Islaml;

(ii) During the period of the Holy Prophet and his rightful companions the duties of Qadi were never entrusted to females since it appears to be a violation of the injunctions of Islam;

(iii) According to Muslim Law the evidence of a woman is half of that of man and her share in the inheritance is equal to half of that of her brother. The judgement of two ladies only can be equivalent to that of a male;

(iv) The ladies do not fulfil the qualifications of Qadi according to the established principles of Muhammadan Jurisprudence.

45. Mr. Justice Aftab Hussain, the Chief Justice, while examining the third argument observed that it is impossible to accept because it means that the number of judges should correspond it the number of witnesses required to prove it. Thus, there should be four *qadis* to decide a case of adultery which is not acceptable to anyone.

46. Mr. Khalid Ishaq submitted that it was not correct that the evidence of a woman is half of the evidence of a male. Referring to verse 6 of Surah Nur about *Lian,* he submitted that it is clear that the oath of a woman is equal to the testimony of one witness. He also submitted that Qadi Shuraih decided a matter on the solitary evidence of a lady. Similar arguments were given by Mrs. Saleema Nasiruddin and Mrs. Rashida Patel.

47. After giving full consideration to, and making an erudite analysis of, all the arguments advanced by the petitioners, the Chief Justice observed as follows:

48. Before finishing this, it may be clarified that we have not been able to find any justification for the imposition of conditions on an appointment of a woman Qadi. In fact, the opinion of Dr. Tanzilur Rahman in his Book, Islam Ka Nizam-e-Adalat, p. 41 is also without any condition since he agrees with the view of Imam Abu Hanifa.

Qadi as a Fasiq

49. No comprehensive and exact definition of *fasiq* is given. It is generally understood that he who commits *Kabair,* major sins, is a *fasiq.* What are *Kabair?* It is also not defined exactly. Probably to neglect an obligation and to commit what is prohibited is a *Kabirah* (grave sin).

50. The author of *Qada dar Islam* gives the following list of grave sins: (1) murder, (2) usury, (3) adultery/rape, (4) sodomy, (5) procurer's job, (6) cuckoldry, (7) drinking of intoxicant,

(8) theft, (9) usurpation, (10) to run away from the battle-field, (11) to give false evidence, (12) disobedience to parents, (13) despair from the mercy of Allah, (14) to deem oneself secure from Allah's scheme, (15) dishonesty in measurements and weights, (16) delaying of performance of obligatory prayer from its proper time, (17) ascribing false statement to Allah and His Messenger, (18) delaying performance of *Hajj* from the year wherein it became obligatory, (19) to beat and torture a Muslim without justification, (20) concealing the evidence, (21) bribery etc. (Sangalaji; *Qada dar Islam,* 192)

51. The list of *Kabair* (major sins) given by Ibn al-Qayyim al-Jawziyyah is too lengthy. He mentions several other sins, apart from the above-mentioned, as *Kabair* e.g., pride, struggle to gain power through violation and breach of peace, to insult the *Sahabah,* dacoity, man's apparel in attire of woman, and *vice versa,* bewailment, sale of a free person, to learn for wordily gains, and for fame and emulation, to deny the Ascension of the Prophet to deny the ascension of Jesus, to listen to them who don't like it, to draw picture of an animal, to let loose the cloth of turban or trouser, to walk proudly, to be double-faced, litigation on false ground, to falsely proclaim to be one of the progeny of the Prophet commission of fraud, to say one thing and do the other, gambling not to participate in Friday congregational prayer, jealously etc.

52. Al-Marghinani says that a person of such character will not necessarily be unjust in his judicial capacity. Bearing his reputation in mind, he will probably be very much scrupulous and as just as possible in his judgments regarding the dignity of the office. In support of the view that a *fasiq* is not qualified for the post, Ibn Qudamah quotes the following verse:

O ye who believe! if an evil-liver brings you tidings, verify it. (XLIX: 6)

53. We think that the opinion of al-Marghinani is reasonable and balanced because it is nowhere stated in the Quran or the Hadith that administration of justice is analogous to evidence, it is just an analogical deduction of the *fuqaha:* On this basis, they said that if a person is not qualified for being witness, he is not qualified for the post of *qadi.* But to maintain *vice versa,* that every one who is qualified for bearing witness is acceptable as *qadi* is injustice. To give judgement is more serious than to provide information about a ruling of the *Shariah.* Litigants and their attorneys may also be well-informed about the relevant instruction of the *Sharah.* The function of a *qadi* is to sift a corn of truth from the jumble and chaff of obscure and conflicting statements and contentions. Only piety, a praiseworthy quality, does not make any one able to find out the truth and announce an equitable decree unless his heart and mind are cleared from caprice and whims, affection and aversion, spite and inclination and personal likes and dislikes. Hence, only those persons should be appointed the *qadis* who are gifted with composure of temper and equanimity of mind; and that is the real meaning of *adalah.* (probity).

Qadi as Mujtahid

54. Ibn Qudamah, the Shafiites and the Shiite Jurists are of the firm view that only a *mujtajid* (well-versed in requisite branches of knowledge) is competent for the office of *qadi* and the *jahil* is by no way eligible for the post. Imam Malik is of the view, as mentioned before, that a *qadi* must be a *faqih*. Al-Marghinani, on the other hand, is equally of the firm view that the appointment of non-*mujtahid* to the post of *qadi* is valid. It means that this is the real point of difference between the two groups of the *fuqaha;* and presumably both the views were correct in respect of the time and circumstances of the aforementioned scholars.

55. In order to understand this, we should have a brief acquaintance with the Hanafite school of law. Abu Hanifah's selfless service to the Islamic law is somewhat astonishing. He earned his livelihood from his private business and imparted the knowledge of law to his disciples as well as to general public without any desire of worldly gains. First of all, the great *Imam* taught his disciples the way and method of deriving law and inferring legal points from the *nusus,* texts of the Quranic verses and traditions of the Prophet. The Hanafite jurists are reported to have said that the textual injunctions are limited, the problems are unlimited. To find out the solution of each new problem in the texts takes much time and requires much elaboration. Hence, they explained the law, either inferred or deduced, as to each problem or each class of problems.

56. There is another particularity of this school that the Hanafite scholars had always been ready to render services, without demand or desire of any compensation, to each one who required their help in connection with any query or legal point. Regarding what has been related above it may be safely gathered that al-Marghinani's view was based on solid ground; and he is justified to say: "we argue that *non-mujtahid* can dispense justice seeking guidance from the *fatwa* of someone. But, the same cannot be maintained in our circumstances. The *Muftis* and the erudite scholars who extend their genuine and selfless help exist no more. On the contrary, it is feared that if the *qadi* himself is not fully conversant with the requisite knowledge, one can easily lead him amiss and make him a tool of tyranny.

57. This conclusion is reinforced by the considered opinion of Ibn Rashid, quoted by Ibn Farhun, as he says: "If a *Jahil* is appointed at a city where no *fuqaha a*re residing, it is feared that he will pass judgements according to his desire and whims as it is prevalent in our cities and time. Knowledge has gone, ignorance prevails; ignorant persons are being brought to the forefrunt and those who are knowledgeable are being rejected.

58. Nowithstanding these strong contentions about *Jahil* and *Mujtahid,* the words are not defined and lengthy discussions made the controversy more confusing and complicated.

If by the word *Jahil* is meant an ignorant one, none seems to recommend him as *qadi*. The antonym of *mujtahid* is *muqallid*, not *jahil*. Hence the real point of consideration is whether the appointment of *muqallid* to the post of *qadi* is valid? Or, to put it in other words, whether the appointment of *mujtahid* to the post will be more advantageous? Now, let us consider who is *mujtahid* and who is *muqallid*? A *mujtajid* is one who by virtue of his vast learning, is capable of making his opinion in accordance with the law regarding a certain situation despite the (different and/or opposite) opinions of the other *faqaha*. He who adheres to the given law (of a certain school of thought) is called a *muqallid*.

59. The purport of suggesting, or asserting, the condition of *ijtihad* for a *qadi* is to confer on him a right to make, and pronounce, his own opinion as what ought to be, and is, the law concerning the dispute to be adjudged by him. This concept is quite different from the modern concept of a judge who interprets the law and not makes it, whereas the result of the former concept is to allow each *qadi* to make law according to his capacity of knowledge and learning; and this will drag us into a troublesome quandary. In this situation, the law will differ from province to province and from town to town; rather from court to court. What is admissible and lawful before one court will be prohibited and invalid before the other. We, therefore, seeking guidance from the ruling of Umar b. Abd al Aziz, suggest that a *qadi* should be a *faqih* and fully conversant with Islamic literature and as far as *ijtihad* is concerned, it should be left for the legislature.

Qadi as Non-Muslim

60. As far as the appointment of a non-Muslim as a judge is concerned, the point is not discussed in detail in the works of *Fiqh*. Abu Hanifah argues on the basis of the following verse:

O Ye who believe! Take not the Jews and Christians for friends. They are friends one to another. (V: 51)

Hence, in his opinion a non-Muslim can perform judicial work among the non-Muslim community.

61. Al-Mawardi does not allow a non-Muslim to be a *qadi* even in connection with the disputes of the non-Muslims residing in a Muslim state.

62. The *fuqaha* do not seem to allow a non-Muslim to administer justice among the Muslims. Their viewpoint was appropriate to their own circumstances when the non-Muslims residing in an Islamic state were mostly the *dhimmis*. Now, the situation is quite different. The non-Muslims residing in a Muslim state are treated as the citizens of the state. Hence, they enjoy equal rights. Strict adherence to the opinion of the *fuqhah*, particularly that of

al-Mawardi, in our quite different circumstances may prove detrimental to the rights, and harmful to the status, of the Muslims residing in a non-Muslim state. It is also pertinent to note that during the British rule of India, the disputes of the Muslims had been correctly decided, according to their personal law, by the non-Muslim judges. This point, therefore, may be reconsidered by the *'Ulama'*.

63. To sum up this discussion, an ancedote is related here that throws a guiding light on the selection of a *qadi.*

A woman came to Umar b. al-Khattab (may Allah be pleased with him) and said as a poet has versified and translate:

O Judge of wise discretion, the mosque and worship has made my companion, neglectful of me; away he keeps from my bed. Neither day or night he sleeps.

Kaab was sitting beside the Caliph. The Caliph admired her comments about her spouse. Kaab said in the Caliph's ear that the woman was making a complaint of her husband. Umar, after confirming this from the woman, summoned her husband who appeared and replied as it is versified:

Aye, that which is revealed in Surah al-Nur, and that which is in the seven long Surahs, for sure has made me abstemious of conjugal relation and in the Book of Allah there is much intimidation, exhort her, therefore, on beautiful toleration.

64. After hearing the reply, the Caliph referred the case to Kaab for decision. Kaab accordingly decided the case and passed the decree as says the poet:

The most competent *qadi* is he who with application of wisdom, decides with right and elaboration and dispenses justice. Against you O husband! she has a right, three are thine, for her the fourth night, make it your practice.

65. The Caliph, regarding the discretion and erudition of Kaab, appointed him a *qadi* at Basrah.

66. As a resume of the discussions dilated upon in the chapter, it seems worth while to quote *qadi* Abu Bakr al-Gharnati (d. 849 A.H.), a Malikite jurist, as he says:

Recommended for him is dignity, and that he be responsible with probity. And that he be a male and free; of sound organs of sight, hearing, piety, being in possession of Jurisprudence in plenty. (Abu Bakr Gharnati; *Tuhfat al-Hukkam, 3*)

67. In Pakistan, nowadays an illiterate person cannot be appointed as a judge. He should hold a law degree and prove himself suitable for the post through a competitive examination held by the Public Service Commission for higher posts. Practical knowledge as an advocate for some years is also prescribed. He should also be of sound health and unblemished character. In case he commits any misconduct, he is liable to dismissal.

Features of Qadiat

He who is entrusted with the function of *Qada'* is slaughtered without knife.

(Waki; *Akhbar al-Qudat)*

68. The customs and the will of the sovereign are the sources of law according to the Western philosophers. Notwithstanding this, they advert, and have adverted, to moral values as a guiding principle of legislation because the laws emanating from these sources should be consonant with morality and, as a result, should generate a good moral character amongst the citizens or the subjects. Otherwise, the laws will be held in derision and dealt with violation. It is feared that people will put up a strong protest against immoral laws. This means that morality is the spirit of law which gives it force and makes it alive.

69. Not only this but a good system based on morality must be run by good people endowed with high moral values and purity of heart. Bad people at the helm of affairs are like wild elephants who would shake the system and run over, exhorted by their mean passions, all that is good and valuable. In Chapter 1, we have stated that administration of justice is the enforcement of good and suppression of evil. Good people, therefore, must be appointed as the administrators of justice. This will ensure the stability and prosperity of a state. According to Muhammad Shahir Arsalan, a complaint of maladministration and disruption in politics was once made to Sir W. Churchill. He reportedly replied that if there was no disruption in the administration of justice, there would be no fear upon Britain. This shows the significance of administration of justice in a state.

70. The *qadis* inspite of their wide learning and probity are human beings, hence not above criticism. Being in high position, they are caught between two sharp extremes. On the one hand, they are under heavy responsibility, representing divine justice with all their human limitations. On the other, they are always the target of blatant criticism of the people who may overlook everything, but never forgive the errors of those who are in high position, always casting doubts on the conduct of those who occupy high positions and are bestowed with gift of knowledge.

71. Regarding this situation, the Messenger of Allah and his successors prescribed a way of conduct for the *qadis* in order to repel doubts and suspicions, founded, or unfounded, real or imaginary. The *fuqaha* have also dealt with this topic at great length. In this chapter, we shall confine ourselves to the analysis of the salient points of the subject, beginning with the relevant excerpt from Ali's letter to al-Ashtar al-Nakhai.

Then select (that one who seems to you) the best of the people for the post of *qadi:* one with whom the matters do not become narrow and difficult and whom do not infuriate the litigants. He who does not brood on greed. He who does not stop at the ordinary understanding afore (reaching) the farthest. He who pauses at doubts (and thinks). He who concedes most to arguments and does not become tired of hearing and the most perseverant in discovering the truth of facts The most expedient when he reaches the final conclusion... Then frequently examine his judicial work and spend on him with bountiful hand that remove his ills and minimise his needs unto people. Confer on him such a high position (in you, hierarchy) that even your most chosen persons do not covet.

(Nahj al-Balaghah, XVII, 58)

Importance of Wisdom

72. Muhammad Shahir Arslan is of the opinion that much wisdom with little knowledge is more advantageous than much knowledge with little wisdom. Knowledge is not to be in possession of vast treasury of precedents and their remembrance as Ibn Masud has said that knowledge is a (divine) light that Allah throws into the hearts.

73. In the previous chapter, we have shown that a *qadi* should be a *mujtahid.* It should be borne in mind that a *qadi* has to deal with two sets of questions, questions of law and questions of fact; and sometimes with mixed questions of law and fact. In order to deal with a question of law he must be fully conversant with the law *(fiqh)* but to deal with a question of fact, he must be wise enough to discern the truth from falsehood, otherwise, he will not be able to pass an equitable judgment.

74. No doubt, wisdom is a divine gift and you cannot make wise of a fool by inculcating much knowledge of law in his mind. However, wisdom may be increased by general knowledge and vast experience, and probably for this reason in some countries Jury system is introduced whose function is to ascertain the truthfulness of facts so that the judge may deal with the question of law involved therein. The following cases may illustrate well the point under consideration.

75. Two friends sat to have a lunch. One had five loaves, the other three. As they started eating, a stranger came there and on their invitation, sat and ate with them. When the lunch was over, the stranger gave the two friends, eight *dirhams.* He who was with five loaves took five *dirhmas* and gave him who was with three loaves, three *dirhmas.* The latter did not agree and demanded the half amount, that was four *dirhmas.* They took the dispute to Ali. Ali said, "This is a petty matter; litigation about it is not good and compromise is better". He advised the latter disputant to remain content with three dirhmas and give up the dispute.

76. The man insisted that he wanted the case to be decided on merits and in accordance with right and justice. Ali announced his decision that the man insisting so, according to the justice, deserves only one dirham; and his friend who had five loaves deserves seven *dirhmas.* After hearing the decision the man protested and demanded reasons of this judgement.

77. Now, no legal point is involved in this case, and man fully conversant with *nasikh* and *mansukh, al-Hidayah* and *Sharai al-Islam* cannot solve the riddle unless he has full knowledge of mathematics and endowed with the gift of wisdom.

78. There is another case well-known as *'Dinariyyah'* because a woman got only one *dinar* in inheritance of her brother about which she besought judgement of Ali when he was about to ride his horse and had put one foot in stirrup. She said, "Commander of the Faithful! My brother has died. He has left six hundred *dinars;* but the heirs gave me only one *dinar"*. Ali asked, "Is it that your brother left behind him two daughters, mother, wife, twelve brothers and yourself:? She replied, "Yes". Ali said, "They gave you justly, and drove his horse away.

79. This judgement is a marvellous example of quick intelligence and full command over the laws of inheritance. It involved an intricate question of law and it was decided in the twinkling of an eye.

80. Imam Malik is reported to have said, "In this period, I don't find anyone possessing all the requisite qualifications and recommended qualities of a *qadi.* Therefore, if we find anyone having two qualities i.e. *al-lim* (learning) and *al-Wara* (piety), we should appoint him a *qadi.* Ibn Habib in this connection has said, "We can dispense with the qualification of learning but *Aql* (wisdom) is indispensable". This is why the Hanafite *fuqaha* have allowed appointment of an illiterate person to the office of *qadi* provided such a man is bestowed with gift of knowledge and deep understanding.

Qadi should belong to a Noble Family

81. A man who is rich and comes of a respectable family should be appointed to the post of *qadi,* as Umar advised his governor, Abu Musa al-Ashaari, because he who is rich does not desire the wealth of other people (to accumulate it by unlawful means) and because he who belongs to a family of high position does not fear the consequences of his decisions that he makes in the capacity of a *qadi.* Much wisdom is contained in this saying of Umar but can no longer be guaranteed that moneyed people are immune from temptation and devoid of avarice.

82. Muhammad Sanglaji maintains that a bastard should not be appointed a *qadi.* To be of pure birth, as says Ibn Farhun, is a quality of perfection (*Kamal).*

Balance of Mind

83. The Messenger of Allah is reported to have said: No Judge should give judgment between two when he is angry. Ali is reported to have advised Shurayh to get up from the seat (of justice) if he became angry or infuriated. Sangalji is of the opinion that if a *qadi* does not feel well or feels tired, or is sad or angry or hungry, or with heavy stomach, or is suffering from ailment or pain, he should not pass judgment in this situation or state of mind or body. This view of the learned writer is supported by a *hadith* of the Prophet that a *qadi* should not adjudicate unless he has taken meals (food and water).

Court-sittings

84. The place of the court should be wide enough so that all the concerned can gather therein. Al-Mawardi recommends that a *qadi,* before sitting for the hearing of the cases, should perform two or four *Rakaat* as supererogatory prayer. Al-Khassaf says that he should entereat Allah to guide him aright and protect him from committing wrong. Sangalji says that it is better that the seat of the presiding officer of the court should face the *Qiblah.* Wahidi, another Shiite authority, is of the opinion that the back of the *qadi* should be towards the *Qiblah* (direction of the Kaaba) so that those who appear before him face the *Qiblah.*

85. Al-Khassaf cites a *hadith* in this connection that the best of the seats is facing the *Qiblah,* and infers that the *qadi* should sit facing the *Qiblah.* Giving account of the practice of his own times he relates that it is the attendants who face the *Qiblah* and the *qadi* sits as does an orator while delivering the sermon on Friday prayer. Hilli, a Shiite Jurist, holds the same view. This seating arrangement gives the judicial work an orientation of worship as the Muslims do in their *Salat* (Prayers).

86. Al-Mawardi is of the opinion that the timings of the court should be the first part of the day, whereas al-Sarakhsi has recommended that a *qadi* should sit at the two (the early and the later) parts of the day to hear the cases.

87. Reports tell us that once Mamun al-Rashid was sitting to hear the complaints after the *Zuhr* (noon) prayer. A woman appeared and asked his permission to present her complaint as is versified by some poet:

    O the best judge, who is guided aright, O the leader, who throws upon cities ample light. Complains before you, a widow poor, offended against; bereft even of her hair. The aggressor has usurped my property and thus separated me from my family. The Caliph mused for a while and said: That which you have stated impressed Me much, my heart bleeds, liver injured. This is the time of the call for the *Asr* prayer. Go back, on the fixed day, bring the defendant here. On Saturday if it is vouchasafed for us. Otherwise Sunday, we shall decide it thus. (M. Shahir Arsalan; *al-Qada wal-Qadat,* 121,122)

88. Al-Mawardi depicts the scene of the court and the *qadi* while performing judicial work. The *qadi* seated with downward eyes, deep silence almost no movement, no gesture and the bailiffs seated before him. The same writer is of the view that the litigants should sit before the *qadi* and not stand. They should sit before him on their knees paying utmost respect to the court and giving the performance a colour of worship unto Allah. Women can sit cross-legged or they deem convenient.

89. Ibn Farhun narrates on the authority of Ibn Abd al-Hakam that a *qadi* should not fix the day of hearing the cases on holidays and the rainy days because this will create trouble for the disputants.

Unprejudiced Treatment

90. The Prophet is reported to have said that if one of you is entrusted with the function of *qada* he should give equal seats to the disputants appearing before him; and he who is assigned this onerous task should fear Allah in his seats, looks and signs.

91. A *qadi* should not smile to anyone nor should he cut jokes with one of the litigants while performing judicial work. This is to save him from unnecessary suspicions and maintain his dignity.

Disadvantages of Bribery

92. The Messenger of Allah is reported to have said that Allah has cursed him who gives bribe and who takes it in respect of judgment or execution of an order. In another *hadith,* it is narrated that one who gives bribe and one who takes it both are in helifire. Again, another *hadith* says that Allah's Messenger has cursed him who give bribe, and him who takes it, and him who plays the role of an intermediary between them.

93. In the Holy Quran, the children of Israel are cursed of several abominable crimes that they used to commit. *Suht* was one of them (V. 42). Abd Allah b. Masud, explains that Suht is equal to bribery. Bribery, according to Sangalji is an act that leads to violation of a right, or establishment of a wrong (that is gained by presentation of money etc. to the authorities).

94. Bribery is a curse and the most abominable act that gives birth to all kinds of corruption and injustice. The house it enters remains firm no longer as Abd al-Malik b. Marwan has versified:

    When bribery enters a house and gets in, to abide there, and leadership is therein. The latter one runs away and diminish, as a wise man turns his face from the foolish.

    (Waki; *Akhbar al-Qudat,* I, 56)

95. Al-Khassaf, on the basis of the practice of a *Sahabi* on a certain occasion, allows to give bribes to a tyrant ruler from whom on justice is expected and thinks that the man afflicted with such situation will not be the sinful.

96. Not only the bribe but acceptance of presents from the public is strictly prohibited for a *qadi* because the Prophet said: "Acceptance of gifts by the functionaries of public affairs (including the *qadis)* is *ghulul* (tantamount to gross misappropriation)". (Waki; *op. cit,* I, 59, 60). It is vehemently condemned in the Holy Quran: whoso deceives will bring his deceit with him on the Day of Resurrection. (III 161)

97. Al-Kasani and al-Marghinani are of the opinion that a *qadi* can accept presents from those who are his relatives and are allied to his within the prohibited degree, or from those who were used to send him gifts before his appointment to the post of *qadi.*

Al-Marghinani argues that to accept presents from the close relatives is strengthening of family relation which is recommended by the Holy Quran, provided that his relatives have no case for decision pending before him, and provided that the friend does not present more than usual. This is because acceptance of present and bribery makes one inclined to that one who offers. In Exodus, it is commanded:

And thou shalt take no gift, for the gift blindeth the wise, and perverteth the words of the righteous.

(20 : 8)

98. Jalal-al-Din Rumi in some moving verses gives the psychological effect of gift and bribery as he says to the effect.

When a Judge is to bribe and present addicted, how will he differentiate between aggressor and afflicted.

Anger and greed leads a man astray, from righteousness his soul doth sway. When there is need competency doth not last. Hundred veils from heart to sight are cast.

(As quoted by Sangalagi; p. 102)

99. Rabia says, as quoted by Ala-ud-Din Ibn Khalil and Ibn Farhun: "Refrain from accepting presents because that is the way to bribery." Umar b. Abd al-Aziz (the Caliph) rejected a present, it was said to him. "The Prophet used to accept presents." He replied: "For him it was a present and for us, bribery."

100. Moreover, a *qadi* should not attend feasts and entertainments except those that are general. This is not meant by all that he should lead a life of recluse; he should attend funerals and visit the sick.

101. If one of the litigants is stranger or a traveller, the *qadi* may invite him as a guest to dinner but it is incumbent upon the *qadi* to invite the adversary of his guest because Ali is reported to have said that the Messenger of Allah prohibited us to entertain a party to the case unless the opponent is also invited alongwith him.

102. Keeping in view these glorious teachings of the Prophet and the admonitions of the sages, we note with regret that in the long run post of *qadi* became a commercial transaction between the ruler or his deputy and the candidate for the post. Thus, the seat of the *qadi* was sold for an agreed amount of money between the parties. This is stated by Arif al-Nakidi; and if so it is the bitter fact of history to be swallowed. A post purchased would have become a hell of corruption.

Qadi's Garb

103. A time-old wise proverb says that when he appears in the seat he is another man; hence a *qadi* should appear in the seat in the best and dignified attire. In this connection, Ibn Farhun says that he should always be clad in the best dress which is becoming of his

position for it is more dignifying, more imposing, and reflecting his wisdom and honour. If he is not so dressed, it will lower his dignity. These recommendations of the *fuqaha* are based on the practice of the Holy Prophet that whenever he received envoys he used to wear a black turban or put on some fine gown. Al-Mawardi says that a *qadi* should put on a dress that distinguishes him from others. Qadi Abu Yusuf is of the opinion that a judge should put on black gown while presiding the court. Although the black turban or the gown has been used by the Prophet at some occasions, Abu Yusuf's recommendations may be taken as token of loyalty to the Abbasides because black dress was symbol and insignia of the Abbasides.

104. Dr. Tanzilur Rahman thinks that no dress was prescribed for a *qadi* before the appointment of Abu Yusuf to the post of Chief Justice. He prescribed the dress for *qadis* which consisted a long gown with wide sleeves open on shoulders and a turban. Its sleeves lay on to the shoulders. The Chief Justice used to wear a shawl in addition.

105. We may suggest that it should be left to the wise discretion of the *qadis* to prescribe a dress becoming of their honourable profession. Al-Mawardi recommends that those who appear as witnesses should put on a dress that may distinguish them from other people, and that there should be a particular place in the court for the witnesses.

Whom to Take First?

106. Those who come first should be heard first. The cases of travellers or strangers may be given priority, as a matter of grace. The *qadi* may fix a day and the time to hear the cases of women and the *dhimmis*.

Qadi should not Indulge in Trade

107. It is disapproved that a *qadi* should sell or purchase or indulge in trade or any other business, it is desirable that he should appoint someone to make purchases for him. This has been suggested by al-Hilli. Ali is reported to have admonished Shurayh for purchasing a house by himself for his personal use.

108. Ibn Farhun and his predecessor Malikite *fuqaha* are of the opinion that a *qadi* should not indulge in sale and purchase in the court, while performing the judicial work. This practice has been denounced. He should refrain from lending or borrowing, for its effects are related to his office and position.

Qadi and Relationships

109. A *qadi* should avoid taking cognizance of the case of his parents and children, and of those in whose favour he cannot appear as a witness. Al-Mawardi is of the view that a decree passed against his parents or children is valid and lawful because his evidence against

the aforementioned relatives is admissible. He further suggests that a *qadi* may take cognizance of the cases of his brother, uncles and other collaterals and his decision in their favour or against them shall be valid. A *qadi* should not hear the case of his enemy and should refer it to some other *qadi* or to the higher authorities. A *qadi* should not contest his own case but appoint someone as his attorney to do the needful on his behalf.

110. Ibn Qudamah has summed up the qualities of a *qadi* and his moral conduct as follows: It is desirable that a *qadi* should be strong without harshness, lenient without weakness, of such a disposition that a strong and influential person may not expect his favour and a weak one may not become disappointed of his justice. He should be sober, intelligent, wakeful, and not to be deceived, of sound hearing and sight, having the knowledge of the dialects of the people of the area. He should be pious and abstemious, smart and fresh, free from greed, truthful of speech, able to give opinion and to take counsel. He should make a soft speech, put up grand threats and fulfil his promise. He should not be tyrant and snubbing.

Ali is reported to have said that a person cannot become a *qadi,* in the true sense of the word, unless he possesses five qualities; i.e. he is pious, sober, possessing the knowledge of the past events, consulting the wise and fearing Allah and none else.

(*al-Mughni,* IX, 43)

111. In Pakistan, the code of conduct for the judges lays down that a judge should be God-fearing, law-abiding, abstemious, truthful of tongue, wise in opinion, cautions and forbearing, blameless and untouched by greed. While dispensing justice he should be strong without being rough, polite without being weak, awe-inspiring in his warnings and faithful to his words, always preserving calmness, balance and complete detachment, for the formation of correct conclusions in all matters coming before him. In the matters of taking his seat and of rising from his seat as a judge he should be punctilious in point of time. In his behaviour, while in his seat, he should be mindful of the formal courtesies, careful to preserve the dignity if the court maintaining an equal aspect towards all litigants as well as all lawyers appearing before him. He must decline to decide a case involving his own interest or his close relatives. He should refrain from entering into a business dealing with any party to a case before him. He should ensure that justice is not only done, but is also seen to be done. As for gifts, it is laid in the code that gifts are to be received only from near relatives and close friends, and only such as are customary.

Nomination and Selection of Judges

A Brief Historical Account

112. During the blessed life-time of the Messenger of Allah both executive and judicial functions were performed and administered by the Prophet himself who at some

occasions entrusted his deputies with judicial powers as in case of Muadh b. Jabal, Abu Musa al-Ashaari and Ali b. Abu Talib.

113. As I have discussed before that for judicial work, the word *qada* as a term was adopted later. In the Holy Verses and the *Ahadith,* we find the words *hukm* and *'qada'* alternately used for this purpose including other connotations. In a battle with Banu Qurayzah, the Messenger of Allah appointed Saad (b. Muadh) to give his decision. These words as narrated by al-Bukhari are:

114. The Prophet entrusted *al-hukm* (the work of decision) to Saad. He said, "I order *(ahkumu)* that the active fighters be killed"— to the end of the *hadith.*

115. The use of word *'hukm'* indicates that judiciary is a part of executive, and judicial work is in furtherance of the duty of the executive. Anyhow the word *qada* for judicial work is also used in the verses of the Quran and the words of the Prophet. The Holy verse IV: 65 runs as follows:

But nay, by thy Lord, they should not believe (in truth) until they make thee judge of what is in dispute between them and find within themselves no dislike of that what thou decidest, and submit with full submission.

It is narrated by Ali b. Abu Talib that the Messenger of Allah sent him to Yemen as a *qadi...* Muadh b. Jabal narrates: "When the Messenger of Allah sent me to Yemen, he asked me, 'How will you decide a matter/dispute when it is referred to you for *qada* (judgment)? I replied. I shall decide *(aqdi)* the matter in accordance with the Book of Allah'.... to the end of the *Hadith*"

116. Another tradition *(riwayat)* narrated by Tirmidhi says:

Uthman (the third Caliph, said to Abd Allah b. Umar, "go and do qada-decide-the disputes-between/among people." He said, "would you accept my apology, O, Ruler of the Muminin". Uthman said, "what makes you avoid it whereas your father had been doing this work (of judgement)"? He said, 'Yes, my father had been doing the *qada,* and if he faced any difficulty he had been seeking guidance from the Messenger of Allah.

(Tirmidhi. I, 170)

117. From the *Ahadith* narrated above, we come to know that the Messenger of Allah entrusted his deputies with Judicial powers and gave them guidance as how to decide the disputes and supervise their performances.

118. After relating the *ahadith* pertaining to the appointment of Ali as entrusted with judicial powers and functions, Muhammad Sallam Madkur concludes as follows:

The traditions indicate clearly that *qada* and *wilayat* were in one hand. To put it in other words, there was no line of separation between the executive and the judiciary. This may be inferred from the words of Ali, if you agree (to my decision) that is judgement *(qada)* otherwise I pass an *ad inte, im* injunction to make you desist from each other till you come to Allah's Messenger so that he may give his decision as to your cause and dispute'.

119. The said writer discusses the point at length. After rebutting the assertion of those who are of the view that the system of judicial work at the blessed period of the Prophet was not known, he says that:

The upshot of the foregoing discussion is that judicial work *inter alia* was mostly administered by the ruler himself and the judiciary was not independent from the executive in the period of the Prophet as we have explained.

(Madkur; *al-Madkhai, 324,* 325)

Similar views are expressed by Abd al-Hayy al-Fasi in *muqaddimah al-Taratib al-ldariyyah.*

120. The perusal of *Akhbar al-Qudat* by Waki brings it to our notice that the pattern of judiciary in the period of Abu Bakr's *Khilafat* was almost the same as in the blessed period of the Prophet. According to the same writer, Abu Bakr, the first Caliph, on a suggestion submitted to him, appointed Umar b. al-Khattab as a *qadi* but for about one year none appeared before him with a case. He also appointed Anas as qadi at Bahrayn.

121. It was Umar b. al-Khattab, the second Caliph, who, first of all, separated judiciary from the executive and entrusted the *qadis* with power of deciding suits of purely civil nature Muhammad Sallam Madkur says in this connection:

Umar b. al-Khattab separated the judiciary from the administration and appointed for judiciary persons who were not the administrators and separated the two offices. He appointed Abu Darda with him at Medina, Qadi Shurayh at Basrah, Abu Musa al-Ashaari at Kufah and Uthman b. Qays b. Abi-l-As at Egypt as *qadis.* It is narrated that Umar said to one of his *qadis,* prevent people from me in (affairs/disputes of) one dihram and two dirhams (petty disputes). (Madkur; *op. cit.,* 325)

122. According to Sallam Madkur the power of the *Qadis* appointed by Ibn Khattab were confined to monetary disputes *(al-Khusumat al-maliyyah)* and that pertaining to punishments and awarding of compensation for damages remained in the hand of the *Khalifa* in the period of the *Khulafa* and their deputies.

123. Not only this but *Hadrat* Umar (may Allah be pleased with him) laid down for the *qadis* a rather detailed code of conduct as it will be reproduced in the forthcoming chapter; and discussed, with reference to J. Schacht, in the ensuing pages.

124. Uthman, the third caliph, as narrated by Waki, formed a judicial council comprised of himself as the head and Ali, Talha, Zubayr and Abd al-Tahman as its members and did not appoint any person as a judge at Medina Al Kufah, as narrated by Ibn Khayyat, he appointed Shuryh as a *qadi.*

125. Waki' who wrote a book with a purpose to give a detailed account of the *qadis* appointed during the early period of Islam, does not give the list of those who were appointed as *qudat* by Ali during his *Khilafat* for the reasons best known to the said writer. Nonetheless, it is very frequently narrated that Ali, during his period of *Khilafat,* appointed Qadi Shuryh as *qadi.* His own case before Shurayh wherein he appeared as a defendant is reproduced by several historians particularly by Waki. Moreover, several maxims pertaining to the procedural law and instructions as to the appointment of *qadis* and their code of conduct are ascribed to Ali that means he also appointed *qadis* during his Caliphate. According to Khalifa b. Khayyat, Abul Aswad Duali, Dahhak b. Abd Allah Hilali and Muhammad b. Zaid b. Khalifa were also appointed as *qadis,* besides Shurayh, by Ali.'

126. *Vis-a-vis* the above there are some other sources that apparently contradict these historical narrations. Zohri and Ibn al-Musayyab are of the view as reproduced below:

Allah's Messenger did not appoint anyone as a *qadi,* neither Abu Bakr nor Umar did appoint till the middle of the *Khilafat* of the latter when he said to Ali, relieve me of some (responsibility of) affairs, because Ali was the best judge from amongst the *Sahabah.* (Waki, *Akhbar al-Qudat,* I, 105)

127. The same view is ascribed to Malik *(Imam* Malik) with the addition that it was Muawiyyah who first of all entrusted someone with judicial function.

128. Joseph Schacht is also inclined to this viewpoint as he opines:

The first Caliphs did not appoint Qadis and in general did not lay the foundations of what later became the Islamic System of administration of justice; this is shown by the contradiction and improbabilities inherent in the stories which assert the contrary; the instruction which the Caliph Umar is alleged to have given to *Qadis,* too, are a product of the third century of Islam.

129. Both sets of opinions are before the reader so that he may himself determine which is more convincing. To me, it seems rather strange that there was a society or state without proper administration of justice however extinct may be its picture. As far as the development of the system is concerned, it is natural process: changing circumstances make modifications in a system. It may also please be noted that the Islamic territory at the blessed lifetime of the Prophet was not vast. People who embraced Islam adopted sublime moral values taught by the Holy Prophet.

130. As far as the period of Banu Umayyah is concerned we are not able to find the whole truth about it because the first sources of their history are those historians who flourished during the reign of Banu Abbas who gave a mighty coup *de pied* to the Umayyad domination and through a bloody revolution ascended the throne. Hence, none could dare to praise the Banu Umayyah during this period without facing bitter

consequences. The Abbasides in their turn were shattered to pieces by the Tartars who, fortunately, themselves embraced Islam.

131. During the course of my study, particularly on the subject-matter of this book, I came to the conclusion that in the Umayyad period judiciary was fully independent from the executive; and no instance of interference with the judiciary by an Umayyad caliph is cited. Anyhow, this independence remained confined to civil cases and private wrongs.

132. In the Abbaside period the system of administration of justice was improved further though it also seems to us that the judiciary was somewhat under their executive control. An office of *Qadi-al-Qudat* was created for the purpose of advising the Caliph on the appointment of the *qadis.* The *Diwan al-Mazalim* established (perhaps initially by the Ummayyads) to hear the complaints against the public functionaries was also improved and a new office called the *Diwan al-Qada* was set up. The Caliphs themselves used to sit on prescribed days and times to hear the appeals and administer justice.

133. The same system *mutatis mutandis* was maintained by the later dynasties who ruled the Islamic world. Very late in the history of Islam and close to the period of modern developments, the laws were codified under the auspices of *Uthmani* caliphs. The *Qadi al-Asakir* was vested with appellate jurisdiction and the office of the Chief *Mufti,* called the *Shaykh al-Islam,* with supreme judicial power was created. Towards the second decade of the 20th century, A.C., almost all the Muslim countries came under the influence of the west. The Khalifa of Turkey was deposed and the *Khilafat* was abolished.

134. When Iran became an independent state the customary law was brought into force side by side with the Shariah law. During the Kingship of late Rida Shah Pehlawi, Iran assumed a Western colour of civilization that was obliterated by the blood of revolution brought about by Ayatullah Khumayni whose speeches overthrew the strongest and the richest monarch of the present world; and the banner of *Islami Inqilab* was hoisted throughout the country.

135. Egypt was conquered during the period of Umar. It remained the part of Umayyad, and then, the Abbaside rulership till the Fatimides, through a successful insurrection and with use of force, became its rulers. The system of administration of justice under the Fatimides was the same as under the Abbasides. The Fatimides were overthrown by the Mamluks who submitted to the *Uthmanis.* During the early decades of the twentieth century, when Egypt was under the influence of the Western colonists, some secular courts of Justice, side by side with *al-Mahakim al-Shariyyah* were established. The West retraced its steps from Egypt but left behind a strong impression of its civilization which was obliterated by the appreciable acholarly works of learned *'Ulama'.*

136. In Saudi Arabia and Arab Emirates, Islamic laws are in force and *qadis* administer speedy justice, an achievement which is coveted by other Muslim countries.

Islamic Laws in Indo-Pak

137. In the indo-Pak Sub-continent, Islamic laws have been in force since the period of Qutub al-Din Aybak and Ghiyath al-Din Balban. The Chief *Qadi* was called *Sharaf al-Mulk* and *Mir Adl* (the Lord of Justice) with addition three more titles i.e., *Sadr al-Sudur, Sadr-e-Kul* and *Sadr-e-Jahan* in the Mughal period. A state compendium of Islamic laws known as *Fatwa Alamgiriyyah* was complied under the auspices of Aurangzeb Alamgir. Only Alauddin Khilji and Jalal ud-Din Akbar *are* reported to be an exception as the former was averse to theocracy and did not care about the *fatwas* of the *'Ulama'* and the instructions of *Sadr al-Sudur* whereas the latter is known as the founder of the greatest secular state in the world though later on he changed his mind and invented a new religion called *Din-e-ilahi* adhered to by his own imperial majesty and a few courtiers. Jahangir, his son, abolished the new religion of his father and restored Islamic way of life. The episode of chain-and bell for the help of petitioners is a renowned fact of history. In the reign of Shah Jahan, a regular system of appeals was introduced. The same policy was followed by Alamgir.

138. When the (British) East India Company took over the administration of India, the Islamic judicial system, for the Muslims, was not abrogated till the Queen of Great Britain extended her sovereign shadows to the borders of India. Thereafter, changes as to *Muhammadan law* and the administration of justice, by and large, took place. The *qadis* and the *Muhtasibs* were replaced by the judges and the magistrates, the *muftis* by the advocates. The picture of Judicial procedure became more clear by the introduction of civil and criminal procedure codes.

139. Soon after the creation of (the Islamic Republic of) Pakistan, an Objectives Resolution was passed whereby it was promised, and proclaimed, that in Pakistan Islamic way of life shall be introduced and adopted. Efforts had been made in this direction since the creation of Pakistan. The period from 1947 to 1956 is understood as the period of constitutional crisis. In 1956, the first Islamic-oriented constitution was framed which was abrogated in 1958 when Martial Law was imposed.

140. In 1962, a new constitution was made whereby Islamic Advisory Council and Islamic Research Institute came into being. This was perhaps the first remarkable step towards Islamisation in Pakistan. The Constitution of 1973 went a step further in this direction and it was provided therein that all the laws shall be brought in conformity with the teachings of Islam within the period of seven years.

141. In 1977, there was a mass agitation in the country which culminated in the movement of *Nizam-e-Mustafa* that ushered in the Military Regime which performed the onerous task of Islamisation. Hudud Ordinances were enforced, *Riba* in Banking was abolished, Zakat and Ushr Ordinance was enacted, penal Code was amended and Federal Shariat Court

was established. All the existing laws were perused in the light of the Quran and the Sunnah and orders were passed for amending those provisions which were found to be repugnant to *Shariah*.

142. Now, every officer of the court is fully conversant with the Islamic laws. The Qadi Courts are in the offing. But here arises an important question about the rationale of the Qadi Courts when the judgments being delivered by the existing courts in Pakistan are not repugnant to the teachings of Islam. It has been explained in this connection that as justice is expensive and has been delayed, the *qadi* Courts will satisfactorily solve the problem. For support, the example set by Saudi Arabia and Arab Emirates is also cited. The other side of the picture is also being taken into consideration and it is hoped that the nation will soon reach a final conclusion.

143. This brief but comprehensive historical survey of the institution of *qada'* leads us to an important natural question, who is the fountain-head of justice? The Western jurists have evolved two theories in this regard. According to one theory, the fountain-head of justice is the sovereign. According to the other, it is the people who are the source of justice. To put it in other words, justice is administered in the name of the king or in the name of the people. It follows, therefore, that the judges will be appointed either by the government or elected by the people.

144. To accept the king as the source of justice means to deem his royal majesty above the law and exempt him from subpoena. Thus, there will be no power to call in question the cruel and tyrannical acts of the king. To accept the people the fountain-head of justice results in dismissal of the judges according to the whims of the masses. In order to avoid this difficult situation another political theory was coined whereby sovereignty is divided into three institutions, *viz;* legislature, executive and judiciary. According to this theory, the legislature enjoys full liberty and power in the hemisphere of legislation. Beyond any check, it can pass cruel and immoral laws. It is, therefore, aptly remarked about some parliament that it can do everything except making a man a woman and a woman a man. The executive, likewise, is independent in its particular field. It means that if in some country the head of the executive happens to be indolent and the public functionaries corrupt, none will be allowed to interfere. The judiciary, according to this theory, is also deemed independent so much so that it can call in question *suo motu* or on a petition, the acts of the executive which reciprocally has no *locus standi* to interfere in the judgements passed by the judiciary.

145. The above is the gist of the Western political philosophy and jurisprudence. On the other hand, according to Islam, sovereignty belongs to Allah. The people as well as the head of the state are bound to obey the commands of Allah. Allah is the fountain-head of law and justice and to carry out the responsibilities of the administration of the state is the

duty of the *Khalifa;* and not his prerogative. It is the duty of the *Khalifa* to interfere if an unjust order, or an erroneous judgement, is passed. Likewise, the judiciary and the people have full power to keep the *Khalifa* on the right path and disobey his orders if the same are tantamount to disobedience to Allah.

146. This is why the Muslim rulers did not remain indifferent to the functions of *qada.* They supervised the work of the *qadis* and sometimes themselves heard appeals and delivered justice.

Appointment of Qadis According to Fiqh

147. The *fuqaha* are of the view that the appointment of the *qadis* is *fard* (obligatory). Al-Kasani says: "appointment of a *qadi* is obligatory". Al-Kasani, after putting forth arguments in support of his assertion concludes:

> The appointment of a *qadi* is one of the indispensable needs of the appointment of the *Imam.* Hence, it is obligatory. *(Badai al-Sanai,* VII, 27)

148. Al-Mawardi who has written a voluminous book on the subject says:

> To entrust someone with the work of judgment is obligatory for the Imam-Caliph-because it is a part of his general duties and powers. *(Adab al-Qadi,* I. 137)

149. Al-Hilli, the Shiite jurist is of the following opinion:

> It is the duty of the *Imam* to appoint a *qadi* at a city where there is no *qadi* and if the inhabitants of the city resist his appointment they will be sinners and it is lawful to wage a war against them in order to force them to accept the order of the *Imam.* *(Sharai al-lslam,* 314)

150. Another Shiite authority, Haji Sayyid Muhammad Wahidi *(Ayatullah)* holds his view in the following words:

> Out of benevolence, it is must for the *Imam* to appoint the *qadis* in cities/populated places, and it is incumbent upon the people to obey the order of the *Imam.* *(Wajizah Nafiah,* 12,13)

Shouldering the Responsibility

151. Acceptance of the post of *qadi* is not obligatory, as held by the *fuqaha,* except in a situation when there is none other eligible and competent for the post. It is recommended to accept the post when the person appointed as such is more capable than other persons. It is permissible in ordinary cases and undesirable when there are others who are more competent for the post. It is *haram* (strictly prohibited) to accept the post when the person so appointed knows within the heart of his heart that he is not eligible and competent for the post.

152. The author of *al-Mughni,* relying probably upon the hadith with effect:

> *Qadis* are of three categories, one of whom will go to Paradise and two to Hell. The one who will go to Paradise is the man who knows what is right and gives judgment accordingly. But, the man who knows what is right and acts tyrannically in his judgment will go to Hell. The man who gives judgment for people when he is ignorant will (also) go to Hell. (Ibn Majah, *Sunan,* 168)

says that acceptance of the post of *qadi* is not permissible for a person who is not eligible. Its acceptance is incumbent upon a person who is competent for the post. In case, there are more than one persons who are eligible and can administer the work, its acceptance is permissible but in this case it is desirable *(mustahabb)* to avoid to shoulder the responsibility because therein is great danger and heavy burden and responsibility. In case, the person who is offered the post is in need of financial help, it is recommended (by the *fuqaha)* that he should join the job because it is the best occupation and therein is virtue and worship *(qurbah* and *taah,* the words used by Ibn Qudarnah).

153. There is another category of the candidates for the post, i.e., those who demand the post: is it permissible? It is the unanimous opinion of the *fuqaha* that demand of the post of *qada* is an abominable act because the Messenger of Allah is reported to have given a warning in this connection that is:

> if anyone desires and asks (influential persons) to recommend him to be appointed as *qadi,* he will be left to his own devices but if anyone is forced to accept it God will send down an angel who will direct him aright. (Ibn Majah, *Sunan,* 168)

154. According to my own humble understanding, its demand is permissible for whom who can administer the work justly. This I inferred from a *hadith* narrated by Abu Daud as follows:

> Abu Hurrayrah reported God's Messenger as saying, "If anyone demands the office of *qadi* till he gets it and his justice prevails over his injustice, he shall go to Paradise, but the *qadi* whose tyranny prevails over his justice, shall go to Hell (fire). *(Sunan,* III, 325)

How to Appoint?

155. *Al-Mawardi* in *Al-Ahkam al-Sultaniyyah* says that a *qadi* may be appointed by means of oral order in case the proposed appointee is present, and by means of written order in case the appointee is not present before the appointing authority. The order should be clear and expressed in words that mean that I (the Imam or his deputy) have appointed such and such person/persons at such and such place/places to administer the work of judgment among the people. The wording of the order, according to al-Mawardi should be like this, I depute you to administer justice, I have appointed you to administer justice instead

of me, I appoint you as a qadi, I have made you to administer justice. Anyhow, the words like and etc., that impliedly mean appointment, are also of lawful authority and legal effect.

156. Ibn Qudamah in *al-Mughni* says that after ascertaining the justness and fitness of the proposed appointee, the anointing authority should give the order in writing after giving the appointee the oath that will remain God- fearing, firm in the administration of justice, consulting the erudite and those who are knowledgeable, judging the witness and analysing the evidence with wise discretion, and will discharge his duties as guardian of the properties of the orphans, and endowments for benevolent purposes.

157. In case, the appointee is to be appointed at some far-flung place from the permanent seat of the appointing authority, the order to this effect should be accompanied by two just witnesses. This Hanafites do not recommend the witnesses. This they have opined relying upon the mode of the appointment of Muadh and Ali by the Prophet'

158. Al-Hilli, the shiite jurist, is also of the same opinion that is put forth by the writer of *al-Mughni.*

Appointment by Sultan Jair

159. Acceptance of the office of *qadi* from a *sultan/ hakim Jair* is permissible according to some *fuqaha* whereas some others are of the opinion that it is not permissible. Those who are of the opinion as to its permissibility rely upon the acceptance of the Prophet Yusuf (Joseph, Peace be on him) *an* office from a sultan who was a *Kafir* (did not believe in Prophethood of Yusuf). In this respect, a rational argument is also advanced that acceptance of the office of *qadi* by a just and pious person from an unjust and tyrant ruler will help to obstruct his injustice and mitigate the effect of his atrocities.

160. Those who are of the opinion that it is not permissible rebutting the above-mentioned arguments contend that the *sultan* from whom Hadrat Yusuf (peace be on him) accepted a post was not tyrant *(taghi),* he was a good man though not a believer. Secondly, the post that Hadrat Yusuf (peace be on him) accepted was that of the office of finance and not that of the office of *qadi.* As to rational argument they contend that it is tantamount to extend help to a tyrant. It is also feared that he can interfere with the administration of justice.

161. The learned readers may decide better which of the arguments are forceful and nearer to the spirit of the Islamic teachings and the settled principles of justice and its just administration.

Qadi's Salary

162. On remunerations of the *qadis,* the *fuqaha* are almost silent though some pieces of historical facts are available which narrate that in the period of Umar b. al-Khattab (the second

Caliph) a *qadi* was paid one hundred *dirhams* and an amount of wheat compatible with his needs per month. The same practice continued on the period of Uthman and Ali. In the period of Banu Umayyah the amount of remuneration was increased to one thousand *dirhams*. In Abbaside period, it decreased to three hundred *dirhams*. Thereafter came a period when the *qadi* himself was the paying one and not the paid one.

Sacking Qadi's Rights

163. The appointing authority can depose a *qadi* from his post but it is not recommendable to depose him without any cogent and convincing reason. Upon the death of the appointing authority, the *qadi* will continue in his office and no fresh appointment by the succeeding ruler is required because the office of *qadi* is a branch of *Wilayat Ammah* and the demise of the ruler does not make any difference to its validity. According to some Shiite *fuqaha* at the demise of the *Imam*, fresh appointment to the office of *qadi* is required.

164. If a *qadi* deems it proper to resign from the post, he should submit his resignation to the appointing authority as has opined Qadi Abu Yusuf. Before his resignation is accepted, he should not leave the office and continue in discharging his function/duties till he is replaced by some other appointed to the same post.

Delivering Justice

165. The sole purpose of the office of *qadi* is to dispense justice. The procedures laid down this connection are to help him and provide him facilities to carry out the judicial work, and not to bind him by the regulations of the work if the same are inconsistent with the fair and speedy administration of justice. Hence, no exhaustive and rigid procedure can be prescribed; and where there are no regulations as to the procedure, the *qadi* can rely upon precedents on his own discretion.

166. Much is said by the *fuqaha* about the conduct and etiquette of the *qadis* but little material is available in the works of the *fuqaha* about the procedure of judicial work. This is perhaps because of two reasons. First, that the concern of the *fuqaha* was with the law and not with the procedure of the *modus operandi* of the public functionaries. Secondly, the society at the time of the early *fuqaha* was much different from ours. Now, the population has increased much, and the problems have grown complicated due to novel political and economic theories and systems, mostly because of materialistic outlook. That is why, the codes of civil procedure introduced nowadays are detailed and based on scientific and universal methods in order to meet the complications-expected and incidental—remove doubts and uncertainties and furnish all essential and relevant details to the judges and the litigants alike.

167. I have tried my best to collect all relevant instructions and material available on the point in the Holy Quran the *Sunnah* and the discussions of the *fuqaha,* picking up pieces of information from here and there and have arranged the same in a systematic shape so that a picture of procedure of *qada,* suitable to our modern requirements, may be drawn therefrom. It seems worthwhile to give at the outset the translation of the letter of Umar (that was reportedly written to Abu Musa al-Ashari). This will help us very much in drawing the outline of the procedure.

(i) Verily *qada* is firm obligation and a followed path and practice;

(ii) Understand when a disputed matter is put up to you because to pronounce a just verdict without its implementation is of no use;

(iii) Consider all the people (and disputant parties) equal in your presence (attention), assembly (court) and judgement so that a man of high position not cherish hope that you will do injustice; and so that a weak one not despair of your (doing) justice (that you will not do justice);

(iv) (Onus of) proof is on him who alleges or claims, and oath on him who denies;

(v) Compromise amongst the Muslims is lawful; except that which makes a lawful prohibited, and render the prohibited one, the lawful;

(vi) He who claims on the strength of an absent evidence, fix a time-limit for him; if he brings his evidence within the limitation-period, grant him his right, if he deserves; if he fails to do so reverse upon him the judgement. This is the last plea and the utmost clarity that dispels the darkness;

(vii) Prevent you not your yesterday's judgement that you have reconsidered afterwards in your conscience and are guided aright, to revert to the right judgement because right is established (of old); and nothing annuls what is right, because it is better to return to right than to continue in wrong;

(viii) Evidence of all the Muslims is admissible in each other's cases except the evidence of the one who is flogged in one of *hudud* cases or experienced of tendering false evidence, or the evidence of the one who is doubted to be a relative or an affiliated one;

(ix) Almighty Allah knows the hidden secrets of His servants and has put a cover upon them in *hudud* except that becomes manifest through evidence or by oath.

None is Condemned Unheard

168. This much recommended principle leads us to give opportunity to both the parties of a dispute to be heard and appreciated so that *exparte* decision not be passed without reasonable cause. This principle may be derived from a *hadith,* reported by Ali b. Abu Talib

in connection with his own appointment in Yemen whereby he was entrusted with judicial powers and instructed by the Prophet as follows:

The Messenger of Allah sent me to Yemen as a *qadi*. I said, 'O Messenger of Allah! you send me and I am young and have no knowledge of (the procedure of) *qada*. He said, Allah will guide you to announce correct judgements. When two disputants appear before you, do not decide for one till you hear the other. It is more likely that by adopting this procedure the reasons of a judgment will become clear unto you'. Ali said, after following this instruction, I was never doubtful about a decision that I made.

(Bayhaqi; *al-Sunan al-Kubra,* X, 137)

169. Ibn Qudamah, a *Hanbali* jurist, is of the opinion that a judgment or a decree pertaining to the rights of human beings *(huquq al-Adamiyyin)* passed against an absentee is valid. This he has opined relying upon and quoting a *hadith* that says:

Hind said, "O Messenger of Allah, Abu Sufyan is a niggardly man and does not give me that may suffice me and my children." The Prophet said, 'Take what is sufficient for you and your son according to the custom'. (*Al-Mughni,* IX, 109, 110)

He further says that an ex *parte* decree without giving the chance of hearing to the defendant is to be set aside if the *ghaib* (he who is not present in the court) appears in the court and proves that the witnesses were not acceptable at the time when they tendered evidence in the court. An *ex parte* decree according to the same writer is not valid when the defendant is present in the city according to the majority of the scholars.

170. To my humble understanding, the *hadith* quoted by the learned writer is not a judicial decree passed by the Messenger of Allah in judicial capacity. At the most, it is a piece of legal advice and a general religious instruction about the rights of the dependents of a person in his property. The opinion of the erudite *Hanabali* jurist is also repelled in the light of another *hadith* that says:

Ibn Abbas narrated that the Prophet said, "If people be given only on the bases of their claims, they would claim the blood and the property of others, but the (onus of) oath is on the defendant," (Muslim; *Sahih)*

171. Al-Marghinani, a *Hanafi* jurist, is of the opinion that an *ex parte* decree is not valid except in presence of the agent of an absent one." Ibn Farhun, *Maliki,* and al-Hilli *jaafari,* are of the same opinion as maintained by Ibn Qudamah.

172. Al-Mawardi has devoted a score of pages to the point and discussed it at full length under a separate topic, *Al-Qada Ala al-Ghaib-Decision* Against the Absentee- Al-Mawardi, being a *Shafii,* is of the view that a decree against a person who is not present in the court is valid, may the suit be pertaining to movable or immovable property, provided it is in the realm of the rights of human beings.

173. To Malik, such a decision is valid pertaining to movable and invalid pertaining to immovable property.

174. Decision against he who is present in the (same) city and not present in the court is not valid according to Shafii and is very much valid according to Ibn Shubrumah, Ahmad and Ishaq as stated by al-Mawardi. Ibn Shubrumah has said, according to al-Mawardi, "I shall decide against a person who is behind the next wall and is not present before me".

175. Al-Mawardi, after recording the opinions of the eminent and leading *fuqaha,* advances arguments supporting the *Shafii* view. These arguments are reproduced below for further clarification. He relies upon the Holy Verse which runs:

O David, Lo! We have set thee as a viceroy in the earth: therefore judge aright between mankind. (XXXVIII : 26)

and infers that when requisite evidence is tendered against the absentee, the *haqq* (right) becomes established and passing the judgement, valid.

176. In my humble opinion, the argument set forth by the erudite writer is irrelevant and does not forcefully support his view because in case of dispute the plain truth does not become manifest, beyond the shadow of doubt, unless and until both the parties are heard and their evidence and contentions appreciated.

177. In support of his view, he further relies upon a *hadith* to the effect that in a case two disputants are reported to have made a promise in presence of the Messenger of Allah to perform their obligations on a certain day. One of them did not fulfil his promise, the Prophet passed judgement and decree against him who did not comply with the promise. The inference from this *hadith* also does not support the view of al-Mawardi. Secondly, the point under discussion is an *ex parte* decree against that one who is *ab intitio* absentee and no opportunity of hearing is provided to him. The position covered by the aforementioned *hadith* is different one.

178. Al-Mawardi's third main argument is the *hadith* whereby the Holy Prophet allowed Hind (wife of Abu Sufyan) to take from the property of her husband will be sufficient for her expenditures according to the custom. The writer lays much emphasis on its being a judgment and decree, and not a *fatwa.*"

179. His forth main argument is *Ijma*- the consensus of the *fuqaha.* No doubt that the majority of the scholars of *fiqh* is almost of the same view that is set forth by al-Mawardi, nevertheless, the *Hanafis* do not allow this and advance arguments in support of their opinion. Hence, to declare that there is *Ijma* of the *fuqaha* that a judgment against an absentee is valid seems to be a statement made with carelessness.

180. These discussions are of little practical value in modern times. In the period of the early *fuqaha,* journey from one city to another was very difficult because there were on vehicles for transportation of the passengers. That is why the *fuqaha* resorted to *qada ala al-ghaib,* in order to expedite justice according to their best discretion. The *Hanafis* adopted and introduced another procedure that when the defendant lived, temporarily or as a permanent resident, at a considerable distance from the court of *qadi,* the plaintiff was allowed to present his suit and evidence in the court of *qadi,* and the *qadi* after recording the evidence and giving due consideration to the truthfulness of evidence should send the record of the case to the *qadi* within whose jurisdiction the defendant was residing. The *Hanafis* have discussed this point at length under the topic of *Kitab al-Qadi lla al-Qadi-* consigning the record of the case to another *qadi.* Al-Mawardi himself has agreed to this procedure.

181. According to my own humble understanding, it is valid in special cases when a defendant leaves his home-country and goes to some far off territory for a long period and is not likely to return in near future, particularly in past days, when journey from country to country was difficult and took very long time. It should be noted that in case of an *ex parte* decree, the plaintiff shall be ordered to furnish sureties lest the defendant appear in future and prove his cause. This interpretation of the opinion of the *fuqaha* satisfactorily solves the controversy and does not seem against the modern norms of judicial procedure.

Issuance of Summons and Processes

182. Bearing in mind the above-explained principle, it is necessary that whenever a party appears before a *qadi* praying for judgment, he ought summon the defendant. The *fuqaha,* however, did not provide sufficient details pertaining to the issuance of summons, except Ibn Qudamah and al-Khassaf.

183. The issuance of summons and sending for the defendant is termed by al-Khassaf as *al-'Adwa wa' I'ada'* (Toiling in Search of the Defendant) and relying upon the ruling of Abu Yusuf has opined that after the suit is instituted in the court of *qadi* and the defendant is mentioned as residing in the same city, the *qadi* shall summon him and send with the plaintiff (a bailiff) who shall bring the defendant along with himself or cause him appear in the court.

184. The procedure of *al-Adwa wa l-lada* according to the author (and the expounder) is based on *Istihsan,* better and facile performance, and not on *qiyas* (analogy); and further that the *Sahabah* did so and none objected.

185. In case the defendant resides away from the city, at a distance of one day's journey, the *qadi* shall record the evidence produced by the plaintiff and then send for the defendant, ordering him to appear and answer the plaint. These provisions, according to the said writers, are inferred from several precedents set forth by *al-Khulafa' al-Rashidin.*

Verification of Summons

186. The summons shall be sent with a strong testimony and symbol of the court of the *qadi* as accompanying the courier or the bailiff by seal or written order.

187. Those who are suffering from illness and are unable to appear, and the ladies who according to custom on serve purdah, shall not be summoned and a commission shall be appointed who shall visit the persons so exempted and shall act as the deputy of the *qadi* if empowered so, otherwise the commission shall record the statements of the persons so exempted and submit it to the *qadi.* If such exempted persons appoint someone as their representative *(wakil),* the procedure shall be carried out as usual and the commission shall not record their statements.

Non-followers of Law

188. If the defendant after being summoned refuses to appear before the *qadi* and two witnesses give their testimony that the defendant refuses to appear, the *qadi* shall inform the *wali* (the local executive authority) about it and the cost and expenditure of the processes shall be borne by the defendant who shall also be punished with beating or slapping or imprisonment according to the discretion of the *qadi,* because by refusing the summons of the *qadi,* the defendant has committed contempt of the court *(isaat al-adab).*

189. The defendant shall be liable to punishment in case he acknowledged the summons and did not appear on the date fixed by the court, because one who does not obey the orders of the court is a criminal *(jani)* of contempt liable to punishment. Anyhow, in the latter case, the punishment will be lighter or less than that in the former case.

190. In case a defendant hides himself from the server of the summons, the *qadi* shall write to the *wali* in order to bring the defendant in the court or cause him appear.

191. In case the *wali* fails to cause the hiding defendant appear in the court and the plaintiff presents two witnesses who state that they have seen the defendant in, or about, his house where he resides within last three days, the *qadi* shall order that the door of the residence of the defendant be locked and sealed. That residence will thereafter deemed to be legally converted into the prison house till further orders. After doing so the *qadi* shall send his messenger alongwith two witnesses to the residence of the defendant so imprisoned who will advise him to appear before the court. This will be done for three days, each day three times, and if in spite of this advice, the defendant does not give his willingness to appear in the court, the *qadi* shall appoint someone as the *wakil* (attorney) of the defendant who will answer the plaint on behalf of the defendant.

192. According to al-Mawardi in case of a refusing defendant to appear, the *qadi* may adopt one of the following ways:

(i) To compel him with help of bailiffs to appear;

(ii) To refer his case to the executive authority who shall forcefully cause him to appear;

(iii) To appoint two just persons who will call upon him at the door of his residence to appear and answer.

193. According to Ibn Qudamah, Imam Malik is of the opinion that on mere application of the plaintiff, the *qadi* should not summon the defendant, unless he is satisfied that *prima facie* there might have been some transaction between the plaintiff and the defendant because someone may file a suit against a respectable person just to disgrace him. Ibn Qudamah himself does not support this view. He is of the considered opinion that on the application of a plaintiff, the defendant, whosoever may be, should be summoned to answer the suit.

194. Imam Shafii is of the opinion that women who observe purdah should not be ordered to appear personally in the court and a commission should be sent to the residence of such women defendants and the case should be decided there because the Messenger of Allah sent Unays to decide a case of a woman at her residence and ordered:

Go, Unays, to the woman (wife) of this, if she confesses (the commission of adultery), stone her to death.

195. According to Ibn Qudamah, a dismissed *qadi* may also be summoned to answer plaint against him.

Raid on the Residence of the Defendant

196. Al-Khassaf says that some of our *fuqaha* allow to make a raid on the residence of a debtor who hides therein. This practice was adopted by Qadi Abu Yusuf in the opinion of al-Sarakhsi this practice is not desirable.

197. The mode of the raid in this case shall be as follows:

The *qadi* shall send two reliable persons escorted by a party comprising of the *aawan* (bailiffs), women and servants. The *aawan* shall stand at the door of the residence of the debtor or defendant, and around it, so that if he tries to run away or escape, they may catch hold of him. The attendants, servants and women shall enter all the rooms of the residence and try to find him out even if he is hidden with women of his family.

198. In support of this practice, several precedents of the *Khulafa al-Rashidun* are quoted. But, in my opinion ail of them are concerning raids on those places where the commission of some cognizable crimes (drinking of wine or dancing) was suspected.

199. If despite this all, the defendant does not appear, the *qadi* shall record the evidence produced by the plaintiff and after appreciation of the evidence pass an ex *parte* judgment.

200. These detailed discussions lead us to the fact that the early Muslim jurists and *qadis* were very much careful about the issuance and service of summons. It was held as the duty of

the court and the executive authority to inform the defendant about the action so that he may appear and answer the allegations. Compare the passing remarks of Joseph Schacht as follows:

Islamic law still envisages the primordial method of starting an action, which consists of the plaintiff seizing the defendant and hauling him before the judge.

(An Introduction to Islamic Law, 16)

Advocating the Case

201. Al-Mawardi deals with the subject under a special excursus with the title *Sayr al-Daawa*-Journey and proceeding of the Suit-According to al-Mawardi and Ibn Qudamah a plaint be in a written form.

202. In the period of the Messenger of Allah and the *Kulafa Rashidun* most of the suits were contested orally judgments and decrees were passed probably by oral orders. In later periods, when facilities of scribing became easily available, the *fuqaha* recommended that pleadings should be in a written form.

203. It must, however, be borne in mind that the Holy Quran lays much emphasis on bringing down the legal transactions to a written form. The Holy verse says:

O ye who believe! when you contract for a fixed term, record it in writing between you in (terms of) equity ... Be not averse to writing down (the contract) whether it be small or great with (record of) the term thereof. This is more equitable in the sight of Allah and more sure for testimony; and the best way of avoiding doubt between you.(II: 282)

204. From the verse cited above, it can be safely inferred that utmost care should be taken to legal transactions and proceedings and the same should be brought to written form.

Minor and the Insane cannot Claim

205. A minor or a person of unsound mind cannot institute a suit unless represented by the guardian. This point is discussed in detail by the *fuqaha.*

Particulars of the Subject-matter of the Suit be Given

206. A plaint should contain all particulars and full description of the subject of suit along with the cause of action and relief prayed for.

207. The author of *al-Hidayah* opines that since no obligation can take place with respect to a matter of uncertainty, the plaint is liable to be rejected if the particulars of the subject-matter of the suit are not stated.

208. Ibn Farhun lays down five conditions of a plaint. (1) The thing sued for be known. (2) If the defendant acknowledges the truthfulness of the plaint, a relief may be granted. (3) The plaint should not be vexatious. (4) The plaint must be brought

with certainty of cause of action (5) The plaint should be of such sort that good reason does not deny its truthfulness.

209. The author of *al-Hidayah* is of the view that in case of movable property it must be produced in the court, if possible, for the purpose of exhibition, certainly and pointed reference. Otherwise the species, the gender, the quantity, the value and the amount of the article sued for must be stated.

210. In a suit of immovable property, a full description of its boundary alongwith the names of persons, adding a description of their families, in occupation of the boundaries must be mentioned. It is sufficient, if only three boundaries of the suit land are defined, according to the majority of the followers of Abu Hanifah. Other *fuqaha,* particularly Ibn Qudamah and al-Mawardi are of the opinion that all the four boundaries must be described.

Defendant in Court

211. When the plaint is presented as mentioned above and *prima facie* is maintainable, the *qadi* shall send for the defendant to appear and answer. Acknowledgment of the Defendant.

212. In case the defendant confesses the truthfulness of allegations of the plaintiff, the decree shall be passed in favour of the plaintiff.

No Answer from a Defendant

213. In case the defendant refuses to give answer, neither acknowledges nor denies the allegations, the *qadi* shall imprison him till he replies the allegations made against him by the plaintiff. This is the opinion of the *Hanafi fuqaha.* The *Shafii fuqaha* according to al-Mawardi, are of the opinion that in this case the defendant shall not be imprisoned and judgment shall be announced against him.

Plaintiff must Prove his Cause

214. In case the defendant denies the truth of allegations made by the plaintiff, the plaintiff shall produce evidence in accordance with the law of evidence. The *qadi* thereon shall put the witness to *tazkiyah* (investigation of their character and demeanour) as explained in detail by the *fuqaha* and shall appraise the evidence, and then pronounce his judgment either in favour of the plaintiff or against him.

Defendant and Oath

215. In case the plaintiff fails, or is unable to produce requisite evidence, the *qadi* shall, on demand of the plaintiff, put the defendant to his oath that is mentioned in the *hadith* and the books of *fiqh.* Al-Mawardi has opined that if the plaintiff does not demand the oath from the defendant his claim shall be rejected. It may be noted that there are some cases wherein oath shall not be given. Nukul.

216. In case the defendant refuses to take oath the case shall be decided against him. Imam Shafii and the majority of the Shiah *fuqaha* are of the opinion that in this case the judgment shall not be passed in favour of the plaintiff unless and until he himself takes the oath. In support of his opinion, Shafii adduces a precedent that Uthman claimed against Miqdad b. Aswad before Umar, the Caliph. Miqdad insisted that let Uthman (the plaintiff) take the oath, let Uthman take the oath and have his right. Thereupon Umar said, 'Miqdad has acted according to justice'.

217. The *Hanafis,* in support of their view rely upon the well-known *hadith* that says:

The onus of proof lies on the plaintiff and the oath is to be taken by the defendant.

218. In further support of the *Hanafis,* the case of Hadrami brought before the Messenger of Allah may be cited. The *Hadith* as narrated by Muslim says:

Two persons, one from Hadramawt, the other from Kindah appeared before the Prophet The Hadrami said, O Messenger of Allah! This man has usurped my land. The Kindi replied, "The suit land is my property in my possession and the Hadrami has no right to claim the same". The Prophet said to Hadrami, "Have you any evidence"? He" said, "No". The Prophet said, "Then you shall have to be content with the oath of the defendant". The Hadrami said, "O Messenger of Allah! the man is not a pious one, hence a false statement under oath makes no difference to him". The Prophet said, "Nevertheless you have to accept his statement under oath". *(Shaih,* I, 80)

219. Sarakhsi, while discussing the point, advances a very suitable and convincing argument that the oath is not a proof of the claim. Only evidence is admissible in proof; when the defendant takes oath that means the assertion of the plaintiff is not proved. Hence, if the plaintiff takes oath that will not prove his case.

Oath and Counter Claim

220. In case there are counter claims and counter assertions, both the parties will have to produce their evidence and administer oath if cannot produce requisite evidence. But, what will be the fate of the case? This depends on the merits and nature of each case and no formula can be set forth in connection with the cases of mutual swearing *(tahaluf).*

Effect of Personal Knowledge of the Qadi

221. According to the majority of the *fuqaha a qadi* can decide the case upon his personal knowledge of the facts. Abu Hanifah says that such decisions are valid concerning only those cases the facts whereof came to the personal knowledge of the *qadi* after his appointment to the office.

222. Qadi Abu Yusuf is of the opinion that such decision is valid except in the *hudud* cases. (the point shall be discussed in the next chapter).

223. Malik is of the opinion that *qadi* will not decide upon his personal knowledge of the facts.

224. Al-Mawardi has opined that in such decisions the *qadi* will mention it in his judgment that he has decoded the case according to his personal knowledge of the facts. Shahid, the Shiah authority, as quoted in *Qada dar Islam,* is of the opinion that if the *qadi* has the knowledge of the right he shall decide (relying) upon his own knowledge without any objection and impediment.

Al-Bayyinah

225. After reading the above discussions of the learned *fuqaha* about proof and evidence, it seems worthwhile to revert to some oft-quoted and well-known *ahadith* that throw a guiding light upon the points discussed afore. The Messenger of Allah is reported to have said:

Onus of proof *(al-Bayyinah)* lies on the plaintiff and the oath is to be sworn by the defendant.

The word *'Bayyinah'* in the *hadith* is from the root of *bayan,* that means to explain in a clear-cut manner. Hence, according to the *hadith,* it is incumbent upon the plaintiff to make out his case crystal clear by giving full description of the claim, adducing all possible and lawful evidence and putting forth forceful and convincing arguments. This explanation leads us to infer that the plaintiff may present documentary evidence, circumstantial evidence and expert opinion in order to prove his assertion.

226. In a case that is known as Zabriqan b. Badr and Hutayah case wherein it was alleged that Hutayah his poem insulted the governor, Zabriqan. Umar called Hassan b. Thabit, a great poet, to give his expert opinion. Hutayah is reported to have said:

Leave high depositions Travel not in their exploration. For sure, thou art the eater, And wearer after the latest fashion.

Hassan opined that Hutayah was guilty of defamation. On this opinion, Hutayah was punished.

227. The Messenger of Allah is reported to have said as narrated by Umm Salamah:

The Messenger of Allah said, "I am only a human being and you bring your disputes to me, some perhaps being more eloquent in their plea than others, so that I give judgement on their behalf according to what I hear from them. Therefore, whatever I decide for anyone which by right belong to his brother he must not take it. For, I am granting him only a portion of hell". (Bukhari, *al-Shaih,* II, 1085)

228. From this *hadith,* it may safely be inferred that advancing arguments in the court, as to the assertions of the parties to the suits are permissible as it is an attempt to solve the riddles and remove the doubts in a case that is under consideration.

229. Ibn Farhun has especially adverted to the point of expert opinion in *Tabsirah.* He says that the opinion of masons/architects in cases of buildings (disputes concerning houses, walls, roof, etc.), the opinions of tradesmen in cases of price and value of things and the opinions of medical practitioners (in matters concerning medical science) are admissible according to several *fuqaha.*

230. It should further be noted that the qualifications of a *shahid* (witness) are the part of the law of evidence and out of the pale of the present discussion. Nevertheless, the *tazkiyah* of a witness is the function of a *qadi,* which is not as easy as it seems. Whether a witness is of good moral character or not; cannot be ascertained particularly in our modern societies. People never commend their fellow inhabitants or the neighbours. And who is protected from sin except the prophets? Ibn Farhun in this connection prescribes a simple procedure that when a witness appears before a *qadi,* he should write down his name, his parentage, his address of residence, the mosque wherein he performs prayers, his face and disposition, his profession and whether the residence is his own ownership or not. This description facilitates the work of *tazkiyah.*

Dispensation of Judgment

231. Judgments should be in a written form according to the opinions of the *fuqaha.* Al-Bayhaqi quotes a *hadith* that says that the Holy Prophet wrote an endowment for the *Ansar* (the helpers of *Muhajirin* at Medina). They requested that the same may be written for their brethren, the Quraish, and infers that a *qadi* may write (his judgment) for a party on his demand. Ibn Qudamah, however, is of the opinion that two copies of judgment should be prepared, one to be preserved in the record room *(diwan),* the other to be delivered, on demand, to that one in whose favour the judgment is passed. Al-Hilli, a *Jaafari* Jurist, has opined that all the judgments shall be kept by the court as record, either in form of month-wise file or year-wise file.

232. Al-Kasani, describing the practice of judicial procedure of his time, records that the plaint with date is written first, then the names of the witnesses and then the reply. This record is kept month-wise or year-wise, in a satchel or a case or a file (that is called *qimatrah)* sealed with seal of the court.

Passing the Judgement

233. Decrees not executed are without advantage as per advice of Umar sent to Abu Musa al-Ashaari as given in the beginning of the chapter. According to al-Marghinani the decree should be executed by the same court that passed it because a decree without execution does not meet the ends of justice. If a *qadi* passes a decree and ceases to be in the office, the succeeding *qadi* shall execute, maintain and enforce the decree passed by his predecessor subject to revision.

Importance of References

234. The *fuqaha* did not deal with reference of cases to some other court or revision thereof at length. Guidance as to this point may be taken from a long *hadith* narrated by Waki' in *Akhbar-al-Qudat* whereby Ali is reported to have said to the disputants whose case was decided by him: Hold fast to my judgment *ad interim* till you appear before the Messenger of Allah and he decides your case. (Waki' *op. cit;* I, 97)

235. From this *hadith* we may infer that (1) *ad interim* injunctions are valid and (2) a *qadi* may refer the case to higher authorities if it does not fall within his jurisdiction or he deems it fit to be decided by the higher authority.

236. With respect to revision, I reproduce the words of Umar from his letter to Abu Musa al-Ashari, "shall not prevent you a judgment that you passed yesterday, and (afterwards) reconsidered it in your conscience and you are guided to correct conclusion, since to come back to right is better than to prolong with (and maintain) what that is wrong".

237. According to al-Marghinani, it is incumbent upon every *qadi* to maintain and enforce the decree of another *qadi,* unless such order be repugnant to the doctrine of the Quran or the *Sunnah,* or a decision against the consensus of *fuqaha.*

238. Generally, it is not desirable to alter the judgment of a foregoing *qadi* upon the ground of difference of opinions in relation with a legal point as recommended in *al-Jami al-Saghir* by Muhammad al-Shaybani (the famous disciple of Abu Hanifah) and recorded by al-Marghinani in *al-Hidayah.*

239. Al-Hilli is of the opinion that if the succeeding qadi finds some error in the decision of some foregoing *qadi,* the succeeding *qadi* should annual that decision *suo motu* or on an application in this behalf.

Court Venue

240. Any place may be declared as the court of *qadi* if it is open and easily accessible for the public. Administration of justice may be carried in a mosque according to the *Hanafi fuqaha.* Shafii does not recommend it. He is of the view that the polytheists, and women during their menses, are admitted into the court, but are not allowed to enter a mosque. Al-Kasani and al-Marghinani, in support of the *Hanafi* view, advance forceful arguments. According to my humble opinion, it is better to prescribe some place, other than a mosque, as the court of *qadi.*

Justice and Factors

241. Either the influx of cases was meager in the period of the early *fuqah* or because of some other reason, they did not comment on adjournment of judicial proceedings and delay in dispensation of justice.

242. From the letter of Umar to Abu Musa, as given in the beginning of the Chapter, we may infer that a *qadi* should apply his mind and full wisdom to a case that is chequered and difficult, and may adjourn the announcement of judgment till he arrives at considered conclusion.

243. In case a plaintiff does not have his witnesses at hand, the *fuqaha* have said that the *qadi* may wait till the appearance of witnesses for three days. That is to the effect that the award of judgment may be adjourned on reasonable grounds.

Scholars of Law

244. A *qadi* may consult the *muftis* and the *'ulama'* regarding the legal points. This is not only allowed but recommended by the *fuqaha.* The opinion is also supported by a *hadith* that is reproduced for advantage.

Uthman b. Affan asked Abd Allah b. Amar to act as *qadi* among the people. He asked the commander of the faithful to excuse him. The Caliph asked him what objection he had to the acceptance of the post whereas his father had been holding such an office. Ibn Umar said, "If anything seemed dubious to my father, he asked God's Messenger but I can find no one to ask".

245. It may, however, be noted that volunteering information or advice to the court is nowhere narrated in our literature.

Council of Experts

246. It is already narrated in Chapter 4, of this work that Uthman formed a judicial council under his own headship. No other precedent concerning this is available.

Role of Translation

247. According to al-Hilli and Ibn Qudamah translations of two just persons is admissible in the court of *qadi.*

Court Employees

248. The *fuqaha* allow that there should be a clerk capable of writing and a strong contingent to assist the service of summons, maintenance of law and order and execution of decrees. The clerk should be a trustworthy person and in possession of good knowledge of *fiqh* and should be seated in such a manner that the *qadi* can, and should, see what he writes.

249. All these details, though collected with much labour and from several sources, point to the fact that judicial system in early and medieval Islamic period was not as simple as it appears to several people. No doubt, it was not a complicated system that involves

technicalities but does not prove to be helpful in solving the problems. Anyhow, full details is a major shortcoming of our historians and the *fuqaha.*

250. Nowadays, there is a general prevalent opinion that such details of Islamic law, and particularly of court procedure, are derived, and borrowed, from the Roman law and the Sasanide laws. As for the *ahadith* in this connection, it is also said that these are invented in order to Islamise the borrowed principles whereas the Muslim scholars assert that the *ahadith* are genuine, the very words of the Prophet transmitted down with utmost care by those ones who were learned and pious.

251. Leaving aside the controversy, which is outside the pale of the present work, let us advert to this point that Islam is a code of life and not code of laws. Religions always give guidance which provides a framework and the followers are instructed and expected to lead their lives remaining within the framework set forth. Islam, from the very beginning, teaches us to lead a systematic life, to observe unity in diversity.

Hence, if the Muslims chalked out a system for their judicial procedure they neither committed sin nor had done any harm to Islam. To adopt modern techniques and systems of works is quite an Islamic act. If the modern Muslims fight with guns they are not to be accused of deviating from the way of their predecessors who fought with swords and spears.

To fight in open field was in vogue among the Arabs but when Salman Farisi suggested that a trench should be dug, which was a Persian strategy of war, the Holy Prophet accepted it as it was the best means to achieve the noblest cause. And who said that all was wrong with the Christians, the Jews, the Arabs, the Romans and the Persians from Islamic point of view? What that was wrong with them it was openly and vehemently condemned by Islam and what that was good with them it was openly appreciated. Islam emphasises learning all that is good with other peoples. The prisoners of war in Battle of Badr were ordered to teach the children of the Muslims how to write. The Holy Prophet is reported to have advised; "Go as far as China in quest of knowledge".

252. Hence, in the sphere of judicial procedure it is no sin to seek guidance from other codes and adopt all those provisions which are not repugnant to the teachings of Islam.

253. Justice delayed is the main, and the most undesired problem of our period. Unfortunately, it cannot be solved through introduction of codes and procedures. No provision and instruction as to the solution of this problem is given in the works of the *fuqaha.* Some quick judgments were delivered by Ali in cases wherein no evidence was produced and the decision was given on merits with application of wisdom. It is hoped that the learned and wise men of all the nations will soon be able to solve the problem.

Justice on Criminal Acts

254. The purpose of this chapter is not to discuss punishments and their quantum as to various crimes because it fails in the realm of substantive law. The purpose is to examine the procedure adopted in a criminal case from trial to execution. But, there are several difficulties facing a *qadi* who is deemed as representing the divine justice. Human beings are the most respectable creatures upon the earth, and perhaps in the whole universe. To inflict punishment on a human body is horrible unless based on solid reason and good justification. Let us, therefore, first of all examine the following three important questions in this connection: (1) What is crime? (2) why punishment; and (3) what quantum of punishment?

255. As for the first question, it has been said that what that is punishable is a crime. But, this definition of crime is not comprehensive and far from convincing because an act or omission punishable in one state may not be punishable in the neighboring country. Also an act or omission punishable in one society may be regarded a virtue worth reward in the other. To slaughter a cow is punishable according to the Hindus but the same may be, and at occasions is, a virtuous deed according to the Muslims. Some people say that crime means public wrong. But, this interpretation also fails when put to test. Suicide, for example, is purely a private wrong. Is it not a crime? A steals the property of B and does not commit any harm to public, is it not crime? The noise of a flying aeroplane over the populated areas disturbs the sleep of so many innocent people and makes babies cry, is it a crime? Several people die of starvation in the neighborhood of a wealthy man who does not bestow donations, is he a hardened criminal?

256. It means that crime and its description differ from country to country and from time to time and depend on the sweet will of the sovereigns.

257. The second question is why punishment? It is said, firstly, that punishment is executed so that people respect the criminal law. Bur is it that a crime is committed only to disgrace the criminal law of the land and is it that those who are released from jail learn to respect the law? Criminals have their own motives. They seldom intend to disobey the law. Again, if an accused says that he respects the criminal law of the land whole-heartedly but he was in need of money so he snatched it from a person who was very much disrespectful to the laws of the land as he has been either criticising the laws or has earned the money by illegal means. Shall this man be not punished? Further, an accused becomes criminal in the eyes of the jury but from within his own heart he deems himself justified because he might have injured the complaint who about some years back injured him but because of the lack of the evidence he kept quite and has been waiting for an appropriate opportunity for revenge.

258. It is said, secondly, that punishment is inflicted so that people be deterred to commit crimes. This justification of punishment has proved more attractive. But, the facts tail to corroborate it. Punishments have been given and have been announced but the rate of crimes is ever increasing. As this theory aims at the infliction of punishment in order to make other people fearful, it sometimes brings forth ironical results. Several times the innocents are punished and the criminals remain free. In this connection an anecdote is also cited that a girl was raped by some negro. This roused the good sentiments of the society and the people taking out a procession demanded action. All of a sudden the governor arrested a negro, sentenced him before them and it was calm and peace all over. Another theory in this connection says that punishments are given as an implementation of the principle of 'tit for tat' so that the revengeful sentiments of the victim and his relatives be requited.

259. The third question is how much punishment? This is a very difficult question to be answered. The ratio of punishments differs from country to country. The utmost that is said in this connection is that the culprit be given a deserving punishment, but who shall determine it? A thief should be sentenced for one year's imprisonment or for the whole of his life?

260. From the above, it becomes clear that while inflicting punishment we should be extremely careful particularly a *qadi* who is deemed to administer divine justice.

261. The word *'uqubat',* (punishment) is very rarely used in our early literature. We find, in our literature, the words *qisas, diyat* (alongwith its minor forms), *hudud* and *taazir.* The later scholars who have studied the modern Western penal codes have very frequently used the word *'uqubat'* and tried to infer similar punishments from the *nusus* under the head of *taazir* and have recommended punishments that are more sever than *hudud.* Such recommendations give a bad impression that bastinado and flogging alone is the most effective way of reformation in Islam.

262. The early *fuqaha* have used the word *tadib* that means to remind someone of good manners and taazir that means to help someone to resume good conduct and high station. The author of *al-Hidayah* devotes only one page to the topic of *taazir.* This is because, the early *fuqaha* believed whole-heartedly in the efficacy of the teachings of Islam which create a noble society, a society that is not jealous to incriminate its brethren, a society whose members are always ready to extend sincere help to the erring brother and fulfil their lawful requirements. Islamic teachings are believed to create a society wherein if someone commits an error he is ashamed of it, and if has committed a wrong he is ready to confess it.

263. Dr. Abd al-Aziz Amir in his book *al-Taazir fi l-Shariat al-lslamiyyah* recommends all those punishments that are covered by the modern penal codes of the Western countries.

Not only this but the quantum of *taazir* is raised to three hundred stripes, life imprisonment and death sentence. If so, then what difference remains between a secular way of life and the Islamic way of life?

264. Much has been written on *taazir*, its justification and its quantum and here we need not repeat the same. For the purpose of caution, the following two points may be taken note of:

   (i) There is a *hadith* in *Tirmidhi* that reads: "Not be flogged (anyone) more than ten stripes but in a *hadd* from the *hudud* of Allah; *(Sunnah,* I, 189)

   (ii) The fuqaha are reported to have said that quantum of *taazir* varies from one category of persons to another, pertaining to the same wrong committed. For respectable people oral admonition is sufficient and the commoners may be punished according to the discretion of the *qadi;* (Ibn al-Humam; *Sh. Fath al-Qadir,* IV, 312)

265. Much wisdom is contained in this saying of the *fuqaha*. Human beings are not infallible, they may err but it does not mean that all of them be beaten with the same rod. To admonish a man of responsible position is a sufficient remedy whereas the coarse and commoners may deem it the weakness of the administration hence their tendency of wrong doing ought to be suppressed with a heavy hand.

266. As for major offences or crimes, a Muslim is not expected to be so vicious and wicked. The Holy Quran says:

It does not become a believer to kill a believer unless it be by mistake. And whoso kills a believer intentionally, his reward shall be Hell wherein he shall abide.

And Allah will be wrath with him and will curse him and will prepare for him a great punishment. (V: 45)

267. Anyhow in cases of injuries inflicted on any person of a human being and in cases of manslaughter the complaint is given the option to choose between loss for loss or gain for loss, that is called *qisas* or *aiyat.* The distinction between secular laws and Islamic laws in this connection is that according to Islam if a murderer is not found the blood does not go waste. Compensation must be paid to the heirs of the murdered by the people living near the place of murder or by the public exchequer. The amount of *diyat* in bodily injuries is quite reasonable, receiving which the grievance, according to the good conscience, is redressed and there remains no scope for further action or revenge. It means that Islam takes efficacious measures to suppress the crime.

268. Hudud are deemed very severe punishments by the secularists but they overlook an Islamic society that fulfils all the lawful requirements of its members. If despite this, there is one so wicked who disturbs the peace of his brethren, he deserves the most

severe punishment, or if he is a *dhirmni* he cannot be allowed to corrupt the society and rouse the good sentiments of the Muslims.

Lawsuit and Mechanism

269. As for the procedure of a criminal court, it is already stated in the previous chapter that the *fuqaha* and the historians disappoint us in this connection. We must confess that for the details of procedure, we are indebted much to the West. Anyhow, we may derive a broad outline of the procedure from the *hudud* cases that were decided by the Prophet.

Maiz Case

270. Maiz was a *Sahabi* who unfortunately fell in a great sin. He appeared before the Prophet and beseeched, "Purify me O Messenger of Allah!" The Prophet replied, "Go, repent and seek forgiveness of Allah. He went away and after a while came back and made the same request. The Prophet again advised him to go back and make repentance. He, in compliance with the order, went back, but again appeared for the third time. This time too, he was turned back. He appeared for the fourth time and repeated the same request. Now, the Prophet asked him, "From what sin do I purify You?" "From Adultery", he replied. The Prophet enquired whether the *Sahabi* so confessing was insane? He stated that he was of sound mind and understanding. The Prophet questioned whether the confessing *Sahabi* was drunk? It was submitted in reply that the above-mentioned *Sahabi* was not drunk.

271. The Prophet after these examinations and cross-questioning, finally asked him whether he means to say that he has committed adultery. Maiz replied, 'Yes', whereupon the Prophet awarded him the sentence of stonning-to-death.

Ghamidiyyah Case

272. Once a woman from the tribe of Ghamid appeared before the Prophet and confessed that she was big with a child of adultery. The Holy Prophet after hearing her confession and advising her to go back and make repentance, ordered her to go back and wait till she gives birth to the child. She, after giving birth to the child, appeared again. The Holy Prophet ordered that her punishment be postponed till her child remains suckling or someone else manage for the suckling and care of the child. One of the *Ansar* undertook to manage this; whereupon the Prophet ordered that the woman so confessing be stonned to death.

273. From these precedents, we come to know that confession in *hudud* cases be discouraged as it is made clear in another *hadith* that reads: "Don't execute *hudud* as much as possible (Abu Yusuf *K. al-Kharaj,* 165). In another *hadith,* it is laid down that *hudud* are not inflicted in cases of doubt. As far as the execution of a *hadd* punishment is concerned it ought not be executed in a mosque. In case of stoning to death, the witnesses (who

tendered evidence against the convict) must take the lead, if they refuse, the *hadd* shall not be executed and it shall be deemed that the evidence was false and the witnesses shall be liable to *hadd al-qadhf.*

274. The orthodox school of thought does not allow any alteration in the quantum of hadd-punishment. Anyhow, it may be derived from the precedents set by Umar and Uthman that the culprit can be given the sentence of imprisonment in addition to a hadd-punishment. Abu Mihjan al-Thaqafi, a drunkad, is reported to have been imprisoned by Umar and *Sabi* b. Hadith, a thief of Banu Tamim, by Uthman. Anyhow, I am not sure that these punishments were in addition to hudd-punishment.

Provision for Appeal

275. I have tried my best and consulted almost all the available original sources in order to find some express guidance or piece of discussion as to the points of appeals but found nothing except some inference that I draw from the *ahadith* and the opinions of the *fuqaha.*

276. Waki has transmitted some *ahadith* wherein it is related that some decisions of Ali, when he was administering judicial work at Yemen were brought to the notice of the Prophet. The Prophet gave an expression of agreement as to the decisions of Ali and appreciated his performance.

277. In the *ahadith* transmitted by Waki', there is no clue that the decisions of Ali were brought to the notice of the Prophet by the parties, or any of the party concerned or by Ali himself or by impartial observers. There is only one case, and actually of rather intricate and dubious nature, wherein Ali allowed the parties to present it before the Prophet and *ad interim* obey his own decision. The case is reproduced as follows:

278. Four persons from the tribes of Yemen went on hunting a lion. The lion fell in a well or a ditch and one of the four slipped. When he was about to fall in the well he caught hold of the other. The second one when inclined caught hold of the third and the third in the some way caught hold of the fourth. All the fourth hunters fell in the well to become an easy prey of the much provoked lion. All of them died. The tribes of the latter three persons demanded blood-money from the tribe of the first poor creature. His tribe replied that they were ready to pay the same for one deceased only because their man caught hold of only one. This dispute and contention gave birth to much fury and bloody feud was likely to begin.

279. The matter was brought to the knowledge of All who passed an injunction that ail the concerned desist immediately from fighting and accept the *ad interim* decision till they come to the Prophet. They all agreed. Ali, after hearing the case, ordered that a full blood-money of all the four deceased be brought together and decided that the heirs of the lowest one in the well be given¼, of the second one 1/3, of the third ½ and of the last

one the full amount. They agreed to obey the *ad interim* order and appeared before the Prophet in the season of *Hajj*. The Holy Prophet maintained the decision of Ali.

280. It also seems to us that the performance of the *qadis* was supervised by the rulers as some *qadis* were dismissed and that cannot be done but on revision of the decisions of a *qadi*.

281. In the Abbaside period there was created for the first time, the post of *Qadi al-Qudat,* that literally means the judge of the judges. But, whether his appointment was to hear appeals, or appoint the *qadis,* it is not clear. No doubt that the *qadis* were appointed with the consultation of *qadi al-qudat* but practically it was just a honorific title conferred on the *qadi* who administered justice at the capital city of the state.

282. Whatever may be the function of *qadi al-qudat,* Mr. CM. Shafqat, a law Consultant, is of the opinion that court of the Muslim *qadi* was normally the final court. Fayzee, another reputed, lawyer, whose book *Outlines of Muhammadan Law* is very popular with the students of law, is also of the same opinion as he writes,...." and his judgement was decisive, there being ordinarily no appeal from it" (p. 328).

283. The pronouncement of Muhammad Iqbal Siddiqui, in this regard, is sonorous and imposing as reproduced hereunder:

"In Islamic law there is no (murafaa: appeal) against the sentence of a *qadi.* The punishment is executed without delay and without any resistance. The *qadi* enjoys the sanction of the Quran, for he has been accepted as the *(Hakam:* arbitrator) by virtue of professing Islam, and the *qadi* decides the case strictly in accordance with the laws of the Quran and the Sunnah. Hence the convict cannot prefer an appeal to the ruler. After that the punishment has been inflicted, the convict may complain against the *qadi* in which case the ruler may investigate into the facts. If the ruler finds that the *qadi* has wrongfully punished the appellant, the punishment will revert to the *qadi (e.g.* if the appellant had been flogged 80 stripes the *qadi* will receive the same number of stripes and *ipso facto* will be deposed.

(The Penal Law of Islam, 183)

284. I have reproduced the original words of the learned author so that the readers may appreciate the wisdom of the verdict.

285. Mr. Anwar Qadiri in his book, *Justice in Historical Islam* narrates that the Caliphs, notably al-Mahdi, al-Hadi, al-Rashid and al-Mamun ordinarily received complaints, and heard appeals to set right the miscarriage of justice. The mother of al-Muqtdir herself presided at the high court of appeals listening to applications, gave audience to foreign envoys and dignitaries. Mr. Anwar Ahmad, however does not give us the particular source of this information.

286. In my humble opinion the right of appeal belongs to rights though compliment of procedure of remedy and to remove error that leads to evil and injustice is one of the

fundamental teachings of Islam as well as the foremost function of the administration of justice. In the context of retributive remedy laid down in the Holy Quran, V, verse 45, the concluding words of the verse are: whosoever judgeth not by that which Allah hath revealed such are wrong doers. Hence, a decision that is repugnant to the teachings of Islam is liable to be set aside.

287. Al-Mawardi in his book *Adab al-Qadi* has adverted to the point of *Naqad al-Hukm*—reversal of the decree—and is inclined to justify it under certain conditions, but he does not come round the point of appeal and revision whereas himself was chief *qadi.*

288. In the works of the *Hanafi fuqaha,* however, the word *rafa al-hukm,* equal to *murafaah* is used and instructions in this regard are given. Al-Marghinani says:

And when put up before the *qadi* the decree of another *qadi* he shall maintain and enforce it unless such decree be repugnant to the Book, the Sunnah or the *Ijma',* in other words, unless it be decision unsupported by authority. *(al-Hidayah,* 141)

289. Whether an erroneous decree is to be reversed or not, al-Marghinani is silent about it. But al-Khassaf and al-Kasani very expressly opine that such decrees are liable to be set aside by *suo motu* power of the other court or on an application made by the complaint, because what is erroneous is *ab initio* null and void.

290. To sum up the discussion, two precedents are reproduced here, one given in the Quran and the other narrated by Muslim in his *Sahih.*

And David and Soloman, when they gave judgment concerning the field when people's sheep had strayed and browsed therein; and we were witnesses to their judgment. We gave Soloman the right understanding of the matter and to each of them gave We wisdom and knowledge. (XXI: 78, 79)

Al-Tarabi relates some traditions whereby a person let loose his sheep, by night, that destroyed crops or grapeorchard of the other. David decided that the goats/ sheep be given to the one whose crops were destroyed and the field be given to the owner of the sheep.

291. The owner of the sheep informed Soloman about it. He decided that the owner of the field whose orchard was destroyed take possession of the sheep and the sheep- owner cultivate the field till the crops take the same standard of maturity wherein it were destroyed. During this period, the original owner of the orchard shall be the owner of the wool, milk and off-spring of the sheep/goats in order to compensate his loss.

292. Abu Hurrayrah narrates from the Prophet that there were two women with their two babies: a wolf came and picked up the son of one of them. One said to the other, wolf has gone with your son; the other said, nay, the wolf has gone with yours. Both brought their dispute before Daud for decision. He gave his judgment in favour of the elder

woman. They went to Sulayman and informed him about the matter. He said, "Fetch me a knife. (should) I sunder the baby in two equal parts". The younger one cried, "No, God bless you, it is her baby". Hence, he passed his judgment in favour of the younger one. (*Sahih,* II, 77). For further enlightenment, the relevant portions of judgment delivered by Mr. Aftab Hussain, the Chief Justice, Federal Shariat Court of Pakistan are reproduced as under:

293. It was urged by the learned judge Advocate General of the Army that in Islam there is no provision of appeal. This argument is fallacious. From the several traditions reproduced above, it may be clear that after the fight was over, in some cases, the decision of Commander was challenged before the Prophet and he set aside the order of the Commander. There is another tradition which was related by Salem on the authority of his father.

The Holy Prophet sent Khalid bin Walid to Banu Jazima. He invited them to Islam but instead of saying "we embraced Islam" they started joking by saying 'sabana', 'sabana' (we got out from our religion to another religion). So, Khalid started killing them and making them prisoners. He handed over to every person his prisoner and ordered that every one of us should kill his prisoner that very day. I (relater) said, "I will never kill my prisoner nor any of my companions will kill his prisoner". Then, we came to the Holy Prophet and informed him of the situation. The Prophet raised his hands and said, "Oh Allah! I am not responsible for what Khalid did in this matter". He said so twice.

(*Fathul Bari,* Vol. VIM, pp. 56, 57)

294. There is yet another tradition that two persons came to the Holy Prophet. One of them charged the other that the latter's cow had killed his donkey. The Holy Prophet ordered Hadrat Abu Bakr to decide this case. Hadrat Abu Bakr decided that animals do not incur any liability for their acts. The Holy Prophet then ordered Hadrat Umar to decide the matter but he decided according to the same principle as emaciated by Hadrat Abu Bakr. Then, the Prophet ordered Hadrat Ali to decide. Hadrat Ali asked the complainant whether both the animals were tethered. He replied in the negative. He then asked whether the cow was tied and the donkey free. He again answered in the negative. He then enquired whether the donkey was tied and the cow was free. This admitted to be the case by both parties. Hadrat Ali decided that the owner of the cow was liable (for damages).

(*Adab al-Qadi* by al-Marwardi, Vol. VI, page 388, printed at Baghdad, 1972)

295. The Hadith amply justifies appellate jurisdiction since the Holy Prophet acted as an appellate court by setting aside the judgments of Hadrat Abu Bakr and Hadrat Umar and approved of the judgment of Hadrat Ali. It also justifies the remanding of the case for retrial by the appellate court since the Holy Prophet had remanded the matter twice when it was decided first by Hadrat Abu Bakr and then by Hadrat Umar.

296. The right of appeal also emerges from the Quran (4: 59) in which it is laid down that in case of dispute with the (the person in authority) the matter is to be refereed to Allah and his Prophet (Peace be on him). This reference is nothing but an appeal to the law of the Quran and Sunnah.

297. The above argument of the learned judge Advocate General of the Army was addressed because no statutory appellate Court was formed during those days but that itself is no reason to hold against the appellate jurisdiction. The formality may not be there but as stated above, if the Holy Prophet (Peace be upon him) acted as an appellate Court in matter of dispute *inter alia* against the order of the Commander, no objection can be taken to the establishment of appellate courts. (P.L.D. 1985 Fsc 365)

Task of an Attorney

298. *Wakalah* is defined by the *fuqaha* as the appointment of another person to do the needful in a known transaction on behalf of the principal. Almost all of the *fuqaha* are of the opinion that it is lawful. Ibn Qudamah, a *Hanbali* Jurist, in this connection, says:

Wakalah is lawful according to the Holy Book, the *Sunnah* and the consensus.

299. *Wakalah* means agency including the act of representing a litigant or appearing on his behalf before the court of justice in order to contest the dispute put up for decision. Ibn Qudamah has put forth the following arguments as to the lawfulness of *Wakalah:*

Significance of Holy Quran

(i) The alms are only for the poor and the needy and those who collect them. (IX: 60)

This inference is for attorneyship at fact.

(ii) Now, send one of you with this your silver coin unto the city, and let him see what food is purest there and bring you a supply thereof. (XVIII: 49)

300. This verse is in the context of the story of the People of Cave *(Ashab al-Kahf)*. They sent one from amongst themselves to the city in order to fetch food. I cannot say whether it was an attorneyship in fact or just an ordinary and friendly request.

Contribution of Sunnah

301. Relying upon the *Sunnah,* the author *al-Mughni* cites three *ahadith.* In the first *hadith,* it is stated that the Messenger of Allah gave Urwah b. Jad one *dinar* and said to him, "Go and purchase a goat for us". He went accordingly and purchased two goats by one *dinar,* then he sold a goat by one *dinar,* and came back to the Prophet with the *dinar* and a goat.

302. According to the second *hadith,* Jabir b. Abd Allah narrates that when I wanted to go to Khyber, I sought permission of the Prophet. He said to me, "You are my

Wakil, take therefrom fifteen *wasaqs"...* (to the end of the *hadith).* In this *hadith,* the word my *wakil* is expressly used.

303. In the third *hadith,* it is narrated that the Prophet appointed Umar b. Umayyah al-Damari (as his Wakil) to accept the (contract of) marriage of Umm Habibah.

Advantages of Consensus

304. After reciting the above verses and the *ahadith,* the writer relies upon the consensus (Ijma) and says: The Ummah has made consensus on lawfulness of *Wakalah* in general.

Role of Wisdom

305. The fourth and wonderful argument of the learned writer is rationale of *Wakalah.* He says that necessity demands it, because every one cannot perform by himself what he has to do out of necessity.

306. Al-Marghinani, the Hanafite, has changed the arrangement of arguments and says:

It is lawful for a person to appoint another as his agent, for the settlement in his behalf of every contract which he might have lawfully concluded himself. *(al-Hidayah,* II, 177)

307. First of all he relies on the rule of necessity that a man sometimes is prevented from performing a task, so, out of necessity, he engages another to perform the needful on his behalf. He seeks support from the *ahadith* that: (1) the Messenger of Allah appointed Hakim b. Hazam to purchase (some animal) for sacrifice and that (2) the Messenger of Allah assigned Umar b. Umm Salamah to conclude the contract of marriage (of his mother).

308. As for the attorneyship at law, the erudite writer says in clear words that it is lawful for a person to appoint another as his agent for the management of a suit relative to any rights whatsoever, and argues that every one is not fully acquainted with the mode of contesting disputes. For support, he adduces the precedent of Ali that he appointed Aqil and then Abd Allah b. Jafar as his attorneys (in disputes).

309. Al-Mawardi, the Shafiite, does not deal with the topic in his well-known book, *K. Adah al-Qadi.* Al-Khassaf, the Hanafite, on the other hand, and the expounder of his work Husam ud-Din, elaborated the point under the topic of *Ithbat al-Wakalah-In* proof of *Wakalah.* They are of the opinion that agency for litigation is lawful and adduce the following precedents and arguments in order to establish their view:

310. Ali used not to appear in *Khusumat-d*ispute- and used to say disputes are dire danger, Satan appears therein.

Because of this, he appointed Aqil and then Abd Allah b. Jaafar as his attorneys to appear in *Khusumat* and contest it.

311. The author of *al-Hidayah,* as already mentioned, has also relied upon this precedent but he does not mention the above-quoted words, hence a joint commentary. The word *"Khusumat"* literally means dispute and is also used for litigation because it is also a kind of dispute. In my humble opinion the words ascribed to Ali are not in the context of litigation. To appear before a court of justice is a religious and moral, duty and in no way a Satanic work. Moreover, it is reported that Ali appeared in person before Qadi Shurayh in connection with dispute of an armour.

312. Narrated from the Messenger of Allah that he said, "Suffice it to be sinful to always remain a disputant".

313. From this *hadith,* it is inferred that one should avoid to participate in dispute; and hence should appoint another to advocate his case.

314. Tirmidhi has narrated this *hadith* and observed that it is a *gharib hadith,* not fortified by other narrations. Again, the purport of the *hadith* is to admonish an one who always remains indulgent in dispute. Moreover, if to remain a disputant is sinful then to appoint someone in this behalf should also be an act of sin; and to appoint an one in this behalf should not be excuse or expiation.

315. The *hadith* narrated by Fatimah bint Qays. She said, my husband divorced me three times and appointed his brother for my expenses, and himself went to Yemen, I put up the case against him before the Prophet. He did not award me expenses and residence (out of the property of my husband). (Khassaf; *Adab al-Qadi*- II 402)

316. The *hadith* is pertaining to attorneyship at fact which is lawful in all cases. As for as his statement as to the judgment pronounced by the Prophet. Tirmidhi has transmitted the comments of Umar b. Khattab to the effect that we do not know whether she remembered or forgot (the words of the Prophet)'. *(Sunan,* I, 152)

317. Abu ishaq al-Shirazi, the Shafiite, in *al-Muhadhdhab,* has made the point of *wakalah* more clear as he says:

318. Lawful is *Wakalah* in transaction like contracts of sale, mortgage, transfer of loans or debts, partnership, lending, partnership in profit on basis of cooperation; investment on the one side and labour on the other, compacts of gardening, tenancy or hiring. It is lawful in matters of torts, deposits, wages, loans, waqf, charity, marriage and dispute or litigation.

319. As far as the lawfulness of attorneyship in litigation is concerned, it is inferred from the precedent of Ali (as quoted in foregoing pages). Moreover, necessity demands appointment of someone in disputes because one may not properly present his case or defend allegations levelled against him. It is lawful without obtaining the consent of the adversary because it

pertains to his own right. Attorneyship at law is lawful in demanding *qisas* and execution of *hadd al-qadhf* (punishment for slandering), provided the complainant (the principal) is present, because these are human rights. But, it is not lawful in other *hudud* cases because these are the rights of Allah.

Anyhow, the *Imam* may appoint someone (as his deputy) to execute the punishment of *hadd* on his behalf because the Prophet appointed Unays and Uthman appointed Ali, for this purpose.

320. Al-Marghinani has also adverted to this point and says that in demand of execution of *hudud* and *qisas,* attorneyship at law is lawful provided the complainant (principal) is present. Because in absense of the complainant, there is doubt of forgiveness; and where there is doubt there is no execution of *hadd* (punishment). This opinion is ascribed to Abu Hanifah. Abu Yusuf says that in cases of *hudud* and *qisas, Wakalah* is not lawful. Abu Hanifah and Abu Yusuf are of the same opinion in case of the defendant in *qisas* and *hudud.*

321. The discourse of Allamah al-Hilli, the *Shiite,* on the point is marvellous. He says that there are actions, performance of which is required by person himself e.g. (ritual) purity, incumbent prayer, fasting, sitting in mosque during the last part of Ramadan, incumbent pilgrimage, vows, division between/amongst the wives, expiation of calling the back of one's wife similar to his mother, deposition in case of slandering the spous *(Wan)* with adultery, accomplishment of the period whereafter a widow or a divorced woman can remarry, etc.

In these and such like affairs appointment of an agent or deputy is not allowed. For example, one cannot appoint another one to take (ritual) bath on his behalf. Besides this, there are actions which should be performed either personally or through an agent. In such matters and affairs, it is lawful to appoint an one to do the needful in behalf of the principal.

322. He is also of the opinion that there are only two requisite conditions of a *Wakil, viz;* (1) being adult and (2) wise. Hence, to appoint a *fasiq* or an infidel or a *murtad* (apostate) as an agent is lawful.

323. These discussions lead us to the conclusion that in the opinion of the *fuqaha Wakalat* is lawful in civil cases as well as in cases of *hudud.* It is, however, ascribed to Abu Hanifah that a party to the case may assign someone as his *Wakil* to contest his case in the court of justice with the consent of the other party or in case of being a woman that observes purdah and does not appear before men, or illness or going on Journey that may take the period of at least three days. Otherwise, the *Wakalah* will not be binding on the other

party. This opinion rests on the reason that the advocates are more eloquent in arguments and the other party may suffer from one-sided strong presentation. Now-a-days, this fear is purged because both the parties to a case do engage well versed and experienced counsellors who extend their invaluable help not only to the litigants but to the court as well and to the society at large.

324. According to the opinions of Abu Yusuf, Muhammad al-Shaybani, and al-Shafii, as narrated by al-Marghinani and Ali b. Khalil al-Tarablusi, one may assign someone as his *Wakil* to contest his case in the court of justice without consent of his adversary because it is purely his own right and he can use it without obtaining the consent of anyone. The latter mentioned also recommends remunerations for the attorneys at law as he says:

The counsellors can take fees from one for whom they work, either the claimant or the defendant. But they shall not take more than two dirhams for each sitting (appearance).
(Muin al-Hukkam, 17)

4

Mechanism of Witnesses

That department of the Islamic legal system which regulates the procedure of the Courts, relating to the trial and proof of claims affords a peculiarly interesting study. Here, as in the other departments, the usages of the people of the age are not altogether ignored, but are to a certain extent still recognised as a sort of ground work on which to base the provisions of a scientific system of procedure.

The Islamic Law requires that a properly appointed judicial officer called Qadi should decide upon the claims of the disputants but, if the requisite number of witnesses testify in support of a claim, the Court must, as a general rule, accept such testimony and decree the claim, a rule which reminds us of the age when witnesses were, in fact, judges of the cause. A new principle is, however, established, namely, that the object of testimony is to furnish information of a fact, and rules are introduced in order to give effect to that principle. Similarly, sanctity is still attached to an oath, but an oath is regarded as a guarantee of truth and not a conclusive test of the nature of an ordeal.

The most noteworthy feature of this part of the system lies in the elaborate rules which have been laid down for the purpose of guiding the Court in determining the general credibility of a witness and the truth of his statements in order to guard against the possibility of the Court being misled by his testimony. Attempts are also made to preclude the possibility of the Court being called upon to decide between the claims of conflicting testimony. In cases where the parties make contradictory allegations and each desires to support his own allegation, rules are laid down as to whose evidence is to be preferred. The cardinal principle underlying the Islamic law relating to evidence is that a decree or order of the Court should be based as far as possible on certainty and not on conjectures. Those who are familiar with the modern system of procedure would be inclined to think that these rules, which leave little or no discretion to the Court in judging of the truth or credibility of testimony, however, much they might eliminate uncertainty, are likely to have the effect in many cases of defeating their own object, namely, a right decision of the claim. On the other hand, it might be said that the Islamic rules of procedure ought to lead to a speedy settlement of claims, an end which the rules of some of the modern system of procedure are ill-calculated to achieve.

The right which the Court may be asked to enforce would be either a private or a public right. In the first case it is for the individual or individuals who complain of the wrong to seek the remedy and in the latter case the representative of the State or his agent would be the claimant. The rules are substantially the same in both classes of cases, with only such variations as are clearly called for by the difference in the character of particular claims.

Judge and Learning

A source of the proof of an offence or a right in Islamic Law is the knowledge of the judge about the case before him in the court. The Jurists differ whether a judge can decide a case on the basis of his personal knowledge or not. There are three view points on this matter. The first prohibited the judge from deciding on the basis of his personal knowledge as to any criminal or non-criminal matter.

This view is founded on the practice of the Prophet and on the following statement by Hadrat 'Umar: "If you wish, I can testify but not render judgement, or I might judge but not testify." This was response to a request that he arbitrated a dispute with which he was familiar. It has been related on the authority of Ikrima that once Hadrat 'Umar said to Abdal-Rahman Bin Awf, If you were Amir (ruler) and I was Qadi and I had seen a man making illicit sexual intercourse with a woman or I had seen him committing theft, (what would I have done)? Abdal-Rahman said to him" your evidence is like the evidence of any other man."

Hadrat 'Umar said, "you are right".

It has been related on the authority of Ibn Juraij that Hadrat 'Umar wrote to Abu Musa al-Ashari, "The ruler (judge) should neither decide on the basis of his personal knowledge nor on weak presumption nor on doubt."

It has been related by Bukhari that once a party said to Qadi Shurai during hearing, "Be our witness (as you have witnessed the incident)". Qadi Shurai said to him, "Go to Amir so that he may appoint another Qadi for this case, then I shall testify in your favour".

Moreover, judgement on the basis of personal knowledge empowers a judge to render judgement without evidence which creates suspicion about the public confidence of the judge. This is the view of Abu Bakr, 'Umar, Ali, Ibn Al-Abbas, Abd al-Rahman Ibn Al-Awf, and Muawiyyah. It is also the view of Malik, Shafii, Ahmad, Shabi, Bukhari, Ibn al-Qayyim and the later Hanafis.

According to the second view which has been advocated by the Zahiris, the judge is allowed to render judgement in accordance with his personal knowledge in criminal as well as non-criminal matters. This view is based on the following Quranic verses:

> "O ye who believe! Stand out firmly For justice, as witnesses To Allah, even as against Yourselves, or your parents, Or your kin, and whether It be (against) rich or poor: For Allah can protect both". "We have sent down To thee the Book in Truth, That thou mightest judge Between men, as guided By Allah: so be not (thou) a pleader for treacherous."

It is based on a *hadith* related on the authority of Abu Saeed Khudri that the Holy Prophet, said, "The status of the people may not prevent anyone to say something about them which one has either seen or known or heard."

Thus, believers including judges are enjoined to do justice, and it would be unjust if a judge, knowing one of the adversaries to be guilty, fails to punish him. In addition, a judge's ruling based on the testimony of two frequently unreliable witnesses, would be less often correct than if he ruled on the basis of personal, though certain knowledge. Furthermore, the judge evaluates the credibility of the witnesses according to his own familiarity with them. Thus, he should also be permitted to decide truth or falsify according to his personal knowledge. This is the view of al-Athra, Abu Thawr, a version of Shafii, a version of Ahmad Ibn Hanbal and Ibn Hazm Zahiri.

Proponents of the third view would prohibit the judge from making decisions according to his personal knowledge only in the cases of *hudud* crimes specially *zina* which have been prescribed as rights of Allah. This is based on the following verses of Holy Quran:

> "If any of your women
> Are guilty of lewdness,
> Take the evidence of four
> (Reliable) witnesses from amongst you,
> Against them; and if they testify,
> Confine them to houses until
> Death do claim them,
> Or Allah ordain for them
> Some (other) way."
> "Why did they not bring
> Four witnesses to prove it,
> When they have not brought

The witnesses, such men,
In the sight of Allah,
(Stand forth) themselves as liars."

This is further inspired by the saying of the Holy Prophet (Pbuh) concerning a woman accused of *liar* (sworn allegation of adultery) because the child whom she gave birth later had great resemblance with the accused (adulterer) about whom the Prophet said: "were I to stone to death without evidence, I would stone her to death". This *hadith* states that the judge is prohibited from judging according to personal knowledge in case of adultery. This rule applies to all the *hadd* penalties and reflects the related precept of forgiveness. This view derives additional support from the *hadith*". Doubts nullify *hudud*". It is further supported by the saying of Abu Bakr who said, "If I saw someone making intercourse with someone (woman), I will not implement *hadd* on (them) until there are witnesses".

Thus, the judge's personal knowledge does not inspire confidence in the public, but instead breeds doubt. The *hudud* are applied by the ruler as Allah's representative, without any other individual demanding them (i.e. a complaining witness) which might make the judge's motives suspect were he to rule on the basis of personal knowledge. Also, a *hadd* is nullified if the confessor retracts his confession, in this case the judge cannot inflict the fixed penalty upon him. Therefore, a *hadd* penalty may not be inflicted on the basis of the judge's personal knowledge if the confessor denies the confession.

Imam Shafii and Imam Abu Hanifa, and the followers of Abu Yusuf, and Muhammad Ibn al-Hassan all have adopted this view. However, though judge cannot decide on his personal knowledge in matters of *hudud and qisas* but he can decide on his personal knowledge in matters of *tazir* and rights.

Imam Abu Hanifa is further of the opinion that a judge is not allowed to decide a case on his pre-trial and extra-judicial knowledge which he has gained before the trial. He is, however, not in favour of the judgement of a judge based on his pre-trial knowledge in matters of *hudud* because *hudud* are removed by doubts. If the judge has seen the commission of adultery and there are three more eye-witnesses on that, he is not allowed to decide by counting his own testimony. He should, however, refuse to judge such case and come as witness in it so that the other judge will accept the testimony of the four witnesses and implement *hadd* on the accused.

According to Shafii school of thought, a judge is authorised to decide a case other than *hudud* on the basis of his personal knowledge whether there is any proof in that matter or not and whether he has got that knowledge before appointment as judge or during his tenure of being a judge.

It is also pertinent to mention here that according to Islamic law a judge is bound to hear the testimony produced before him and not to postpone pronouncing judgement after hearing it except to bring about an amicable settlement or unless requested to delay judgement by the plaintiff. The Islamic law, however, embodies safeguards to insure that testimonies be truthful to the greatest possible extent. Several prerequisites have been laid down for acceptance of testimony including the trustworthiness of witnesses. This stipulation of trustworthiness gives the judges a wide latitude in rejecting witnesses for reason of bad character or undependability. Thus, a judge, in Islamic legal system, is entitled to evaluate the testimony so that if its authenticity is established for him and his conscience is satisfied, he could give judgement in accordance therewith. If, on the other hand, there is any doubt in his mind, he may turn it down.

Various Issues

According to Islamic law, possession in case of a disputed property will be considered as evidence of ownership. For example, if two persons claim ownership of the same property and one of them has its possession and the other couldn't prove that his possession was illegal, decree will be given in favour of the one who has the possession of the property in question. However, if it was proved that the possession was illegal, decree will be given in favour of the other one provided he has produced authentic evidence, in support of his ownership of the property in dispute.

If two persons claim ownership of the same property and both produce evidence but the evidence of one of them indicates that his ownership of this property was earlier than the other one, decree will be given in his favour. And if the evidence of both of them was equal in all respects, then either the property may be equally divided between them or the property may be given to anyone of them on the basis of casting lot or their claims may be discharged keeping in view the circumstances of the case and the authenticity of the evidence.

The court may in case of various proofs or conflict among various proofs for the same property or fact, prefer anyone of them or annul them, keeping in view the circumstances of the case and the authenticity of the evidence.

The court may, in case of the possession of one person or more and the proof of ownership by another person or persons of the same property, prefer anyone of them or retain the possessor or possessors as they are or divide the property between them or annul their possession and evidence, as the case may be, keeping in view the circumstances of the case and the authenticity of the evidence. For the purpose of exploring facts, the judge may, after he has recorded the statement of every party and witness, put them questions according to his discretion in the circumstances of the case and decide when the authenticity of the evidence appears to him. The opponent party can question the witness as well as its oponent party for the sake of its defence and the exploration of the facts of the case.

Appropriate Court: a Choice

The person who wants his claim to be heard must first of all select the proper Court, that is, the one which has jurisdiction to hear the suit. But this is a more or less simple affair under the

Islamic system. Except so far as the jurisdiction of a particular Qadi may have been limited by his order of appointment as regards the class of cases he is to try, a plaintiff is entitled to institute his action in the Court within whose local jurisdiction he and his witnesses reside. And it would make no difference in this respect if the subject-matter of litigation, for example, land be situated elsewhere or the person against whom the claim is made resides within the jurisdiction of another Qadi.

Definitions of Claim, Plaintiff Defendant: A claim (dawa) is defined as demand by a person of his right from another in the presence of a judge. The man making the demand is called Muddai that is, plaintiff or claimant and the person from whom the demand is made is called Muddaalaihi or defendant. These definitions of plaintiff and defendant are as given in Al-Majalla.

According to 'Hedaya' the claimant is the party who is entitled to abandon the action if he so chooses and the defendant is the party who cannot, at his mere pleasure, avoid the suit being pursued. According to other definitions the claimant is the party who cannot succeed without proving his allegation and the defendant is the party who may have a decision in his favour without adducing evidence, and according to Muhammad the defendant is the party who denies.

Who may Prefer a Claim: A claim can only be preferred by a person possessed of understanding. Hence the claim of a minor or a lunatic will not be heard except through the intervention of a guardian, nor will a suit be heard against him without such representation.

A Claim must Conform to Certain Rules: A claim must conform to certain rules. For instance, the individual or individuals against whom it is preferred must be ascertained. The thing or right claimed must also be ascertained with sufficient distinctness; for instance, if it be landed property its boundaries ought to be specified though its value need not be mentioned; nor is it necessary for the plaintiff to state how he came to acquire the property which he claims, it being sufficient for him to state that it is his property. If the claim relates to a debt he ought to say how it arose, whether on account of money lent, purchase money or wages, and so on and the amount.

What is claimed must be possible, so that if it be impossible according to our experience or judgement, for instance, if a person claims a man older than himself or one who is known to be the son of somebody else as his son, the claim will be rejected.

The statement of a claim, if self-inconsistent, is to be rejected. For instance, if a man takes steps to buy a certain property and, subsequently there to and before making the purchase, puts forward a claim that the property belonged to him, his suit will be rejected because of inconsistency. So also if a person claims certain property on behalf of somebody else, he cannot, at the same time, claim it for himself, but if the allegations of the plaintiff may be reconciled, his suit ought not to be dismissed for inconsistency.

A claim may be made verbally or in writing. If verbally, the Court ought to record it.

The claim must disclose a good cause of action against the person against whom it is made, the test of which is whether, if such person admitted the allegations in the claim, a decree would be passed against him. If it would, and he denies the allegation, the suit will proceed against the defendant as the opponent (Khasm) of the claimant and the defendant will be called upon for an answer. Suppose, the plaintiff states that an agent of the defendant purchased certain goods from him, and he demands the price, but the defendant denies the claim, the defendant will be regarded as the opponent and the suit will proceed against him. On the other hand, if the plaintiff merely alleged that the defendant's agent purchased the article without at all alleging that he did not pay the price and the defendant denies the claim, the suit will fail and will not be heard as the plaintiffs allegations do not disclose a good cause of action against the defendant.

Coupling Parties

It may happen that two or more persons were concerned in violating, or interested in denying the right of the claimant, some more directly than the others or all in the same degree, or more than one person are interested in the establishment of the claim. Then the important question arises as to the selection of parties and the law lays down rules for the purpose of such selection. For instance, when a claim is made with respect to a specific article, the person who is in possession of it is alone to be made the defendant. Thus, if a person has taken wrongful possession of a horse belonging to another and sold it to a third person and the owner wants his horse back, he must sue the person who has possession of the animal. The person that has possession will be entitled to sue his vendor for recovery of the price he has paid. A bailee for hire, a person having the use of an article, and a lessee, when the property in their possession has been wrongfully taken by another, may sue the wrong-doer for recovery of the article without making the owner a party.

In matter relating to the estate of a deceased person the general rule is, that one of the heirs may be a plaintiff or defendant with respect to a claim which could have been made by or against the deceased, except where the claim is for the recovery of a specific property from the estate of the deceased when the proper defendant is the person in whose possession it is and an heir who is not in possession cannot be made a defendant. The admission of an heir in possession will not, however, bind the other heirs. It is likewise competent for one of the heirs to sue on behalf of the deceased for something which was due to the latter from the defendant, in the form of a debt or similar latter from the defendant, in the form of a debt or similar obligation and if the claim is established, a decree will be made for the entirely of what was due for the benefit of all the heirs. The plaintiff himself will, however, be allowed to realise only his portion. Similarly, if a person has a claim for money against the estate of the deceased, he can establish his claim in the presence of only one of the heirs whether such heir is in possession of the estate or of any portion of it or not, though an admission by one of the heirs will not bind the other heirs. If the defendant heir does not admit the claim and the plaintiff proves his claim in his presence, the decree will be made against all the heirs and the other heirs will not be entitled to require the plaintiff to prove his claim against them with respect to their portions. It is, however, open to them to meet such a decree by a plea in the way of avoidance.

When there are several sharers in a specific property but not by right of inheritance, one of the cosharers cannot represent the others as defendant in a suit with respect to such property, but if he is sued alone a decree will be made against him to the extent of his share.

One member of the public may sue with respect to a property or matter the benefit from which is derived by the public generally such as a public road; and a decree in his favour will accrue to the benefit of all members of the public. In a suit with respect to a thing the benefit of which is participated in by the inhabitants of two villages, such as a stream or a common, it will be sufficient if some inhabitants of each village be made parties; unless the number of inhabitants be limited when all of them must come before the Court. If the number exceeds one hundred it is regarded as unlimited.

Proceedings of Law Suit

Rules are then laid down regulating the hearing of a claim. An important general rule in this connection is that a claim must be heard in the presence of the parties or their representatives. The plaintiff, if he can, may bring the defendant with him to the Court at the time of presenting his claim. If he cannot bring the defendant, the Court is to issue summons to secure his attendance.

If the defendant refuses to come or to appoint a representative, he is to be brought up under compulsion, and if his presence cannot be secured then a copy of the plaint is to be sent thrice to him at different times and if he still does not come it is to be notified to him that an agent will be appointed on his behalf by the Court and the claim and the evidence will be heard. If he does not still come or send his representative then the Court will itself appoint a person to watch his interests, and after hearing the claim and the evidence in the presence of such person and scrutinizing the same, pass its decision.

But if the person against whom an *ex-parte* decree has been made appears afterwards and objects to the correctness of the decree, he will be allowed to meet the claim, and his defence will be hear. If his allegation is established the decree will be set aside. *Ex-parte* proceedings are not permitted in charges for offences punishable with hadd or retaliation because in such cases there must be no doubt as to the proof.

Avoidance in Court Proceedings

When both the parties are present in Court, the claimant will be asked to state his case and if he has written out his claim to verify it. Then the Court will call upon the defendant for his answer, if necessary. The defendant may merely deny the claim or meet the claim by a plea in the nature of avoidance (dafa). A reply of the latter character consists of an allegation put forward by the defendant, which would be sufficient to meet the claim of the plaintiff, for instance, where a man claims from another a certain amount of money as a debt owing to him and the defendant states that he owed the money but has paid it or that the plaintiff has released him from the debt or that he and the plaintiff have settled the matter or that the amount was not a debt but the price of certain goods which he, the defendant, bought for the plaintiff. If the defendant establishes his allegation the plaintiffs suit will fail.

When the defendant disputes the claim the plaintiff will be called upon to prove his allegations. If the claimant is able to adduce admissible and sufficient evidence he will be entitled to a decree in his favour and if he is not, he can only call upon the opposite party to take the oath in support of his denial. If the opposite party thereupon takes the oath the claim against him will be dismissed, but if he refuses to take the oath, it will be decreed. The Qadi, according to the old rule, can base his order on his personal knowledge of the facts. But nowadays, says the author of 'Durrul-Mukhtar, this would not be allowed because of the corruption of such officers.

Procedure, where Defendant Resides beyond Jurisdiction: According to the general rule of law, founded upon analogy the decree of a Qadi is only binding against a defendant who resides within his jurisdiction, but upon juristic preference which had the concurrence of the Companions and their successors and is based on necessity, if the defendant is within the jurisdiction of another Qadi, the plaintiff may file his suit in the Court of the Qadi in whose jurisdiction he resides and his witnesses are available. The Qadi in whose Court the suit is filed may record the evidence and also pass his order provided the absent defendant has either appointed an agent to represent him or the Court itself has appointed some one to watch his interests.

But the validity of appointment by the Court of an agent for the defendant in such a case does not seem to be free from doubt. If the evidence adduced by the plaintiff proves his case the Court may record its finding and pass a decree and after property sealing and securing the record in presence of two witnesses of unimpeachable character, remit the same with the plaintiff and those two witnesses to the Qadi within whose jurisdiction the defendant is to be found. If the absent defendant is not represented by an agent of his own the Court before whom the suit is filed may if it so chooses only record the evidence and forward it to the Qadi of the place where the defendant resides for the latter to pass order thereon in presence of the defendant.

These proceedings are allowed only in cases which involve the establishment of private rights, such as the recovery of a debt, the establishment of marriage or paternity, the recovery of immovable property and the like and not in matters of hadd and retaliation.

Decrees: A decree (hukm) is defined as that which settles or terminates a dispute. The decree may be directory directing the judgement-debtor to give something to the judgement creditor, or prohibitive, as when the case is decided against the plaintiff the judgement being that he is not entitled to the right which he claims. The decrees and orders of Court are to be preserved.

When a decree is made the question arises, whom does it bind. The general rule is that it binds the parties and also those whom the law allows them to represent, but not the others. As between them the matter is said to be finally settled so that it cannot be litigated afterwards except in some particular cases.

Thus a decree with reference to property against the man in possession of it binds him alone and those who derive title from him but not the others. A decree against a person in possession declaring that the property is waqf is, however, according to 'Ruknul-Islam', binding on all people, but not so in the opinion of Abu Laith and Sadrush-Shahid. And as already mentioned a decree against an heir will, generally speaking, bind the estate.

A decree of the Court may be void in certain circumstances. For instance, if it is contrary to a rule of certain law or if it is based on inadmissible evidence or if it is in favour of some person in whom the Judge is interested, such as his parent, wife or children.

Proof and Priority

Suppose both the parties make contradictory allegations of a positive nature in relation to the same matter and both are prepared to adduce proof, the question then arises whose proof is to be preferred or heard (tarjuhul-bayyinat). The general rule is that the evidence of the party whose allegation is supported by certain general presumptions (istishabul-hal) will be preferred. The Court, as we have seen, cannot hear evidence in support of the allegations of both, because the allegation of one must be false and the testimony in support of it cannot be information or evidence.

Thus, if one person wishes to produce evidence that a person was in good health at a particular time and the opposite party wants to prove that he was then seized with death-illness, there being nothing else, the evidence of the former will be accepted in preference to that of that of the latter. The reason is that in the absence of proof to the contrary a man will be supposed to continue in good health.

Similarly, evidence of the party who wants to prove that a man was possessed of understanding will he heard in preference to that of the party who alleges that he was insane or idiotic at a particular time. The evidence that a certain property was purchased will be preferred to the evidence that it was a gift or a pledge or hired, and the evidence that it was hired would be preferred to the evidence that it was a pledge.

If both the parties are in possession of a certain property and one of them claims that it belongs exclusively to him and the other alleges that it belongs to them jointly, the evidence of the former will be heard, the reason being that his right is partially admitted by the latter. If, on the other hand, both claimed exclusive rights, they will be declared to be joint owners as there is no reason for preferring the proof of one to that of the other.

When the Word of One Party is to be Accepted: In certain cases where both the parties are unable to adduce proof, but there is a presumption in favour of the allegation of one of them arising from circumstances (tahkimul-hal) the statement of that party is to be accepted.

In such cases the law will sometimes require the party in whose favour the presumption is raised to take the oath and sometimes not. For instance, when there is a dispute between the husband and the wife regarding certain goods in the house, if they are articles like swords and lances and the like, they will be presumed to belong to the husband and his word will be accepted and a decree will be made in his favour if the wife is unable to adduce any proof and the husband is prepared to take the oath.

A similar presumption will be made in favour of the wife in respect of things like household utensils, carpets, and so on, If a donor applies for revocation of his gift and the done says that the thing has perished, his word is to be accepted without his being asked to take the oath. If a bailee says that he has returned the goods entrusted to him. his word is to be accepted if he takes the oath.

If a Christian dies and his wife alleges that she became Muhammadan after his death, but his heirs say that she became a convert to Islam before his death, the statement of the heirs is to be accepted. The reason is that, at the time the woman comes to Court, she being a Muhammadan, this fact confirms the allegation of the heirs. Sometimes when the parties to a transaction cannot agree and neither of them is able to adduce evidence, but both are prepared to take the oath is support of their respective allegations, the Court will set aside the transaction itself.

For instance, when the vendor and the buyer of an article cannot agree as to the amount of consideration or as to the thing sold or both, and none of them can adduce evidence, but both are prepared to take the oath in support of their allegations, the Court will set aside the sale. The reason is that there is no ground for preferring the bare statement of the one to that of the other.

Proof by Circumstances

Besides human testimony facts and circumstances (Qarinat) may also be relied upon as a proof. But circumstantial evidence will only be acted upon if it is of a conclusive nature (Qatiatun). For instance, if a person is seen coming out from an unoccupied house in fear and anxiety with a knife covered with blood in his hand and in the house a dead body is found with its throat cut, these facts will be regarded as a proof that the person who was seen coming out murdered him.

Documentary: Sometimes documents are accepted as a substitute for oral testimony. But the Court is not to act on a sealed deed or any other document unless it is free from the suspicion of being forged and is such as is customary for people to enter their transactions therein. For instance, official documents and the records of a Court of Justice can be accepted. Books of account kept in course of business and documents executed in presence of two witnesses are also admitted in evidence.

Admission: The Court generally accepts an admission without requiring any further proof from the claimant. An admission must, however, be unconditional, and it must be voluntary, so that if obtained by coercion it is not binding nor if made in jest. Similarly, if the fact admitted is contradicted by apparent and obvious circumstances of the person making the admission, it will not be accepted.

Role of Circumstantial Evidence

The next source of the proof of a crime or a right is circumstantial evidence *(Al-Qarain). Qarina* literally means connection, conjunction, relation, union, affiliation, association, linkage, indication. In term it is the logical inference to be drawn from something done, or from circumstances by virtue of which the matter becomes definitive, a sign which makes the matter certain. A presumption may be weak or strong, sometimes it is considered conclusive while on the other occasion it might be only probative. When it is strong it is accepted as evidence for the relevant fact.

Islamic *Shariah* recognises presumption as evidence in a number of diverse situations. The Holy Quran says, "At last Joseph and she raced towards the door one behind the other and she rent his shirt (pulling it) from behind and then met her husband at the door. Seeing him, she cried out, 'what punishment does the one deserve who shows evil intentions towards your wife? What else than that he should be put in prison or tortured with painful torment. At this, a witness of her own folk testified. If his shirt is torn from front, then she speaks truth and he is of the liars. And if his shirt is torn from behind then she tells a lie and he is of the truthful. 'When the husband saw that the shirt was torn from the back, he said, 'This is one of your cunning devices, your devices are indeed very cunning'.

The Holy Prophet Muhammad (Pbuh) has Admitted the Presumption as Source of Proof in many Cases: It has been related that in the battle of Badr the two sons of Afraa claimed that they have killed Abu Jahl. The Holy Prophet said to them, "Have you cleaned your swords". They said, "No". The Holy Prophet said, "Show me your swords". When Holy Prophet saw the swords being bloodstained, he said, "You have killed him".

It has been related on the authority of Numan Ibn Al-Jaria who relates from his father that some people brought their dispute about a hut to the Holy Prophet. The Holy Prophet sent Hudhayfa to decide their dispute. Hudhayfa decided in favour of those to whose side the bamboos of the hut had come out. When he returned and told the Holy Prophet, the Holy Prophet said, "Your decision is correct."

It has been related on the authority of Abu Hurrayrah that Holy Prophet (Pbuh) said, "There were two women who had small sons. A wolf came and took away the son of one of them. One of them said to other, It was your son'. The other said, 'No, it was your son'. They brought their dispute to Prophet David and he decided in favour of the elder one. Then they went to Prophet Solomon and related to him their dispute for decision. He ordered to provide him a knife to make two pieces of the child so as to give one piece to each of them. On this the younger one said, 'Don't cut him into pieces; this is the son of the elder one'. Hearing this Prophet Solomon decided in favour of the younger one".

It has been related on the authority of Wail Ibn Hajar that a woman was going in the dark to the mosque for her morning prayer in the period of the Holy Prophet (Pbuh). Suddenly, a person met her on the way and made sexual intercourse with her forcibly and then ran away. She cried and meanwhile another person came to her and she related to him the whole story. That man went in search of the culprit. Then, other persons came to her and she also related the whole incident to them and they also went to search the actual culprit. But this group met the second person who was searching the actual culprit (and was in a terrible situation).

They caught him and brought him before that woman. She also confirmed that he was the man who had committed the illicit sexual intercourse with her. Then, they brought him to the Holy Prophet. The Holy Prophet (Pbuh) asked him, "Have you committed this offence". He remained silent and didn't answer the question. The woman admitted before the Prophet that he was the person who committed the illicit sexual intercourse with her. Seeing the circumstances i.e. the silence of that person, the confirmation of the woman and the plea of those persons who told that they found him in a terrible condition, the Holy Prophet ordered to stone him to death (because he was married). On this, another person stood and confessed that he, and not the person who was sentenced, has committed the offence."

The Holy Prophet has also used the world *"Bayyina"* for the proof of an offence or right which means anything that indicated and proves the commission of an offence or violation of a right whether it be witness or something else like circumstantial evidence, oath, documents etc. Thus, the Muslim jurists concur that circumstantial evidence is acceptable in *tazirat* and rights. But they, however, differ in accepting it in the crimes of *hudud and qisas.* There are three views in this matter.

The Hanafis and Shafii's and with one exception Hanbalis reject the use of presumption in *hudud* and *qisas,* allowing only witnesses and confession as evidence. This view is based on the *hadith* of the Holy Prophet (Pbuh) who said, "Were I to stone anyone without evidence, I would stone so-and-so *(fulana),* for her speech, appearance and cohabition are such which raise suspicion". This reinforces the rule that doubt nullifies *hudud.* Since a presumption is always doubtful it cannot be the basis for judgement in *hudud.*

The second view would permit certain types of presumption to be used in proving *hudud* cases. Thus, for example, pregnancy of an unmarried woman is sufficient proof of her adultery provided she does not claim rape. The smell of alcohol or regurgitated wine presumptively proves drinking. This is the view of Imam Malik and a reported view of Imam Ahmad and is based on the statement of Hadrat 'Umar who said, "Adultery is public (proved) when pregnancy appears (in case of an unmarried woman without being coerced) or confession is made."

The third view freely recognises the validity of presumption in all cases including *hudud.* It is argued that evidence is whatever brings the truth to light including presumption. It is argued that if a presumption is susceptible of doubt, so is the testimony of witnesses and it should, therefore, be judged in the same manner. Indeed, testimony by witnesses is more susceptible to illusions, lies and errors than presumptions. Thus presumptions have at least as much validity as testimony by witnesses. Practically the Muslim judges, throughout the Islamic history, have relied upon the circumstantial evidence.

Majalla Al-Ahkam Al-Adliyya, a Codified law of the Ottoman Empire of Turkey, has Accommodated Presumption in Section 1741 which is as under:

"Section 1741:- A complete presumptive proof is an inference which attains the degree of positive knowledge.

"For example: On someone's going into an empty house, immediately after a man has come from the house with fear and haste, and with a bloodstained knife in his hand, if there is seen a person with his throat recently cut, there is no doubt that man is the murderer of the person.

"No attention is paid to the mere possible chance that person perhaps killed himself."

The postmortem examination, dying statement, recovery of blood-stained clothes, razor, spear, lathi, chopper etc., injury on the body of the suspect or accused, recovery of a gun or other weapon can be considered in a murder case as circumstantial evidence which can be linked and corroborated with other circumstances. The principle forms of the circumstantial evidence in criminal cases are:- the motives of the accused, his threat, his opportunities, his attempts, false statements, his silence, his preparations, his fabrication or distribution of evidence, his flight, his possession of stolen or other property etc. In case of *zina,* the pregnancy of the accused woman who is unmarried, existence of semen on the body or clothes of the accused man or woman etc. and in case of drinking wine, the odour of wine in the mouth of the accused or his vomiting is suspected being of wine etc. — all these are considered as circumstantial evidence which is admissible in Islamic law. However, no *hadd* punishment shall be given on such evidence and the accused shall be punished with *tazir* in case of an offence liable to *hadd* if his offence is proved by the circumstantial evidence.

Documentary proof:- One of the circumstantial evidences is documentary proof. "Document" means any matter expressed or described upon any substance by means of letters, figures or marks, or by more than one of these means, intended to be used, or which may be used, for the purpose of recording the matter. According to Islamic law, it includes any written, printed or inscribed material which gives information.

The jurists concur that a letter of a judge to another judge about a case before the judge to whom it is sent is sufficient proof in matters other than *hudud* and *qisas.*

The majority of the jurists are of the opinion that a right or a *tazir* crime can be proved by documentary evidence provided it is free from forgery. Describing the opinions of the jurists regarding the documentary proof, Ibn Al-Qayyim writes, "According to Imam Abu Hanifa documentary proof is sufficient proof for rights and *tazir* crimes provided the judge is satisfied about it. Imam Abu Yusuf and Imam Muhammad maintain that if a document is found in the official record of a court duly signed by the authorised officer, it is sufficient proof in civil matters and *tazir* crimes even if the judge does not know something about that. Imam Malik is of the opinion that a document cannot be considered sufficient proof until it is known to the judge.

According to one view of Imam Shafii, a document can be treated a sufficient proof provided it is free from forgery. According to one view of Imam Ahmad a document is considered sufficient proof provided it is known to the judge". He further observes that an obvious feature of Islamic Law as applied in practice as a whole, is its reliance on documents, right from the start. Even strict theory designed to recognise the existence of documents and to admit them as valid evidence specially when they had been attested by qualified witnesses, the Malikis to the widest extent, the Hanafis and Hanbalis with some hesitation, whereas the Shafi is continued to regard them strictly as accessories, but the actual use of documents was equally extensive among the adherents of all schools.

In the modern period, during which the application of Islamic Law has been started by the independent Muslim states like Saudi Arabia, Egypt, Kuwait, Jordan and Pakistan, documents have been generally admitted as valid proof for rights and *tazir* crimes, and sometimes the competence of the judges is restricted to cases in which documentary evidence is produced.

Professional and Scientific Witness

One of the sources of the proof of a crime or a right in Islamic law is evidence by expert i.e. expert's opinion. Expert's evidence means the testimony which is given in relation to some scientific, technical or professional matter by experts i.e. persons qualified to speak authoritatively by reason of their special training, skill or familiarity with the subject. It assists the trier to determine a fact in issue. A witness qualified as an expert by knowledge, skill, experience, training or education may testify thereto in the form of an opinion or otherwise.

Opinion of experts has been given due importance in Islamic Law. The Holy Quran says:

> "We granted inspiration: if ye realise this not, ask of those who have knowledge".

The *Sunnah* of the Holy Prophet (Pbuh) has also recognised the expert's evidence. It has been related on the authority of Hadrat Aishah who said that one day the Holy Prophet came to her and said with extreme happiness, "Oh Aishah . Don't you see that Mujazzaz Al-Mudlaji came and saw Usama and Zaid, lying being covered with a sheet in a position that their heads were covered but their legs were not covered, and said, "These legs are from one another." Mujazzaz Al-Mudlaji was an expert of lineages.

Hadrat 'Umar practically introduced the testimony of experts in suits involving questions of techniques. Experts of the particular science or art in question were called to give testimony in the court. For instance, Hutaia wrote against Zabarqan b. Badr a satirical couplet, in which, however, the point of satire was not apparent. Zabarqan lodged a complaint in the court of 'Umar himself.

It was a case of poetical technique, and poetical terminology and terms of expression are different from those of common speech. 'Umar, therefore, invited Hassan Ibn Thabit, a poet of great distinction and eminence, to give evidence, and delivered judgement in accordance with his expert opinion. Similarly, experts of physiognomy were called as witnesses in cases of disputed heredity.

It has been related on the authority of Jafar Ibn Muhammad who said, "A woman and young man from Ansar were brought to 'Umar. Actually she loved that young man but he did not like her. So she used strategy and took an egg and broke it on her clothes and thighs. Then she came to 'Umar crying and said, "This man tried to make sexual intercourse with me and this is the sign of his offence". 'Umar asked some women.

They said to him, "There is semen on her clothes and thighs". So 'Umar intended to punish him. On this, young man said, "Oh Amir al Muminin. Don't hurry, I have not committed any offence. She has made device". Then 'Umar asked Hadrat Ali about that. Hadrat Ali saw her clothes and body and ordered to bring hot water. Then he threw that water on her clothes and thighs and collected that material and tested it. By tasting, he knew that it is an egg. Thus Hadrat Ali threatened the woman and she confessed.

It has been related in *Muwatta* Imam Malik on the authority of Abdullah Ibn Abi Bakr who relates from his father who relates from Amra bint Abdal-Rahman who said that a thief stole some fruits *(cetruja)* in the period of Hadrat 'Uthman. Hadrat 'Uthman ordered that its value should be fixed by the experts. Thus, its value was fixed by three dirhams equal to 12 dinars. Hadrat 'Uthman ordered to amputate his hand.

It has been related that a black man complained to Hadrat 'Umar and said, "I am black and my wife is black. But my wife gave birth to a red child". His wife said to Hadrat 'Umar, "I swear by Allah that I have not committed illicit sexual intercourse (with anybody) and this is actually the son of this husband". Hadrat 'Umar asked Hadrat Ali about this case. Hadrat Ali said to the man, "Will you give me the true information if I ask you anything." He said, "Yes". Hadrat Ali said to him, "Have you met your wife when she was in menses". He said, "Yes". Hadrat Ali exclaimed with joy and said, "When human sperm mixes with blood, it gives birth to a red child, so don't deny your son. You have done wrong with yourself.

The jurists are of the opinion that when a judge faces any difficulty in some scientific, technical or professional matter he should seek the opinion of the expert to determine the fact in issue. Only one expert is sufficient in any case if more than one are not available.

Imam Sarakhsi States: "When Imam faces difficulty about the value of the stolen property and the experts differ in fixing its value some fix it as ten dirhams and other fix it by less than that, *hadd* will not be implemented on the accused because *hadd* is implemented when the *nisab* (prescribed limit) of the stolen property is completed and it is not completed when there is difference between the experts in its value".

Allama Ibn Al-Qayyim writes, "The opinion of one doctor is sufficient in serious hurts if two are not available. Similarly the testimony of one veterinarian is sufficient in case of the disease of an animal".

The opinion of the expert was given great importance by the later Muslim jurists and they relied upon it in adultery, theft, drinking wine, murder, hurts and all civil matters. It is stated in *Majallatul Ahkamil Adliyya,* a civil codified law of Ottoman Empire of Turkey, that reports of the skilled persons are acceptable as authentic testimony even if they did not use the word *Shahadah* (testimony).

Thus the report of a doctor, the opinion of an expert of foot-prints, arms, lineage or laboratory test of blood, semen etc., shall be considered for the purpose of disposing the matter under dispute. However *hadd* punishment will not be given on such evidence but *tazir* punishment will be given to the accused in the crimes liable to *hadd.*

Role of Confession

Another source of the proof of a crime or a right in Islamic law is confession in criminal matters and admission in civil matters. "Confession" means the evidence of a person against himself. Thus it signifies a statement made by a person charged. "Admission" means statement made by a person acknowledging the right of another person upon himself.

Confession and admission have been recognised as sources of proof of a crime and a right by the Holy Quran and the *Sunnah* of the Holy Prophet (Pbuh). The Holy Quran says, "O ye who believe! Be ye staunch injustice, witnesses for Allah even though it be against yourselves". The Holy Prophet (Peace be upon him) has considered confession and admission a conclusive proof in many cases and he implemented *hadd* merely on the confession of the accused. It has been related on the authority of Jabir Ibn Abdullah who said that a man from the tribe of Banu Aslam came to the Holy Prophet (Pbuh) and confessed to have committed *zina* and gave testimony against himself four times. The Holy Prophet then ordered to stone him to death.

Conditions for Confession/Admission: The following are the conditions for the validity of confession and admission:

(i) The person who confesses or admits must be adult and sane. Thus the confession and admission of a minor, mad person, sleeping person, intoxicated person etc. is not admissible. It is based on the *hadith* of the Holy Prophet (Pbuh) who said, "Three persons have been exempted (i) the minor until he attains puberty, (ii) the mad until he recovers and (iii) the sleeping person until he awakes".

(ii) The confession and admission must be explicit as to the commission of the crime and violation of the right. Any ambiguity in the confession or admission renders it inadmissible. It is based on the *Sunnah* of the Holy Prophet (Pbuh) who asked several questions about the commission of *zina* from Maiz Ibn Malik who confessed to have committed *zina* and when he answered all the questions, then Prophet (Pbuh) ordered to stone him to death. A confessor in case of *zina* liable to *hadd* must confess the act of penetration.

(iii) The person who confesses or admits must be capable of self-expression. According to Imam Malik, Imam Shafii and Imam Ahmad the confession and admission of a deaf and dumb person is admissible provided he or she can write his or her confession or admission or his or her signs are intelligible. But according to Imam Abu Hanifa his or her confession is not acceptable in *hudud.* The admission of writing, signature or seal shall be considered the admission of the writer or executant of the document. The jurists concur that the confession or admission of a blind person is admissible in all matters.

(iv) The confession and admission must be with free consent without any pressure or compulsion. It is based on the *hadith* of the Holy Prophet (Pbuh) who said, "My *Ummah* has been exempted from (the liability) of the action done by mistake, forgetfulness or for which they have been forced to do". Thus the confession or admission given under threat, inducement or promise is not admissible. Dr. Awad A. Awad, while discussing the views of the jurists regarding confession under compulsion, writes:

"Under *Shariah,* the accused has the absolute right to answer or refuse to answer the investigator's questions. If he admits guilt, he has the right to change his mind. If he does so, his admission becomes invalid and cannot be used as evidence at trial.

"It is universally agreed among Islamic jurists that the accused cannot be forced to admit guilt. Ibn Hazm suggest in *Al-Muhalla* that neither the Quran, nor the *Sunnah* nor *Ijma'* (consensus) allow examination by beating, imprisonment or threat. And the Malikis require that admission be voluntary, otherwise it is invalid even if it would have led to the recovery of the victim in a murder or of stolen goods in a robbery.

The Hanafis also reject as unjust an admission obtained by torture or threat even though it might be true. However, some later Hanafi jurists would permit coerced admissions. Thus Ibn Al-Abidin in his *Hashiya* (commentary) relates that Hasan Ibn Ziyad allowed the beating of the accused to force him to admit guilt provided this did not lead to wounding the flesh and exposing the bones. Ibn al-Abidin adds that without beating, it is rare to get confession of guilt, arguing that there is a special need for this measure during interrogation due to the spread of corruption. However, those who hold this opinion qualify it by limiting it to the known evil immoral men.

"Some jurists adopt a middle view by not permitting involuntary confession while admitting its true results (except in *hudud* crimes). Among these are Ibn Al-Qayyim and Ibn Hazm. Ibn Al-Qayyim points out that if the accused is tortured in order to obtain his confession of stealing, and he does confess and the stolen property is found in his possession, his hand should be cut. This is not punishment on the basis of the confession he was forced to make, but rather the fact that he was caught with stolen possessions. Ibn Hazm expresses this opinion more clearly and logically, arguing that such forced confession by itself has no legal weight according to Quran *Sunnah* and *Ijma'* (consensus).

The skin, blood and honours of the accused are inviolate and cannot be otherwise affected except by text or consensus. If there is evidence consistent with accused's confession, then he deserves the *hadd* punishment for whatever the crime *{hadd* or *tazir).* On the other hand, the accused has the right or redress against those who ordered his torture, whether this be the ruler or any other person in authority, since beating him unnecessarily is an illegal and oppressive act. The fact that he committed a crime does not negate the fact that an illegal act was committed against him, nor does the commission of a crime deprive him of his basic rights.

The opinion of Ibn Hazm leads to a legal dilemma, for he does not rely upon the invalidity of the involuntary confession, but at the same time he does rely on its results as self-sufficient evidence and a valid basis on which to base a conviction. Nevertheless Ibn Hazm, with the institution of a jurist, tries to balance the requirements of justice necessitating the punishment of the guilty and the protections afforded by the *Shariah* against harming a person to obtain a confession.

"An assessment of these views suggests that the majority opinion is more consistent with the *Shariah.* The second opinion clearly stands on a weak and unsound foundation and the fact that it is result-oriented conflicts with the *Shariah,* which requires that the means and the objective be equally legitimate. The third view is defensible, and its practical benefits may be justifiable. However, it is indefensible for two reasons: first, it conflicts with the established doctrine of *Shariah* as expressed by jurists using it as a basis for several secondary judgements. The rule states that 'right cannot arise out of wrong and the 'source determines the offshoot.

"The second reason is that the use of illegal means to achieve legal ends requires the exclusion of what is obtained through coercion because reliance on the result of an involuntary confession will tempt weak souls to torture the accused. Furthermore, the accused is not protected sufficiently from this danger simply by affording him a subsequent opportunity to retaliate against his torture. His injury may not be adequately redressed in that manner. He is better protected if involuntary confessions are held invalid and their results or consequences are nullified.

"Confessions obtained by deceit were, however, allowed and preferred by Ibn Hazm, since no coercion is involved. On this question he criticised Imam Malik by commenting the *deceit* is not forbidden. Ibn Hazm attributes the use of trickery to the Holy Prophet (Pbuh) and Hadrat Ali who used it to obtain the confession of certain suspects. Ibn Hazm argues that trickery is not like force, for force is that which harms a person's body or belongings or threatens him or his family. No harm is effected by trickery. Thus trickery is not coercion.

"However, Imam Malik's view seems the more acceptable, for it is not true that the investigator's resort to deception and deceit is not prohibited. Furthermore, coercion nullifies a confession by invalidating the element of choice and negating the voluntary nature of the confession which is a requirement of its validity. This defect is likewise present in a confession obtained through trickery. Thus, the latter must be considered the same in effect as an involuntary confession. Ibn Hazm viewed harm or the threat or harm as the defect of involuntary confession. While a confession gained through deceit is not without harmful consequences, it is more important to recognise the effect of the means employed as the means of coercing the accused to submit to the will of the confessor."

Extra-Judicial Confession: The confession and admission must be before a court. If the confession took place outside the court, there is difference of opinion about its validity. According to Imam Abu Hanifa, if the confession took place outside the court, it is not valid and no evidence will be accepted on that because if the confessor confessed before the court then the offence will be considered proved by his confession and not by the evidence of the witnesses, and if he refused to confess before the court, his refusal will be considered his retraction from the confession which is admissible in the offences of *hudud* which relate to the rights of Allah like *zina.* However, his refusal will not be considered retraction from his confession in the offences which relate to the rights of individuals like murder, hurts etc."

But according to Imam Malik, Imam Shafii and Imam Ahmad extra-judicial confession is valid if it is witnessed by two witnesses. Further, Imam Malik and Imam Shafii apply it to all cases, and according to Imam Ahmad four witnesses are required in case of *zina* on the basis of the requirement of four witnesses for its proof by testimony. If the confessor retracts his extra-judicial confession, Imam Malik considers it a withdrawal of his confession that nullifies it, but Imam Shafii does not consider it withdrawn unless the confessor contradicts himself in his confession.

The concept of extra-judicial confession in the contemporary law is not more different than its concept in the Islamic law. In this connection Dr. CM. Hanif writes, "The law in regard to extra-judicial confession may be stated thus: An extra-judicial confession, if voluntary, can be relied upon by the court along with evidence in convicting the accused. Usually, and as a matter of caution, courts require some material corroboration to an extra-judicial confessional statement.

Though it cannot be laid down as an extra-judicial confession affords the sole basis for conviction. In cases of homicide and such other grave offences, it would not be safe to convict a person on the confession alone unless corroborated by other evidence. This is a rule of prudence rather than of law. The nature and the quality of corroborative evidence must depend upon the facts of each case. The extra-judicial confession of an accused cannot be taken into consideration in determining his guilt when it is not put to him in the examination Under Section 342 of the Code of Criminal Procedure".

Quantum of Confession: According to Imam Abu Hanifa and Imam Ahmad it is necessary in the case *of zina* that there must be four separate confessions as four witnesses are necessary for its proof by testimony. They base their opinion on the tradition of the Holy Prophet (Pbuh) related on the authority of Abu Hurrayrah that when Maiz came to the Holy Prophet (Pbuh) and confessed his guilt four times, Prophet (Pbuh) ordered to stone him to death. It is further supported with a *hadith* related on the authority of Buraida Al-Aslami who said that a Ghamidiyya, who was a woman from the clan of Ghamid, came to the Holy Prophet (Pbuh) and confessed four times that she has committed *zina.* The Prophet ordered that as she was pregnant she will be punished when she given birth to the child and when the child becomes grown enough to carry on without mother.

But according to Imam Malik and Imam Shafii only one time confession is sufficient in all offences including *zina* because confession is an information and it does not need repetition. They base their view on the *hadith* of the Holy Prophet (Pbuh) wherein Prophet ordered Unais to go to that woman and stone her to death if she confessed. The Prophet (Pbuh) did not mention four times in this *hadith* and thus only and time confession was considered sufficient.

According to Imam Abu Hanifa confession must be repeated on different occasions even though within the same sitting. It is based on the practice of the Holy Prophet (Pbuh) in the case of Maiz who confessed his offence on four different occasions.

In this connection, a famous Hanafi jurist, Ali Al-Marghinani, writes, "The reasons for establishing four appearances of the person confessing as a condition are two-fold:- First, the tradition of Maiz as already related; Secondly a plurality of confessions is made a condition, and that cannot be obtained without a plurality of appearances on the part of the confessor, since one effect of an unity of place or appearance is to render the separate declaration of the same thing as one declaration; and hence four confessions, in a single appearance, amount only to a single confession; and as confession relates only to the person confessing, the unity or otherwise of his appearance is regarded, and not that of the *Qadi's* assembly; and this appearance is made four separate times by the *Qadi* repelling the person's first confession, and saying to him "you are mad!" and such other words, the person, upon the *Qadi* thus repelling his confession, going forth, so as to be out of the *Qadi's* sight, and returning again, and repeating his confession, and so on to the fourth time.

This is recorded from Imam Abu Hanifa, on the authority of the conduct of the Prophet (Pbuh) in the instance of Maiz whom he thus sent out of his sight three different times." But according to Imam Ahmad four confessions are necessary whether on one occasion or on different occasions.

Prior Complaint: It is necessary for the validity of confession and admission in the rights and the offences regarding human rights like *qisas,* theft etc. that there must be a prior complaint against the accused or the defendant in a court by the victim or his heirs or representatives. It is based on the reasoning that when the victim or his heirs do not complain or put any claim against the accused or the defendant, it would be presumed that they might have pardoned the accused or the defendant and thus no proof is required. If a person confessed to have committed theft, *hadd will* not be implemented on him until the victim files a complaint against him.

The jurists however concur that no prior complaint is necessary for the confession in the offences which relate to the pure rights of Allah. It is based on the reasoning that it is the duty of every Muslim to safeguard the rights of Allah and whenever he violates any right of Allah, he should confess the offence before the court irrespective of whether the victim has filed any complaint against him or not. This is based on the practice of the Holy Prophet (Pbuh) that he implemented *hadd* on Maiz Ibn Malik Aslami on his confession without any complaint from the opposite party.

But according to Abu Yusuf, Malik, Abu Thaur and Ibn al Munzir no prior complaint is required for the validity of the confession or admission in all criminal and civil matters; so if a person confessed to have committed theft from the property of such person who was absent, *hadd* will be implemented on him though there has been no complaint filed against him prior to his confession in the court. They argue that the order of theft is general in the Holy Quran and not conditioned with prior claim in court. Moreover when the offence is proved then its punishment must be implemented and must not be removed for want of complaint.

It is also necessary that what is confessed or admitted must be practicable for the person who makes it. So if an impotent man or such a woman who has no capability of sexual intercourse confesses to have committed *zina,* the confession is not valid. Moreover confession proves guilt and incurs penalty only when the judge is convinced of it. It is thus necessary for the judge not to wholly depend on the confession of the accused but to find in other circumstances corroboration of the fact confessed. The jurists hold that the judge should also suggest to the accused the possibility of retracting his confession. Allama Amir Kehlani, after relating the *hadith* of Maiz, writes; "This *hadith* is an argument on the point that the accused must be suggested to adopt a way which removes *hadd* from him".

Similarly Allama Al-Kasani has related from Hadrat 'Umar who said, "Drive away the confessors". Another Hanafi jurist, Ali al-Marghinani, writes, "It is laudable in the Qadi or Imam before whom confession of whoredom may be made, to instruct the person confessing to deny it, by saying to him, "perhaps you have only kissed or touched her", because the Holy Prophet (Pbuh) spoke so to Maiz.

Delay in Confession: The jurists concur that unlike evidence delay in confession does not affect its admissibility and the confession after delay is admissible like admission. It is based on the reasoning that delay in evidence amounts to malice and suspicion while there is no such possibility in confession because no sensible person confesses what is harmful to him and thus one is not considered suspicious in what he confesses to have committed.

But according to Abu Hanifa and Abu Yusuf delay in the confession of drinking wine nullifies it and delay in it is the ceasing of the smell of wine from the mouth of the confessor. So if a person confessed to have drunk wine after passing the smell of wine, his confession is not valid.

In this connection a famous Hanafi jurist Ali Al-Marghinani comments, "If a man makes confession of having drunk wine, after the smell has ceased, in this case punishment is not to be inflicted upon him, according to the two Elders. Imam Muhammad maintains that it is to be inflicted. The same difference of opinion obtains in a case where witnesses bear evidence against a man that he has drunk wine' after the smell has ceased. The reason of this diversity of opinion is that *Taqadum,* or lapse of time, forbids the accepting of evidence in a case of wine-drinking, according to all the jurists: but Imam Muhammad fixes the limitation of *Taqadum,* in wine-drinking, to a certain time, namely, one month (according to the most approved authorities), he conceiving an analogy between this, and a case of whoredom, because delay is established by lapse of time, and not by the ceasing of a smell; and the existence or non-existence of a smell is of no weight, as there are other things the flavour of which resembles that of wine.

According to the two Elders, on the contrary, *Taqadum* is established by the non-existence or departure of the smell, for two reasons:— a decree of Abdullah Ibn Masud who, when certain person brought before him a man charged with drinking wine, directed that they should examine his breath, and that if any flavour of wine were discovered, punishment should then be inflicted upon him'; secondly the existence of the effect (namely the smell), is an irrefragable proof of wine having been lately drunk. And as to what Imam Muhammad advances that 'there are other things the flavour of which resembles that of wine it may be replied that the difference between the smell of the wine and other articles, may be easily distinguished by one who is possessed of judgement and discernment, nor can any but ignorant persons be doubtful concerning it. Thus according to Imam Muhammad confession of wine-drinking is not rendered ineffectual by distance of time, in the same manner as (according to him) confession of whoredom is not rendered ineffectual by distance of time, agreeable to what was before advance. With the two Elders, on the contrary, punishment for wine-drinking is not to be inflicted but on the conditions that the smell still remains because Ibn Masud stipulated that condition, as before stated".

Confession of Co-Accused: In Islamic Law a confession is a conclusive proof only against the confessor and it is not a proof against his co-accused. It is based on the following *Ahadith* of the Holy-Prophet (Pbuh):

1. It has been related on the authority of Sad Al-Saidi that a man came to the Holy Prophet (Pbuh) and confessed that he had committed *zina* with a woman whom he named. The Holy Prophet (Pbuh) sent for the woman and enquired from her about that. She denied the allegation. The Holy Prophet punished the man and acquitted the female.
2. It has been related on the authority of Abu Hurrayrah and Zaid Ibn Khalid that while they were with the Holy Prophet (Pbuh), a man stood up and said to the Prophet (Pbuh), "I beseech you by Allah that you should judge us according to Allah's law". Then his opponent, who was wiser than him, got up saying, "Judge us according to Allah's law and kindly allow me to speak". The Holy Prophet (Pbuh) allowed him to speak. He

> said, "my son was the servant of this man and he committed *zina* with his wife and I gave one hundred sheep and a slave as a ransom for my son's offence. Then I asked a learned man about that and he informed that my son should receive one hundred lashes and be exiled for one year, and the man's wife should be stoned to death." The Holy Prophet (Pbuh) said, "By him in whose hand my soul is, I shall judge you according to laws of Allah. Your one hundred sheep and the slave will be returned to you and your son has to receive one hundred lashes and be exiled for one year. Oh Unais! go to the wife of this man and if she confessed, stone her to death". Unais went to her and she confessed. Thus he stoned her to death.

If a man confessed to have committed adultery with a woman who is absent, *hadd* will be implemented on him. Similarly if a man confessed to have committed *zina* with a woman whom he does not know, *hadd* will be implemented on him. In the same way if a man confessed to have committed *zina* with a woman and she denied the allegation, *hadd* will be implemented on him and not on her. This is the opinion of Imam Malik, Imam Shafii and Imam Ahmad. But according to Imam Abu Hanifa in case where one party confesses and the other party denies the charge, *hadd* will not be implemented on both of them because the denial of the other creates doubt in the confession of the first party.

It is pertinent to mention here that according to some of the jurists if a man and a woman who are charged for having committed *zina* stated that they are wife and husband, their statement will be considered sufficient proof of their marriage and they will not be punished provided there is no evidence on their *zina.* But according to Imam Malik they have to prove their marriage failing which they will be punished.

Retraction from Confession or Admission: Retraction from confession in *hudud* is admissible before or after the announcement of the judgement or during the execution of the punishment and it nullifies the *hadd* punishment. But retraction from confession in matters which relate to the rights of individuals like *qisas, diyat* etc. is not admissible. Retraction from admission is not admissible in all matters and once a person makes an admission, he shall be liable for the right created therein even if he retracts it.

But according to some jurists like Hasan, Said Ibn Jubair and Ibn Ali Laila retraction from confession is not admissible in any offence whether it relates to the rights of Allah or rights of individuals, and when the offence is proved by the valid confession, the confessor must be convicted even though he retracts the confession.

According to Imam Abu Hanifa, Imam Malik and Imam Ahmad merely running away during the execution of punishment amounts to retraction from confession irrespective of whether he expressly retracts the confession or not. But according to Imam Shafii merely running away during the execution of punishment is not retraction unless he expressly retracts. And the execution of the punishment will be stopped by his running away. It is based on the tradition of the

Prophet related on the authority of Jabir Ibn Abdullah that when they started stoning Maiz Ibn-Malik Aslami, he ran away and said, "O People! return me to the Prophet. My people killed me and deceived me because they told me that Prophet will not kill me." But we stoned him to death. Later on when we informed the Prophet of his running away, he said, "Why didn't you leave him and bring him to me".

A Hanafi jurist, Ali Al-Marghinani, writes about retraction from confession, "If a person confessing should deny the fact, and retract from his confession, either before or during the inflicting of punishment his retraction must be credited, and he must forthwith be released. Shafii and Ibn Abi Laila have said that retraction after confession is not to be credited, but that the punishment must be inflicted, since as it has been already incurred by the confession, it cannot be done away in consequence of denial; as in a case where whoredom is established against a person upon the testimony of witnesses;— or as in case of retaliation, or of punishment for slander;— that is to say, when retaliation or punishment for slander are once established upon the confession of the offender, they do not drop in consequence of his subsequent denial of the fact; and so in this case likewise.

The argument of our doctors is that denial after confession is an intimation, which (like the confession) may be either false or true; and there is no person to disprove such denial; and hence, from the inconsistency between the confession and the denial, a doubt arises concerning the confession; and punishment drops in consequence of any doubt contrary to intimations which involve the rights of individuals (such as retaliation, and punishment for slander), as the claimant of the right in those cases, is the disprover of the person who has confessed, when he afterwards denies, which is not the case in any matter involving merely a right of the law".

While discussing *hadd* of drinking wine, the same author writes, "If a person makes confession to the drinking of wine, or any intoxicating liquor, and afterwards retracts from such confession punishment is not to be inflicted upon him, as the punishment of wine drinking is purely a right of God."

If a person confessed the commission of theft which relates both to rights of Allah as well as rights of human beings and then retracted the confession, *hadd will* not be implemented on him and he will be held responsible for the stolen property or its compensation.

It may also be mentioned that some Malikis have conditioned the admissibility of retraction with sound ground. In this connection al-Qarafi writes in his book *Al-Zakhira,* Retraction from confession in the rights of Allah like theft, drinking wine etc. is admissible provided there is sound ground for that". If there is no ground then there is difference of opinion in its admissibility. If it relates to both rights of Allah as well as rights of individuals like confession of theft, in this case the right of the person is due on him whether he offers some grounds or not, and so far right of Allah is concerned if he offered any ground, his retraction will be admissible but if he didn't offer any ground *hadd* will be implemented on him. Ibn al-Qasim Maliki is of the opinion that *hadd will* not be implemented on the person who retracts the confession in the offence of *qadhf*, while Ashhab Maliki is of the view that *hadd* will be implemented on him.

Contradiction and falsification in the confession also render it retracted and withdrawn; for example if a person confessed to have stolen the property of a specific person and afterwards said, "No I have stolen the property of another person". So this creates doubt which nullifies confession.

If a person confessed to have committed *zina* and also confessed that he is *muhsan* (married) but afterwards he retracted the confession of being *muhsan* (married) he will not be stoned to death and will be whipped 100 stripes.

If an offence is proved both by evidence as well as confession and then the accused retracts the confession before judgement, there is consensus of opinion among the Hanafi jurists that confession nullifies the evidence and thus retraction from confession at this stage will remove *hadd from* the accused. But if he retracts the confession after judgement which was based on evidence then according to Imam Abu Yusuf *hadd* will not be implemented on him because the evidence is only effective when there is no confession at any stage. But according to Imam Muhammad *hadd* will be implemented on him in this case because the offence is proved with the evidence.

When the *zina* is proved by the evidence of the witnesses and then the accused confessed the commission of the offence and he is not yet punished with *hadd* punishment and then he retracts the confession whether expressly or impliedly, according to Imam Abu Hanifa *hadd* will not be implemented on him. But according to Imam Malik and Imam Ahmad when *zina* is proved by the evidence of the witnesses and then the accused confesses the commission of the offence validly and afterwards retracts the confession, *hadd* will not be removed from him by his retraction because it has been proved by another independent source i.e. evidence of the witnesses.

Imam Shafii is also of the view that if a *hadd* offence is proved by the evidence of witnesses and then the accused confesses the commission of the offence and later on retracts the confession, *hadd* will not be removed from him as it is proved with the evidence of the witnesses. They argue that if retraction nullifies the evidence then it will be made a source for removing of *hadd* punishment in all cases.

But if a person confesses the commission of adultery and later on the witnesses also give evidence on his adultery then there is difference of opinion among the jurists of Shafii School of thought. According to some of them if the accused retracts the confession *hadd* will not be removed from him because of an independent proof still existing there i.e. the evidence of the witnesses, and it is like the case *of zina* in which eight give evidence on it and than four of them retract their evidence, so even then *hadd* will be implemented because four witnesses which is an independent source of proof for adultery are there. But according to some of them if the accused retracts the confession *hadd* will be removed from him because evidence is ineffective with retraction.

According to some of them it depends upon the judgement whether it is based on both evidence and confession or on evidence only, so in these cases *hadd* will not be removed from him by his retraction. If the judgement is solely based on confession only then retraction from it will remove *hadd.* But some of them believe that when a case is proved both by confession as well as evidence, the judgement will be based on the evidence in the offences which relate to the rights of Allah because the evidence is more powerful source of proof than confession in these offences. But in the offences which relate to the rights of human beings the judgement must be based on confession because confession is more powerful than evidence. Moreover, retraction from confession in the rights of human beings is not effective. And according to some of them the judgement must be based on both confession and evidence in all offences.

It is also to be mentioned here that according to Imam Abu Hanifa, Imam Malik and Imam Ahmad if a judge heard an extra-judicial confession of an accused, he is not authorised to base the judgement on that in the court. But there are two views in Shafii school of thought in it, the preferred one is that judge will not base his judgement on what he has seen or known or heard while another view is that the judge is authorised to base his judgement on what he has seen, or heard or known.

If an accomplice has been promised to be pardoned if he confesses and tells the whole story of the commission of offence and the parts played by him and his co-accused, there are two things to be looked into on Islamic point of view, (i) whether the promise of pardon by State is right or not; (ii) whether his confession is an evidence against his co-accused or not.

So far the promise of pardon of a confessor is concerned, it is not valid in the offence of *hudud* because *hudud* being rights of Allah cannot be remitted by the State or victims or their heirs/ guardians. But if the victim or his heir/guardian promises pardon to an accomplice in the offence of *qisas, diyat,* hurts and stolen property etc. and after that he confesses and identifies his co-accuseds and other circumstances of the commission of the offence, the victim or his heir/ guardian can pardon him, but the State cannot pardon an accomplice in the offences of *qisas, diyat,* hurts and stolen property because these are the rights of human beings.

However State can pardon an accomplice in an offence of *tazir,* if it is in the larger national interest. In this connection Allama Ibn Abidin writes, "The difference between *hadd* and *tazir* is that unlike *tazir hadd* can neither be remitted by the recommendation nor can the State remit it and that it is also not removed by the passage of time".

So far the evidence of the confession of the accomplice to whom pardon has been tendered is concerned, it is to be pointed out that in Islamic Law the confession of the accused is conclusive proof against himself and it cannot be extended to his co-accused. And the offence of the co-accused will be proved by his own confession or the evidence of the witnesses against him. However the confession of the accomplice can be considered as presumption *(Qarina)* which can be accepted for *tazir* punishment if it is corroborated with other circumstances.

The Witness

One of the sources of the proof of a crime or a right in Islamic law is taking oath or its denial before a judge or an authorised person. The words *Qasam, Yamin* and *Half* are used for oath which means a solemn pronouncement in the name of Allah or His Attributive names to affirm the truth of one's statement".

The Holy Prophet (Pbuh) said, "Proof is on the complainant and the oath is on the one who denies". Thus, if the plaintiff is unable to produce any proof, oath will be administered on the defendant and if he takes oath, decree will be given in his favour, and if he refuses to take oath then, according to Imam Shafii, the plaintiff will be asked to take oath and if he takes oath, the claim against the defendant will stand proved except in *hadd* and *qisas?*

Majalla says, "The object of evidence is to prove what is contrary to the apparent fact, and the object of the oath is to ensure the continuance of the original state".

According to some jurists oath is taken by the following persons: (i) The complainant or plaintiff. (ii) The accused or defendant. (iii) The witness.

So far the taking of oath from the complainant is concerned, it is taken in the following cases:

(a) When a person accused another person for stealing his property and the accused denies the charge and takes oath that he has not stolen his property. But later on stolen property is found with the accused. The complainant will be asked to take oath and if he takes oath the stolen property will be restored to him.

(b) When the accused refused to take oath and the matter related to human rights like theft, *qadhf* etc., the accuser (complainant) will be asked to take oath for gaining his right.

(c) When there is one witness in support of the claim of the plaintiff in matters other than *hudud and qisas,* he will be asked to take oath. It is based on the *hadith* of the Prophet that he decided on the basis of one witness and the oath of the plaintiff.

(d) When husband accuses his wife, both will be asked to take oath four times.

(e) Oath will not be demanded in a case liable for *hadd* except in the case of theft where it can be demanded to make a decision in respect of the stolen property on the basis of refusal to take oath by the accused.

So far taking oath from the accused or defendant, it is based on the tradition of the Holy Prophet (Pbuh) who said, "Burden of proof is on the accuser (claimant) and the oath is on him who denies (the charge)". But the jurists are unanimous that if the accused denied and refused to take oath in matters of *hudud,* decree will not be given against him except in case of theft wherein if the accused refused to take oath and there is no evidence he will be held responsible for the stolen property and his hand will not be amputated. However jurists differ in matters of *qisas, diyat* and *tazir.*

According to Malik no case of *hudud, qisas* and *tazir* will be decided on the refusal of the defendant from taking oath. But according to Shafii the case will not be decided on the refusal of the defendant from taking oath but will be decided on taking oath or refusal from taking oath of the complainant/plaintiff after the refusal of the defendant from taking oath in matters other than *hudud and qisas.* But Abu Hanifa opines that if the accused refused to take oath in hurt case he will be punished with *qisas* or *tazir.*

It is important to mention here that according to Shafii and the preferred view of Imam Ahmad when defendant refuses to take oath (and there is no evidence) then the plaintiff will be asked to take oath and judgement will be given in his favour on the basis of his oath and not on the refusal of the accused or defendant in all matters except *hudud* and *qisas.*

Imam Ahmad has two opinions in this regard, (i) Judgement will be based on the refusal from taking oath in the matters which relate to money. So according to this view judgement can be based on the refusal of the accused in matters relating to murder and hurts when it is punished with compensation (money). (ii) Judgement will not be based on the refusal of the accused or defendant or the complainant or plaintiff from taking oath in matters other than money.

But according to Imam Abu Hanifa, judgement in matters other than *hudud* and *qisas* will be based on the refusal of defendant or accused from taking oath and not of the complainant or plaintiff. The complainant or plaintiff will in no case be subjected to take oath.

Ibn Al-Qayyim has related many versions regarding oath from the witness. He stated that Ibn-Hazm has related from Ibn-Waza that he was in favour of taking oath from the witness. It has been related on the authority of Abul Haris that Imam Ahmad was asked about *Fasiq* (bearing bad character) witness and a slave witness. He said, "take oaths from them".

Allah has laid down taking oath from the non-Muslim witnesses when they testify to a will of a Muslim during a journey. So Muslims are more liable for taking oath in any civil or criminal case.

Moreover, as the *Qadi* can separate the witnesses when he deems it necessary, he is more competent to" take oath from them when he deems it necessary.

The judge can also take oath from the complainant, the witnesses and the accused or defendant in the same case if he deems necessary.

A non-Muslim is allowed to take oath according to his own religion or belief.

The later jurists concur that due to the change in the social life of the people, the judge has to evaluate the oath taken by a person and make himself satisfied of its authenticity before giving judgement on the basis of the oath.

Withdrawal of Witness

The juristic effect of testimony may be revoked by the witness himself by retraction of what he testified to. Such retraction must be made in Court, otherwise it will not be taken into account at all. If the witnesses retract their testimony before the order is passed such testimony will be rejected, but if afterwards, it will not affect the order. If in the last case their evidence has caused any loss, the witnesses will be held liable.

Estoppel: The law sometimes does not allow evidence being given of a certain fact having regard to the conduct of the party desiring of adduce such evidence. This, as I have stated elsewhere, is called bayanud darurat which corresponds to estoppel of the English law. For instance, if the owner of a certain property sees another person selling it and keeps quiet, he will not be allowed to prove that the man who purported to sell was not authorised by him to do so.

Importance of Witness

The first source of the proof of a crime or a right in Islamic law is *Shahadah* i.e. Testimony. *Shahadah* literally means "information of what one has witnessed or seen or beheld with his eyes, declaration of what one knows, decisive information. It also means to be present". In term of law it means to give true information before a competent court of law what one has seen or known for the purpose of proving or disproving a right or a crime. In Islamic Law great importance has been given to evidence. The Holy Quran says,

> "O ye who believe! Be steadfast witnesses for Allah in equity and let not hatred of any people seduce you that ye deal not justly". "O ye who believe! Be ye staunch injustice, witnesses for Allah, even though it be against yourselves or your parents or your kindred".
>
> "And call to witness from among your men, two witnesses. And if two men are not available, then one man and two women whom you approve as witnesses, so that if the one makes an error the other will remind her and have witnesses when you sell one to another."
>
> "And for those of your women who are guilty of *zina* call to witness four of you against them."
>
> "And those who accuse chaste women and then couldn't produce four witnesses (in support of their accusation), whip them eighty strokes."
>
> "And call to witness two just men among you, and keep your testimony upright for Allah. "

Concealment of evidence is a great sin. The Holy Quran says, "Don't conceal testimony. He who conceals it, his heart is sinful."

When a case is brought before a court and the court requires evidence for its decision, it is compulsory for a witness in such case to give evidence before the court. The Holy Quran says, "And the witnesses must not refuse when they are summoned."

The Holy Prophet (Pbuh) has made it obligatory for the plaintiff/complainant to produce proof (evidence) in support of his claim/complaint. The Holy Prophet (Pbuh) said, "Burden of proof lies on the plaintiff/complainant and the oath is on the person who denies".

The Holy Prophet has also given great importance to the evidence. It has been related on the authority of Wail ibn Hajar who said, "A man from Hadarmut and a man from Kinda came to the Holy Prophet. Hadrami said, "Oh Prophet! this man has wrongfully possessed my land." Kindi said, "This is my land and is in my possession. He has no right in it." The Holy Prophet said to Hadrami, "Have you any proof. He said, "No". The Prophet said, "Then you have to accept his oath."

The evidence must be clear and explicit in respect of the facts for which it is given. The Holy Prophet (Pbuh) said, "if you see a thing like the sun, give evidence on that and not otherwise."

Conditions for a Witness: (i) A witness must be adult and sane. This is the unanimous view of the jurists of all schools of thought. It is based on the *hadith* of the Holy Prophet (Pbuh) who said, "Three persons have been exempted (from every kind of obligation), (i) the minor until he attains puberty, (ii) the mad until he recovers, (iii) the sleeping persons until he awakes".

A Witness After being Adult and sane must be Adil: *Adil* means a person of irreproachable and serious character and not to be liable to suspicion. According to Shafii school of thought it means a person who abstains himself from capital sins and does not insist on minor sins and thus models his conduct upon the respectables among his contemporaries and fellow-countrymen. Reconciling the various definitions of *adil* it is to be concluded that *adil* means a person who is generally considered a reliable person in his society and is not notorious.

A Witness to be a Muslim: According to Imam Malik, Imam Shafii and Imam Ahmad the evidence of a non-Muslim is not admissible neither for and against a Muslim nor for and against a non-Muslim. They base their view on the verse of the Holy Quran. "And call to witness two *Adil* persons among you". And a non-Muslim can't be *Adil.* But according to Imam Abu Hanifa the evidence of non-Muslim is admissible for and against each other. He bases his view on the reasoning that though they are not *Adil* for Muslims but they may be reliable for one another. Moreover the Holy Prophet (Pbuh) has accepted the evidence of Christians among themselves. This is also one view of Imam Ahmad and the view of Ibn Al-Taimiyya and Ibn Al-Qiyyim.

The situation in the present day has greatly changed. Many Muslims reside in non-Muslim states and many non-Muslims reside in Muslim states, and all the countries of the world are connected and tied with one another through mutual contracts and different international and territorial organisations under which every state is bound to give rights to all its residents which are available to the residents of the other states. Moreover all the nations of the world specially all Muslim countries have signed Geneva Convention, Charter of Human Rights, which obliges them to treat non-Muslims like Muslims to a possible stage keeping in view the laws of Islam.

Thus depriving non-Muslims of giving evidence for and against one another is not fit in the present day circumstances. It will be in the interest of the present day situation in Muslim countries to allow non-Muslims to give evidence for and against one another in matters other than *hudud.* So far *hudud* crimes are concerned, their evidence for and against each other will be acceptable but the accused shall not be punished with *hadd* but will be punished with *tazir.* Moreover the evidence of a non-Muslim may also be accepted for and against a Muslim in matters other than *hudud* because there is no express verse of the Holy Quran and *hadith* of the Holy Prophet (Pbuh) which prohibits the acceptability of the evidence of a non-Muslim. On contrary according to verse 5:106 of the Holy Quran, the evidence of two non-Muslims for a Muslim is acceptable in connection with his will at the point of his death during a journey when Muslims are not available there.

Evidence of Woman: According to the majority of the jurists including Imam Malik, Imam Abu Hanifa, Imam Shafii and Imam Ahmad a witness in *hudud* and *qisas* must be male and thus the evidence of a woman is not admissible in *hudud and qisas.* In cases other than *hudud* and *qisas,* the evidence of two women arid one man is admissible. Only in matters which are generally known to women like virginity, menstruation, suckling etc., the evidence of only women is admissible in them; further according to Imam Abu Hanifa and Imam Ahmad the evidence of only one woman is sufficient in these matters, and according to Imam Shafii the evidence of four women is necessary in these matters.

According to Ibn Taimiyya and Ibn Al-Qayyim the evidence of a woman is admissible even in *hudud and qisas* if her evidence is otherwise authentic and the evidence of the men is not available in that case. It has been related that Hadrat Muawiyyah decided a case of a house on the single evidence of Umm Salama.

Ibn Qayyim in his book *Al-Turuq al-Hukumiyya* has discussed at length the opinions of the jurists about the testimony of the woman. He writes, "it has been related from Makhul who said, "the testimony of women is not acceptable except in loan matters". According to a version Ibn 'Umar said, "the testimony of the women is not acceptable except in cases which cannot be investigated by the men like pregnancy, menses and other special matters of the women". It has also been related from Hadrat Ali who said, "the testimony of the women is not acceptable until there is a man with them." It has also been related from Hadrat 'Umar and Hadrat Ali who said "the testimony of the women is acceptable in divorce, marriage, *qisas* and *hudud".*

It has also been related from Zuhri who said, "it has been the practice since the period of the Prophet and the two Caliphs after him not to accept the testimony of the women in *hudud,* marriage and divorce". It has been related from Shabi that the testimony of one man and two women is acceptable in divorce and unintentional hurts. According to Sufyan Thauri "the testimony of a man and two women is acceptable in *qisas,* divorce, marriage except in *hudud.* And the testimony only of the women is acceptable in matters which are out of the approach of men".

According to Abu Hanifa the testimony of one man and two women is acceptable in the matter of suckle and completion of *iddat.* The only testimony of the women is, however, acceptable in matters of birth and secrets of the women. According to Imam Malik the testimony of the women with one man or without is not acceptable in *qisas, hudud,* marriage, divorce, parentage etc. Their testimony with a man is acceptable in matters of loan, property, agency, wills. And the testimony of only women is acceptable in the secrets of the women, birth, suckle and the noise of the child at the time of his birth."

It has been related by Ibn Hajar that Taus accepted the testimony of women alongwith men in every offence except *zina* (adultery).

It has been related from Ata ibn Abi Raba who said that if eight women gave testimony on the adultery of a woman, I shall punish her with stoning to death.

Ibn Shahab said that Allah has directed that the matters are to be decided by the evidence of two men and in the absence of two men by the evidence of one man and two women and did not prohibit the evidence of women alongwith men. He also stated that evidence of women alongwith a man is sufficient to prove a case of murder.

It has been related from Hammad ibn Abi Sulaiman who said, "the testimony of one man and two women is admissible in *hudud* and *qisas.*

In the matter of *Wali* the Holy Quran has equated the evidence of a man with the evidence of a woman. The Quran says:

> "As for those who accuse their wives but have no witnesses except themselves; let the testimony of one of them be four testimonies, (swearing) by Allah that he is of those who speak the truth. And yet a fifth invoking the curse of Allah on him if he is of those who lie."
>
> "And it shall avert the punishment from her if she bear witness before Allah four times that whatever he said is indeed false. And a fifth time that the wrath of Allah be upon her if he speaks truth."

Regarding the validity of the evidence of the women in original, a Hanafi jurist Allama Ali Al-Marghinani writes, "The reasoning of our doctors is that testimony of women is originally valid, because testimony is founded upon three circumstances, namely sight, memory and a capability of communication; for by means of the first the witness acquires knowledge; by means of the second he retains such knowledge; and by means of the third he is enabled to impart to the Qadi; and all these three circumstances exist in a woman (where it is that her communication of a tradition or of a message is valid); and with respect to their want of memory, it is capable of remedy by junction of another; that is, by substituting two women in the place of one woman, and the defect of memory being existence of a doubt, namely, retaliation or *hudud* thus supplied, there remains only the doubt of substitution; whence it is that their testimony is not admitted in any matter liable to drop from the existence of a doubt, retaliation or *hudud* in opposition to marriage, and so forth, as those may be proved notwithstanding a doubt, whence the testimony of women is admitted in those instances".

Thus not accepting the evidence of women may at the most be restricted to the offences of *hudud.* But in *tazirat* and other matters, the evidence of women is acceptable and the court is authorised that if it is satisfied it may award *tazir* on the evidence of a woman specially when it is corroborated. The court is also authorised that if the prescribed *quantum* of evidence is not available in civil, fiscal and personal matters, it may decide on any available evidence which, in its opinion, is authentic and sufficient for the proof of a claim or a part thereof. So far the evidence of women in the offences of *hudud is* concerned, it is acceptable but the accused shall not be punished with *hadd* but shall be punished with *tazir.*

It is important to mention here that there is no expressed or implied text of the Holy Quran and the *Sunnah* of the Holy Prophet which prohibits the acceptability of the evidence of a woman and except for documentation of certain monetary transactions no discrimination has been made in the evidence of a man and a woman. Thus, the evidence of a woman is basically acceptable in all matters if her evidence is otherwise authentic as that of a man.

As regard the evidence of two women being equal to the evidence of one man in documentation of certain monetary transaction as mentioned in verse 2:282, it is to be pointed out that even in this case the witness is only one woman the second is only to remind her if the first makes an error. Moreover in matters of *liar* the evidence of a woman has been equated to the evidence of a man by the Holy Quran (verses 24:6-9). It is also necessary to mention here that the Holy Prophet (Pbuh) said to a delegation of women "Is the evidence of one male not equal to the evidence of two women?" They said, "yes". According to Imam Bukhari this *hadith* is in respect of verse 2:282 in which the evidence of one man is equal to the evidence of two women for the proof of the document of certain monetary transactions.

It is pertinent to mention here that though *Shariah* doctrine is all-embracing, Islamic legal practice has always recognised the larger jurisdiction of the courts than that has been prescribed. It is due to the fact that sometimes the courts, while adopting the prescribed procedure of evidence, don't prove a satisfactory organ for the administration of justice in all respects, particularly as regard criminal, land and commercial law. It is for this reason that special courts were constituted even in the period of *Khulafa al-Rashidun,* known as *Mazalim* courts, which were later on developed and organised in the period of Banu Abbasides.

These courts were not strictly bound to follow the prescribed procedure and evidence and were authorised to decide on any evidence which, in their opinion, was authentic. Ibn Al-Qayyim is also of the opinion that the claimant or complainant is obliged to produce the prescribed *quantum* of evidence in support of his claim or complaint, but the courts are not obliged to decide only on the prescribed *quantum* of evidence; they may decide on any other available evidence, which, in their opinion, is authentic and sufficient. Thus the testimony of a woman is acceptable if, according to the court, she is credible and her testimony is authentic and sufficient. The testimony of a woman which is based on sight and hearing is acceptable in any matter. Moreover according to the majority of the jurists the single evidence of a woman as expert is admissible and shall be based for the decision of any disputed matter.

Proof of Rape: According to some jurists if a woman was subjected to *zina* by force whether through abduction or otherwise her single testimony as victim will be sufficient proof for the offence of the offender and he shall be liable to *hadd of zina* or any other grave punishment and she shall not be punished at all. It is based on the *hadith* of the Holy Prophet related on the authority of Wail Ibn Hajar who stated that a woman was going to mosque for her morning prayer in the period of the Holy Prophet. While she was on the way in darkness that a person met her and made sexual intercourse with her forcibly and then ran away.

She was there when a person came to her and she told him the incident. He went in search of the culprit. Meanwhile some other persons came to her and she related the incident to them. They also went in search of the actual culprit. On the way they met the first man who was also searching the actual culprit but was in terrible condition. They caught him and brought him to the woman. She confirmed that he is the same person who committed sexual intercourse with her forcibly. Then they all came to the Holy Prophet. The Holy Prophet said to him, "Have you committed this offence". He remained silent. The woman admitted before the Holy Prophet that this is the same person who made illicit sexual intercourse with her. The Holy Prophet ordered to stone him to death". However such testimony must be supported with other corroborations failing which the accused shall not be punished with *hadd.*

A witness in *hudud* and *qisas* must possess the power of seeing and faculty of speaking. Thus the evidence of a blind person and a deaf and dumb person is not admissible in *hudud* and *qisas.* This is the view of Imam Abu Hanifa. But according to Imam Malik, Imam Shafii and Imam Ahmad, the evidence of a dumb and deaf is acceptable in *hudud and qisas* if he can write his evidence or his signs are intelligible. The evidence of a deaf and dumb person, is however, acceptable in other matters if he or she can write his or her evidence before a competent court. Similarly the evidence of a blind person is admissible in matters concerning hearing.

Blood Relations: The majority of the jurists with the exception of some Shafii argue that the testimony of the major and minor branches of families for each other is not admissible. It is based on the *hadith* of the Holy Prophet (Pbuh) who said, "The testimony of a treacherous man and a treacherous woman is not admissible not of a man on whom *hadd* of *qadhf* has been implemented, not of a man who has enmity with his brother, not a slave who attributes his freedom to another person, not of the servant of a family for the members of that family.

According to a narration from Imam Ahmad the testimony of the major and minor branches of families like father for son or son for father is admissible in marriage, divorce, *qisas* and property if they are *adils* (bearing good character). This is the opinion of Hadrat 'Umar and it has been related from Qadi Shurai and this was adopted by 'Umar bin Abdul Aziz, Abu Thawr and Muzani.

This view is supported by verse IV: 135 which is reproduced as under:

> "O ye who believe! Be ye staunch injustice, witnesses for Allah, even though it be against yourselves or (your) parents or (your) kindred."

Abu 'Ubaidah said, "According to Hadrat 'Umar the testimony of father for his son, son for his father, and brother for his brother is admissible provided they are *adils* (bearing good character).

There are not two opinions of 'Umar in this matter. He has only rejected such testimony when they are blamed and are *ghair adils*".

Ibn al-Qayyim writes, "There is nothing in the verses of the Holy Quran which relate to the testimony that reject the testimony of near relatives for each other. It is supported by the judgements of Hadrat Ali, Qadi Shurai, 'Umar Ibn Abdul Aziz and Abu Bakr Ibn Muhammad bin Amr Ibn Hazm. It is based on the principle of *Shariah* that all Muslims are *adils* (bearing good character).

Actually such testimonies became doubtful when the people started giving up the requirements of justice and they started giving preference to the relations than to justice. But this does not mean that it is an established rule of judiciary in Shariah. However, if the testimony of a relative is based on the relationship and not on justice, his testimony will not be admissible. This is left to the *Qadi* to look into the testimony of the relatives and differentiate between the one based on justice and the one based on relation and accept the first and reject the second."

Ibn Al-Qayyim has related that a woman produced two witness in the court of Qadi Shurai; one was her father and the other was her husband. The opponent party said to Qadi Shurai: "How do you accept their testimony, one is her father and the other is her husband" Qadi Shurai said, "Is there anything which denotes the inadmissibility of their testimony? If not, then every Muslim is *adil* (just) and his testimony is admissible".

According to some Malikis if a father and his son testified in a case they will be considered one witness. But according to Sahnun, Muttarif, Ibn Al-Farhun and Ibn-e-Asim among Malikis they will be considered two witnesses.

According to Abu Hanifa, Malik and the preferred view of Ahmad the testimony of spouses for or against each other is not admissible. But according to Shafii it is admissible.

Enmity: The majority of the jurists agree that enmity between a witness and a party to a case arising out of worldly matters disqualifies that witness. Enmity by reason of matter involving the rights of Allah does not disqualify a witness if he possesses the quality of *adl* (justness or fairness). This is why the testimony of a Muslim for or against a non-Muslim is admissible.

Imam Abu Hanifa and the earlier Hanafis were in favour of the admissibility of the testimony of a witness who is in enmity with the party to a case provided he is *adil* (just or fair). But the later Hanafis changed this view and adopted the view that the testimony of a witness who is in enmity with a party in not admissible. Like other jurists they based their view on a *hadith* related on the authority of Amr Ibn Shuaib who related from his father and grandfather that Holy Prophet said, "The testimony of a treacherous man or woman is not lawful nor of a man having enmity with his brother". The Holy Prophet has also rejected the testimony of a servant of a family for the members of that family. *Majalla* states, "It is a condition that there must not be enmity as regards temporal things between the witness and the person against whom evidence is given.

"Enmity of worldly nature is known by custom".

According to Zahiris only such enmity disqualifies a witness which is suspicious and if the testimony is not suspicious and the witness is just, it is admissible. They base their view on the following verse of the Holy Quran:

> "O ye who believe! Be steadfast witnesses for Allah in equity, and let not hatred of any people seduce you that ye deal not justly. Deal justly, that is nearer to your duty. Observe your duty to Allah. Lo! Allah is informed of what ye do."

So this verse clearly shows that Allah has ordered to be just with the enemies and this qualifies a witness to testify for or against an enemy if he is just person.

Suspicion: A claim of suspicion exists when there is any kind of relationship between the witness and one of the parties which suggests suspicion or a personal interest that may be advanced by the witness through his testimony.

This is the opinion of all jurists except Zahiris and is based on the following verse of the Holy Quran:

> "Be not averse to writing down (the contract whether it be small or great, with (record of) the term thereof. That is more equitable in the sight of Allah and more sure for testimony, and the best way of *avoiding doubt* between you.

Among the testimonies which are not admissible on this base include the testimony of the partners for each other, the testimony of a master for a slave or vice versa, the testimony of an agent for his client, the testimony of friend for friend etc.

It is pertinent to reproduce section 1700 of *Majallatul Ahkam al Adliyya:* "As regards the giving of evidence it is a condition that there be no cause arising from the avoidance of loss or the accruing of gain, i.e., the avoidance of harm or the production of benefit.

> "Therefore, the giving of evidence of ancestor for descendant or descendant for ancestor, i.e., the evidence of father and grandfather and mother and grandmother on behalf of children and grandchildren, and also of children and grandchildren on behalf of father and grandfather and mother and grandmother, and also of one spouse for the other, is not admitted."
>
> "But except these, the evidence of relatives is admissible on behalf of one another."

> "Likewise, the evidence of a man who subsists on the food of someone, and of a person employed privately on hire, is not admissible. But the evidence of fellow servants on behalf of one another is received."

Likewise, the evidence of partners for one another in respect of partnership, property, and of a surety for the payment of the thing, for which he was surely, by the principal are not admissible. But in other matters their evidence on behalf of one anotheris admissible."

False Accusation of Adultery: All the jurists concur that the testimony of the person who accuses another person of committing adultery and then fails to produce four witnesses on his accusation and is punished with *hadd qadhf* is not admissible. This is based on the following verses of the Holy Quran:

> "As for those persons who charge chaste women with false accusation but do not produce four witnesses, flog them with eighty stripes and never accept their evidence afterwards, for they themselves are transgressors, except those who repent and reform themselves: Allah is forgiving and merciful".

There is difference of opinion among the jurists as to whether his testimony after repentance is admissible or not. One group says that this sentence is related only to the last command. That is, a person who repents and mends his ways, will no longer be a sinner in the sight of Allah and the common Muslims, but the first two commands will remain effective, i.e., the sentence will be enforced on him and his evidence will never be accepted in future. To this group belong eminent jurists like Qadi Shurai, Said Ibn Musayyab, Said bin Zubair, Hasan Basri, Ibrahim Nakhai, Ibn Sirin, Makhul, Abdur Rahman ibn Zaid, Abu Hanifa, Abu Yusuf, Zufar, Muhammad, Sufyan Thauri, and Hasan bin Saleh.

The other group says that the clause ".... except those who repent...." is not related to the first command but is related to the other two. That is, after repentance, not only will be evidence of the offender who has been punished for *qadhf* be accepted, but he will also not be regarded as a sinner. This group comprises jurists of the status of Ata', Taus, Mujahid, Shabi, Qasim bin Muhammad, Salim, Zuhri, Ikrima, 'Umar Ibn Abdul Aziz, Ibn Nujai, Suleiman Ibn Yasir, Masruq, Dahhak, Malik Ibn Anas, Uthman al-Batti, Laith Ibn Said, Shafii, Ahmad Ibn Hanbal and Ibn Jarir Tabari.

Among other arguments, these scholars cite the verdict of Hadrat 'Umar which he gave in the case of Mughira Ibn Shuba. For, according to some traditions, after enforcing the punishment, Hadrat 'Umar said to Abu Bakra and his two companions: "If you repent (or confess your lie), I shall accept your evidence in future, otherwise not". His companions confessed not Abu Bakra.

Prima facie, it appears to be a strong argument. But from the details given above of Mughira Ibn Shuba's case, it would become obvious that it is not correct to cite this precedent in support of this view. For in that case, there was complete unanimity as far as the act (of sexual intercourse) was concerned and Mughira Ibn Shuba himself did not deny it.

The point of dispute was the identity of the woman. Mughirah said that she was his own wife, whom the accusers had mistaken for Umm-Jamil. Then the wife of Mughira and Umm Jamil resembled with each other to a degree that from the distance and in the kind of light that they were seen, the former could be mistaken for the latter. But the circumstantial evidence was wholly in favour of Mughira Ibn Shuba, and a witness of the case also had admitted that the woman was not clearly visible. That is why Hadrat 'Umar decided the case in favour of Mughira Ibn Shuba, and after punishing Abu Bakra, said the words as mentioned in the above quoted tradition. This clearly shows that the real intention of Hadrat 'Umar was to impress on the accusers that they should confess that they had given way to undue suspicions and that they should repent of accusing people on the basis of such suspicions in future, otherwise their evidence would never be accepted.

From this it cannot be concluded that in the eyes of Hadrat 'Umar the evidence of a person whose falsehood had been established, could become acceptable just after he had repented. The truth is that in this matter the view of the former group is more sound. None except Allah can know whether a person has repented sincerely or not. If a person repents before us, we may not consider him as a transgressor afterwards, but once his falsehood has been established, we cannot afford to trust him in future simply because he has uttered repentance. Moreover, the words in the text themselves indicate that".... except those who repent ...." is related only to "they themselves are transgressors".

The reason is that the first two things, in the sentence "....flog them with eighty stripes, and never accept their evidence afterwards ...." have been given in the imperative form, while the third thing".... they themselves are transgressors...." is a predicate. Then the clause".... except those who repent ...." just after the predicate and not to the two imperative sentences. Nevertheless, if it is conceded that the exception is not confined to the last sentence, one does not understand why it should be made to apply to "never accept their evidence" only and not extended to "flog them with eighty stripes" also.

Allama Ali Marghinani Hanafi writes, "the testimony of a person that has been punished for slander is inadmissible, even though he should afterwards have repented; because God has said in the Quran".... But as to those who accuse married persons of whoredom and produce not four witnesses of the fact, scourge them with eighty stripes, and receive not their testimony forever for such are infamous prevaricators, excepting those who shall afterwards repent...." The rejection of his evidence, moreover, is included as a part of the punishment prescribed for the crime, as this tends to prevent the commission of it in future; and as the rejection of the evidence is a part of the punishment, this effect must evidently remain after his repentance, on the same principle as the punishment itself is not remitted although he repents, it is otherwise with respect to a person punished for any other crime; for the evidence of such a person is admissible after repentance, since the rejection of it, in regard to him, proceeded from the stigma attached to his offence, which is done away by repentance.

According to Shafii, the evidence of a person punished for slander is admissible, provided he has afterwards repented because God, in enjoining the rejection of the evidence of such, has particularly excepted penitents. Our doctors, on the other hand argue that the exception in the divine ordinance relates to that part of it which declares slanderers to be infamous prevaricators, and not to that part which declares them to be incompetent as witnesses; penitence, therefore removes the stigma from the character of such a person, but does not restore his competency to give evidence.

If an infidel, who had suffered punishment for slander, and afterwards becomes a Muslim, his evidence is then admissible; for although, on account of the said punishment, he had lost the degree in which he was before qualified to give evidence (that is, in all matters that related to his own sect), yet by his conversion to the *Musalman* faith he acquires a new competency in regard to evidence (namely, competency to give evidence relative to *Musalmans),* which he did not possess before and which is not affected by any matter that happened prior to the circumstance which gave birth to it.

It is otherwise with respect to a slave, who having suffered punishment for slander, afterwards becomes free; for his testimony is not admissible after emancipation; because in his former condition of slavery he did not possess, in any degree, ability to give evidence, and consequently the punishment was incomplete, since it was impossible to subject him to any greater degree of discredit than what was before imposed on him; the credit, therefore, which he would otherwise have acquired afterwards in virtue of his emancipation, if taken from in order to complete the prescribed punishment.

Quantum of Evidence: The Holy Quran has prescribed the number of witnesses for the proof of *zina,* document of certain monetary transactions, will and divorce. The relevant verses are as under:

a. "O ye who believe! when ye contract a debt for a fixed term, record it in writing. And call to witness, from among your men, two witnesses. And if two men be not available, then one man and two women, of such as ye approve as witnesses, so that if the one make error the other will remind her".

b. "And for those of your women who are guilty of lewdness, call to witness four of you against them".

c. "And those who accuse chaste women but bring not four witnesses, whip them eighty strokes".

d. "Then, when they have reached their term, take them back in kindness or part from them in kindness, and call to witness two just men among you, and keep your testimony upright for Allah."

e. "O ye who believe! Let there be witness between you when death draweth nigh unto one of you, at the time of bequest—two witnesses, just men from among you, or two others not among you in case you are compaigning in the land and the calamity of death befall you".

In other than the above mentioned matters no number has been prescribed for their proof. It has been related that Holy Prophet (Pbuh) decided on the evidence of one witness alongwith the oath of the plaintiff.

The Holy Prophet has also considered one witness sufficient provided he or she is just. It has been related that once the Holy Prophet purchased a horse from a bedouin. Later the bedouin denied the purchase and asked the Holy Prophet to produce evidence. The Prophet said, "I have purchased it from you but there was no witness". On this Khuzaima Ibn Thabit, who was present there, said, "I am your witness". The Holy Prophet said, to Khuzaima, "How you are witness?" Khuzaima said, "Because I believe in your truthfulness". The Holy Prophet declared his evidence equivalent to the evidence of two persons. Interpreting this *hadith,* Abu Daud argues that if a judge is aware of the truthfulness of a witness, he can decide on his evidence even if he is the single witness in that case.

It has been related by Bukhari that the sons of Shuaib came to the court of Marwan and claimed that the two houses alongwith a drawing room be given to them because these have been given to Suhaib by the Holy Prophet. Marwan said to them, "Who will testify to that". They said, "Abdullah Ibn 'Umar". So Abdullah Ibn 'Umar came and testified that these two houses alongwith the drawing-room have been given to Suhaib by the Holy Prophet. This Marwan decreed in their favour on the single evidence of Abdullah Ibn Umar.

It has been related that the Holy Prophet (Pbuh) accepted the evidence of one woman in suckling and birth of the child.

The Holy Prophet has relied upon circumstantial evidence in many cases.

The jurists have prescribed *quantum* of evidence for different crimes and rights. Al-Nawawi, while describing the *quantum* of evidence, writes, "In order to prove the crime to *zina* four male witnesses must be produced, and two to prove the culprit's confession, though in this latter case also one jurist considers that four are necessary. Real property claims, and contracts having consequences that are merely pecuniary, such as sale, cancellation by consent, transfer of debts due to one, and security, as well as the rights resulting form these contracts, such as right of opinion, or a term for payment, may all be proved by the testimony of two male witnesses, or of one male witness and two women.

Two male witnesses are rigorously required in all other contested cases, whether it be a matter of non-remissible penalties, except that for *zina,* or of remissible ones, or of some dispute as to an act of private life ordinarily effected before men and in their sight, such as marriage, repudiation, return to conjugal union, conversion, apostasy, notorious misconduct, irreproachability, death, insolvency, appointment of an agent, testamentary disposition, and the testimony which two witnesses have made a certain deposition. On the other hand, what is specially liable to come under the observation of women, and in general, facts which do not usually take place in the presence and in the sight of men, such as the existence of virginity, accouchment, menstruation, suckling, redhibitory defects in women and in parts of the body usually covered, are proved by the evidence of four women. Matters other than *hudud* and *qisas* are also proved with one male witness and the oath of the plaintiff.

According to Imam Abu Hanifa the evidence of only one woman is sufficient in matters which are proved with the evidence of the women only.

But if the prescribed evidence is not available in a case and lesser authentic evidence is available, the evidence will be accepted and the accused will be punished with *tazir* or the defendant will be obliged for the restoration of the right accordingly.

The number of witnesses depends upon the types of cases. The determination of truth depends upon the trustworthiness of witnesses and not upon their number. Ibn Taimiyya says that the Holy Quran makes no mention of the testimony of two males or one male and two females, concerning the procedure by which a judge arrives at his decision, and that the Holy Quran merely mentions this procedure in connection with a person's endeavour to safeguard his rights. The Holy Quran has only fixed number of witnesses for the proof of *zina,* divorce, will and documentation of certain monetary transactions and has not fixed number of witnesses for the proof of any other crime or right.

If the number of witnesses in case of adultery is less than four then the witnesses will be guilty of defamation and *hadd* of *qadhf will* be implemented on them. This is the opinion of Imam Abu Hanifa, Imam Malik, some Shafii's, some Hanbalis and Zaidis and this is based on verse 24:4 which is reproduced as under: "and those who accuse honourable women but bring not four witnesses scourge them (with) eighty stripes".

This view is also supported by the judgement of Hadrat 'Umar about Mughira Ibn Shuba about whom Abu Bakra, Nafi' and Shibli ibn Mabad testified that he (Mughira) had committed adultery with Umm Jamil but Zaid said that the woman was not clearly visible and that he could not say definitely whether she was Umm Jamil or not. Moreover he had only seen that the legs of a woman were lying on his shoulders and he has seen not more than that. On this Hadrat 'Umar released Mughira and implemented *hadd* of *qadhf* on Abu Bakra, Nafi and Shibl.

But according to Zahiris, some Shafi is and some Hanbalis, the witness or witnesses will in no case be punished with *hadd* of *qadhf* whether the number of the witnesses is less than four, or their testimony differs from one another or they are not able to prove the guilt. They say that they come as witnesses and not as complainants (accusers) an the Holy Quran and *Sunnah* have clearly differentiated between the accuser (complainant) and the witness. Moreover if the witnesses are to be punished like this, nobody will come forward as a witness in cases of adultery, for nobody can be certain that there will be three more who will testify and that all the four will be unanimous in their testimony.

A critical study of the case of Mughira Ibn Shuba, in which Hadrat 'Umar punished Abu Bakra and the other two eyewitnesses on the charge of false accusation, shows that this precedent is not applicable to every case where the crime is not proved by the prescribed testimony.It is, therefore, pertinent to reproduce the facts of this case as explained by Ibn al-Arabi in *Ahkamal-Quran:* "The facts of the case are that Mughira Ibn Shuba, the governor of Basrah, did not have good relations with Abu Bakra, whose house was opposite to his house across the same street. One day the windows of the two houses were opened by a strong current of wind. When Abu Bakra got up to close his window, he saw, through the opposite window across the street, Mughira in a state of sexual intercourse. He asked three of his friends (Nafi' bin Kalada, Zaid and Shibl bin Mabad) who were also sitting with him to stand up and witness what Mughira was doing. The friends asked him who was the woman. Abu Bakra said that she was Umm Jamil. The next day a complaint to this effect was sent to Hadrat 'Umar, who immediately suspended Mughira and appointed Abu Musa Al-Ashari as Governor of Basrah. Mughira along with the witnesses was called to Medina. When they were asked about the case, Abu Bakra said that they had seen Mughira actually committing sexual intercourse with Umm Jamil, but Zaid said that the woman was not clearly visible and that he could not say definitely whether she was Umm Jamil or not.

During cross-examination, Mughira proved that they could not have seen the woman distinctly from the place where they were standing. He also proved that there was a close resemblance between his wife and Umm Jamil. Besides this, circumstantial evidence also showed that during the caliphate of Hadrat 'Umar, the governor of a province could not have committed this crime in his official residence, especially when his wife was also living with him. Thus the supposition of Abu Bakra and his companions that Mughira was having sexual intercourse with Umm Jamil, instead of his own wife was nothing but a misplaced suspicion. It was for this reason that Hadrat 'Umar not only acquitted the accused but also punished Abu Bakra, Nafi' and Shibl as slanderers. It is obvious that this isolated decision was based on the specific circumstances of the case and not on the principle that the witnesses must be punished when they are not able to prove the charge by their evidence".

It is important to explain that *zina* in Islamic criminal Law means wilful sexual intercourse between a man and a woman without being validly married or suspected to be married to each other in a way that the male part of the man penetrates in the female part of the woman. Thus the accuser and the witness of *zina* liable for *hadd must* have to mention in their accusation and evidence that they have seen the accused making intercourse and the male part of the man has penetrated in the female part of the woman. If a person accused another person of less than that like accusing him of kissing a woman, sitting with a woman in a doubtful place, travelling with the woman and keeping her with himself even at night, lying with a woman on one bed — it will not be considered accusation of *zina* liable for *hadd* for which four witnesses are required. And if it was proved the accused will be punished with *tazir* and whether it was proved or not the accuser will not be punished.

Conditions for the Evidence:

(i) The evidence must be in conformity with the claim/complaint in respect to the subject matter. But any difference between evidence and the claim/ complaint which can be reconciled does not render the evidence inadmissible. The evidence against a fact which is perceptible or generally admitted is not admissible.

(ii) *Testimony to be Relevant:* The testimony must be in respect of the facts in issue and of such other facts which are relevant to the facts in issue and of no other fact.

(iii) *The Forum:* Imam Malik, Imam Abu Hanifa, and Imam Ahmad Ibn Hanbal maintain that the witnesses to adultery must present their testimony at the same legal session, while Imam Shafii finds testimony presented at separate sessions acceptable. According to the view of the majority when the hearing is concluded, the absent witness is not allowed thereafter to present his testimony, and the accuser who does not have all four witnesses to support his claim of *zina* is considered a defamer. Imam Malik and Imam Abu Hanifa further opined that all witnesses must be present when the testimony of each one of them begins.

(iv) *Prior Claim:* Prior to giving evidence in offences which relate to the rights of human beings like *Qisas, Diyat, Hadd of Qadhf, Hadd of Saraqa* etc., as well as the civil rights there must be a claim from victim or his heirs or his guardians in the court. In this connection *Majalla* states "As regards the giving of evidence *(Shahadah)* in private actions, it is a condition that there should be a claim in court first".

If there is no prior claim in such offences and rights, it would be presumed that the victim or his heirs might have pardoned the offender and thus no evidence is then required. Moreover it is based on the tradition of the Holy Prophet (Pbuh) who said, "(In later period) telling a lie will spread among the people and a person will take oath before he is required to do so. And a person will give evidence before he is summoned for that".

This is the opinion of Imam Abu Hanifa, Imam Shafii and Imam Ahmad, but according to some Malikis no prior claim is required for the evidence in offence and rights and any offence or right can be proved by the evidence without prior claim in the court for that.

The jurists, however, concur that no prior claim is necessary in the offence which relate to the rights of Allah. It is based on the reasoning that it is the duty of every Muslim to protect the rights of Allah and whenever he witnesses an offence he has to inform the Qadi of that to enable him to implement its punishment and protect the rights of Allah and establish peace in the society.

The jurists differ whether the presence of victim is necessary in a theft case liable for *hadd* or not. According to Ibn Abi Laila it is not required and the evidence, if authentic, will be accepted like that of adultery because both are the rights of Allah. But according to Imam Shafii if the theft is proved by the confession of the offender then the presence of the victim is not required. And if the theft is proved by the evidence then the presence of the victim or his agent is necessary because offence is based on the complainant's complaint and if he is not present evidence cannot be considered authentic.

But according to Imam Abu Hanifa the presence of the victim is necessary whether the theft is proved by the confession of the offender or by the evidence of the witnesses because complaint is a condition in the offence which relates to the rights of human beings and this is considered completed when the victim is present.

(v) *The Evidence must be before a Qadi in the Court:* It is necessary for the evidence that it should be given before a Qadi and as such the evidence given outside the court is not acceptable.

(vi) *The Evidence must be Conclusive:* In order to become a base for the judgement the first condition that evidence must satisfy is that it must be conclusive. This means that the evidence must clearly and explicitly prove the occurrence of the criminal act or violation of a right without any need of explanation or interpretation. The fundamental principle on which it is based is that certainty can only be negated by another certainty. And since every man is inherently innocent, only clear and convincing evidence can overcome that presumption. On this Imam Abu Hanifa, Imam Shafii, Imam Malik and Imam Ahmad Ibn Hanbal all concur. Thus, for example, if the act in question is adultery, the testimony of every witness must clearly and explicitly prove the act of adultery. The criminal act must be described explicitly by each witness so as to substantiate each element. Applying these rules, 'Umar Ibn al-Khattab imposed the *hadd* penalty for defamation on three witnesses who testified against a person accused of adultery when the testimony of the fourth witness clearly failed to corroborate theirs. The witnesses in a contract must be unanimous in respect of the terms of the contract.

In order to achieve conclusiveness in evidence, the time and place of the crime or the right in dispute must be specified, and must be consistent with the other evidence accrued by the judge pertaining to the circumstances of the crime or the right in dispute. This is also true of evidence obtained through confession. As a result of this condition, the judge in Islamic law *(Shariah)* has the authority to evaluate the evidence, despite the principle of restricting the evidence that can be considered. The principle of restriction generally required the judge to render a decision, not whenever some of the evidence would be sufficient, but rather when he believes all the evidence clearly and convincingly proves the commission of the crime or violation of the right. The burden of proof is consistent with the Prophetic *hadith:* "Doubt nullifies *hudud*", *i.e. hadd* punishment will not be imposed in case of doubt, and conflicting evidence precludes a *hadd* punishment. For example proof of virginity is a conclusive defence even when the witnesses testify to adultery, or if the accused confesses. It is essential, therefore, that the judge should strictly and conscientiously evaluate the evidence.

Moreover, the evidence must remain conclusive until the execution of punishment in criminal matters. If the evidence loses its conclusiveness during any stage of the trial prior to sentencing, as when the witness changes his testimony and deprives it of its clear and convincing quality, then neither the evidence nor verdict based thereon is valid. The same is true when the evidence loses its conclusive quality after sentencing but before execution. If the witness changes his testimony, or if new facts not known to the judge during sentencing come to light which might have cast doubt on the testimony of witnesses then the evidence lacks credibility and the verdict must be reversed. If punishment has been imposed, it must cease.

(vii) *The Evidence not to be delayed:* It is a condition that the presentation of evidence should not be delayed. Some jurists have raised the issue of delay of evidence as equivalent to doubtful evidence which is sufficient to preclude punishment for *hudud* crimes.

Islamic jurists have approached this problem from four distinct perspectives. The first, as represented by Muhammad ibn al-Hasan, considers testimony inadmissible if the witness fails to come forward and submit his testimony within a specified period of time. This applies to all *hudud* crimes. Confessions are always admissible except of the crime of drinking. The second view also considers testimony inadmissible when it is delayed and applies to all *hudud crimes.* However, a confession is never nullified in crime of *hudud,* including drinking, because delay does not affect the validity of the confession. The third view holds that any delay in the presentation of the confession and testimony creates sufficient doubt so as to invalidate the evidence in *hudud* crimes. As for other crimes and rights the evidence can be used irrespective of time.

These three view-points are based on the theory that where the rights of God are affected, testimony is the providence of God. Concealment is a necessary element in crimes which predominantly violate the rights of God. Therefore, if the witness hesitates before the two commands of God not to withhold testimony in order to prevent corruption in society and supply the *hudud* of God, and to protect believers by preventing the spread of evil, then this testimony becomes suspect. Although he may hesitate because of just concern for those who inadvertently fall into disobedience, it creates the suspicion that behind his motivation lie ulterior motives whose source is hatred or enmity. 'Umar Ibn al-Khattab has stated: "Those who testify to a *hadd* not at the time of its occurrence testify out of hatred and their testimony is invalid." Thus, such testimony is inadmissible if it is suspected of being motivated by hatred. And while delay of testimony in cases involving the rights of men does not affect its admissibility, such delay in cases of crimes of *hudud* leads to the nullification of delayed testimony because of the principle of invalidating conviction of *hadd* penalty may not be inflicted even though restoring the stolen possession to the rightful owner is permissible.

In addition, jurists who maintain that delay of confession casts doubt on the *hadd* of drinking reflect the consensus that the *hadd* is proved only when the drunkard is caught with smelling of wine. Obviously delay necessarily *attenuates* all signs of intoxication. Abdullah Ibn Masud made it a condition of proving drunkenness that the culprit be brought to him while drunk.

Those who consider that a delayed confession nullifies all *hudud* penalties except defamation, deterrence is impossible unless punishment is imposed at the time of the crime or as quickly thereafter as possible. In addition, delay of confession encourages repentance, which according to some jurists, constitutes grounds for repeal of the *hadd* punishment. As for the *hadd* of defamation unaffected by delay in testimony or confession because defamation involves the rights of men. This right encompasses the protection of man's honour and the exoneration from the accusation of adultery. This can be achieved only by inflicting the penalties on the defamers.

Finally, the fourth view expressed by many jurists, including Imam Malik, Imam Shafii and Imam Ahmad Ibn Hanbal, suggests that delay of testimony or confession does not necessarily cast doubt on the evidence. Proponents of this view claim that delay of confession does not directly affect any right because proof by testimony or confession is based on their inherent credibility, which is a question determined by the judge. Thus testimony or confession cannon be nullified by mere presumption but is left to the judge to determine its credibility. Islamic jurists have expressed three views concerning Imam Abu Hanifa's analysis of the extent of the delay required to invalidate the evidence or render it doubtful. First, recognizing that societies differ, it is left to the discretion of the judge to determine the proper extent according to his knowledge of the circumstances and customs of the people. The second view is that the period of limitations is six months. This last view is that of Abu Yusuf based on the authority of Abu Hanifa. These periods of limitation apply to all *hudud* crimes, except drinking, where delay is determined by the absence of the smell of alcohol.

It is important to note that causing doubt does not include excuse acceptable to the judge, such as travel, sickness, distance, and mental distress due to threats and terror, although the effect of such factors is for the judge's evaluation. According to the Hanafis and some of the Shafii's, the trial judge must verify the evidence himself. Generally the trial judge is not permitted to consider evidence sent to him by another judge, since the trial judge cannot make a personal evaluation in the light of the totality of evidence. This would constitute a form of *transmitted testimony* (hearsay) which is inadmissible in *hudud* and in most other crimes. However, Imam

Malik allows judges to render judgement on the basis of transmitted testimony in *hudud* and other crimes. Similarly, Imam Ahmad bin Hanbal admits this type of evidence, but only in *hudud* crimes and in some *qisas* crimes.

In any event all schools of jurisprudence agree that the judge must be convinced on the basis of the evidence submitted during the criminal proceedings. The fact that the majority of jurists restrict criminal evidence to testimony and confession does not mean that the judge is constrained to impose punishment once the legal elements of proof have been established, for the judge still has the authority to evaluate the persuasiveness of the evidence. He may discard the testimony of witnesses if he is not convinced of its validity, credibility or reliability and he may reject confessions if they are inconsistent with the facts revealed during the proceedings.

There is, however, disagreement among jurists as to inflicting the *hadd* penalty for defamation where the judge rejects the testimony of a witness due to conflict with the testimony of other witnesses or other substantive differences. Some believe in applying a *hadd* punishment to the witness; others do not, and a third group leaves the matter to the judge's discretion. In other words, if there is perjury or false testimony it is a matter for the discretion of the judge.

So according to Imam Abu Hanifa the delay in testimony without any reasonable ground renders it doubtful which removes *hadd* punishment from the accused except in the matter of *hadd* of *qadhf* where delay in testimony is not effective. However, Ibn Abi Laila among the Hanafis is of the view that delay both in testimony as well as confession renders them inadmissible. But according to Imam Abu Hanifa delay in testimony is not effective if it is based on a reasonable ground like long distance from the court, serious illness etc.

But according to Imam Malik, Imam Shafii, Zaidi Shia and one of the two views of Imam Ahmad the delay in testimony does not render it inadmissible and the delayed testimony is sufficient proof for even *hadd* punishment if it is otherwise authentic. Imam Ahmad in one opinion agrees with the opinion of Imam Abu Hanifa.

Tazkiya al-Shuhud: *Tazkiya al-Shuhud* means the mode of enquiry adopted by a court to satisfy itself whether a witness/witnesses is/are *adil* or not. According to Imam Abu Hanifa *tazkiya al-Shuhud* is not required except in *hudud* and *qisas.* But according to Imam Al-Shafii if the court is otherwise satisfied of the witness or witnesses as being *adil* or *adils* then *tazkiya al-Shuhud* is not required in any case.

The mode of *tazkiya al-Shuhud* is that if court is not satisfied of a witness or witnesses as to being *adil* or *adils,* it shall through a confidential letter addressed to two *muzakkis* seek their opinions regarding the witness/witnesses as to his/her or their being *adil* or *adils* or not. The aforesaid letter shall contain the names of the parties to the case, names of the witnesses and their such other particulars to identify them and the nature of the case. This letter shall be delivered in a sealed cover to the *muzakkis* through the representatives of the court and the *muzakkis* shall, in answer to the letter, express their opinions in writing about the witness or witnesses as to whether he or they is or are *adil* or *adils* or not. The court may call two *muzakkir* to the court and ask them before the court in the presence of the witnesses as to whether the witness or witnesses is or are *adil* and *adils* or not.

If one of the *muzakkis* declares a witness *adil* and the other declares him *ghair-adil,* the court may, if it deems fit in the circumstances of the case, decide on the opinion of the one who has objected on the credibility of the witness.

A *Muzakki* must be an *adil,* sane, adult Muslim having full knowledge about the background of the witness or witnesses about whom he has been asked by the court to give information as to his, her or their being *adil* or *adils* or not. However, if a witness is not Muslim the *muzakkis* may be non-Muslims and the credibility will be according to their religion or faith.

Shahadah ala al-Shahada: If a real witness in a case due to being dead or seriously ill or is on a long distance from the court or, by any other sound reason, can't appear before the court, he can direct another person to give his evidence before the court. But the real witness must tell the second witness that he has witnessed such and such fact and authorise him to give his evidence before the court. The seconded witness must have to identify the original witness before the court by stating his name and other particulars. According to Imam Al-Shafii and Imam Abu Hanifa *shahadah ala al-Shahada* is admissible in every case except in *hudud* and *qisas."*

Retraction from Testimony: Retraction from the testimony in matters related to the rights of individuals is not admissible. But retraction from evidence in *hudud is* admissible at any stage even during the execution of the punishment, and after retraction the *hadd* punishment is nullified. If a witness retracts his evidence in a civil matter before the announcement of the judgement, the evidence stands revoked and the court shall not make it a ground for its judgement.

But the witness will, however, be liable to *tazir* and if she retracts after the judgement, he will be liable for the right created therein. If a witness in a case of *zina,* retracts his evidence prior to the announcement of the judgement or prior to the execution of the punishment, he shall be liable to *hadd* of *qadhf.* If the witnesses in the case of *qisas, zina* liable to *hadd,* apostasy, theft liable to *hadd* retract their evidence after the execution of the punishment and declare that they had intentionally given false evidence, they shall be liable to the punishment as was given to the executed person and if they say that they had made mistake, they will be liable to *diyat,* compensation, or *ta'zir* as the case may be."

In this connection Allama Ali Marghinani writes: "The retraction of evidence is not valid, unless it be made in the presence of the *Qadi:* because being a destruction of evidence, it must consequently be restricted to that place which is particularly appointed for the reception of evidence: namely, the assembly of the *Qadi* (that is to say, of any *Qadi* whatever). Besides, retraction of false evidence resembles repentance of a crime; and repentance of a crime, if committed privately, must be performed openly— as, therefore, retraction of evidence is not valid, unless made in the assembly of the *Qadi,* it follows that if the defendant should say that the witnesses had retracted their testimony somewhere out of the assembly of the *Qadi,* and should either require that an oath to this effect be administered to them in the assembly of the *Qadi,* or offer to produce witnesses there to prove his assertion, yet neither would the oath be administered to those witnesses, nor would the evidence he offers to produce be accepted, since the plea on which he proceeds (namely, an invalid retraction) is of no effect.

If, on the contrary, his plea be of an effectual nature (as if he should assert that the witnesses had retracted their testimony before a certain *Qadi,* who had in consequence passed a decree for their making separation) the evidence he offers must be admitted because he in this instance grounds his plea upon a valid retraction".

He further writes about retraction of testimony in the matter of *qisas:* "If two witnesses bear evidence against a person, in a case of retaliation for murder, and then retract their testimony after the person has been put to death, they are in that case bound to pay *Diyat,* or fine of blood, but are not to suffer death by way of retaliation. Shafii maintains that they are to suffer death, since they were the efficient cause of death, inasmuch as the retaliation was executed on the strength of their evidence and they therefore resemble a *Mukri,* or compeller (in other words, they compel the commission of murder) nay, they are still more criminal than a *Mukri* inasmuch as the avenger of blood in a case of murder is aided in bringing the murderer to justice, whereas a person under compulsion is prohibited, by the Law, from putting to death.

The reasoning of our doctors is that the witnesses, in this case, cannot be considered either as actual perpetrators, or as instrumental causes of the bloodshed: for nothing can be considered as a case except such a thing as presses upon, and joins to, the agent; and the testimony of the witnesses cannot be considered in this light, since notwithstanding they furnish legal grounds for the relation, yet pardon and forgiveness being equivalent acts, the probable consequence is that the avenger of blood will pardon the person against whom they bore evidence.

It is otherwise in a case of compulsion; for person compelled is induced to execute the murder with a view to save his own life, which the compeller threatens to take from him in case of his refusal; whereas, in the case in question there is no compulsion on the avenger of blood to execute the retaliation; on the contrary, he is at free liberty either to pardon the other, or to execute the retaliation; and where a man acts from free liberty, and not from any necessity, the cause of his actions cannot be ascribed to the witnesses; at least, it must be allowed that there is a doubt with respect to their being the cause; and the existence of a doubt is preventive of retaliation. The *diyat,* or fine of blood, however, takes place because that is a matter of property, and as such, may be established, notwithstanding any doubt which may happen to attend it".

It has been related that two men testified before Hadrat Ali that a person whom they named had committed theft. Hadrat Ali ordered that his hand be cut and thus his hand was cut. Later on they retracted and testified that the theft had been committed by another person and they were at fault to accuse the first one. Hadrat Ali said to them, "I don't accept your this testimony also and impose *diyat* of the first man on you. And if I had known that you had intentionally testified about the first man, I would have cut your hands". Basing on this practise of Hadrat Ali, Imam Ahmad is of the opinion that if the witnesses retracted and admitted that they had made mistake in their testimony they will be held responsible for compensation and if they admitted that they had intentionally testified falsely, they will be subjected to *hadd*.

If four witnesses testify to the adultery of a man and he is stoned to death then one of them retracts his testimony, the retractor will be punished with *hadd* of *qadhf* and will be responsible for 1/4 of *diyat*. And if all the four re tract, all of them will be punished with *hadd of qadhf and* will be subjected to *diyat*.

If five witnesses testify to the adultery of a man, and being unmarried, he is punished with 100 stripes. After that it is disclosed that one of them had been punished with *hadd of qadhf and* the other four retracted their testimony. So the four witnesses will be punished with *hadd of qadhf and* fifth one will not be punished with *hadd* of *qadhf*.

According to Abu Hanifa if four men and four women testify to the adultery of a man and *hadd* is implemented on the accused on the basis of their testimony and then all the witnesses retract their testimony, the male witnesses will be punished with *hadd of qadhf*. However if all of them retract their testimony before the implementation of the punishment, all will be punished with *hadd* of *qadhf*.

If five witnesses testify to the adultery of a man and then one of them retracts his testimony, *hadd* will be implemented on the accused.

If during retraction from the testimony it is proved that a witness had given false testimony either by his own confession or by other reliable corroboration, he will be subjected to the punishment of false testimony. The false testimony has been declared a punishable offence by the Holy Quran and *Sunnah* though its punishment has not been prescribed. It has been mentioned in verse 22:30 as follows: "and refrain from all false statements". Giving false testimony also comes under the commandment.

A tradition from the Holy Prophet says: "A false testimony is equal to *"shirk"* with Allah".

That is why according to the Islamic Law, a false witness should be punished and disgraced. Imam Abu Yusuf and Imam Muhammad have expressed the opinion that a person who gives false evidence in the court should be publicly exposed and sentenced in imprisonment. This was the actual practice in the time of Hadrat 'Umar. According to Makhul: "Such a person should be whipped, his head shaved and face blackened and he should be sentenced to a long imprisonment". Abdullah Ibn Amr has reported from his father that a person's false testimony was established in Hadrat 'Umar's court, whereupon the caliph kept him exposed to public for a day, saying that he was so and so and a false witness so that people might recognise him, and then he imprisoned him". Thus the witness who gives false evidence must be punished with *tazir*.

Allama Ali Al-Marghinani Hanafi writes about the punishment of false testimony: "Imam Abu Hanifa is of opinion that a false witness must be stigmatised, but not chastised with blows. The two disciples are of opinion that he must be scourged and confined; and this is also the opinion of Shafii. The arguments of the two disciples upon this point are two fold. First, it is related from 'Umar that he caused a false witness to be scourged forty stripes, and to have his face blackened with the soot of a pot. Secondly, false testimony is a great crime of which the evil results to other; and as no stated punishment has been ordained for it in the law, it must therefore be punished by *tazir* or discretionary correction.

The arguments of Imam Abu Hanifa are also two fold:—First, Shurai stigmatised a false witness, but did not scourge him. Secondly, prevention of the crime in future may be effected by stigmatizing, and it ought therefore to be adopted as sufficient; for beating or scourge enjoined in such cases might operate to the concealment of the crime and the consequent destruction of the rights of others. In other words, as being a grievous punishment, the fear of it might deter false witnesses from a confession of their falsehood. With regard to the transmission related from Hadrat 'Umar, it evidently alludes to the infliction of punishment on a criminal, as appears by the number of lashes (namely forty), and the blackening of the countenance.

The mode of stigmatizing a false witness, as prescribed by *Shariah,* is this:— If the witness be a sojourner in any public street or market place let him be sent to his own tribe or kindred, after the evening prayers (as they are generally assembled in greater numbers at that time than any other); — and let the stigmatiser inform the people that *"Qadi* Shurai salutes them, and informs them, that he has detected this person in giving false testimony; that they must therefore beware of him themselves, and likewise desire others to beware of him".

Shams al-Aimma has said that a false witness ought also to be stigmatised, according to the two disciples, and that the degree of correction and imprisonment ought (according to them) to be left to the discretion of the *Qadi.* (The nature of discretionary correction has been already explained under the head of punishment). It is related in the *Jami al-Saghir* that if two witnesses confess that they have given false testimony, they must not be scourged. The two disciples maintain that they are to be scourged as the disciples maintain that they are to be scourged at the discretion of *Qadi".*

Evaluation of a Judgement

The law allows a review of a decree in cases where it is in violation of the principles of law; the case will then be heard over again.

Execution of Decrees: When a decree is obtained by a party, the law also provides for its enforcement and realisation through the agency of the Court, that is, by execution (tanfid). A decree is to be executed by compelling the judgement-debtor to comply with it and such compulsion is generally exercised by imprisoning the debtor until he obeys. If a decree can be satisfied by delivery of certain property or by the sale of the judgement-debtor's property, the Court will order such delivery or sale if the judgement-debtor does not otherwise satisfy the decree.

In execution of a money decree the debtor will be imprisoned if he makes delay in satisfying the decree; but if he is able to satisfy the Court that he has no property or means, there will be no order for imprisonment. If the Court finds that the judgement-debtor has concealed his property or refuses to pay the decretal amount in spite of his having sufficient means he may be imprisoned until he pays. But if the Judge thinks that the debtor has been for a sufficient length of time in imprisonment, he will be discharged.

The Follow-up

The Court is empowered to make certain ancillary orders with a view to preserve the subject-matter of litigation. For instance, it may sometimes happen that all the parties who may be interested in certain property may not be before the Court or their whereabouts may not be known. In such cases the Court secures the protection of the interests of others by appointing a receiver or by taking security from the party in possession.

For instance, if a property be in the possession of a certain person and another person adduces proof that it belonged to his father who died leaving himself and a brother who had disappeared, the Qadi while making a decree for a moiety of the house in favour of the claimant should according to Abu Hanifa leave the other share in the hands of the person in whose possession it is without taking from him any security. But according to his two disciples, if the person in possession of the property disputed the fact that it belonged to the deceased, it should be removed from his possession and made over to a trustworthy person to hold it on behalf of the absent heir.

Similarly, when the Court makes over a runaway slave or a trove to the owner or orders maintenance for a woman who alleges to be wife of a person, who has disappeared from the latter's property, it ought to take security.

Arbitration: The Islamic law allows the parties disputing about claims in respect of property and other similar private rights to refer their dispute to an arbitrator. Such reference is called tahkim. The arbitrator must possess the qualifications which are required of a Qadi, for in fact he exercises the same function, but the dhimmis may appoint a person of their own pursuasion as an arbitrator. In certain matters, such as offences entailing hadd and retaliation, no arbitration is allowed. The arbitrator is empowered to hear the evidence and to administer oaths just like a Court, and on the award of the arbitrator being filed in Court a decree will be passed in accordance with its terms if does not contravene the law.

Limitation: In Turkey periods of limitation for the hearing of suits have been laid down by the order of the Sultan so that if a plaintiff comes to Court after the lapse of the prescribed period his suit will not be heard.

The order is justified on the ground that as the head of the State has power under the law to make the appointment of Qadis limited to particular matters, an order to the effect that a Qadi is not to hear suits instituted after a certain time is within his competence. The learned of the present day apparently agree that such an order is in accordance with the principles of Islamic law. The old theory of the law undoubtedly was that a person's right would not be lost because of lapse of time and that it was incumbent on the Qadi to hear his claim. However, that may be, the introduction of the law of limitations is a forcible illustration of the fact that law in the long run tries to find out some means of adapting itself to the circumstances of the time and Islamic law is no exception to this rule.

Evidence Juristic Theory Relating to Testimony: Let us now consider the general features of the Islamic law of evidence and the theory on which it is founded. Testimony of a witness (shadat) is a juristic act of the category of informations (akhabarat). When a right is originated or translated either by an event of nature or act of man, it is the State as representing the community that gives effect to such a fact when it occurs. When a fact has given rise to a right of an individual the State takes notice of it when moved by him and when to a right of its own it takes notice of it of its own motion. But in either case the official of the State in this connection, that is, the Judge, if he himself has no personal knowledge of the occurrence which he mostly has not, has to depend upon information or evidence. This information may be supplied either by the statements of some one who perceived the fact or by perceptible signs or traces accompanying or immediately following the event or by both. If the fact is of an imperceptible nature or all traces of it have been removed or disappeared, it is necessarily beyond the ken of a human tribunal. For this reason there can, generally speaking, be no evidence of a bare negation or denial.

When a perceptible fact originating or translating a certain right has occurred, it is a right as well as a duty of every member of the society who perceived it to give information of it to the State. But as the witness may choose not to give a correct account of what happened and such account alone can be said to be information, the duty or obligation to give evidence is regarded as of an imperfect character so far as its enforcement by the human tribunals is concerned. False testimony is not regarded as evidence by the Islamic jurists, as the very object of information is to disclose what occurred. In fact according to them false testimony or false evidence or false information would be a contradiction in terms.

The necessity for evidence mostly arises when the fact in question has originated a right in some one against another and the latter denies it. And as it is in the very conception of evidence that it gives information of that fact its practical effect is to originate liability against the person of incidence taking the place of the fact itself so far as a human tribunal is concerned.

The Islamic jurists, therefore, say that to give evidence is the right of a person who has seen an occurrence to fasten liability upon the person against whom a right is claimed. So far as the Court is concerned its only function is to enforce such liability on a demand to that effect being made by the claimant and on being furnished with the information or proof. The right of the witness, however, is to give true evidence (shahadat), but as men do not always give correct information either from error of perception or some moral aberration, it is incumbent on the law to take precautions with a view to prevent the Court as far as possible from being misled by falsehoods.

True information alone being regarded as evidence, there can be no conflict of evidence though there may be a conflict of statements, one of which alone can be called evidence, the other being either a falsehood or an error. As regards falsehoods or errors it cannot be the right or duty of anyone to place them before the Court not can the Court admit them.

Hence on principle, evidence relating to a fact must necessarily according to Islamic jurists be one-sided. Having regard to these principles the law makes provisions for excluding as far as possible mistakes and falsehoods. Some of these are mere matters of procedure, but the others indicate the nature and extent of testimony as a juristic act.

Classification of Testimony

The highest kind of oral testimony having regard to its value as a proof is known as tawatur or universal testimony. Such proof consists of information given by such a large body of men that our reason cannot conceive that they would combine in a falsehood or agree in an error. When testimony is not of this notorious and universal character it is called isolated or single testimony. When a man testifies against himself in support of a claim made against him, it is called admission (iqrar).

Conditions Relating to Capacity of a Witness: Regard being had to the various reasons which induce men to tell falsehoods or the circumstances which prevent them from giving correct and reliable information, the law insists upon certain conditions as necessary for a jurists act of this class:

(1) Freedom from bias and prejudice; hence, testimony is not admitted of the father in favour of the son and *vice-versa*, of a slave in favour of his master, of parties in support of their own case, of a person who bears a grudge against the opposite party, of a non-Muslim against a Muslim and so on.

(2) General reliability of character; hence, persons carrying on certain professions of a degrading nature, such as professional dancers, persons known to be habitual liars, drunkards or gamblers, persons who are not of virtuous character being in the habit of committing such breaches of religious injunctions as would entail hadd, that is, men who are fasiq as opposed to adil or as the compilers of Al-Majalla' say, those whose bad actions outweigh their good ones and unscrupulous officers employed for purposes of oppression are not admitted as witnesses. Abu Yusuf is, however, of opinion that though a man be not of virtuous character, yet if he is of such a position in life that he is unlikely to depose to a falsehood, he ought to be admitted as a witness.

(3) Maturity of the understanding and power of perception; thus, a small child, a lunatic, or a blindman in matters which have to be proved by ocular testimony, are declared unfit giving testimony.

As a further precaution against the chances of mistake or false testimony and also because otherwise there would be the word of one man against another, testimony of a single witness is generally regarded as insufficient to prove a claim.

Hence claims belonging to the category of rights of men are not established except by the testimony of two male or one male and two female witnesses. But certain matters which women alone are likely to know such as whether a particular child was born to a particular woman, can be proved even by the testimony of a single woman. Matters which are of the category of public right and require absolute certainty of proof, such as offences entailing the punishment of hadd can only be proved by the testimony of two male witnesses and in one case, namely, that of whoredom by four male witnesses. A woman is regarded as of inferior competence in respect of giving evidence because of her weak character.

Inquiry into the Competency of a Witness: It is one of the important duties of a Judge, if the witness who is put forward by the party going into evidence as eligible, has given relevant evidence against the opposite party and the latter challenges the evidence by alleging that his evidence is false or due to his having forgotten the occurrence, to make inquiries into the witnesses' competence and particularly as to the fact of his being a man of rectitude. The inquiry is to be made by him either privately or in Court with the help of persons whom he knows to be reliable and who are acquainted with the life and character of the witness cited.

The other party is also at liberty to take exception or objection (jarh, tan) to such evidence by showing that the witness is disqualified such as by reason of bias or interest or otherwise. Public investigation into a witness's character which prevailed in the early days of Islam has, it is said, been discontinued because of the strifes and disturbances which it led to . If a witness is a stranger to the place the Qadi of the locality where he resides should be asked to make the inquiry. The Qadis are also required to keep a register of persons who are proved to be adil or men of rectitude and to revise the register from time to time.

Direct and Hearsay Testimony: Again direct testimony alone, generally speaking, has any probative value. Hence a fact must be proved by an eyewitness if it be one which could be seen, or if it consisted of spoken words, by the person who heard them. But sometimes indirect testimony is also admitted. For instance, the facts of paternity, death, marriage, appointment of a Qadi, can be proved by a person who received information with regard to them from men of reliable character. Even in those matters a mere statement by a witness that he heard so and so will not be accepted by he must be able to depose to the fact itself, for instance, that on a particular date so and so was the Qadi of such a place or so and so died on such a date and that he knew it although his knowledge might be based on here say.

In other words his information must have produced such belief in his mind as to be accepted by himself as knowledge. Similarly, if he says I did not see this but know it and it is a notorious fact the statement will be accepted. Such evidence is also admissible to prove the fact of a property being waqf but not to prove the conditions of the grant. If a person sees another in possession of a property other than a slave, he would be justified in deposing that it belongs to the man in possession because possession indicates ownership.

It may sometimes happen that the persons who witnessed a transaction may not be available owing to their being dead or being at such a great distance that it is not practicable to produce them; then evidence may be received of a person who heard them state that they witnessed the transaction. This is called 'evidence of testimony' (Shahadat ala Shahadat), and is allowed by juristic equity because of necessity.

Testimony must Agree with Claim: Legal testimony must also agree with the claim; otherwise it has no effect. For instance, when the claim is that a certain property has belonged to the plaintiff for two years and his witnesses say that it has been his for above two years, it will not be accepted; though, if they had said that the property had been owned by the plaintiff for less than two years the testimony would not be discarded, because their knowledge might have fallen short. Similarly, if a plaintiff claims a thousand rupees and the witnesses speak to five hundred, the evidence will be accepted for five hundred, but not if they speak to more than a thousand. Suppose a man's claim is for a thousand rupees for property sold and the witnesses depose that the defendant owes a thousand rupees to the plaintiff on account of a loan, it will not be accepted. Similarly, if there is conflict of testimony among the witnesses of the claimant such evidence will be rejected. If evidence be opposed to a visible or notorious fact it will have no operation.

5

Law for Inheritance

Basis and Purpose of the Laws of Succession: Muhammad (SAW), the greatest benefactor of mankind, the Saviour of mankind, the Messenger of Allah, is reported to have said:

> Learn the laws of inheritance, and teach them to people; for they are one half of useful knowledge.

The purpose and importance of the laws of inheritance and succession have been clearly emphasised by the Prophet of Islam (SAW), in numerous traditions like the one quoted above. His emphases on learning and teaching the laws of inheritance was not only because it is half the knowledge of faith *(Iman)* but also by way of precaution so that it may not be forgotten by 'Umma' (the followers). He also warned his followers that the first part of the useful *ilm* (knowledge) which will be taken off my Umma (the followers) will be this, the *ilm-ul-fraiz* (the laws of inheritance). Colbrook observes:

> No branch of jurisprudence is more important than the law of succession and inheritance; as it constitutes that part of any national system of laws which is the most peculiar and distinct, and which is of most frequent use and extensive application.

The subject (succession) unquestionably is of the greatest importance as affecting the interest of all description of people and deserves special notice. In the words of S.V. Fitz Gerald "in all systems of law the doctrine of succession is, it has been said, the touch stone of the lawyers, the legal mind delights in its inevitable intricacies, the layman is repelled".

It is usual to divide the law of succession into two main branches, namely: (1) the law of testamentary succession—regulating the devolution and distribution of the property of a person who dies having made a valid will; (2) the law of intestate succession—regulating the devolution and distribution of the undisposed part of the properly of a deceased person.

Testamentary power gives an individual a personal right to determine the devolution of his property after his death according to his wishes and preference. But the law of intestate succession *i.e.* inheritance lays down compulsory rules of succession for the security of the family of the deceased. The security of the family and society requires that property should on the decrease of its owner, be transmitted in a forcible way to those held by nature as best entitles to it rather than to those whom the deceased might personally prefer.

The law itself takes into account the fact that the properly of the deceased should be applied primarily to the support of persons who were entitled to be first supported by the deceased in his lifetime and who have greatly suffered, emotionally and financially, by his death. Therefore, naturally and historically intestate succession gets precedence over testamentary succession. The right of testamentary succession was only to meet exceptional cases for reasons best known to the testator himself.

In the following words, Mr. N.J. Coulson has correctly summed up the basis and object of the law of succession in Islam:

> "The supreme purpose of the Islamic law of succession is material provision for surviving dependents and relatives, *for the family group bound to the deceased by the mutual ties and responsibilities which stem from blood relationship.* The manner in which this provision is to be made is prescribed by the law in rigid and uncompromising terms. The power of the deceased to dispose of his property by will is recognised but is restricted to safeguard, substantially, the basic interest of dependents and close relations. Accordingly, the transmission of property by way of testamentary succession, or in accordance with the wishes of the deceased is of secondary importance and the central core of the system of succession is formed by the compulsory rules of inheritance designed for the material benefit of the family group."

From the sociological stand point, the Islamic laws of inheritance reflect the structure of family ties and the accepted social values and responsibilities within the Islamic community. For in the eyes of the law rights of inheritance are generally regarded as the consideration for duties of protection and support owed to the deceased during his lifetime, so that the stronger the family bound, the greater the right of inheritance. In Islamic legal philosophy the rules of inheritance propound the ideal way for the deceased to fulfil his duty to his surviving relatives and members of the family."

In early communities the power of divesting property, through will was usually limited in its operation to a part only of the disponer's property. It was seldom allowed to interfere with the right of heirs.

Traces of the predominating claims of members of the family still persist in the laws of many states in the from of 'legitism'

To achieve the end of *natural law,* that the primary dependents must be provided out of the property left by the deceased, Roman Law also imposed restrictions on the testamentary powers. Justinian provided by the 18th Novel that testator should leave at least one-third or one-half of the estate if he has four or more children.

Islamic law, which takes into consideration the welfare not only of the children but of all relatives, goes further and requires that at least two-third should be left for the near relations of the deceased.

By contrast, succession under most of the modern systems rest firmly upon the freedom of the individual to determine the devolution of his property upon his deceased. Under English law, for example, the wishes of the deceased as expressed in his will are paramount, and the law only intervenes to specify the manner in which the property shall devolve when a person died wholly or partially intestate.

This in the opinion of Sir D. Hughes Parry the modern English legal system has perhaps tended to regard succession under a will as normal or natural and intestate succession as exceptional or accidental. Holdswoth observes that at one time to die intestate other than in cases of sudden death was regarded with horror, because it was practically tantamount to dying unconfessed. While on the other hand distribution of property, on an intestate's death, had been regarded in English law as a legacy of ancient system, as complementary to testamentary disposition, that is to say, as taking effect in the absence of and subject to any intention manifested by a testator in his will. It is only under the comparatively recent and limited terms of the Inheritance (Family Provision) Act, 1938 that the court may vary or override the will of the deceased in order to make reasonable provision for the assistance of family dependents.

In Nigeria, the succession under statutory law, is based on English legal system and has followed the same line of approach relating to testamentary and intestate succession. As a result, the intestate succession is not only of secondary importance but in the words of Mr. E I. Nnogugu it is in a state of utter confusion.

Under other modern system like Common Law, American, Russian French and Hindu legal systems, the same approach has been adopted. As a result the laws of inheritance have lost their importance and practical utility under these systems, and have been relegated to secondary position in the scheme of legal education.

In addition to the aforesaid overemphasis of testamentary succession given under modern legal systems there are some distinctive features of the laws of succession and inheritance under these systems which have also been responsible in making these laws less or more important for the people governed by them. Let us briefly examine some of these distinctive features of some relevant legal systems with a view to assess the relative practical value of these laws under these systems.

Right to Birth

Right or interest by birth is peculiar concept of Hindu law *(Mitakshara* School). It is an incidence of Mitakshara coparcenary. The concept in Hindu law means acquiring interest in the family property by mere birth in the family. The right or interest by birth is an automatic consequence or incidence of joint-tenancy in the form of Mitakshara coparcenary. The interest is acquired by birth and extinguishes on death and under this phenomenon the member of a coparcenary is treated as *born with property.* In no other system (except Hindu law) one is born with property. It is in contradiction with the rule of Spes Sucessionists and also in some respect resembles it. A direct and logical 'corollary of this rule' *i.e.* the right by birth, is the rule of survivorship.

Muslim law does not recognise this Hindu concept and theory of right by birth. Islam believes that every one is born empty handed and so he/she dies. The right of inheritance, in Islam, arises only on the death of a certain person. This is one of the reasons why Muslim law does not recognise the doctrine of representation. The right of an heir-apparent or presumptive comes into existence for the first time on the death of the person through whom he/she claims and he/she is not entitled until if he /she interest in the Property to which he would succeed as an heir if he/she survived the deceased. For example: *A,* who has a son *B,* makes a gift of his property to *C. B,* in alleging that gift was procured by undue influence sues C, in *A's* lifetime, on the strength of his right to succeed *to A's* property on *A's* death. The suit must be dismissed for *B* has no cause of action against *C. B* has no cause of action, for he is not entitled to any interest in *A's* property during *A's* lifetime.

Degrees of Nearness

In determining the preferential claim of various relations of a deceased some rule of preference has to be applied. Nearly all the legal systems of the world recognise the nearness of blood relationship as the basis and principle of preference. This preference based on nearness of blood is technically called the 'Rule of Propinquity'. It is another thing that different system adopted different principles to decide the nearness of blood. The rule of propinquity is not absolute but qualified and subject to other rules of preference recognised by various systems.

For example a system believing in the preference of agnates will not treat a very near cognate as nearer by blood in comparison with a remote agnate *e.g.* between a daughter's son and a son's son's son's daughter, the former though nearer in blood will be considered remote being a cognate. Similarly a system preferring male agnates will deny the nearness of blood of a female relation however close she may be *e.g.* in such system between a daughter and brothers son's son the latter though very much removed by blood will be treated nearer by blood tie because he is male agnate. So in spite of recognizing the rule of propinquity *i.e.* the nearness of blood, by all the systems of the world, they have evolved different rules of preference.

Under Islamic legal system Shias and Sunnis have adopted different approaches in recognizing the rule of propinquity or consanguinity (blood relationship). The Shias, rejecting the rule of agnacy recognised the rule of propinquity the sole criterion to determine the priority of claim. They prefer the nearest blood relation irrespective of the sex of the claimants and the sex of the intermediary links.

The Sunnis on the other hand, fully recognise the distinction between agnates and cognates. The rules of nearer excludes the more remote *i.e.* the rule of propinquity is applied to the kindred of the same class only.

So if the class of the two claimants is different, the preference may not be decided simply on the basis of propinquity. Rules of Exclusion discussed (infra), explain the other rules affecting the question of preference. The following provisions and illustrations governing the distribution among *'Asaba'* (Residuaries) may explain the point more clearly.

Among different kinds of residuaries the preference is given to propinquity to the propositus. So in case of a female inheriting as a residuary (by conversion due to the presence of another heir) is preferred over an ' Asaba' or Residuary in his own right *i.e.* on MA (male agnate), provided she is nearer to the deceased *e.g.*

SD	Sis_b	and	B_c
1/2	1/2		x

In the above example Sis_f is converted into a residuary due to the presence of SD and B_c is an 'Asaba', residuary, in his own right, being an MA. So to decide, out of the two residuaries (Sis_f and B_c) who is to be preferred to take the residue *i.e.* 1/2. Here Sis_f (sister full) is preferred over B_c (the brother consanguine) on the basis of propinquity (based on blood strength).

Thus the theory of propinquity or nearness in blood is fully recognised by Shias but only partially by Sunnis.

Right to Inheritance

It is a well established rule of Muslim law that the property never remains in a state of abeyance, but on the death of the proprietor, it vests at once in his/her own heirs in accordance with the law of succession and inheritance. A 'vested inheritance' is the entitlement which vests in an heir at the moment the propositus dies. The right of succession vests in heirs immediately on the death of the propositus. It cannot under any circumstances, remain in abeyance in expectation of the birth of a preferential heir where such heir was not conceived at the time of the death of the propositus. The vesting of inheritance does not depend on the payment of debts or satisfaction of legacies, if any. The vesting, a legal phenomenon, takes place immediately on the death of the propositus though the heirs are only entitled to take out of the residue left after the payment of debts and satisfaction of legacies.

If an heir dies before actual distribution, the share of inheritance which has already vested in him/her on the death of the propositus, will now pass on his/her death. The share will be determined at each death. For example *A* dies leaving a son *S,* and a daughter *D. S* dies, before the estate of *A* is actually distributed leaving behind his *(S's)* own son Ss. In this case, on the death of *A* two-third (2/3) of his estate vests in .V and one-third (1/3) in *D.* The S's death before the actual distribution makes no difference, the 2/3 share which had already vested in him *(S)* simply passes on to his heir *Ss* at the time of allotment.

It means mere chance of an heir apparent succeeding to the estate of living person. The right of a person to succeed as a heir on the death of an owner of property is a mere spes successionis, *i.e.* a mere chance of succession. Unlike other legal systems under Muslim law there is no concept of an would be heir dealing, in any way, with his/her expected future right or interest in the inheritance. Spes successionis is not recognised, in Islam, as a present or vested interest so the heir apparent cannot make a valid transfer of it. For the same reason, any agreement entered into by such an heir in respect of the expected right of inheritance cannot bind persons who actually inherit when the succession opens. It, therefore, follows that in the life time of a Muslim a very close relation of his/her *e.g.* son or daughter or spouse cannot legally interfere, with the use and transfer on the part of the owner on the basis of his or her having an expected chance of inheritance. The cardinal principle of Muslim law is that the succession for the first time opens on the death of the propositus. Before, his/her death no one can claim any right in the property on the basis of being the heir-apparent. Right of inheritance, under Muslim law, arises for the first time only after the death of the propositus. No one is an heir of a living person. The following example may make it further clear.

An extravagant and irresponsible father spends recklessly or meddles with the property in a way which threatens the very existence of the property the only son who is definitely to succeed the father cannot *legally* check the father's actions. He can simply request and advice the father because in the father's life time he has a mere chance to inherit but not a right in present. A Muslim heir has not even a nominal right to the property of his/her ancestor or any other relative until the death of that ancestor or relative. Straight J. rightly remarked "The Muslim law does not recognise any reversionary or contingent interest expectant on the death of another and till the death occurs which, by the force of law, gives birth to the right as an heir in the person, entitled to it according to the rules of succession, he/she possesses no right at all".

Waiver of Hereditary Rights by a Heir: Renunciation, Relinquishment, Release or Transfer of spes successionis *i.e.,* contingent or future chance of inheritance by a presumptive heir of a Muslim is void. An agreement where such an heir agrees to disclaim his/her expectant interest in the property of the would be propositus when it devolves on him/her *i.e.* when the propositus dies. Or where in lieu of a particular item of the owner's property waives his/her expected share in the rest of item are acts in futile having no legal bearing. The question of consideration is immaterial.

The transfer, disclaimer or waiver of spes successionis even for consideration has no sanction of Shariah (Islamic law). But in India, under the impact of English and Hindu legal systems, courts have deviated from this clear and unambiguous position of Shariah where the disclaimer or waiver is supported by good consideration, and not necessarily valuable consideration and forms part of a valid family settlement it has been held effective. Such deviation is an innovation in Shariah, totally uncalled for and amounts to clear interference in the sacred laws of Muslims and must not be allowed to form a precedent.

Privilege of being the First

Under the doctrine or rule of primogeniture the eldest son of the deceased, if there are more than one, is allowed to exclude others from inheritance. The rules sometimes means preference for the eldest son either completely or partially. The rule entitled only the eldest son to inherit the whole of the deceased father's property or to get the lion's share. The rule owes its origin to the ancient feudal system. In most of the ancient societies there existed a rule of preference in favour of the eldest son. This rule of primogeniture was prevalent among Jews under Mosaic laws.

The eldest son enjoyed exclusive right of inheritance in respect of landed property coupled with certain responsibilities towards other members of the family specially unmarried females. In respect of other properties he used to get double share. Roman law also recognised the rule of primogeniture. It was recognised in African countries and was prevalent among Maori of New Zealand and in the Western Europe. Chinese also recognised this doctrine.

In England the doctrine applied to real property only. Free hold real estate descended undivided to a single heir, the eldest son. The rule of primogeniture extended to collateral heirs in the absence of descendants. Nobility and gentry adhered to it. Later on English system recognised another favourable rule—estate entail. From 18th century some changes and modifications in the application were introduced in England. It was also recognised in France and America. In America, the American Revolution and in France and Western Europe, the French Revolution, through the Napoleonic code radical changes were introduced to abolish this discriminatory rule. But in Australia, Germany and Scandinavian countries the rule continued upto 1918.

Maine, on the authority of saints like Baudhyana, Gautama, Apasthana mentions the recognition of this doctrine from ancient time. The preference of eldest son was recognised by ancient Hindu law. The doctrine of primogeniture which is a clear cut rule of discrimination and injustice is not tolerated by Islam and is rejected out right from the very beginning. Sunni law completely rejects this pre-Islamic rule or mode of preference and discrimination. But under Shia law it is nominally applied. Under Shia law the eldest son, if of sound mind, is exclusively entitled to the wearing apparel, the Quran, sword and ring of the deceased father provided the deceased has left some other property besides those articles. By discarding this doctrine Islam laid down and set the pattern of equitable and democratic concept of distribution of heritage previously unknown to the world.

British India provided the system of 'Royal Succession', the special rule of succession applicable to the Estate of Rajas, Nawabs and Principalities. The rule lost its practical importance only after the Abolition of Zamindari Act. But Muslims considered it un-Islamic and violative of Divine laws of succession. Maine has rightly remarked:

> "Indeed, of all systems of succession to property, the Muhammadan system is the most-difficult to adjust to royal succession, an off shoot of primogeniture".

Disowning in Islam

Repudiation literally means the act of disowning or refusal to accept or acknowledge. In the context of inheritance and succession it means disowning an heir-apparent, son, grandson or any other relative. It is a declaration of one's intention that he or she has no more connection with such and such a person and is no more responsible for any act or behaviour of such and such person and after his or her death such and such person will not inherit from his or her property. In fact it is an act to disinherit an heir apparent.

According to Juri Zaydan it is the opposite of adoption, in effect. The act of adoption converts a stranger into an heir but by the act of repudiation an heir is converted into a stranger. Zydan observes that if a person was offended, for any reason, with his son or any relative (presumptive heir) he should repudiate *i.e.* disown him and thereby ceased to be responsible for the mischief wrought by that son or relative. This practice was customary in pre-Islamic time.

Through the act of repudiation the following two objects are intended to be achieved:

(i) the disowning of the responsibility of acts done by the relative, disowned, and

(ii) the exclusion of the heir-apparent (disowned) from the heritage.

Islam appears to have no objection to the act of repudiation if it is intended to achieve the object mentioned in clause (i) above. It cannot be blame worthy for a gentleman and true believer to disassociate from an undesirable, wicked and disobedient relative however close he or she might be. It is always commendable to severe connection with such persons.

But Islam does not recognise the legality and validity of the repudiation if it is intended to disinherit or debar a prospective or presumptive heir. This will amount to change and modify the rules of inheritance directly ordained in the Holy Quran. It amounts to dictate a new and different rule of succession opposed to the ordinance of Allah, the Law Giver of Islam. No one including the Holy Prophet (SAW), is allowed to undo what Allah has done.

So in Islam such a declaration is meaningless and ineffective. It carries no weight. The prospective heir, so disowned and disentitled, can legally claim his or her rightful share, if otherwise entitled, notwithstanding such declaration or repudiation (technically called *'Aaq'* by Muslims). It is a fact that *some* Muslims, without knowing its religious and legal implications, take help of this sword to axe (cut) an heir to size. It is to be well understood and remembered that repudiation *(Aaq)* is an un-Islamic, anti-Islamic, illegal and ineffective act. It is of *no* legal consequences. Not only it is an exercise in futile but is a grave sin and bound to attract the wrath of Allah, the Almighty. Allah, after laying down the laws of inheritance and succession, made it plain that these rules set limits which must not be crossed, transgressed or disobeyed and the transgressors and wrongdoers will be severely punished. Allah declares:

> "These are the limits imposed by Allah...."
>
> "And whoso disobeyeth Allah and His messenger and transgresselh His limits, He will make him enter Fire, where such will dwell for ever; his will be shameful doom."

Muslims are, therefore, warned not to resort to an act (repudiation—*Aaq)* bound to attract the punishment mentioned in the above verse of Sura *al-Nisa.* This practice must be strongly condemned and immediately discarded by Muslims. Muslims must be properly educated about the religious and legal aspects of this institution *(Aaq)* which is an innovation.

Factors of Inheritance

Blood Relationship (Nasab): Rights of inheritance arise from blood relationship, and not from relationship by affinity or by fosterage. According to traditional Sunni law from social rights and obligations family group has been extended to agnatic family of males linked through males to a common ancestor. Hence although maternal relatives do have rights to inheritance, the main emphasis lies on the paternal connection, and the primary significance of the word 'nasab' is that of paternity.

The supreme purpose of the Islamic law of succession is material provision for surviving dependents and relatives for the family group bound to the deceased by the mutual ties and responsibilities which stem from blood relationship.

Basis of Inheritance: The cause and basis of hereditary rights in Islam is blood relationship and relationship of husband and wife (existing at the time of death). Every one being a descendant of Adam *(Alaihissalam)* and Amma Hawwa Allaihissalam is related to each other. If no rule of priority or preference is evolved the distribution and devolution becomes impossible and impractical. So as a principle, every system of inheritance must have some far and objective principle and method to select, the persons, out of numerous relations, who should receive a share and who be excluded. The principle and the method employed should not only be objective but also logical, least controversial and natural. Islam adopted *'nearer must exclude more remote'* the most natural, logical, objective and least controversial principle for the purpose. No system has yet evolved a better principle.

The Holy Quran lays down *'Tarakal Walidan Walaqraboon' i.e.* blood relationship as basis of inheritance. *'Aqrab'* means near, so Muslim jurists derived the rule *'Al-aqrab fal aqrab'* As a result the relation who possesses greater basis of inheritance *i.e.* who is nearer, is preferred. Legitimacy is the basis of right of inheritance. Legitimacy is the legal prerequisite for admission to family group. Illegitimacy does not constitute paternity or nasab. Illegitimacy precludes the existence of any legal bond between the blood relatives of the father on the one hand and the illegitimate child and its issue on the other. A limited tie is recognised by Sunni Schools between the mother and the illegitimate child and maternal relatives.

Except for maternal relatives in Sunni law, therefore, rights of inheritance depend upon the relationship between the propositus and the claimant heir being a legitimate relationship.

The owner must have died and the heir must have been alive at such death.

No heir can be excluded from inheritance except by a rule of Islamic law. The propositus, by his/her direction or declaration, can neither exclude an heir nor alter the sharers of heirs. The concept of *'Aaq'* is an innovation, and has no sanction of Shariah. A Muslim can in no way interfere with the course of devolution of property recognised by Islamic law. His/her wishes, preference and choice have no legal value in connection with the law of inheritance. A child not conceived in the life time of the propositus cannot be his/her heir. But a child in the mother's womb is an heir and entitled to inherit if born alive. A childless widow, under Sunni law is treated at par with the widow(s) having issues. But under Shia law, a childless widow is debarred from the share in the landed property of her deceased husband except that she shares in buildings and trees thereon.

Dual Basis of the Muslim Law of Inheritance: The Holy Quran establishes rights of inheritance between husband and wife and in favour of certain close female blood relatives—the mother, the daughter and sisters—by prescribing fixed fractional parts *(faraid)* of the deceased's estate as their entitlement. However, these rules in the enslaves do not form a complete system of succession. In the Sunni view they do not altogether abrogate but merely modify the existing customary system of succession by superimposing upon it a new class of legal heirs. The male agnates still inherit, but now after the satisfaction of the claims of those relatives specified by the Quran.

Thus the Islamic law of inheritance rests basically upon the recognition of two distinct categories of legal heirs—the male agnates or 'asaba', the heirs of tribal customary law, and the new Quranic heirs who arc called *ahlalfaraid'* ("those entitled 10 prescribed shares"). Through the work of Muslim Jurists these two distinct basic elements were gradually fused together into a cohesive system. But this process of amalgamation was not a simple one, and almost all the major complexities of the law stem from its dual basis and the attempt to harmonise the claims of these two categories of heirs.

The system therefore has dual basis as regards the rules governing it. It is based primarily on:

1. The rules laid down in, the Quran or by the Prophet (SAW) *i.e.* Traditions; and
2. The pre-Islamic Arabian Customs and usages in so far as they have not been altered or abrogated by Quranic injunctions or Prophetic traditions.

Estate Organisation

'Administration' means management and disposal of an estate whether it be that of a deceased person or of any other person. Here we are concerned only with the administration of the estate of a deceased Muslim. On the death of a Muslim the questions like who get the right to share the property of the deceased? What happens to the unpaid debts of deceased and legacies left by him or her?; are questions of substantive nature. But questions like who should immediately take charge of the property of the deceased? How to deal with claims for and against the deceased? etc. are the questions of procedural nature. Shariah while governing substantive as well as procedural aspects allowed discretionary powers to *Qadi* in procedural matters.

It is this discretionary power, vested in a *Qadi,* under Shariah, which prompted and encouraged the colonial powers to modify and abrogate Shariah rules and introduce their own in their respective colonies. India is one of such colonies. So the substantive aspect (as explained above) is still governed by Shariah, the Muslim Law, but since British rule in India, the procedural aspects came to be controlled by State through statutory provisions. Taking help of the discretionary powers vested in the Qadi, British parliament passed many statutes to deal with the disposal or application of the estate left by a deceased Indian Muslim.

Administration, as understood in modern law, was unknown to Islamic jurisprudence. In Islam there is a mere distribution of property of the deceased, by the State if not by the heirs themselves. Unlike other modern systems to dispose of the estate of a deceased Muslim neither there is a need of Executor or/and Administrator nor Probate or/and Letters of Administration. In the absence of an Executor, appointed by the will of the deceased, heirs of a Muslim have the right and capacity to dispose of the estate of the propositus according to law. In case they fail or refuse to do so the Qadi (Magistrate) may appoint an Executor. Unlike other legal systems, the estate immediately on death vests in the heirs. Under other systems, based on English Common Law, the estate vests in the Executor. Nothing like Probate or Letters of Administration are required to dispose of the estate under Shariah. In India this aspect of Shariah is modified and replaced by English Law through The Indian Succession Act 1865, The Probate and Administration Act 1881. These Acts were later on repealed by the Indian Succession Act 1925 which incorporates the main provisions of the two repealed Acts. Even after the enactment of the 1925 Act, it remains optional for Muslims to have a recourse of the provisions of this Act.

A Muslim heir or executor is not required under the Act, to procure letters of Administration or Probate. The need of these certificates or permits is felt mainly in cases where the help of State machinery *e.g.* court of law, is sought. For example where a suit for the recovery of debts is to be filed in a court of law. (S.214)

The Holy Quran itself lays down the manner in which the estate of a deceased Muslim has to be disposed of. In verses 11 and 12 of *Surah al-Nisa* the use of phrases:

"*.....Mim badi Wasiyatin Yooswee biha audain.....*" (Verse 11)

"…..after any legacy he many have bequeathed or debt (hath been paid)…."

"…..*Mim badi Wasiyatin Yooswoon biha audain*"…. *"Mimbadi Wasiyatin yooswa biha audain…."* (Verse 12)

"…..After any legacy they may have bequeathed, or debt (they may have contracted, hath been paid…..after any legacy that may have been bequeathed or debt (contracted) not injuring (the heirs by willing away more than a third of the heritage) hath been paid…."

clearly and emphatically provide the obligation or repayment of debts and satisfaction of legacies, if any, before the heirs take their shares according to law. The priority of discharge of debts and legacies constitute prior charges on the property of a deceased viz a viz the right of heirs. Payment of debts and satisfaction of legacies have, therefore, priority over the claim of heirs. Prophet Muhammad (SAW) himself settled the priority between debts and legacies by explaining and commenting on the said phrases used in verses 11 and 12 mentioned above.

Abu Hurrayrah (RA) reported that when the body of a dead person having burden of debt upon him was brought to Allah's Messenger (SAW) he would ask whether he left property enough to clear off his debt, and if the property left had been sufficient for that purpose (payment of debt), he observed funeral prayer for him, otherwise he said to his companions: you observe prayer for your brother.

But when Allah opened the gate of victory for him he said: "I am nearer to the believers than themselves, so if any one dies leaving debt, its payment is my responsibility, and if any one leaves a property, it goes to his heirs". Allah declares: "The Prophet (SAW) is closer to the faithful than their own selves".

It is mentioned that Hadrat Ali (R A) reported "you know the Quranic Verse" *Mim badi Wasiatam yusoon beha awdain*, the Prophet of Allah (SAW) ordered the payment of debts prior to legacies.

Even without this tradition of the Prophet (SAW) the precedence of debts over legacies is quite obvious because in Islam debts constitute an obligation of utmost importance and priority. The above mentioned traditions reiterate this obvious position.

Legacies, on the other hand, are not obligations because their discharge depends completely on the testator's leaving some property. If there is no property left, the legacies, if any, become ineffective and inoperative. But the case of debt is different in the sense that its non payment attracts indignation of Allah and His Prophet (SAW). On the Day of Judgement Allah will see that the debtor or someone on his/her behalf repays the unpaid debts and claims to the rightful creditors and claimants. On non payment the debtor is to be penalised. The first tradition quoted above also points towards the seriousness of the obligation.

The author of *Hedaya* has rightly stated: "If a person deeply involved in debts bequeaths any legacy such bequest is unlawful and of no effect; because debts have a preference to bequests, as the discharge of debts is an absolute duty whereas bequests are gratuitous and voluntary, and that which is most indispensable must be first considered".

It is also obvious that the corpse of the deceased is to be disposed of (buried) without delay and no one is responsible to meet the funeral expenses if the deceased has left any property, otherwise the burial is the responsibility of Umma (the follower of the Prophet (SAW) of Islam) because the Prophet (SAW) declared "I am nearer to the believers than themselves, if anyone dies leaving debt, its payment is my responsibility."

So the Umma, as his true followers, is obliged to shoulder this responsibility (the like of that he undertook to discharge himself), in the absence of *Bait-ul-Mal.*

It is, therefore, well settled question of Islamic law that funeral expenses form the first charge on the estate of a deceased Muslim. The reasonable funeral expenses must be reimbursed from the estate before any claim of creditors, legatees and/or heirs is taken into consideration.

On the basis of the aforesaid discussion there should not be left any doubt in the minds of our readers that under Shariah there is a well established principle for the application and disposition of the estate of a deceased Muslim. Shariah recognises four main charges on the estate of a deceased Muslim. In order of priority these may be enumerated below:

1. Funeral expenses.
2. Debts.
3. Legacies.
4. Claims of heirs.

The author of *al-Sirajiyyah* has summed up these charges and their priorities in the following words:

> "There belong to the property of a deceased person four successive duties (to be performed by the Magistrate (Qadi): first, his funeral ceremony and burial without superfluity of expenses, yet without deficiency, next, the discharge of his just debts from the whole of his remaining effects; then, the payment of his legacies out of a third of what remains after his debts are paid; and lastly, the distribution of the residue among his successors, according to the Divine Book, to the Traditions and to the Assent of the learned".

So the Muslim law recognises the above mentioned four distinct purposes to which the estate of the deceased is successively applicable. In India the Muslim law in this respect has now been replaced by the Indian Succession Act of 1925, the effect of which is that the following claims are paid in the order.

(1) Funeral expenses and death bed charges, including fee for medical expenses, board and lodging for one month prior to his death. (Sec. 320)

(2) Expenses of obtaining probate or letters of Administration. (Sec.321)

(3) Wages for services rendered to the deceased within three months of his death by a labourer or servant. (Sec. 322)

(4) Debts of the deceased, if any, according to their priorities. No creditor shall have a right of priority over another, but the executor or administrator shall pay all such debts as he knows of, including his own, equally and rateably, as far as the assets of the deceased will extend. (Sec. 323)

(5) Legacies, not exceeding one-third of the residue (called the net estate), after all the above payments have been made. "Debts of every description must be paid before any legacy." (Sec. 325)

The debts are chargeable and throw the liability against the estate of the deceased so they must be paid before the distribution of the estate among the heirs.

(6) The distribution of the residue among the heirs of the deceased. By residue is meant, the residue of the *partible* estate and cannot include any portion of the impartible estate, left after the above mentioned five charges have been met.

Under the Act the person primarily entitled to administer the estate of a deceased Muslim, that is, to apply in the manner set forth above, is the executor appointed under his will. If the deceased left no will, the person entitled to administer his estate would be the persons to whom letters of administration are granted. In the absence of an executor or administrator the title of administration vests in the heirs of the deceased.

In India fundamental principles of Muslim Law relating to the administration of estate revolve round the rules laid down by Justice Mahmood in the leading case of Jafri Begum. The considered judgement of Mahmood deals with the law on the subject exhaustively. The following were the important propositions laid down:

Rule I: Devolution of Inheritance: When a Muslim dies leaving debts unpaid, his estate devolves immediately on his heirs and such devolution is not suspended till or contingent upon the payment of debts.

Rule II: Binding Nature of a Creditors Decree against Only one Heir: A decree for a debt passed against such of the heirs as are in possession of estate does not bind the other heirs.

Rule III: Proportionate Liability of the Heirs: If one of the heirs, who was out of possession and who was not a party to the proceedings, brings a suit against the decree-holder for the recovery of his share of the estate, he must pay his proportionate share of the debts before recovering possession of his share of inheritance.

Deceased's Estate and Law

The Rule II in Jafri Begum's case establishes the following principles:

> The theory of representation is not known to Muslim Law. Under Muslim law, each heir inherits a separate and defined share in the estate left by a deceased Muslim. One heir has no right or interest in the share inherited by another heir and can in no sense be said to represent the estate that was devolved on the other heirs. The principle of representation can have no application to such a case. The decree obtained against one of the heirs cannot, therefore be binding on the shares inherited by another heir. One heir cannot represent his co-heir.

In addition to the above guiding rules the following principles of administration relating to the estate of a deceased Muslim in India may also be taken as well established.

1. The estate of a deceased Muslim from the moment of his/her death belongs to the heirs according to law.
2. The proportionate interests of the heirs, if more than one, comes into *separate* existence as from the moment of death, irrespective of any interval that may lapse before the charges on the estate are paid off and the residue actually distributed.
3. Devolution is not contingent upon or deferred to any subsequent happening.
4. There is no intermediate vesting of the estate in anyone, not even in the executor or administrator. But see section 211 of the Indian Succession Act 1925 modifying this rule.
5. The payment of charges (funeral, debt, legacies) should precede appropriation by individual heirs.
6. If the division precedes the payment of debt, each individual heir is liable only to the extent of the portion of outstanding debt proportionate to the share he or she has actually received or allocated from the heritage of the deceased.

Role of Islam

Islam imposed clear cut restriction on the testamentary powers of a Muslim to dispose of his or her property in accordance with his or her whim and caprice.

By discarding the doctrine of primogeniture Islam laid down and set the pattern of equitable and democratic concept of distribution of heritage.

Parents, grandparents, daughters, grand-daughters, sisters, widows and many close relatives who were excluded in pre-Islamic time were made heirs. As a general rule Islam conferred new right of inheritance only on persons who were nearer, though excluded, than the customary heirs.

So the disqualification and incapability to inherit attached to females and cognates was abrogated by Islam. *Sura Nisa,* specially provides the right of inheritance to females and cognates:

> "... and unto the women belongeth a share of that which parents and near kindred leave ... a legal share."
>
> "Allah chargeth you concerning your *children* ... if there be women (female children) more than one then 2/3 for them and if there be one (only) then 1/2 ... and to parents a sixth each if there is a son and if no son then 1/3 to mother..."
>
> "...And unto them (widows) belongeth - l/4th... ...if ye have no child, but if ye have a child then l/8th of what ye leave..... and if a man or women have (neither parent nor child) and he (she) have a brother or a sister (only on the mother's side) then to each of them the sixth (1/6) and if they be more than one then 1/3..."
>
> ".... If a man die childless and have a sister, hers is half (1/2)... and if there be two sisters then two third 2/3..."
>
> "Unto each We have appointed heirs of that their parents and near relations (kindred) leave...."

The above verses were revealed to recognise the hereditary rights of females, cognates and parents.

The Holy Prophet (SAW), the real interpreter, the best interpreter and commentator of the Holy Quran and the best knower of the intention of Allah, the Law Giver of Islam, recognised the right of inheritance of females and cognates. *Sahih al Bukhari, Sunan Abu Daud* and other books of ahadis narrate many sayings of the Holy Prophet (SAW) to this effect.

Islam enhanced family dignity by abolishing the custom of inheriting -women including step mothers and prohibiting 'levirate marriages' in principle.

"O Ye who believe, It is not lawful for you forcibly to inherit the women (of your deceased kinsmen)...."

"And marry not those women whom your fathers married..."

By specifying clear cut entitlement and specific shares of female relatives Islam not only elevated their position but simultaneously safeguarded their social and economic interests. Islamic method of distribution of shares intended to break up the concentration of wealth in one or few hands thereby ensuring the socio-economic welfare of the family and society at large.

The distinctive features of Islamic law of succession may be summarised below.

Distinctive Features and Perfection of Islamic Law of Succession (Mirath): We have already seen the pathetic situation prevailing under Roman Law, Mosaic Law (Jewish Law), Hindu Law and English legal system. The inequalities and exclusion of parents and women from inheritance thereby degrading women to the position of chattels or if more to the barest status prevailing under the above mentioned legal systems have been removed by the revolutionary message of the Holy Prophet (SAW) and a more, equitable and just principle is established, to the astonishment of all systems, past and present, thereby ensuring the absolute right of women in different capacities, as mother, sister, daughter and widow. One of the great reforms introduced by Islam was to raise women in scale of civilization by elevating their moral and social position and giving the widows, the mothers, the daughters and sisters heritable rights.

Under Islamic law of succession the competitive claims of descendants, ascendants and collaterals have been satisfied in most equitable, practical and rational way. Macnaghten admits that it is difficult to conceive any system containing rules more strictly just and equitable than these under Islamic system.

Parents' Position: Islamic law takes note of the right of children and descendants to inherit from their parents and ancestors and at the same time places the parents in the first rank of heirs along with descendants. The Holy Quran itself safeguards the right of parents in the following verse:

> "... And the parents of the deceased shall have, each of them, a sixth part of what he shall leave if he has a child, but if he has no child and his parents be his heirs, then his mother shall have a third part... ye know not whether your parents or your children be a greater use unto you."

Thus under Islamic law the parents inherit simultaneously with children and descendants of the deceased and are never excluded by them (unlike other legal systems). It is natural that when grown up children die the parents arc generally old and infirm and therefore are more in need of assistance, and further the care, sacrifices and advice bestowed by the parents on their own children in the past can never be nullified by any consideration of preeminence in the matter of affection in favour of children.

It is unhappy contingency for the father and mother to inherit from their own children, the parents themselves anticipate that their children would inherit from them, but if they should, unfortunately survive, it is only fit and proper fair and equitable that they should have the right of immediate succession to their deceased children's property. Islam has adopted this attitude because any other course would have been against the laws of nature. In deed it may be noted that no other system of jurisprudence except Islamic law provides for the parents to succeed simultaneously with children and never to be excluded by them.

Nature and Kind of Property: We have seen that in almost all systems the distinction is made between real and personal property. The natural law of succession refers to personal property. The succession to personal property is governed by one set of rules while succession to immovable (real) property is based on different principles.

Hindu law, similarly, distinguishes between ancestral and self acquired property and provides different sets of rules of succession for the two categories of property. However, the Muslim law makes no distinction between various kinds of properties for the purpose of succession. Under Islamic law whether the property is real or personal, ancestral or self-acquired, corpus or usufruct, movable or immovable, is immaterial, the rules of succession are one and the same.

Rules of Primogeniture: The well known rule of primogeniture which is the incidence of real property in various systems, as discussed above, is not recognised by Islam and is completely foreign to Islamic law. Islam prohibits preference between same class of heirs *e.g.* sons. Macnaghten observes: "The apparently unjust preference of the older son, to the exclusion of all the rest which in our own law had its origin in the feudal policy of the times; is rejected by Islam and the equitable principle of equality obtains in its stead. Black-stone informs us that "the Greeks, the Romans, the Britons, the Saxons and even originally the Feudalists do not recognise the rule of primogeniture." He admits that this (the non-recognition of this rule) is the most obvious and natural way.

Males and Females: In principle males do not exclude females. Males share with their female counterparts. The difference in their shares is based on the natural difference in their basic needs to discharge their primary obligations in the society.

Spouse's Position: Quran fixes the right of spouses under different situations. The share and attention provided to them is both natural and just, they arc neither excluded by any other heir nor can they exclude others. Considering the relative position of spouse on one hand and that of the other heirs on the other there could not have been any better approach than the one adopted by Islam.

The systems attaching undue importance to the hereditary rights of the spouses should have taken into consideration the most likely situation where the surviving spouse after getting the lions share marries another person and acquires additional rights in the property of new spouse. This to many may suit to be the best method of acquisition of property. One of the main causes of high rate of divorces, in so-called civilized countries of the West (including those who imitate them) is this unduly advantageous position of spouses under the laws of succession. Quran by natural and reasonable course has closed the doors of any such temptation.

The policy of unrestricted testamentary power and over emphasis of testamentary succession adopted by English law, Common law, Roman law, Nigerian statutory and Customary law, Hindu law and many other modern systems has relegated the laws of intestate succession and their practical importance to the secondary position. It negates the very basis and purpose of intestate succession.

Due to unnatural, unequitable and arbitrary approach in distribution of property of deceased adopted by the above mentioned legal systems, the scope, the usefulness and the practical value of the laws of succession has been considerably restricted. This branch has, consequently, lost its significance and utility in the present time and ceased to be one of general interest and utility. Intestate succession still occupies the place of pride under Islamic jurisprudence. The testamentary succession is of only secondary importance.

The natural, just, equitable and rational approach coupled with perfection and precision in the distribution of shares of various heirs adopted by Islamic law of succession has rendered it most significant and valuable aspect of Islamic jurisprudence. By virtue of affecting the interest of all description of people it is unquestionably of great importance and utility to every Muslim.

Coulson has correctly assessed the nature importance and scope of this branch of Islamic jurisprudence in the following words:

> "Above all, however, the great esteem which this branch of legal science enjoys among Muslims stems from its particularly strong religious significance. True knowledge, or '*ilm*', in the Islamic view, stems from divine revelation, and according to a statement of the Prophet (SAW) the laws of inheritance constitute 'half the sum of 'ilm'. Nowhere is the fundamental Islamic ideology of law as the manifestation of the divine will more clearly demonstrated than in the laws of succession and inheritance. The system is firmly based on the very words of Allah Himself and this is reflected in the terminology of the law, *i.e.*, 'ilm-ul-Faraid'. This epitomises the notion of religious obligation. The laws of succession are vital aspect of the individual's supreme duty to the religion of Islam. In many modern Muslim Countries whole spheres of traditional Islamic law have been abandoned and replaced by laws of European origin. But the law of succession still continues to be generally applied in practice throughout the Islamic world mainly because it constitutes such an integral and deep-rooted part of the religious ethic." The same was the main consideration which guided the policy of noninterference in the Muslim law of succession adopted by the colonial powers in the administration of their colonies.

Excellence and Importance of Islamic Law of Succession

On the death of a Muslim how his or her property is to be distributed among the surviving heirs is elaborately provided in the Holy Quran itself. The provisions, the Holy Quran make, are both fundamental and comprehensive. Their correct interpretation, proper explanation and practical demonstration by the Prophet (SAW) and systematic exposition and development by his illustrious companions have made them most practical and precise. In appreciation of these provisions of Shariah Macnaghten remarks:

> "In these provisions we find ample attention paid to the interests of all those whom nature places in the first rank of our affection; and indeed it is difficult to conceive

> any system containing rules more strictly just and equitable. The obvious principle of preferring the nearer kindred to claimants whose relation to the deceased is not so proximate, seems to have been adopted as the invariable standard for fixing the portion; and the rules for the succession of several heirs and the order of preference assigned to the different degrees of consanguinity seems to be exactly what would be most consonant to the general inclination of mankind."

The Islamic law of succession, Mirath, is a great achievement of Muslim jurist. In its minutest detail it is a system rendered to perfection, and thus deserves our admiration and attention.

Fayzee rightly observes that Muslim jurists gave a great deal of importance to the laws of inheritance (Ilm-ul-Fraid); and they are never tired of repeating the saying of the Prophet (SAW) "Learn the laws of inheritance, and teach them to people; for they are one half of the useful knowledge. Many renowned modern authors of Islamic law have admired the system for its utility, logic, perfection and formal excellence.

Tyabji observes: "The Muslim Law of Inheritance has always been admired for its completeness as well as the success with which it has achieved the ambitious aim of providing not merely for the selection of a single individual or homogeneous group of individuals, on whom the estate of the deceased should devolve by universal succession, but for adjusting the competitive claims of all the nearest relations."

As to the excellence of the system in a formal sense, Sir William Jones said: "I am strongly disposed to believe that no possible question could occur on the Muhammadan Law of Succession which might not be rapidly and correctly answered."

The fundamental principles of Islamic law of inheritance are well explained by that master mind, Justice Mahmood, in the leading case on pre-emption:

> "I may observe that the law of inheritance was founded by the Prophet (SAW) upon republican principles at a time when the modern democratic conception of equality and division of property was unknown even in the most advanced countries of Europe."

Mr. A. Rumsey is of the view that "the Muhammadan law of inheritance comprises beyond question the most refined and elaborate system of rules for the devolution of propert that is known to the civilized world." Coulson remarks: "juristically, the law of succession is a solid technical achievement, and Muslim scholarship takes a justifiable pride in the mathematical precision with which the right of the various heirs, in any given situation, can be calculated."

According to Rumsey, "Islamic law of inheritance in its present form, is a fixed scientific and beautifully harmonious system." He further observes:

> "Rules governing the distribution among Distant kindred constitute most curious and interesting system of devolution which the world has yet seen."

The Rulings

Heritable Property: Muslim law makes no distinction between: (i) Movable and immovable property; (ii) Ancestral and self acquired property (as is the case under Hindu law); (iii) Joint and separate property (as is the case under Hindu law); and (iv) Real and Personal property (as is the case under English law).

All the above categories of property, including actionable claims and interests, short of ownership, constitute the heritage of a deceased Muslim. Thus in Islam the concept of property is very simple but its scope very wide. It comprises all forms of property, and includes both corpus *(ayn)* and usufruct *(manafi).*

So the 'estate' of a deceased Muslim means and includes all types and categories of property left by him or her on death. After the payment of funeral expenses, payments of debts, if any, and satisfaction of valid bequests, if any, the remaining property is the net property available for distribution and allocation among heirs (relations entitled to inherit). This net property is the heritable property which devolves or descends on the heirs according to law. All female heirs, like male heirs are entitled to have their shares out of all categories of heritage *i.e.* heritable. Perfect equality between male and female heirs is provided in this respect.

Partnership in Islam

When two or more persons hold and own the same property, without having specific and defined shares they are called joint tenants, the property as joint property and their interest as joint interest. The joint property is commonly owned property, the common owners are co-owners and their joint interest is co-ownership. The essence of joint tenancy is unity of ownership. The nature of ownership of joint tenants in the joint property is communal ownership. Their interest is joint and not separate. Each joint tenant has an interest in the whole but does not enjoy an exclusive right to any part thereof. While joint ownership of the property belongs jointly to all joint-tenants. No such tenant can predict that he/she has a definite share, say, one-fourth or one-sixth. In other words the interest of joint tenants is unpredictable and unspecified.

Another aspect of a joint tenancy and joint interest is the right of all the joint-tenants to the common use and enjoyment of all the joint properties. None of them can claim exclusive possession or ownership against others. Similarly common enjoyment and common use cannot be denied to any one joint-tenant. The possession of one tenant is deemed to be possession of all others, so the actual possessor cannot claim adverse possession. The above concept of joint property, joint interest and joint-tenancy is peculiar to Hindu Law. In spite of many enactments to modernise and rationalise Hindu law, the joint property and joint interest are still recognised by modern Hindu law.

The Hindu law concept and principle of jointness of property and interest is unknown to Muslim Law. From the mere fact of commonality no presumption as to the existence of joint family, joint property or joint interest can arise in Islam. Under Islamic law on the death of an owner his/her heir at once become entitled to specific shares. Some of them or all of them may not actually divide the property and continue managing jointly.

Such arrangement unlike Hindu law does not create joint-tenancy or joint family. They are only tenants-in-common owning well defined and specified shares. They can actually and physically separate and take possession of their specific shares, any time they like, without any technical or legal formality. Before actual separation and division if any such heir dies his or her undivided but specific and well defined interest devolves on the heirs of the deceased and is not taken by the surviving co-heirs.

In case of any additional acquisition of property by an individual there is no presumption that the same is joint acquisition. Such acquisition belongs to the heir acquiring it. The heirs so joint are free to deal with their respective shares. These heirs have exclusive right of possession, use and enjoyment as well as alienation without the consent or concurrence of the other heirs.

Concept of Survivorship

The main characteristic of the joint-tenancy is the right of survivorship *i.e.* on the death of one joint-tenant the whole property becomes vested in the surviving tenants. The joint tenant so long as is alive has a joint interest in the property and a right to common use and enjoyment but once he/she dies, he/she goes away and leaves nothing behind. The entire property now belongs to the surviving joint-tenants. The legal heirs of the deceased joint-tenant cannot claim the specified and undivided interest of the deceased. Rule of survivorship being a logical corollary to the joint tenancy and jointness of interest is an integral part of Hindu legal system (Mitakshara System). The rule of survivorship is still recognised as one of the modes of devolution of property of a deceased Hindu under the Hindu Succession Act 1956, an Act introducing radical changes in the Hindu law of inheritance and succession.

But Islam rejects the rule of survivorship as it has rejected the concept of jointness of property and interest. Under Islamic law the death of an heir who has not separated his or her share from those of others does allow the surviving co-heirs to get the deceased's share by survivorship but it goes to the heir of the deceased co-heir.

Laws before Islam

Distinctive Features of English Law of Succession

Inheritance Descends Iineally: Children and descendants completely exclude ascendants and collaterals. Even parents cannot succeed simultaneously with descendants. What a disregard and disrespect to the laws of nature. A scholar of the calibre of Bentham tried to justify the exclusion of parents by children. This position did not change even after the Acts of 1925, 1952, 1966, 1969. Now even in the presence of surviving spouse the parents and collaterals are practically excluded from inheriting anything in the face of undue weightage given to the right of the surviving spouse.

Males Preferred to Females: Males in equal degree of relationship to the prepositions were, till recently, preferred to females. This rule applied not only to issues but extended to heirs in ascendant and collateral line. This precedence is far older than feudalism, but the feudal influence made for its retention.

Rule of Primogeniture: The recognition of this rule is a clear example of discrimination and injustice under English legal system. On the basis of this Rule eldest son and his issues were preferred to all other children and their issues. The combined effect of this rule and the rule of Representation was to exclude, completely and forever, other children and their descendant.

Distinction of Real and Personal Property: This is a feudal principle of the laws of succession under English Legal System and those based on it. This distinction breeds jealousy and hatred among the heirs. The distinction unnecessarily evolved two sets of rules governing succession to the two kinds of properties. The one known as Rules of Inheritance, regulating the mode in which real estate on the death of its owner dying intestate descended to his blood relations, the other set of rules called the Rules of Succession, determining the manner in which the personal property of the deceased who died intestate was to be distributed among his next of kin. The administration of Estate Act, 1925 S. 46(1) ultimately merged the two sets and removed the unnecessary bone of contention.

Undue Weightage to the Right of Spouse: The enactments of the Intestate Estate Act, 1952, Family Provision Act, 1966 and Family Law Reform Act, 1969, gradually tilted the balance in favour of surviving spouse, vis a vis issues and other heirs. Personal Chattes absolutely belonged to the surviving spouse. In addition to this privilege the surviving spouse is guaranteed a minimum interest in the property of the deceased spouse even at the cost of children. At common law as well as under the Married Women's Property Act, 1882 husband used to enjoy greater rights.

Distinctive Features of Statutory Law of Succession in Nigeria

Being based on the English legal system it embodies more or less the same governing principles. The following features of this system provide enough proof that it has honestly and faithfully tried to follow the system of the past colonial masters.

1. It recognises in principle right of the children and descendants to exclude parents, ascendants and collaterals.
2. Males are generally preferred to females of the same class.
3. Rules of primogeniture is recognised and applied.
4. Distinction of Real and Personal Property with all their incidents is recognised and applied, even though it is now merged under English law.
5. Over emphasis of the right of spouse is reflected.

Distinctive Features under the Customary Law of Nigeria

A. *Yoruba System*

1. Children and descendants exclude other blood relations.
2. Management remains in the hands of the eldest son—an offshoot of the Rule of primogeniture.
3. Parents are excluded even by brothers and sisters.
4. Equal share irrespective of sex of the heirs.
5. Surviving spouse completely excluded even by distant collaterals.

B. *IBO system*

1. Children and descendants exclude ascendants and collaterals. Parents are excluded even by brothers and their issues.
2. Males exclude females.
3. Widows are completely excluded.

C. *Bini and Ishan systems.*

1. Rule of Primogeniture recognised.
2. Males excludes females.
3. Parent are excluded by children and their issues.

Jewish Law: *Mosaic Law* on the subject of succession and inheritance is more brief and less comprehensive. "And thou shalt speak unto the children of Israel, saying, if a man die, and have no son, then ye shall cause his inheritance to pass unto his daughter, and if he have no daughter, then ye shall give his inheritance to his brethren. And if he have no brethren, then ye shall give his inheritance unto his father's brethren..."

Macnaghten commenting on the above passage observes that here we find no provision whatever made for parents. Even if we presume that at least father gets before his brethren but at any rate he and mother arc excluded by children, their issues and at least by brothers of the deceased. The Jewish law also does not contain express provision for the spouse. It definitely prefers males over females (son over daughter). Daughter had no interest in the property of their mothers.

Among Israelites right of inheritance belonged to agnates only. The wives in early times, were considered as property of the husband and on his death were inherited by his heirs. These heirs had an obligation to marry these widows. Even sons of the deceased father had the same obligation towards father's widows (step-mothers). Such marriages are called 'levirate marriages'. Right of primogeniture was recognised. Females including daughters whether married or unmarried had no right of inheritance. As a later development, in the absence of sons, daughters were allowed to inherit conditionally. Hebrew antiquity did not recognise any difference between legitimate and illegitimate blood tie.

Hindu Law: In Indian sub-continent under the ancient Hindu system right of inheritance was confined to male agnates. Cognates were excluded by agnates. Ascendants, including father, were completely excluded by male agnatic descendants. Rule of Primogeniture was recognised. Joint family property, right by birth and rule of survivorship governed the devolution among Hindus. Females in all capacities were generally deprived from hereditary rights. Only in 1937 widows were allowed to enjoy a limited interest in their deceased husbands' property.

Even this right was not absolute and was limited to their life time. It was only in 1956 that females *i.e.* mothers, daughters, widows and sisters, were included in the category of heirs. There were two different sets of rules of devolution of property separately applicable in cases of male and female deceases. Hindu legal system recognised the distinction between ancestral and self acquired property. The succession differed according to the nature of property. Even after the radical reforms and changes effected by the Hindu succession Act, 1956, the distinction based on ancestral and self acquired properties, the sex of the deceased, the injustice to father have not been abolished. The retention and continuation of these unnatural distinctive features have considerably minimised the importance and practical value of this reformed legal system. To illustrate the unreasonable and unnatural approach of the system, even after the recent effort to modernise and rationalise the existing Hindu law of succession, father's case is enough. He, even today, stands excluded not only by male agnates but even by daughter's children and son's and grandson's widows. What an irony, an injustice and a clear contradiction of the laws of nature.

Other Legal Systems: Under the succession laws of Russia the inheritance is limited to descendants, surviving spouse, disable bodied parents and other persons who were actually dependant upon the deceased for the year prior to his or her death.

In the early stage of the Bolshevik revolution the inheritance was limited to close relations provide they were in need. This limitation and condition of need was lifted in 1926.

Pre-Islamic Arabian Customary Law: Before Islam succession to property of a deceased both among Arabs and non-Arabs was quite unsatisfactory and not well defined. Both testate and intestate succession were prevalent among Arabs. Like other ancient societies, Arabs also enjoyed the complete freedom of testamentary disposition.

In the tribal society of pre-Islamic Arabia the system of inheritance was designed to keep property within the individual tribe and maintain its strength as a fighting force. The object and purpose of inheritance under the customary rules of Arabs was the maintenance of the goods in the family. Concept of tribalism and corresponding responsibilities did not permit the inclusion of maternal or uterine relations in the scheme of inheritance. Notion of kinship were based on the blood feud which gave rise to the principle of comradeship. The right of succession depended on comradeship in arms. The basic principle of inheritance among them was the criterion that one must be capable of defending the honour of the family and tribe. So the property of a deceased Arab devolved on his male agnates capable of bearing arms and as a result all females, minors, infirm and old persons incapable of bearing arms were excluded. Among early Arabs, the comradeship in arms *i.e.*, the tie of war or revenge, was considered more important than family or blood tie.

The heirship was determined by consanguinity, adoption or contract. Only male agnates enjoyed the right of inheritance and nearest of them used to exclude the rest. In spite of recognizing both, agnatic and cognatic, relationships they preferred agnates over cognates. Female had no right of ownership and, therefore, were not allowed to inherit. Daughters and sisters were excluded because they ceased, upon their marriage, to be members of their natural (paternal) family. Wives had no separate entity due to merger of their personality, on marriage, into that of her husband. Consequently she as widow, formed an integral part of the estate of her husband, and subject of inheritance. On the death of a person his sons and, in their absence, his brothers inherited these widows like any other property. They descended to them as heritage of their father or brother as the case might be. The inheritors treated them their wives. This particular custom was the cause of origin of 'levirate marriages' not only among Arabs but also among other nations.

Females were not allowed even a limited right. Uterine brothers and sisters were also not considered heirs. The result was complete exclusion of females and cognates from inheritance and complete monopoly of hereditary rights by male agnates. Among agnates Descendants were preferred to Ascendants and Ascendants to Collaterals. Male agnates of equal degree of nearness, capable of bearing arms, shared the estate per capita.

Law Applicable to the Indian Christians: Before the enforcement of The Indian Succession Act, 1865, Indian Christians, like many other communities in India, were governed by the Common Law of England including the law of succession, both intestate and testamentary. But from 1st January 1866 provisions of the 1865 Act were applied to the Indian Christians. This Act was repealed in 1925 by The Indian Succession Act, 1925. The main features of the intestate succession applicable to the Indian Christians today may be summarised below:

According to the Provisions of the Indian Succession Act, 1925 amended upto date they are as follows:

1. Equal shares to males and females.
2. No distinction between agnates and cognates.
3. Doctrine of representation applies in a modified form.
4. Doctrine of primogeniture not recognised.
5. No simultaneous succession of parents and descendants. Descendants completely exclude parents and other heirs except spouses.
6. Father excludes mother (just opposite in Hindu law).

7. Adoption does not create the tie capable of giving right of inheritance.
8. No distinction between full blood and half blood tie (either from father's or mother's) side.

Law Applicable to the Indian Parsis: At present Succession among Indian Parsis is governed by the provisions of The Indian Succession Act 1925. Prior to 1837 Indian Parsis were, in the matter of succession, governed by English Common Law. The Parsee Chattels Real Act 1837 exempted the Parsis to a great extent, from the operation of English law of primogeniture. But in all cases of intestacy, they were still to be governed by the English Statute of Distribution. Parsis persistently demanded their separate personal law and freedom from English laws and statutes. Their efforts bore fruit in the form of Parsee Intestate Succession Act, 1865.

Under the 1865 Act, widows and daughters were for the first time, allowed to inherit. Mother and other females were still had no right of inheritance. Many provisions of English law continued to be applied to Parsis particularly relating to succession of immovable property even after the enactment of The Indian Succession Act, 1925.

The widows and daughters were given very small share under the 1925 Act. Parents were excluded in the presence of descendants till 1939.

In 1939 the 1925 Act was substantially amended to give a better deal to the right of parents and females. The amended Act of 1939 introduced the widows of predeceased lineal descendent as heirs and excluded the widower of a predeceased daughter from the category of heirs.

Main features of the Parsi succession law as it stands today (under the Indian Succession Act, 1925 as amended up date) may be summarised as under.

1. There are two sets of rules of succession one for a male decease and the other for a female decease like Hindu law.
2. Parents are allowed to inherit simultaneously with lineal descendants only on the death of a male Parsi. But on the death of a female Parsi parents are excludes in the presence of descendants.
3. In the case of a male decease the rule of double share to male (a peculiarity of Islamic law) is followed. But in case of a female decease equal shares are given to males and females.
4. Adoption is not recognised a cause of inheritance.
5. Since 1837 application of the rule of Primogeniture is discarded.
6. There is no distinction between different kinds of properties *e.g.* real, personal, ancestral, movable, immoveable etc.
7. Distant relations are entitled to inherit in the absence of descendants and parents but take simultaneously with widows (entitled to inherit).

6

Will of the Departing

All Muslims were urged by the Prophet to write his will as soon as possible and to have it certified by two qualified witnesses. The Muslim was forbidden to make wills in favour of any would-be heir, or to dispose by will of more than one-third of his net property without the future heirs' approval. The reason given by the Prophet for restricting the right of will is that it is better to leave one's heirs comfortable than destitute.

> "It is prescribed for you that when one of you is face to face with death, if he leaves any goods he should make an equitable legacy in favour of his father and mother and kinsmen". (Quran, 2 : 176)

A will is a transaction to come into operation after the testator's death. It means an endowment of a right in property which is to take effect on the death of the person conferring the right. It means in common language to "convey", the root being "Wassa", (he conveyed), and in a legal sense, it means a gift of property by its owner to another contingent on his (the giver's) death.

The Person Who Wills

Any person capable of entering into legal transactions is capable of making a bequest. But the following conditions must be observed:

(a) Sanity. He must be sane, but a Safih-imbecile, is capable of making a bequest.
(b) The testator must be the owner of the subject-matter or the bequest.
(c) A person being in debt to the full amount of his property cannot make a valid bequest.

Recipient of the Legacy

A *wasiyya* may be made to any person or object actually or constructively in existence at the time of the disposition.

A *wasiyya* is lawful for any purpose which is considered proper under the law, and which may be carried into effect at the time of the testator's death.

1. *Non-Muslims:* A bequest to a non-Muslim who does not reside in an enemy country is valid.
2. It is lawful to make a bequest in favour of an embryo. But it must be born alive and born within such a period as establishes its existence at the time of the bequest or the testator's demise.

   Where a bequest is made in favour of an embryo and it turns to be twins the bequest is shared between them. If one is born alive and the other dead the bequest automatically goes to the survivor.

   But where one dies immediately after his birth his share goes to his heirs.
3. A bequest in favour of a deceased person is valid if the testator knew of the legatee's death, in which case it passes to the latter's heirs. If he did not know of the legatee's death, the bequest lapses.
4. It can be made in favour of the poor generally or a particular body of them.
5. It can be made in favour of the children or one's heirs, kindred, neighbours, etc.
6. It can be made to satisfy one's debts.
7. It can be made in favour of a mosque or any other public institution.
8. Where a bequest is made in favour of another person's child and the testator is not aware that, that person had no child at the time of making the bequest, then it passes to any child that the person may later have.

   But if he knew that the person had no child, existing or in embryo; then the bequest lapses.
9. Where a bequest is made in favour of "Legatee's relatives" all of them share equally in the bequest.
10. Where the testator makes a bequest in favour of his own relatives, only those who are not entitled to inherit, can share in it.
11. "No bequest to an heir". This is an express prohibition by the Holy Prophet (S.A.W.). But where a bequest is made in favour of an heir, the remaining heirs may give their consent to it (such consent must be obtained after the testator's death) and the bequest will be regarded as gift to the heir, i.e. legatee from the consenting heirs.

The consenting heirs must be adult and *sui juris*, and the general rules of gift will apply.

Whether a person is an heir or not, must be considered with reference to his right of inheritance at the time of the testator's death.

Therefore, when a person leaves a legacy to his brother at a time when he has no son, and afterwards a son is born to him and he, the testator, dies, then the brother's legacy is valid since in the presence of the son, the brother has no right to the inheritance.

On the other hand, if the testator makes the legacy to the brother when he has a son and the son dies before the testator dies, then the brother becomes an heir and the rule applies to him.

When some of the heirs consent and others do not, the legacy will be valid in proportion to the share of the consenting heirs.

A bequest in favour of the person who intentionally causes the death of the testator is invalid.

If the act which caused the death, was not intentional, the bequest is valid.

If the testator knew that it was the legatee who inflicted the mortal wound on him but pardons the assailant-legatee, or makes the bequest in his favour after the infliction of the injury, the bequest is valid.

This may be regarded as an act of condemnation. Bequests may be either:

(a) entirely for religious purposes, or

(b) for mundane purposes, or

(c) for both jointly.

Bequests for religious purposes take precedence over all.

Examples of bequests for religious purposes are bequests for the performance of Hajj-pilgrimage to Mecca, or payment of Zakat - alms or fasting.

These are further divided into:

(a) Those providing for obligatory duties *(farz)* such as for the performance of pilgrimage or payment of Zakat;

(b) Those providing for obligatory duties such as payment of expiation-Kaffere fulfilment of vows, e.g. *fitr*, alms; and

(c) Performance of super-erogatory duties (Nawafil), e.g. the umra pilgrimage of Mecca.

In all these bequests if the testator did not expressly give preference for the execution of any of them, preference will be given to category (a) then (b) and then (c).

The Rituals

1 *Offer:* A will may be made either verbally or in writing. It may be constituted by the use of any expression that sufficiently indicates the intention of the testator, so long as it is apparent that the intention of the testator is to make a disposition operative on his death, e.g.:

"I have bequeathed such a thing to so and so" or "I have bequeathed towards such a one".

A bequest may also be made by signs, as in the case of a dumb person who does not possess the faculty of speech but who can express his meaning by signs. So also in the case of a person who is sick suffering from death sickness.

A wasiyya may be conditional or contingent. Its operation therefore is dependent upon the happening or the contingency, and if the contingency does not happen, it will not be given effect. For example, if the testator says, "Should I die from this illness" or "Should I not return from this journey, I bequeath such a thing to so and so". The wasiyya in either case will not take effect, if the contingencies apprehended do not happen.

Whether the will be in words or in writing.

However, Imam Malik himself and other authorities maintain that where such a contingent-bequest is reduced to writing to which witnesses have testified and the written document handed over to the legatee or a third person, the bequest is valid even though the contingency does not happen, provided the document is not withdrawn.

2 *Acceptance:* The validity of a wasiyya is subject to will of the testator.

If the legatee should reject part of the bequest and accept the remainder, such partial acceptance is valid.

If a legatee should die before acceptance, his heirs take his place and may accept the bequest.

But where a bequest is made to a body of people, or a general class, such as the poor, or is in favour of a general religious or pious purpose, the acceptance of the legatee is presumed.

3 *Revocation:* A will is essentially revocable either expressly or by implication. It may be revoked at any time, even during the last illness of the testator. The testator may during his lifetime, either by express language or by any act which ignores or contradicts the wasiyya, revoke his offer of the wasiyya.

Among the various acts of implied revocation are sale and gift of the subject-matter. A bequest lapses by the apostasy of either the testator or the legatee. But where the legacy has been made in writing it does not lapse by the apostasy of the testator.

A bequest lapses if the legatee rejects it.

Object of the Bequest: Anything movable, over which the right of property may be exercised, or which may form the subject of exchange or barter or a fractional share thereof or the usufruct of a thing, e.g. land, trees, etc., may be lawfully disposed of by will.

A bequest remains valid and operative, though the subject matter should undergo a change or improvement after the constitution of the will, unless the alteration is so substantial as to give rise to the presumption that the testator in making such a change or improvement, intended revocation. In the same way, the legatee bears any loss or deterioration to which the property may have been subjected during the interval.

When a piece of land has been bequeathed to a person, and subsequently a building is erected upon it by the testator, the land should, upon the death of the testator, go to the legatee and the building to the testator's heirs.

When a person bequeaths a house to another and later the house falls down, the legacy is void because its subject-matter no longer exists.

A testator has the power to dispose of not more than one-third of the property belonging to him through will, at the time of his death and after his funeral expenses and his debts are paid. This limitation is based on the authority of the Holy Prophet (S.A.W.).

But the heirs may assent to the excess bequest, in which case it will be treated as a free gift from the heirs to the legatee and rules of gift will apply, e.g. inter-alia, the heirs must be adult and capable of making gratuitous dispositions.

When the testator leaves no heir, he cannot make a bequest exceeding one-third, because in the absence of the natural heirs, the rest goes to Bait-ul-mal (public treasury) as quasiasaba.

How to Make a Will?

The testator should be sane, major and possessed of ownership of property. While making a will, there should be an expression of clear intention which may be oral or in writing. According to the Shafii law, even a feeble-minded person may make a "wasiyat", though of course a lunatic or a madman cannot make.

There should be an acceptance of the legacy by the person in whose favour it is made and which may be expressed or implied as the case may be.

A Wasiyat may be made in respect of:

(1) The corpus of any property capable of being transferred and is in existence at the time of the testator's death; or

(2) Of the usufruct of such property for limited period or for the lifetime of the legatee.

It can be made for any purpose which is not prohibited by religion or the Islamic law.

The Arabs of Jahaliyya had unlimited power of disposing of their property by will. The first restriction came by the above verse of the Quran. So far it appeared to concern legacies in favour of heirs. But some people have argued that this Quranic verse stands abrogated by the subsequent texts on the law of inheritance. However, no verse of the Quran abrogates another verse, but it merely restricts its scope.

Nevertheless, the restrictions on legacies or wills rest on the traditions of the Holy Prophet (S.A.W.).

The Holy Prophet (S.A.W.) is said to have forbidden Saad b. Abu Waqqas from bequeathing more than one-third of his estate, He says, this "is ample" although Saad had no heir except a daughter.

On the basis of juristic equity, Wasiyat or will, with regard to spiritual wants, enables the testator to make up his shortcomings during life by pious work.

Definition: It affords the testator the means to circumvent the law of succession in order to help somebody not normally entitled to inheritance.

Any person or institution capable of holding property may be a legatee, provided that the legatee is in existence at the time of the testator's death, or is in the womb and is born within a period of six months of the date of the Wasiyat.

However, a Wasiyat cannot be made in favour of any heir, i.e. Mafqud-ul-Khabar, a murderer under Hanafi law, but not under Shafii law, an animal and the unknown.

Allotment of Property by Will

Wassiyya or Testamentary disposition is the conferment of a right of property (tamlik) in a specific thing or in a profit or advantage, to take effect after the death of the testator.

The Quran first recommended that bequests should be made in favour of near relatives and later laid down certain specific rules for the distribution of a deceased person's estate on the strength of these rules. The Holy Prophet (S.A.W.) in one of his traditions, prohibited bequests being made in favour of heirs.

However, this prophetic tradition was interpreted by most jurists to mean that bequests to heirs were valid if they had the consent of other heirs.

But the Maliki jurists gave a rigid interpretation of this prophetic tradition, and maintained that where a bequest is made in favour of an heir, and the other heirs consent to this bequest, then the transaction must be regarded as a gift from the consenting heirs.

A bequest, from the Muslim point of view, is a divine institution, because its exercise is regulated by the Quran. It offers to the testator the means of modifying to a certain extent the law of succession, and of enabling some of those relatives, who are excluded from inheritance, to obtain a share in his property. It may be necessary to recognise the services rendered to him by a stranger, or reward him for the devotion shown to him during his last days.

At the same time, the Holy Prophet (S.A.W.) has declared that the power should not be exercised to the injury of the lawful heirs.

Wasiyya - Bequest: There are four essentials to bequests:

1. Testator (Musi).
2. Legatee (Musa Lahu).
3. Formalities (Sigha).
4. Bequest Object (Musa Bihi).

7

Usefulness of Fatwas

Saudi Arabia's legal system is governed by the traditional corpus of Islamic law, *fiqh*, to an extent equalled by no other existing national legal system. Saudi Arabia was never colonised, and, unlike virtually every other Islamic country, it has not replaced its legal system with a Western-model constitutional and legal order. Still, the Saudi system has been considerably modernised in two respects. First, the prevailing law, the *fiqh* of the Hanbali school, has been extensively supplemented by decree-laws issued by the king in areas where modern arrangements demand new legal provisions. Second, the legal system has undergone considerable administrative and institutional development and rationalisation. Even with these changes, however, the Saudi legal system remains at heart animated by Islamic legal conceptions and practices very close to those that shaped the first Saudi state many years ago.

Religious Format

The Bedouin of the Judean Desert are subject to the jurisdiction of the Shariah courts of Jerusalem and Bethlehem. Since the annexation of the West Bank by the Kingdom of Jordan, the Jordanian law of personal status has applied in these courts. Alongside the courts, tribal arbitrators act without any statutory status. The Bedouin of the Judean Desert resort to both the *qadi* and to the tribal arbitrator. In matters of personal status, the arbitrator gradually has been superseded by the institutionalised *qadi*, whose position has been reinforced by the execution of his judgments and by civil regulations (such as the requirement that marital status be recorded in identity cards and that government licenses be obtained for various day-to-day activities) that have prompted the Bedouin to resort to the court.

In Jordan, muftis linked to Shariah courts in the main districts are found throughout the country. Staff lists and salary records suggest that the formal status of these muftis in the hierarchy of religious scholars is lower than that of the *qadis* in their respective districts. Nevertheless, the mufti's public status may be higher than that of the *qadi*, depending on the former's personality and legal and moral authority. In addition to the appointed muftis, religious scholars ('*Ulema*') and jurists (*fuqaha*) serve as muftis without appointment. They are not integrated into the establishment; their status is based on their personal authority. They regard themselves as competent to decide, at the request of members of the public, all matters to which the Shariah applies, not just matters that fall within the jurisdiction of the Shariah court (Layish 1977:97-108).

The applicant for the legal opinion in the case under discussion here, Sheikh Ali Hasan, belongs to a clan (*hamoula*) of the al-Radaida Arab al-Ubaydiyya. This tribe is located east of Bayt Sahur in the Jerusalem-Bethlehem region. The sedentarisation of the tribe began in the 1920s and is now almost complete (Layish and Shmueli 1979:30). It seems that Sheikh Ali Hasan chose to apply to the mufti because he surmised that he could not expect the Shariah court to extricate him from the predicament into which he had stumbled.

The resulting fatwa was later given to me by Sheikh Ali Hasan. It belongs to a collection of legal documents gathered from tribal arbitrators in the Judean Desert and from the archives of Shariah courts. Although the scholar who signed the fatwa is unknown to me, references in the legal opinion to the religio-legal literature indicate that he had a sound traditional training in Islamic law. In any case, the scholar, who identifies himself as a Shafii, appears not to be a mufti by appointment, because his opinion is not written on official stationery and is not dated. This indicates that he was not affiliated with an institution but rather was acting in a private capacity. His authority derives from his generally recognised learning and probably also from his reputation as a pragmatist who resolves legal situations involving hardship. Such an independent mufti gives an opinion to every comer, in the best classical tradition, and probably receives a fee for his trouble.

Logic and Setting of a Decree

The *sharii* mechanism of suspended repudiation distinguishes between repudiation intended to ensure the wife's obedience to the husband and repudiation involving an oath, lending additional weight to some utterances of the husband, in which case there is no intention of divorce. In both cases, the divorce becomes effective upon the fulfilment of the condition or contingency mentioned in the oath (Layish 1975:137ff., 156ff.; Anderson 1976:123ff.; Anderson 1970, 362-363). Sheikh Ali Hasan had divorced his wife by an oath of suspended repudiation intended to emphasise his determination in a matter that had nothing to do with his wife. He had repeated the oath several times. The condition of the repudiation materialised, and it was pointed out to him that his wife was now divorced by three successive repudiations, even though he had not intended to divorce her. It seems that the sheikh's attention was drawn to the position of the Shariah in this matter—namely, that the only way to rehabilitate his marriage would be to have his wife marry a third party, who would then divorce her.

All the schools agree that the intermediate marriage must be contracted in good faith and must be consummated before it can be dissolved. The woman can remarry her former husband only on the expiration of the waiting period (*idda*). However, there are differences between the schools regarding the application of this principle. The Hanafi school holds that the intermediate marriage is valid even with the (unexpressed) intention to render the woman lawfully permitted again to her former husband (*bi-qasd al-tahlil*), while other schools hold that such a marriage does not meet the requirements of the intermediate marriage and hence is null and void (Layish 1991:173ff.). The Shariah Court of Bethlehem was bound by the Hanafi doctrine, which attaches no importance to the element of intent (*niyya*) in the oath.

In other words, the wife was divorced even though there had been no intent to divorce her. Under these circumstances, the sheikh sought a remedy that would spare him the need to separate from his wife and to surrender her, albeit only temporarily, to another. It is doubtful whether the sheikh was fully aware of differences between the Hanafi doctrine prevailing in the courts (a heritage from the period of Ottoman rule in the region) and the Shafii doctrine followed by the local Muslim population in matters other than personal status. It seems, however, that from the experience of other Bedouin, he had good reason to believe that a Shafii mufti could solve his problem one way or another, and for this reason he decided to resort to him.

The mufti proposed a solution to the sheikh's predicament that was based on three alternative legal determinations:

(1) The sheikh had not intended to divorce his wife when he uttered the suspended repudiation, which means that the marriage remains valid as if nothing had happened;

(2) The divorce was a revocable divorce, which does not dissolve the marriage immediately and enables the husband to reinstate the wife within the waiting period; and

(3) The sheikh conceded that the original marriage had not conformed with the requirements of Islamic law but was based on tribal custom. This conception of the matter indeed makes it necessary for the sheikh to separate from his wife and to remarry her in accordance with *sharii* requirements, but it does not involve heavy legal costs, because the couple's children would be considered legitimate on the strength of their being acknowledged, and, most important, the wife would not have to contract an intermediate marriage in order to be permitted again to the husband.

Being unfamiliar with Islamic law and technical terminology, the sheikh probably asked his question orally in colloquial Arabic, whereas the mufti formulated and wrote down the question very succinctly in the technical language of the law, in the third person, adding introductory and closing formulas interspersed with religious elements, as are usual in legal documents.

The style of the fatwa is professional and matter of fact. The alternative determinations are formulated very succinctly, but in such a way as to be intelligible only to those familiar with

Islamic law and Islamic legal literature. The name of a famous scholar is invoked, probably in order to lend greater authority to the legal opinion. The fatwa concludes with religious formulas expressing, *inter alia*, the mufti's humility and his praise of Allah as the source of all wisdom.

The Translation of the Fatwa Follows; the Arabic Text can be Seen on the Facing Page.

(1) What is your opinion (*ma qawlukum*)—may your excellence endure.

(2) concerning a man between whom and between whose brother's son-in-law (or brother-in-law, *sihr*) ill-feeling and conflict arose because of the former's objection to the (amount of the) dower of the bride?

(3) The germane brother of the groom lost his temper. His temper got the better of him; he became very angry at the bride's father.

(4) and said: "(I swear that) my wife, so-and-so, shall be forbidden to me (*alayya al-haram*); my brother shall not marry (*yatahallal*) that man's daughter." When (people) approached the person who swore the oath, (trying to persuade him to desist from speaking as he did).

(5) he repeated the oath of prohibition (*haram*) and the divorce (utterance) again and again: "The groom shall not marry the bride; she shall not enter my house." Afterwards.

(6) the contract (*aqd*) with the bride was concluded and, of course, his brother married her and consummated the marriage, and the bride entered the house concerning which an oath had been taken.

(7) that she should not enter it. Under these circumstances, we beg you to direct us by a responsum (*jawab*), and yours are the wages and the reward (*al-ajr wal-thawab*).

(8) The inquirer.

(9) Ali Hasan.

(10) *Answer* (*jawab*): As he has repeated the oath of prohibition and the divorce (utterance), the repudiation has become a fact. This conclusion is inescapable, because the condition to which the oath relates (the marriage and the entry of the bride into the house) has been fulfilled. As regards the oath, it is an implicit declaration (*kinaya*).

(11) which, to be effective, requires (the ascertainment of) the intent (*niyya;* Schacht 1964:116) to dissolve the marriage (*qat al-isma*). If he had such an intent, that declaration entailed repeated (*mukarrar*) repudiation, and if he uttered it three times, the one who renders her (again) lawfully permitted (*muhallil*) (to her former husband) is required.

(12) but if he did not utter that declaration three times, he may reinstate (*murajaa*) the wife without her permission before the expiration of the waiting period (*idda*) and without her being entitled to a dower'.

(13) new dower and a new contract with her permission and consent. An intermediate marriage designed to render the divorced woman lawfully permitted (to her former husband) (*tahlil*) is required where the nature (*asl*) of the (original) contract was valid (*sahih*), fulfilling all the legal conditions (*wajibat*).

(14) where one of the essential elements (*ruku*) (of marriage) was infringed, the marriage is defective or void (*fasid*) and it is permissible to follow (the Imam) al-Shafii, (who, under these conditions, prescribed) a new contract and dower. In this connection, the Qadi Abu Shuja wrote in his book.

(15) *al-Ghaya wal-Taqrib:* "A contract (of marriage) is not fully valid unless it is concluded by a guardian (*wali*) and in the presence of two witnesses of good character (*adl*)"; if the requirement of good character (*adala*) has been met, the contract is valid.

(16) many and well-known. No one but the nearest agnate (*asabat*) may assume the office of marriage guardian unless a stranger has been permitted (by the court) to assume it. Nor may the woman herself act as guardian, for the hadith says:

(17) "A woman may not give a woman away in marriage, and a woman may not give herself away in marriage." And it is Allah who knows. Written by the poor man (who resorted) to Him (God).

(18) Jabir Ibrahim Abu Shabana (?)

(19) Al-Shafii

Evaluation of Fatwas

The legal opinion of a mufti is not binding on either the person who commissioned it or on the Shariah courts; its acceptance is purely voluntary. In the present case, the sheikh obtained full satisfaction. His wife was not divorced, and his sensitivity to Islamic norms was set at rest. There was no reason to ask the Shariah court to confirm the fatwa, nor was the fatwa confirmed or registered with any state institution.

It was deposited with the man who commissioned it, as evidence that his marriage was valid notwithstanding the three successive repudiations. If the sheikh had requested confirmation from the court before the enactment of the Personal Status Law of 1951 (Layish 1991b:451ff.), the qadi—bound by the Hanafi school—would have rejected the fatwa, ruling that the wife must separate from her husband, marry another man, and be divorced by him before being permitted to her first husband again.

Although the legal opinion reflects the particular circumstances of the sheikh, it is of use to the general public, since it is couched in general terms and not limited either personally or territorially. Reliance on the legal opinion of a scholar who is not officially appointed as a mufti is in itself an indication that formal status is not particularly important in the eyes of the

Bedouin. What matters most is the recognised personal authority of the scholar. This resembles the institution of the independent mufti of the classical period, who was unaffiliated with any official agency.

Although the fatwa establishes no new legal norms, it plays an important role in bringing the Bedouin closer to normative Islam by bridging the gap between the Shariah in its formal, Hanafi version and customary tribal law, under which three successive repudiations or a triple repudiation pronounced at once are not grounds for intermediate marriage. The religious transformation of the Bedouin is accomplished in several ways: through Islamic indoctrination via religious education in schools and mosques, modern communications media, the marriage solemnisers, and, of course, the shariah courts. Though the Bedouin may to some extent be conscious of this process, it seems that it results primarily from pressures that forcibly direct the Bedouin towards the orthodox Muslim way of life. Such pressures include the strengthening of the central authority, which in turn strengthens the religious establishment; the abolition of the tribal courts (Oweidi 1982:85ff.) and the subjection of the Bedouin to *Sharii* justice; and, finally, the geographical proximity of the Bedouin to religious, administrative, and economic centres.

The readiness of the Bedouin to accept Islam as a way of life is conditioned on its not being markedly contradictory to the way of life reflected in their customary law. In other words, the shariah is observed not for its own sake but to the extent that it is consistent with custom (Layish 19918:205). The requirement that an intermediate marriage take place after three successive repudiations or a triple repudiation—a requirement which, according to the Hanafi school, must be met under any circumstances, even if the marriage is contracted with the (unexpressed) intention to render the woman lawful once again to her former husband (*bi-qasd al-tahlil*)—is a hardship for the Bedouin community. The Shafii fatwa, which takes the element of intention into account, makes it possible to render religious law more flexible, to mitigate it to such a degree that the community can digest and absorb it. Paradoxically, an institution such as the fatwa, so patently legal by Islamic standards, is enlisted by the Bedouin to uphold custom while nominally acknowledging the supremacy of the shariah. The Shafii mufti uses the mechanism of the legal opinion as a sort of legal device (*hila*) to soften harsh precepts with which the community cannot live. It is known that such devices were used by jurists in classical times as a means of bridging the gap between established legal doctrine, on the one hand, and social and economic reality, on the other (Schacht 1964:78ff.).

The utilisation of the fatwa as an instrument to bring the Bedouin closer to normative Islam takes place on the private rather than the official level. Private resort to Shafii jurists in order to avoid the pain of an intermediate marriage after three repudiations or a triple repudiation is a common practice, attested to by the records (*sijill*) of the Shariah Court of Bethlehem, to which the Bedouin of the Judean Desert are amenable (Layish and Shmueli 1979:52.ff.; cf. Ziadeh 1990:13). This practice is quite natural, because the Bedouin are unaware of the differences between the schools of law and so, obviously, do not regard themselves as tied to a particular school. They seem to have discovered empirically the advantage of resorting to the Shafii scholar rather than to the shariah court to avoid an intermediate marriage, after failing to obtain relief from the court; they had no notion of the doctrinal differences between the schools represented by the qadi and the mufti, respectively (Layish and Shmueli 1979:45).

It is easy to imagine that the qadis of the Shariah courts, charged with applying Islamic law in matters of personal status (with the changes required by statutory legislation), do not look favourably upon the Bedouin's resort to Shafii jurists, which detracts from the court's status as the sole authority for the application of the law. An inevitable consequence of simultaneously resorting to the shariah court and Shafii jurists is perplexity and confusion due to the reference to different legal norms (reflecting differences between schools), some of which are sanctioned by the state and thus enforceable, and some of which are derived from the religio-legal authority of the jurists and thus are not enforceable. However, this situation is not new; in fact, it has always existed, because Islamic law was developed by the jurists outside the establishment.

Eleven Fatwas of the Ottoman Sheikh ul-Islam

In the Ottoman Empire, collections of the *fatwas* issued by the *sheikh ul-islams* from the second half of the sixteenth century until the end of the nineteenth came to form a distinctive branch of legal literature. Although some were anthologies, most contained the fatwas of a single sheikh ul-Islam, together usually with the fatwas of his predecessors that he too had signed. The usually anonymous compilers of these collections grouped the fatwas under chapter headings, such as "Marriage," "Sale," or "Evidence," which correspond to the chapters in standard works of *fiqh*, beginning always with the "Chapter on Ritual Purification." Within each chapter, the compilers grouped fatwas together under headings and subheadings according to the subject matter. These usually reflect a division of material familiar from manuals of fiqh, although sometimes they relate to topics such as military fiefs or tax farming, which are specific to Ottoman law. In some collections, the compilers have added proof texts to some or all of the fatwas. So too have some of the owners of the volumes.

The careful and systematic arrangement of the collections is a testimony to the legal skills of their compilers. The same skill is evident in the drafting of the fatwas themselves. This—and probably also the compilation of most of the collections—was the work of the permanent officials at the Fatwa office who, under the superintendence of the *fatwa emini,* received the original questions from members of the public, the legal profession, or the government, and recast them in the form in which they came before the sheikh ul-Islam.

The establishment of the Fatwa Office, which survived as long as the empire itself, I was largely, it seems, the work of the great sixteenth-century sheikh ul-Islam Ebus-suud (in office 1545-1574), and it is clear that from his time the issue of fatwas became a routine procedure. In Ebus-suud's own fatwas, the text of the question is often fairly circumstantial and the text of the answer often detailed, as though he were trying to educate the questioner. However, the tendency after Ebus-suud's time was for the *fatwa eminis* to draft the question so as to omit any detail that was not strictly relevant to the legal point at issue, and usually in a format that required the sheikh ul-Islam to add no more than a yes or no answer.

Furthermore, given a knowledge of the law, the form of the question usually presupposed the answer. It is clear, too, that, in most cases, the *fatwa emini* saved the sheikh ul-Islam time by indicating to him in advance what answer was required (Heyd 1969). A result of this standardisation of procedure is that after the time of Ebus-suud, and especially from the early seventeenth century, Ottoman fatwas were the work not so much of the sheikh ul-islams who signed them as of the legal bureaucracy at the Fatwa Office. It is the procedures of this bureaucracy that the collections reflect, and that the following fatwas exemplify.

The popularity of the collections was perhaps due in part to a respect for the office of the sheikh ul-Islam—the supreme legal authority in the Ottoman Empire—and to the dignity attaching to the fatwas that its holders had signed. They must also have served the very practical purpose of providing a source of reference for the solution of legal problems. The arrangement of material according to familiar legal categories makes them easy to use, and since the fatwas by and large present solutions to practical problems that had arisen in an Ottoman context, they may, at least to practising members of the Ottoman legal profession, have seemed more relevant, if less revered, than the classic works of fiqh.

Above all, almost all the fatwas are in Turkish, the language in which most legal proceedings in the Ottoman Empire were conducted, and for Turkish speakers they were easier to use than the standard manuals of *fiqh*, which are invariably in Arabic. It is possible, too, to imagine students of the law familiarising themselves with legal problems through the medium of Turkish fatwas before graduating to the authoritative Arabic texts.

The fatwas discussed in this chapter are from an anonymously compiled collection of the fatwas of Abdurrahim (1827, 2:214-215), who held office as sheikh ul-Islam from 1715 to 1716. They appear in a single block and illustrate how a compiler would group together a series of fatwas relating to a specific legal problem. The question here is the legal status of mother and child when a man produces offspring by a female slave belonging to his wife.

The status of a female slave who has given birth to a child by her own master is an important feature of Islamic family law. If the master acknowledges the child as his, the child is free and the mother becomes his *umm walad.* He may not transfer ownership of her to another person, and on his death she too becomes free. The case of a man who has a child by a slave belonging to his wife might seem more problematic, but the law is equally clear. An earlier Hanafi mufti, the Transoxanian jurist Qadi Khan (d. 1196), gives an excellent summary of the rules, which apply equally if the slave belongs to the man's wife, parent, or grandparent (Qadi Khan 1973,1:569):

(A man) has intercourse with a female slave belonging to his wife, or with a female slave belonging to a parent or grandparent. If (the man) acknowledges the child as his, (the child) is not affiliated to him, but he avoids the fixed penalty (for unlawful intercourse) because of a *shubha.*

If he says: "The owner of the female slave made her licit to me," there is no affiliation unless the owner confirms that she made (the slave) licit to him, and that the child is by him. If she confirms him in both these things, (the child) is affiliated (to him); but otherwise, it is not. But if the slave's owner contradicts him (in his claims), and he then acquires possession of the slave for a single day, then the child is affiliated to him.

Qadi Khan's first concern here is to establish whether a man's sexual relations with the slave attract the fixed penalty for illegal intercourse. They do not, since he has "quasi-ownership" (*shubhat ul-milk*) of a slave belonging to his wife, parent, or grandparent. If the slave belonged to a stranger, he would, in theory, be liable for punishment. Qadi Khan's second and, in practice, most important concern is to establish the rules for the affiliation of the child. First, the man must declare that the owner permitted him to have intercourse with the slave, and the owner must confirm him in this. Second, he must acknowledge that the child is his, and again the owner must confirm his acknowledgment. The child is affiliated to him only when these procedures are complete. The other route to affiliation is for the man subsequently to acquire ownership of the slave.

In his exposition of the case, Qadi Khan omits an important question that occurs in the Ottoman fatwas. This is whether, on affiliation, the child becomes free or remains a slave. The answer is that, since the mother does not become the mans *umm walad* and a child inherits its mother's status, the child is a slave. In an earlier section, however, Qadi Khan rules (1973, 1:569) on the case of a man who has a child by a female slave in quasi-ownership, when the child is affiliated to him and he subsequently takes possession of the slave. In this case, the slave becomes his *umm walad* and the child is freed. In brief, if a man has a child by his wife's slave, the child is affiliated to him, provided he claims that his wife gave him permission to have intercourse with the slave and that the child is his, and provided that his wife confirms him in both these claims. The slave, however, continues in the possession of his wife, and the child too becomes his wife's slave. However, if the child is affiliated to him and he acquires ownership of the slave, she becomes his *umm walad* and the child is freed.

Abdurrahim has eleven fatwas on this problem. The compiler has included them as a sequence in the "Chapter on Affiliation and the Status of the *umm walad* (*bab fil-nasab wal-istilad*)." The eight cases in which the husband claims that his wife gave him permission to have intercourse with the slave he has placed under the heading "Concerning a wife's permitting her husband to have intercourse with her female slave." The three cases where the husband has not made this claim he includes as the first items under the heading "Concerning intercourse with the female slave of a wife, father, son, etc., with and without permission." All the questions except for one are problems of affiliation, succession, and the legal status of the mother and child as slaves or free persons. The answers conform exactly to the Hanafi rules as Qadi Khan presented them.

The First Two Questions Concern Affiliation

(1) Hind grants her husband Zaid permission to have intercourse with her female slave, Zeyneb. Zeyd has intercourse with Zeyneb and impregnates her, and she gives birth to a child. Zeyd claims: "The child is by me." Hind confirms that she granted permission and that the child is by Zeyd. Is the child affiliated to Zeyd?

Answer: Yes. (3)

Here the Man and his Wife have Met all the Conditions for Affiliation, Which is not the Case in the Next Example:

(2) Zeyd takes possession of (*tutub*) his wife Hind's wholly owned female slave, Zeyneb. When Zeyneb produces a child, Zeyd claims: "I had intercourse with Zeyneb and made her my concubine with Hind's permission. The child is by me." However, Hind does not confirm that she granted Zeyd permission or confirm Zeyd in his claim (that the child is by him). Is the child affiliated to Zeyd?

Answer: No. (7)

There can be no affiliation because the wife has contradicted both of the relevant claims of her husband.

The next problem on affiliation is anomalous in that it refers to a man's child not by his wife's, but by a stranger's slave. The compiler no doubt included it here because there was nowhere else to put it, but in fact it is not out of place, since the two problems are identical.

A wife's slave, like a stranger's, is separate from her husband's property, and the same rules for affiliation apply:

(3) Zeyd has intercourse with Amr's wholly owned female slave, Hind, and says: "Amr permitted me to have intercourse with her." When Hind produces a child, Zeyd claims: "The child is by me." However, if Amr did not grant Zeyd permission and does not confirm him in his claim, is the child affiliated to Zeyd?

Answer: No. (8)

If the slave's owner had confirmed the man in his claims, then the child would have been affiliated. The only difference between this case and the case in which a man has a child by his wife's slave, is that a man does not have quasi-ownership of a stranger's slave and is therefore technically liable for the fixed penalty for unlawful intercourse. However, since the fixed penalty can never in reality be inflicted (Imber 1982), it is for practical purposes irrelevant, and the only legal distinction between intercourse with a wife's and a stranger's female slave disappears.

After affiliation, the next problem to worry questioners was the legal status of mother and child. Even when her child was not affiliated to the husband, some seem to have suspected that the slave mother might nonetheless become the husband's *umm walad* and that the child might, therefore, be free. This view presumably arose from an exaggerated respect for male authority and a belief that a man had rights over his wife's property, but it was plainly wrong:

(4) Without Hind's consent, Zeyd has intercourse with and impregnates his wife Hind's wholly owned female slave, Zeyneb. When Zeyneb produces a child, Zeyd dies. Did Zeyneb become Zeyd's *umm walad?*

Answer: No. (10)

(5) Zeyd has intercourse with and impregnates his wife, Hind's wholly owned female slave, Zeyneb, without Hind's permission. If Zeyneb produces a child, is the said child Hind's slave?

Answer: Yes. (9)

In these two cases, the child is not affiliated to the husband, but even if it were, it would make no difference, as the following fatwa implies:

(6) Hind permits her husband, Zeyd, to have intercourse with her female slave, Zeyneb. Zeyd has intercourse with Zeyneb and impregnates her, and she produces a child by Zeyd. Is Hind still able to employ Zeyneb and her child as slaves?

Answer: Yes. (5)

Here the text of the question does not make it absolutely clear that the child is affiliated to the husband, but this is the obvious implication of the statement that the wife permitted her husband to have intercourse with the slave. In any case, the question is irrelevant. Whether the child is affiliated or not, both it and its mother are slaves.

In the next two fatwas in the series, the questioner, after enquiring whether the child is affiliated to the husband, does not ask whether the child is a slave, but whether it is an heir. The two questions are, however, related. If the child is affiliated but still a slave, it is not an heir, because a slave cannot own or inherit property. If the child is affiliated and free, it is automatically an heir:

(7) Hind permits her husband Zeyd to have intercourse with her wholly owned female slave, Zeyneb. Zeyd has intercourse with Zeyneb and impregnates her, and she gives birth to a child. If Zeyd now dies, is the child affiliated to Zeyd, and does it inherit from Zeyd?

Answer: If Zeyd claims (that the child is by him) and Hind then confirms (both) that she gave permission (for intercourse) and (also) that Zeyd claimed (paternity), then the child is affiliated to Zeyd. But if the child is not freed, then it is not an heir. However, only the owner—in this case the man's wife—can free the child, either by manumission or by transferring ownership of the slave to her husband. Furthermore, as the next fatwa makes clear, manumission must take place before the husband's death:

(8) With his wife Hind's permission, Zeyd takes her female slave, Zeyneb as a concubine. When Zeyneb produces a child, Zeyd claims (that it is by him). Hind then confirms that she granted Zeyd permission and that the child is by Zeyd. However; Zeyd dies before Hind has freed the child. Is the said child affiliated to Zeyd and does it inherit from Zeyd?

Answer: It is affiliated, but does not inherit.

The child is not an heir, because it was still a slave at the time of its father's death. Subsequent manumission does not retroactively entitle it to a share in the estate.

The fatwas so far given seem to indicate that the normal procedure to establish affiliation was claim and confirmation. The less common method was to transfer ownership of the slave from the wife to the husband:

(9) Zeyd has intercourse with his wife Hind's female slave, Zeyneb, and impregnates her. Later; when Zeyneb is pregnant, Hind sells her to Zeyd. Then, when she gives birth, Zeyd claims: "(The child) is by me." Is the said child affiliated to Zeyd?

Answer: Yes.

In this case, the slave gave birth when she was in the husband's ownership, and the husband acknowledged the child as his. She, therefore, by the normal rules, becomes his *umm walad,* and the child is both affiliated and free. If, however, the husband acquires ownership of the slave after the birth of the child, Abdurrahim offers a different solution:

(10) Zeyd has intercourse with his wife Hind's female slave Zeyneb, without Hind's consent. When she later produces a child, Zeyd claims: "It is by me." If Zeyd then buys the child and Zeyneb from Hind, is the child affiliated to Zeyd and, when Zeyd dies, does it inherit from Zeyd?

Answer: No, but when he buys the child, it becomes free. (11)

In this case, had the child been affiliated, the slave would have become the husband's *umm walad* at the time of purchase. The child would have become free and, therefore, entitled to inherit. However, since the wife did not consent to her husband's having intercourse with her slave, there is no affiliation. In the absence of her consent, intercourse with the slave was unlawful, and this explains Abdurrahim's answer to the question. He is simply invoking the rule to be applied in a case in which a man fornicates with a female slave, which Qadi Khan (1973, 1:570) presents as follows: "A man fornicates with a female slave and she gives birth. He then buys her. By juristic preference (*istihsan*), she does not become his *umm walad.* (But) if he buys the child, it becomes free."

One fatwa does not, strictly speaking, belong with the others in the group, since although the case arises when a man fathers a child by his wife's slave, the problem has nothing to do with affiliation, manumission, or inheritance:

(11) Zeyd says to his wife Hind: "Permit me to have intercourse with your female slave, Zeyneb. Let me have intercourse with Zeyneb. If Zeyneb produces a child, I'll pay you so-and-so many akces." Zeyd has intercourse with Zeyneb and she produces a child. If Zeyd dies before paying the (specified) sum of akces, is Hind, on the basis of the aforementioned promise, able to take the (specified) sum of akces from Zeyd's estate?

Answer: No. (4)

The crux of the question here is whether the husband's promise is binding. If it is, then he becomes his wife's debtor and, on his death, she is entitled to receive the debt from his estate. The circumstances in which he made the promise are irrelevant to the solution of the problem, which is why the fatwa is out of place in this series. Instead, the key to the question lies in whether the precise words the husband used in making the promise constitute a binding oath (*yamin*). The query is a reasonable one, since in one form of an oath the swearer imposes on himself a penalty to be activated on the fulfilment of a specified condition. In Qadi Khan's formulation (1973, 2:2), "An oath ... is the stipulation of a valid condition and a valid penalty on which the oath is sworn." The husband's promise—"If Zeyneb produces a child, I'll pay you so-and-so many akces"—takes the form of a penalty dependent on the fulfilment of a condition, and so there are grounds for considering it an oath.

However, juristic discussion of oaths usually restricts the sense of a "valid penalty" to divorce (Imber 1993), manumission, and religious impositions (al-Marghinani 1965, 2:74, 87-89): for example, "If I do X, my wife is divorced/ my slave is free/ I am an infidel / I shall go on the Hajj." In this instance, Abdurrahim has clearly taken the restricted view and does not regard the payment of money as a valid penalty. The husband's promise is, therefore, non-binding, and the debt cannot be deducted from his estate.

A salient feature of Ottoman fatwas, as these examples demonstrate, is their anonymity. The identities of the original questioner, the officials who drafted the question in its existing format, and the protagonists in the case are all usually unknown. Another feature is their brevity. Both the question and the answer normally omit everything but the essentials of the case. A consequence of their brevity is that the fatwas illustrate points of law with great clarity, while a consequence of their anonymity is that they emphasise that the rulings of the sheikh ul-islams have a general validity, rather than a validity in a particular case.

For a modern reader with an interest in legal history, anonymity and concision have their drawbacks, since they obscure the processes whereby the fatwas came into existence. It is, therefore, impossible to comment with any real certainty on the social or legal background of the fatwas given here. The circumstance that they describe, of a man's producing a child by his wife's slave, cannot have been rare in Ottoman society, where slave ownership was commonplace. It was, however, as these fatwas show, a situation that caused problems of legal status and succession, and one may presume that these problems would come from time to time before the qadis' courts. If the *qadi* was uncertain of the solution to such a case, he could apply to the sheikh ul-Islam's office for a fatwa and pass judgment on the basis of the answer he received.

This certainly appears to be what has happened in (1) and (2), for example, where the texts of the questions appear either to reproduce or to summarise statements that the husband and wife had made in court. In these two cases, the qadi presumably had passed the problem, together with the statements of husband and wife, to the Fatwa Office, and later passed judgment in accordance with the sheikh ul-Islam's reply. One may assume, too, that the important question of the child's status as an heir in (7), (8), and (10) had come before the qadi when the father died and his estate was divided.

The form of the question in (8), for example, seems to suggest that a qadi had been asked to rule on whether a child was an heir of its father. He had before him evidence of the child's affiliation, but no evidence of manumission. Unable to decide on the case, he applied for an authoritative ruling from the sheikh ul-Islam, who then issued a fatwa.

If these assumptions are correct, these fatwas illustrate how, in Ottoman law, court cases could, in a sense, come to form legal precedents. Faced with a difficult case, a *qadi* might apply to the sheikh ul-Islam for a definitive ruling. The sheikh ul-Islam would issue a fatwa. The proceedings would then conclude with a judgment given on the basis of this fetva, in which the question, although presented in concise and stylised language and cloaked in anonymity, would in fact reflect very precisely the particular legal problem that had arisen. The qadi's judgment, pronounced in court, had no validity beyond the case at hand, but the fatwa, based on the same case, had a general validity and would provide *qadis* with authoritative guidance in similar cases in the future.

Importance of Fatwas

In Saudi Arabia fatwas can be obtained from religious scholars either privately or through public agencies established for that purpose. In either case, the authority of a fatwa derives from the reputation for learning and piety of the person who issues it. Even fatwas issued by members of the public agencies for *ifta* are associated with their issuers.

Two public agencies exist to issue fatwas (Kingdom of Saudi Arabia 1971). The first is the Board of Senior '*Ulema*', composed of about fifteen senior religious-legal scholars appointed by the king. The board conducts studies and adopts formal fatwas on major public issues, acting either in response to an inquiry from the king or independently.

The second agency for fatwas is the Standing Committee for *Ifta*, made up of four members of the board, selected by the king, who work full-time responding to requests from private citizens for guidance on their personal affairs. The Standing Committee is administratively part of a larger independent government agency, a "General Presidency," responsible not only for private *ifta* but also religious research, "call" (the propagation of Islam), and "guidance" (public instruction in religion). The Presidency also provides administrative support to the Board of Senior '*Ulema*'.

Sheikh Ibn Baz is the most famous and powerful contemporary *Alim* in Saudi Arabia. He holds a number of important positions, including that of head of the General Presidency just mentioned, member of the Board of Senior '*Ulema*', and member of the Standing Committee for *Ifta*. Owing to these positions and his general influence, he is unofficially called mufti of Saudi Arabia.

The fatwas treated here are taken from Sheikh Ibn Baz's regular column in the Presidency's weekly magazine, *al-Dawa,* in which he answers fatwa requests sent in by readers.

The fatwas all concern divorce by *talaq*—that is, divorce by the husband's repudiation. *Talaq* is a purely verbal act, the pronouncing of words conveying divorce, and it requires no formality, not even witnesses. The insubstantiality of the act of *talaq* occasions many difficult legal problems, three of which are dealt with in these fatwas.

Talaq by Oath

A long-standing practice in Muslim societies is the fortifying of vows by invoking the penalty of divorce from one's wife should the vow be broken. This can be done by conditional *talaq:* for example, "My wife is divorced if I ever drink wine again" or "if my wife ever talks to so-and-so." Most early *fiqh* authorities held that such a divorce was operative automatically on fulfilment of the condition, and this is the view generally applied in the Saudi courts.

The Board of Senior '*Ulema*' undertook to study this issue and, based on an extensive research report, adopted a fatwa favouring the traditional ruling (Board of Senior '*Ulema*' 1980). A minority of the board, however, including Sheikh Ibn Baz, differed and adopted a dissenting opinion. In the following fatwa Sheikh Ibn Baz states this position:

Reader Kh. Kh. H. from al-Qasim sends us a question in which he states: "I made an oath against my younger brother upon divorce (*talaq*) if he went out of the house. Despite this he went out. When I made this oath upon divorce, I did not intend divorce, but merely intimidation, and I was in great anger. But after my anger subsided, I forgave him. I request a fatwa: has a divorce occurred or not? May God preserve and keep you."

Answer: If the facts, questioner, are as you have described them, and you did not intend the occurrence of the divorce if your brother went out, and you intended only to restrain and frighten him, then you are obliged to perform the atonement (*kaffara*) according to the more correct of the two opinions of the *'Ulema',* and no divorce of your wife occurs thereby. God is the giver of good fortune. (Ibn Baz 1986 AD)

Talaq Uttered in Anger

Many questions arise as to the validity of divorces uttered when the husband is not aware of, or does not intend, the consequences of his act. *Fiqh* works discuss the validity of *talaq* issued by a husband who is mentally deficient, intoxicated, or jesting. A related problem, very commonly occurring, is the effect of *talaq* uttered in a state of extreme anger. May the husband avoid *talaq* on the ground that his anger was a sort of temporary insanity? What if he simply lost his head and now regrets what he did?

The Hanbali school as applied in Saudi Arabia's shariah courts is strict on this point. It nullifies the divorce only if the speaker was so angry as to have virtually lost consciousness, and, in particular, to have had no recollection of his act, drawing here an analogy to divorce uttered by one asleep or in a swoon or faint (al-Bahuti 1982, 5:235; al-Bahuti n.d., 3:120; Ibn Qudama 1983, 8:254-255).

Sheikh Ibn Baz again differs, adopting a minority view that avoids the divorce if the husband's true intent was not to divorce. This position is reflected in the following fatwa:

Reader Muhammad al-Umari sent us a question, in which he says: "I became extremely angry at my wife, because of a small thing she did, and after my anger subsided, my wife told me that I pronounced a divorce during my anger, a single (and therefore revocable) divorce. I sat down to remember if this divorce had issued from me, and then remembered it, but I was not sure of it completely. I do not have the intention of divorcing my wife, but my tongue slipped, and anger overcame me without any object, while I have confidence that my wife was not lying. I retracted the divorce at once ... I request from Your Eminence your fatwa whether the divorce occurred".

Answer: The safer course for you is to count this divorce (towards the maximum of three divorces) and consider it as having occurred, because of what you wrote about remembering it, and your confidence in the statement of your wife, in fulfilment of the Saying of the Prophet (Pbuh), "One who is wary of dubious cases is delivered in his religion and his honour," and his Saying, "Leave what causes you doubt for what does not cause you doubt." (Ibn Baz 1986b)

Note that Sheikh Ibn Baz in this fatwa reveals his own more lenient position in that he does not hold the requestor's remembering the act to be conclusive. In the cautelary tradition of fatwas, he adverts to the majority view as a warning that there is an authoritative view stricter than his own.

Ruling for a Triple Divorce

Talaq divorce may be revocable (for the period of the wife's waiting period, or *idda,* usually three months), or irrevocable. Irrevocable divorces are in two degrees: the lesser, which permits the parties to remarry, and the greater, which bars remarriage until after the wife has married another man and that marriage is consummated and terminated. A husband may divorce his wife twice, either revocably or irrevocably in the lesser degree, but upon a third *talaq,* the divorce is of the greater degree of irrevocability. Early in Muslim history the practice arose of issuing three divorces at once, the husband ridding himself of his wife in one dramatic, fatal stroke.

Historically, Sunni *fiqh* authorities have almost universally held that such a triple divorce has full effect as triple, even though they decry it as sinful and even forbidden. However sinful, this form seems always to have been in common use, to the extent that many Muslim men today seem to know of no other form.

In Saudi Arabia this view of triple divorce has always been the majority view, being early endorsed by leaders of the Wahhabi movement (Ibn Qasim 1965, 8:379-380). It is the rule applied by most qadis in the shariah courts. There is, however, a minority view, even in the courts, that owes its persistence to the great Hanbali Taqi ud-Din Ahmad Ibn Taymiyya (d. 1328), whose influence over the Wahhabis of Arabia has always been great. In one of his most famous opinions, Ibn Taymiyya held that the triple divorce should be counted only as a single, revocable *talaq.* He was able to cite as authorities in his favour the earliest practice of the Muslim community and the opinions of a number of Companions, Successors, and early jurists (Ibn al-Qayyim al-Jawziyya 1973, 3:30-50).

Once again, the Board of Senior '*Ulema*' chose this issue for study and adopted a decision endorsing the majority view (Board of Senior '*Ulema*' 1977a). And, once again, a minority of the Board differed, among them Sheikh Ibn Baz.

Thus, on all three issues, Sheikh Ibn Baz adopts positions lenient towards husbands wishing to avoid the consequences of their acts of *talaq.*

Complementarity of Ifta and Qada as Methods of Applying Law

Before considering the role of Sheikh Ibn Baz's fatwas in the Saudi legal system, it is useful to review key functional distinctions between *ifta* and *qada'* as institutions for the application of the shariah. The following statement by Ibn al-Qayyim al-Jawziyya (d. 1350), Ibn Taymiyya's great pupil and successor, gives a good summary:

> The (mufti's) fatwa is a law (shariah), which is general and concerns both the requestor and others. The mufti opines in a ruling that is generally worded and generally applicable (*amm kulli*), that to one who does so-and-so is applicable such-and-such, or one who says so-and-so is obliged to do such-and-such. The qadi makes a particular judgment upon a particular person, (not extending to anyone but the two parties,) and his judgment is specific in terms and obligatory. The fatwa of the scholar is general in terms and not obligatory. (Ibn al-Qayyim al-Jawziyya 1973, 1:37-38)

Ibn al-Qayyim al-Jawziyya identifies as key distinctions the following:

(a) the fatwa states a *general,* abstract rule, while the judgment is *particular* and concrete;

(b) the fatwa has a potentially *universal application* to the class of persons to whom the abstract ruling applies, while the judgment has *unique application,* to only the parties and event judged;

(c) the fatwa is *not obligatory,* but is only advice to the person requesting it, who has the responsibility to apply it to himself or herself (in his or her "inner forum," so to speak), while the judgment is *compulsory* and enforced (in the "external forum"). I would add to this list several other distinctions, which are partly implied in Ibn al-Qayyim al-Jawziyya's statement and partly obvious;

(d) the mufti deals only with *abstract fact,* as stated to him by the requestor, while the qadi engages *concrete fact;*

(e) the mufti leaves the truth of *facts* to be *determined by the requestor,* while in court the *facts are tried* through evidentiary procedures;

(f) the fatwa is relatively *personal and singular,* in respect to both the mufti and the requestor, while the judgment is relatively *public and multiple,* involving the qadi, the two litigants, and the functionaries of the state.

Islamic law, of course, demands application not only in matters of "law" in the Western sense, but also in matters of religious conscience, ritual observance, ethics, family relations, and social manners. Given this comprehensiveness of the shariah, *ifta* is a natural complement to *qada'* in securing the Shariah's application. The most obvious examples are the detailed laws governing the validity of rituals like prayer, fasting, or the pilgrimage. Such laws depend ultimately on the individual's conscience for their implementation, relatively remote from issues of compulsion and proof.

The individual is his or her own fact-finder and verdict-giver, guided as to the law by a fatwa (just as an Anglo-American jury decides the ultimate issues of a case, guided by the judge's instructions). But beyond such clear cases of conscience, fatwas are very often useful where more persons than one are involved and even are in contention. When the issues raised are particularly charged with religion and morality or involve psychologically subtle facts, difficulties of proof, concerns for privacy and intimacy, or strong group pressures towards conformity, resort to fatwas instead of adjudication may be natural. Here the clear example is family law. Saudi families very often forgo a binding judgment and submit internal disputes to the fatwa of a religious figure whom all members respect. Given these two examples of fatwa use, for enforcing ritual observance and resolving family disputes, it is not surprising to learn that in Saudi Arabia the great bulk of fatwas concern the laws of either ritual or the family (Puin 1977).

Complementarity between Ifta and Qada Institutions

Besides providing fatwas for individual or private applications of the law, how else does the Saudi legal system employ fatwas? In particular, are there institutional arrangements in place that exploit the complementarity of *ifta* and *qada*? The most obvious place to look for these is in dealings between the two major institutions responsible for *ifta* and *qada*, the Standing Committee and the shariah courts. Some observations he made in the Marriage Court of the Great Shariah Court of Riyadh are suggestive, and call for further investigation. I found the *qadi* of that court not only paying respect to Sheikh Ibn Baz's fatwas on divorce, but also actively assisting parties to take advantage of those fatwas. This was made clear on two occasions.

The first occasion concerns the issue of triple divorce. A married couple came before the *qadi* and related that the husband had uttered a triple divorce, which they wished to avoid. It turned out that the pair had already been to Sheikh Ibn Baz, who instructed them to ask the *qadi* to prepare for them a statement of the facts of their case, on the basis of which the sheikh would then issue his fatwa (Marriage Court 1983). The *qadi* explained to me that, had the parties instead tried their case before him (as might have occurred had the wife insisted on the fact of divorce), he would have been obliged to give effect to the triple divorce.

The second occasion involves the issue of the husband's intent in uttering *talaq*. Appearing with his wife and their respective families, a husband stated that he had divorced his wife by *talaq* three times on three different occasions. This would ordinarily entail that she is forbidden to him until after her marriage to another man. But, he added, the first divorce had been the subject of a fatwa from Sheikh Ibn Baz nullifying it on the ground of his state of anger. The *qadi* credited this result without further investigation, and suggested that the parties remarry (that is, conclude a new marriage contract). The wife, however, would not consent to the remarriage, which left the husband helpless and terminated the case (Marriage Court 1983).

In these two cases, the parties' invocations of Sheikh Ibn Baz's advice are accepted as valid dispositions not open to reversal or upset in court—and this although the qadi himself would have reached opposite results had the cases been tried in his court.

In a number of respects, arrangements such as those exhibited here are extremely practical and useful, and deploy ifta and *qada* effectively according to the complementary functions of each. First, note that parties who desire a particular result are able to obtain it, if that result enjoys the support of a respected religious figure—even when it is in conflict with the law as applied by the courts. Second, note that such fatwa-mediated outcomes, while they add flexibility to the standard law, do not undermine it or, with it, long-standing family and social arrangements and expectations. For example, the law of the triple divorce has been intimately involved in the workings of families for centuries. Even if a Saudi *qadi* is attracted to Sheikh Ibn Baz's view as a matter of principle, he may, out of concern for the law's stability and predictability, feel reluctant to adopt it as his own general ruling.

If the parties agree on that outcome, however, such concerns are far reduced. Third, note how Sheikh Ibn Baz's outcomes, particularly on such issues as divorce by oath or in anger, are much better suited to application in the "inner forum" than in the "outer," depending as they do on exquisitely subjective facts (chiefly, the husband's intent to divorce). If the context were instead a dispute in court about whether divorce occurred, how could the husband's claim be proved or disproved?

The rule might become a blank check to avoid divorce, or to make *talaq* the husband's plaything, destructive of family stability and the wife's peace of mind. Fourth, a mufti, to the extent that he has interaction with the requestor or can otherwise divine the nature of the case, may be able to tailor the ruling to the moral circumstances, accounting for such factors as a wife's reluctance to resume the marriage or a husband's violence, better than a court could, with its external procedures and compulsory judgment.

From these observations, hypotheses of various types are suggested. One has to do with applications of the Shariah in private, familial, and communal spheres, where the fatwa is used to resolve disputes by voluntary or consensual ordering, without state compulsion.

Such practices should be studied and reassessed as to their significance in the application of the Shariah. Another type of hypothesis concerns use of the fatwa method to lend flexibility even to compulsory legal determinations—indeed to make available for such determinations multiple legal outcomes on any single issue. We should look carefully for further instances of such use, re-examining particularly those procedures, common enough historically, in which a mufti (or muftis) worked hand-in-hand with the *qadi*, even to the point of observing cases and offering opinions that the latter would enact as his judgment. Investigations into both these types of hypotheses could well lead to results altering certain long-standing Western judgments about *fiqh*, particularly as to its rigidity, idealism, and impracticability.

Role of Fatwa

In this chapter He wishes to examine the fatwa as an instrument used to bring a semi-nomadic tribal society within the orbit of normative Islam. Though the influence of Islam on Bedouin law dates back many centuries, orthodox Islam, with its system of beliefs and institutions, plays no central role in shaping a nomadic Bedouin society. Though the Bedouin are Muslims, they generally do not fulfil ritual precepts properly or regulate matters of personal status or succession in accordance with the Shariah. As they grow progressively more sedentary, however, the Bedouin draw closer to normative Islam, which gradually becomes their binding lifestyle as regards worship, pious duties, and law, and they express increasing acceptance of Islamic institutions and of religious functionaries as the guardians, exponents, and practitioners of the Shariah (Layish and Shmueli 1979:31-42; Layish 1980-1982:206-221).

The fatwa is the legal opinion of a mufti. It is intended to elucidate, at the request of an inquirer, a position on a legal issue. Unlike the judgment of a *qadi*, it binds neither the inquirer nor anyone else. The *qadi* bears the primary responsibility of applying the Shariah to a nomadic, tribal society in the process of becoming sedentary (Layish 1984:41-50; Layish, 1991a:85ff.).

The mufti also plays an important role in bringing the Bedouin within the orbit of the Shariah. He replaces the *qadi* where the formalities of the latter's office, and especially the school of law to which he belongs, tend to discourage the Bedouin from turning to the Shariah for help in settling their disputes. The mufti's main function with respect to bringing the Bedouin closer to the Shariah is to enlist the religio-legal literature in support of a mitigation of the Shariah and a reduction of its severity so as to enable the Bedouin to absorb it into their lifestyle without undue conflict with their customary norms and rules.

The Decree

Although the source contains no direct information regarding subsequent events, these may be partially reconstructed from the fatwa itself. Uthman b. al-Hasan died some time after 1475 but before 1496 (the latter being the year in which al-Wansharisi completed the *Miyar*), leaving as his heirs an unspecified number of sons and daughters. If Uthman did not convey the properties to al-Nasiri and did continue to use them until his death, then his children, who may have been minors at the time of the "sale," may have viewed the properties in question as part of their father's patrimony, to be inherited by them—as his heirs—upon his death. Be that as it may, the properties in question apparently were not treated as part of Uthman's estate (which would have comprised only those assets acquired subsequent to the date of the sale in question).

For this reason, at his death, his children protested, alleging that the sale had been undertaken with the intention of disinheriting them in favour of al-Nasiri, who was not related to their father by ties of blood. In an attempt to recover what they considered to be rightfully theirs, they approached the jurist, al-Ghasawi, presumably the *qadi* of the locale in which they lived.

In accordance with the rules of judicial procedure, al-Ghasawi would have summoned al-Nasiri. When both parties to the dispute were present, they would have told their stories to the *qadi* in the language of everyday discourse, of which no record survives, and in terms of the relations that existed between and among them, about which we can speculate: Uthman b. al-Hasan's honorific title (al-Mahdi al-Kaniksi) and al-Nasiri's status as a jurist suggest that the two men were situated in a network of religio-legal authority (a network that included al-Ghasawi and al-Wansharisi).

As for the relations between Uthman and his children, the source does not indicate whether the children were minors dependent on their father when the sale was made or adults who were economically secure and self-sufficient, whether Uthman had made any provisions for his children in the form of pre-mortem transactions, or whether he was known to have displayed any bias in favour of or against his children.

After listening to the respective claims and counter-claims, reviewing the documentary evidence, and, perhaps, asking some questions of his own, al-Ghasawi determined that the case raised a difficult point of law, and he decided to consult with a legal expert before issuing his judgment.

He, therefore, sent the above-mentioned judicial certification to al-Wansharisi. Written at the bottom of the *ishhad* was his undated request for a legal opinion. In the *Miyar,* al-Wansharisi reproduces the istifta as follows:

The Text of the Question: Praise be to God. My Lord—may God be pleased with you (pl.)—your (pl.) response (is requested) with regard to the above document: Is it legally effective, (and) may it serve as the basis of a judicial decision, despite the fact that the witnesses were unaware of the amount of the price for which it was sold (and despite their not having) seen (the actual sale price)? Is the acknowledger's acknowledgment sufficient (to render) the sale valid, or not? How (should one treat), my Lord, the claim of the seller's heirs, who are the male and female children of his loins, that (the sale properties) were part of their inheritance, but (were sold) to the buyer by way of *Al-talij* (*ala wajh al-tawlij lil-mubta*)? Should one accept their claim, and should the buyer—or his heirs after him—be required to establish the price that was paid on the basis of eyewitness testimony? Or should no consideration be given to their claim, and should the sale be assessed to be valid on the basis of his acknowledgment of their inheritance? Your (pl.) response (is requested), my Lord—may you (pl.) be rewarded. Farewell—and may the mercy and blessings of the exalted God (be upon you). (al-Wansharisi 1981-1983, 6:83-84)

The istifta is carefully formulated, short, and to the point. Conscious of the conventions relating to a request for an advisory legal opinion, al-Ghasawi begins and ends his letter with conventional pious invocations, thereby situating the activity of consultation in a proper Islamic framework. Noteworthy is the manner in which he signals his subordination to al-Wansharisi, whom he addresses as "My Lord" and to whom he refers in the second person, plural. Also noteworthy is the manner in which the mustafti transforms the names of the litigants and whatever stories they may have told him into the abstract and impersonal language of legal discourse, as required by the conventions of futya: Uthman b. al-Hasan, (the) Mahdi al-Kaniksi, becomes "the seller"; the scholar, al-Nasiri, becomes "the buyer"; and Uthman's children become his "heirs" and "the children of his loins." The translation of the "facts" of the case into legal categories has the effect of masking status, gender, and age differences, thereby facilitating al-Ghasawi's adoption of an impartial attitude towards the litigants, as reflected in his alternately taking into account both sides of the dispute. Indeed, striving for impartiality appears to be a distinctive feature of the activity of Islamic justice.

Al-Ghasawi asks two questions. The first relates to the *ishhad* of 1475: Is the judicial certification a legally effective document on which a judicial decision may be based, its alleged defect notwithstanding? Al-Ghasawi subdivides this question into two parts:

(a) Does the witnesses' ignorance of the sale price and their failure to observe its receipt invalidate their testimony—and, by implication, the sale?;

(b) Is the seller's acknowledgment regarding the sale price sufficient to render the sale legally valid? The second question, which relates to the notion of *tawlij*), is formulated carefully.

> Properly speaking, the sale transaction does not fall into the category of *tawlij*) because it does not involve a parent's shifting of assets from one child to another. But the plaintiffs sought to have the Muslim judicial authorities extend the meaning of the term *tawlij*) to include this type of transaction, for it was all the same to them whether their father had disinherited them in favour of another relative or of a total stranger.
>
> In this regard, al-Ghasawi asks whether one should accept the children's claim that their father had "sold" the property to al-Nasiri in an attempt to disinherit them (*"ala wajh al-talij*) *lil-mubta"*). If so—and in the event that the buyer is unable to establish the sale price on the basis of eyewitness testimony—should one pass judgment in favour of the children? If not, is the seller's acknowledgment regarding the sale price sufficient to maintain the sale as valid?

In the *Miyar,* al-Wansharisi informs us that he offered the following response:

> Praise be to God—may His majesty be exalted. We have studied the copy of the purchase document (*sic*) that is recorded above and the question that follows it, and We have examined their contents. The response—God, praised be He, is responsible for success, in His benevolence:
>
> Al-Matiti and the author of *al-Kafi* stipulated that it is not necessary to mention the eye witnessing of receipt, in a valid sale. They said, "There is no reason for that (viz., eye witnessing) unless the purchaser is an arrogant person who is known (to engage in) coercion, compulsion, and violation (of the law) and (unless) the person who alleges that about him produces something by means of which his accusation may be confirmed, in which case, (the buyer) must then swear an oath that he paid the amount of the sale price confirmed by the testimony (*bayyina*), in the event that the attestation did not mention the eye witnessing of the seller's receipt of the price."

However, some of the writers of legal documents maintain that the eyewitnessing of receipt is incumbent upon every person who takes possession on behalf of someone other than himself, like the father, the executor, the proxy, and the custodian. (Eyewitnessing) also (is incumbent) with regard to the interdicted person's receipt of his maintenance, or (his receipt) of wealth for the purpose of testing him in commercial activity; for the post-pubescent virgin's receipt of the prompt portion of her dower; and for the dumb and the blind. (The requirement also applies to) a person on his deathbed (who) sells (something) to his child. (ibid., p. 84)

The response, which opens with the customary pious invocations, was addressed specifically to al-Ghasawi and would have been fully intelligible only to a jurist familiar with legal discourse, the sources of legal authority, and the art of legal reasoning. Significantly, al-Wansharisi allowed al-Ghasawi to establish the terms of the argument, organising his response in the order of the questions posed by the mustafti. Confident of his reader's ability to follow the thread of his reasoning, al-Wansharisi shifts abruptly from one topic to the next without signalling the direction of his argument (that is, without using verbal cues, such as, "in response to your first question," common in other fatwas).

The starting point of al-Wansharisi's substantive response to al-Ghasawi's query may be significant. Without making any reference to either the Quran or the hadith, the mufti finds textual authority for his response to al-Ghasawi's initial subquestion (Is the validity of a sale conditional on the witnesses having observed the receipt of the sale price?) by citing a statement attributed to two jurists who lived in the middle of the eleventh and twelfth centuries, respectively: Ibn Abd ur-Barr (d. 1070), the author of *al-Kafi,* a systematic treatise on Islamic law, and al-Matiti (d. 1174), the author of a treatise on legal documents. These two authorities held that eyewitnessing is required only in the abnormal circumstance of a buyer's being reputed to engage in "coercion, compulsion, and violation (of the law)." This observation implicitly touches on a potentially relevant issue, namely, the character of al-Nasiri, who had been accused of colluding with Uthman b. al-Hasan to deprive the latter's children of their lawful inheritance—behaviour which, if substantiated, no doubt would qualify as a "violation of the law." Curiously, al-Wansharisi completely disregards this issue, passing immediately to the observation (in this case, irrelevant) that some notaries require eyewitnessing of a sale in which one of the parties to the transaction is acting on behalf of a third party—as, for example, a father acting on behalf of his child, an executor, a proxy, or a custodian (clearly not the case in the sale in question).

Turning Next to al-Ghasawi's Second Question, Relating to Tawil), al-Wansharisi Writes, in the Continuation of his Response

If this has been established, we say, next: If the purchaser immediately received all the properties to which reference was made that are specified in the document, the seller being in the described state, namely, full competence, then the seller's heirs who allege *tawlij* have no argument, and the claim is absolutely without foundation. However, if he did not immediately receive that which was mentioned, but, rather, the "seller" continued to use, cultivate, and freely dispose of (the properties) until his death, (then there is merit to the claim). This (view) is similar to what was stated by Ibn At in his *Turar,* on the authority of Said b. Malik:

(1) Someone sold land to his son and summoned (witnesses to hear him attest) that he received the sale price (viz., on behalf of his minor son), but he did not bring forward the price (*mal*) and he did not show it to the witnesses; following his death, his heirs arose, claiming *tawlij.* (The sale) is effective if (the witnesses) acknowledged receipt (of the sale price)—even if the son was of the age of legal majority and the land remained in (the father's) possession until he died.

(2) Some of the judges (discuss) the case of a person who purchased (something) from himself, on behalf of his minor son who was not known to possess any assets; when the father died, the heirs arose and claimed, "(The sale was intended) as *talij.*" Their claim has no basis, and that (sale) to the son is effective.

(3) Then (Ibn At) said, on the authority of the legal adviser (*mushawar;* viz., Said b. Malik): If a man buys properties and records them in the name of his son, who is not known to possess any assets, Malik requires that (the father) acknowledge (the sale) and attribute (the properties) to the son, even if the father cultivates them or resides in them until his death. This is the correct (opinion), which is in conformity with the judicial practice (*wa-bihi al-amat*), because it is possible that the son possesses assets in a manner that is not known. Asbagh, (however) treats it as *tawlij*—(but his opinion) is of no consequence. End (of quote).

If the sale is binding in these three cases, and the acknowledgment of the receipt of the sale price is effective—even if no testimony confirms the presumption of receipt (*asalat ul-qabd*), together with the fact that the person on behalf of whom the acknowledgment was made in all (three cases) is a child, which, generally, constitutes cause for suspicion of *tawlij* and deception—then the binding nature of (the sale) in your (pl.) case, in which the buyer is a stranger with respect to the seller, is more appropriate and stronger. This is because no one would be suspected of diverting his wealth from a child of his loins to a stranger, because this is the opposite of human nature, namely, sympathy and affection (for the child). Be that as it may, if the persons who allege *tawlij* produce the testimony (of two witnesses) whose moral probity is satisfactory and whose testimony is acceptable, who testify on their behalf that they mediated the contract between the buyer and the seller, and they both concur that the apparent sale that they negotiated was merely a thing heard (*suma*), without any basis in reality—or they say, "He acknowledged that (viz., the fictitious nature of the sale), in the presence of the buyer, subsequent to the sale"—or they say, "So-and-so and So-and-so summoned us (as witnesses to hear) their testimony in one of the two (above-mentioned) respects"—then they have grounds for a claim, as stated by Ibn Harir on the authority of Ibn Harith. (The transmission) was cited by Ibn At and others. (ibid., pp. 84-85)

To determine whether the sale should be classified as *tawlij*), it is necessary to establish whether or not the seller immediately conveyed the fields and the date palm orchards to the buyer. As already noted, this detail is not specified in the *ishhad,* for which reason al-Wansharisi considers two alternative scenarios. If the seller did convey the property immediately, then there is no force to the claim of *tawlij*. But if he did not—that is, if the seller continued to use the property in any way whatsoever—then there may be force to the claim. Al-Wansharisi finds textual authority for this formulation in three cases mentioned in the *Turar* of Ibn At al-Shatibi (d. 1212.), itself a commentary on *al-Wathaiq al-majmua* of Ibn Fattuh (d. 1069). All three cases deal with a father who purchased property from himself on behalf of his minor child.

In the first case, the witnesses did not observe the sale price, and the father retained possession of the property until his death; in the second and third cases, it is further specified that the minor on behalf of whom the purchase was made did not have any assets at the time of the transaction.

In all three instances, when the father died, one of his heirs challenged the transaction on the ground that it constituted *tawlij.* The legal authorities, however, upheld the validity of each transaction. (In the third case, a minority opinion is attributed to Asbagh (d. 839), who classified the sale as *tawlij.* Ibn At, however, states that "his opinion is of absolutely no consequence." Significantly, al-Wansharisi does not pursue Asbagh's line of reasoning, which represents an alternative view).

Commenting on the statement attributed to Ibn At, al-Wansharisi reasons that if an argument can be made for the validity of the sales mentioned in these three cases, an even stronger argument can be made for the validity of the sale in the case at hand (an example of an argument *ad minorum ad majorum*). At this point in the argument al-Wansharisi makes a subtle but important shift from the formal language of legal discourse to the simpler expression of everyday speech, observing that in the three cases mentioned by Ibn At, a father attempts to transfer assets from one child to another, whereas in the present case the buyer and seller are "strangers" who are not related to one another by blood. Al-Wansharisi makes a key cultural assumption, based on his understanding of human nature. Invoking the natural sympathy and affection that parents have for their children, he asserts that the absence of a blood relationship between the buyer and the seller creates a presumption of validity, for under normal circumstances, there is no reason to suspect that a father would disinherit his children in favour of a stranger.

That is, al-Wansharisi assumes that because he knows who the seller is in relation to both the buyer and the plaintiffs, he can know with certainty how the seller will behave and what the seller would or would not do. On these cultural grounds, anyone who would argue that the sale in question should be classified as *tawlij* goes against the normal presumption and bears the burden of proof. Such a claim must be substantiated by the explicit testimony of upright witnesses who attest that the buyer and seller colluded with one another and that the sale was intended as a legal fiction.

In the Present Case, al-Wansharisi Continues, the Claim of Tawlij is not Supported by Such Evidence

As for the mere allegation of *tawlij* by the claimant—as appears from the weight (*quwwa*) of the question, it should not be taken into consideration and it should not be relied upon, unless circumstantial evidence (*qarain*) manifests something that renders doubt, in which case the buyer should be offered the decisory oath regarding the true nature (*batin*) of the case. If the testimony supports (the claim) of *tawlij* in a general manner, without mentioning anything that was specified above, Ibn Harith said, "Most of the distinguished legal authorities (maintain: it) is not accepted unless given by scholars in the form of testimony." But Ibn Zarb held for the acceptability (of testimony given by non-scholars), giving as a reason for his position the fact that the moral probity of testimony should be presumed (*yuhmal*) (here) to the extent that it is presumed with respect to someone whose lying is not evident. (ibid., pp. 85-86)

Here, al-Wansharisi appears to have arrived at the determination that the claim of *tawlij)* in the present case should be rejected because it is not supported by testimonial evidence. Seeking to make his answer as comprehensive as possible, however, he immediately presents a countervailing consideration: an unsubstantiated claim of *tawlij)* may be accepted if circumstantial evidence signals cause for suspicion. Unfortunately, al-Wansharisi does not specify what this circumstantial evidence might be, although we assume that he had in mind either the witnesses's failure to specify the sale price, or the seller's continuous use of the property until his death. In the event that circumstantial evidence does point towards *tawlij)*, the case would be resolved by having the buyer swear a decisory oath confirming the legitimacy of the sale; only if the buyer refused to swear would the presumption shift in favour of the plaintiffs. This procedural strategy would appear to favour al-Nasiri, who, merely by swearing the oath, could render the sale legally valid even if circumstantial evidence suggested that it was fictitious.

An Additional Level of al-Wansharisi's Reasoning Incorporates a Fatwa Issued by the Andalusian Jurist Ibn Al-Makwi (d. 1010) that Introduces a Distinction between Deathbed and Inter Vivos Transactions:

In some of the *Nawazil* books (there is a case relating to *tawlij)*: Ibn al-Makwi was asked about someone who summoned (witnesses to hear him attest) with regard to himself, during his deathbed illness, that he had sold all his properties to his daughter's husband, and that he had received the sale price from him—it was such-and-such—and that he had no (heirs) other than that daughter and his wife, her mother. Then he died. He responded: If the seller feared (that he would die) from his sickness, then his (mere) acknowledgment of having received the sale price is not legally effective, unless eyewitnesses attest to its having been paid. End of quote.

The meaning is: had (the transaction taken place) while he was healthy or during the course of an illness that was not life-threatening, then the acknowledgment would have been effective (viz., without yewitnessing). This understanding is widespread and it is supported by the preceding transmission of Ibn At.

In a manner similar to this response by Ibn al-Makwi, a fatwa was issued by Ibn al-Hajj and Abu Muhammad b. Attab in the case of a man who sold a female servant to his wife during the course of the illness from which he died; the sale was certified, but receipt (of the sale price) was not seen (by the witnesses). Ibn al-Hajj and Ibn Attab issued a fatwa, when (the case) occurred in Cordoba, after the *qadi*, Ibn Hamdin, had consulted with them (*istasharahum*), holding for nullification of the sale and (recommending) that the female servant revert (to the estate as part of) the inheritance. But the two of them were opposed by Ibn Rushd and Asbagh b. Muhammad, who issued fatwas holding for the effectiveness of the sale and (the sale object's) belonging exclusively to the wife. As a result (of the disagreement), the *qadi* recommended a compromise solution: one-half of the servant was awarded to the wife and the other half was awarded to the estate. Some say: This was a good choice. (ibid., p. 86)

The case referred to Ibn al-Makwi deals with a father who, during his deathbed illness, summoned witnesses to hear him attest that he had sold all his properties to his daughter's husband, that he had received a specific sale price from the buyer, and that he had no heirs other than his daughter and his wife. When the sale was contested (presumably by his wife), Ibn al-Makwi reasoned that because the statement was uttered by the father on his deathbed, his acknowledgment (*iqrar*) of receipt of the sale price was legally effective only if the exchange had been observed by the witnesses. The relevance of this case to the case at hand (in which the acknowledgment was not made on the seller's deathbed) is immediately clarified by al-Wansharisi. Ibn al-Makwi required eyewitnessing of the sale price only because the sale was acknowledged on the seller's deathbed.

Otherwise, al-Wansharisi observes, the father's acknowledgment of his receipt of the sale price would have been legally effective without eyewitnessing of the exchange (as in the first of the three cases cited above). As further support for this conclusion, al-Wansharisi refers to another Andalusian fatwa, issued about a century after that of Ibn al-Makwi. During his final deathbed illness, a husband sold his slave girl to his wife. Although the sale was certified, witnesses did not observe receipt of the sale price. Subsequently the sale was contested, and the case was brought before the Cordoban *qadi* Ibn Hamdin, who, before issuing his decision, consulted with the muftis Ibn al-Hajj and Ibn Attab (both men died in 1126). The muftis advised the *qadi* that the sale was null and void and that the slave girl should revert to her master's estate. This case also suggests that if the transaction had not been conducted on the man's deathbed, the sale would have been valid, even though the witnesses did not observe the receipt of the sale price.

Having nearly finished his analysis, al-Wansharisi tests it by constructing the following hypothetical objection to his line of reasoning.

Objection: Why did you not treat—in the case in question—the properties' remaining in the possession of the seller until his death (as a factor that) weakens the sale contract and nullifies it—if it is established that (the properties) did remain in his possession until his death; and (why did you not) construe the seller's acknowledgment of the sale and receipt of the price in the sense that he intended not to give the buyer the aforementioned properties and (in the sense) that his summoning (of witnesses) for that purpose was a legal fiction, designed to circumvent the law governing property conveyance (*hiyaza*), which is the established legal custom (*sunnah*), in the absence of which neither a gift nor any other type of unilateral monetary transaction becomes complete? This is the sense conveyed in the fatwas issued by all of the most eminent authorities and the leading muftis, (including) Abu Muhammad b. Attab, Asbagh b. Muhammad, Abu Abdullah b. al-Hajj, Abu ul-Walid b. Rushd, when (a case) occurred in Cordoba, during the days of the *qadi* Abu al-Qasim b. Manzur, regarding a man who sold to a wife or to his female slave who had borne him a child (*umm walad*) half of his house, while he was in a state of health. He summoned (witnesses to hear him attest) to the sale for one hundred and fifty *ibddiyya mithqals*, and to the receipt of the entirety (of the sale price), but he continued to reside there until he died.

(This is) also (the sense conveyed by) the transmission of Hussain b. Asim on the authority of Ibn al-Qasim, which is the source text (*mustanad*) on which these noble legal authorities rely in their fatwa. The text of (the transmission) reads: Hussain said:

> I asked Ibn al-Qasim about someone who, while he was in a state of health, summoned (witnesses to hear him attest): "I have sold this residence of mine to my wife, to my son, or to my heir, for a large sum of money"—but not one of the witnesses saw the sale price, and the residence remained in the possession of the seller until he died. (Ibn al-Qasim) replied: That is not permissible and that is not a (valid) sale. Rather, it constitutes *tawlij*, an (act of) deception, and a bequest to an heir. End (of quote).
>
> (ibid., pp. 86-87)

Here, al-Wansharisi asks his reader to imagine that the following facts have been established: the seller in the case at hand retained possession of the sale object until his death and admitted, in his acknowledgment of 1475, both that it was his intention not to give the properties to the buyer and that his summoning of witnesses was a legal fiction designed to circumvent the legal requirement relating to the conveyance of property. Under these circumstances, one might argue, the sale should be declared null and void. Indeed, this argument finds support in two cases. The first case occurred in twelfth-century Andalusia. While in a state of health, a man sold half of his house to either his wife or his *umm walad.* He summoned witnesses to hear him attest that the sale price was 150 *ibadi mithqals* and that the sale price had been received. The seller, however, continued to reside in the house until he died.

The sale was invalidated by Ibn Attab, Asbagh b. Muhammad, Ibn al-Hajj, and Ibn Rushd, presumably on the ground that the man's failure to convey the house to the buyer served as an indication of *tawlij.* The second case, related by a certain Ḥussain b. Asim on the authority of Ibn ul-Qasim (d. 806), is the source text on which the four Andalusian jurists based their decision. While in a state of health, a man summoned witnesses to hear him attest that he had sold a residence belonging to him to his wife, to his son, or to his heir, for a large sum of money. But the witnesses did not see the sale price, and the residence remained in the seller's possession until his death. The sale was contested, and Ibn al-Qasim declared it invalid on the grounds that it constituted *tawlij,* a deception, and a bequest to an heir.

Al-Wansharisi's hypothetical objection was constructed so that it would collapse on inspection, as follows:

> ***Reply:*** In the case (discussed by) the distinguished legal authorities, the heir is a brother, and a document containing secondary testimony confirmed that the deceased brother had (manifested) continuous enmity for (the surviving brother) and that (the former) used to say, while he was alive, that he would not allow (his brother) to inherit any property from him. The buyer is either a wife or an *umm walad,* and in both cases this constitutes grounds for suspicion of bias and *tawlij.* In the case in question, on

> the other hand, it is posited that the buyer is a stranger and that the heir is a child. As (in the case discussed by the distinguished legal authorities), in the case of Hussain b. Asim, the buyer is a wife, or a child, or a parent. Therefore, it is necessary to nullify the sale in these two (cases) on account of the suspicion of *tawlij,* because of the (three) aforementioned qualities (viz., *tawlij,* deception, and a bequest to an heir). Its nullification in the case in question is a consequence of (only) one of those qualities, namely, the seller's misappropriation of the sale object and its continuing in his possession until his death—if he (in fact) did so, because the consideration of something that relates to a third party does not necessitate its being taken into consideration with regard to himself—despite the fact that the transmission of Ibn Asim contains exceptions in the school. The distinguished legal authorities followed (his transmission) in their case only because of the magnitude of the intent to (engage in the practice of) *tawlij* in their time and its diffusion in their place, and out of deference for the opinion of the Medinese— Ibn Kinana, al-Makhzumi, Ibn Abi Hazim, and Ibn Maslama—in the case of a man who, while he was in a state of health, acknowledged that he owed a debt to his child, to his wife, or to one of his heirs. Then, years later, he died, whereupon the heir demanded the (debt) that he had acknowledged in his favour. The Medinese said, "(The claim) is of no consequence, even if he made the acknowledgment on his behalf while he was in a state of health." Ibn Rushd said, "That which is known and widespread is that he possessed assets with regard to which he made an acknowledgment on his behalf, while he was in a state of health. God—praised be He—knows best. In Him resides success."

Signed by the one who submits to You (pl.) frequently, the servant who asks for forgiveness, the one who is in need of God—praised be He: Ahmad b. Yahya b. Abd ul-Wahid b. Ali al-Wansharisi—may God grant him (*sic*) success. (ibid., pp. 87-88)

Bringing to bear his expert knowledge of Maliki fatwas, al-Wansharisi turns the tables on his imagined "opponent" by saying that he has failed to convey all of the facts relating to the first supporting case. The plaintiff was the seller's brother, and witnesses attested, after the fact, that the two men were known to have hated each other and that during his lifetime the seller used to say that he would not allow his brother to inherit any property from him (these details can be found in ibid., p. 79, where the fatwa is cited in full). The latter statement, viewed in conjunction with the fact that the "buyer" was the seller's wife or *umm walad,* strengthens the presumption that the seller was attempting to disinherit his brother. In other words, this case (as well as the source text related on the authority of Ibn al-Qasim) constitutes a textbook example of *tawlij,* which explains why the jurists nullified the sale. Indeed, al-Wansharisi adds, the practice of *tawlij*) was widespread in twelfth-century Andalusia, where Maliki jurists sought to eradicate it out of deference to the Medinese jurists whom they regarded as their authorities. In the present case, on the other hand, the facts are different. Because the seller and the buyer are strangers who are not related to one another and the heirs are the seller's children, the sale in question cannot, properly speaking, be classified as *tawlij*) or even, as the plaintiffs had argued, quasi-*tawlij*. It might still be invalidated—but only if the plaintiffs can demonstrate that the seller misappropriated the sale object by retaining possession of it and freely disposing of it until his death (and if, as al-Wansharisi fails to remind us, the defendant refuses to swear an oath attesting to the legitimacy of the transaction).

Al-Wansharisi's distinctive and characteristic signature, which emphasises his subordinate and supplicatory status with respect to the Divinity, signals the end of his response—and of the documentation. Presumably al-Wansharisi sent the fatwa to al-Ghasawi, who, after studying it and seeking to determine which of the legal issues raised by the mufti were relevant to the case, issued his judgment, or *hukm*.

In issuing a fatwa, the jurisprudent is summoned to draw on his expert knowledge of the multiple layers of the Islamic legal tradition in an effort to identify the legal rules and categories that govern a particular case. Like jurists in other cultures, the mufti locates legal authority in established sources that are external to himself. Inasmuch as Islamic law commonly is characterised and perceived as a sacred law in which legal doctrine invariably is grounded in the authority of the Quran and the prophetic Sunnah, it is noteworthy that al-Wansharisi makes no reference whatsoever to either of these two sources, but rather situates the authority of his response in an impressive range of Maliki sources that includes doctrinal law books, treatises dealing with legal formularies, earlier fatwas, and court practice, especially as manifested in eighth-century Medina and twelfth-century al-Andalus.

Drawing on his extensive knowledge of these sources—knowledge that was sharpened as he compiled the *Miyar*—al-Wansharisi articulates the contemporary Maliki legal tradition by selecting from the thousands of available cases those he considered relevant to the case at hand, carefully arranging them in a unique narrative context. The rhetorical art by which he proceeds in this particular literary performance involves the frequently abrupt and unannounced juxtaposition of parallel and contrasting cases, a characteristic form of Islamic legal argumentation (cf. Schacht 1964:205). Treating these cases as the relevant sources from which legal rules may be construed, al-Wansharisi applies the resulting rules to the case at hand. The mufti's contribution is to bring earlier cases to bear on the present case through an interpretive act embedded in a new literary composition, the fatwa, which, because it is formulated in general terms, has a timeless quality that facilitates the citation of other cases—formulated in similar terms—from, in this instance, eighth-century Medina, twelfth-century al-Andalus, and fifteenth-century Fez. By its very nature, such a literary work displays a dense intertextuality that is mediated and controlled by the mufti, through whom there emerges a layered voice representing the consensus of Muslim jurists as formed over a period of nearly eight centuries. Herein lies the authoritative nature of the mufti's discourse.

The juristic style adopted by al-Wansharisi in this particular fatwa appears to be characterised by openness, even handedness, and a willingness to suspend judgment. Rather than commit himself to one or another version of "the truth," al-Wansharisi outlines the legal parameters of the case, tacking back and forth between the perspective of the plaintiffs and that of the defendant and between factual configurations found in earlier cases, so as to provide as full and comprehensive a statement as possible of the legal issues that must be taken into consideration before any judgment is issued; he also takes care to mention his doubts and uncertainties (Further research may establish whether this juristic style is particular to al-Wansharisi, or characteristic of muftis in general.).

Running below the linguistic surface of the text, however, are crosscurrents that one discerns when taking account of the information in the document attached to the istifta and, fortuitously, transcribed by al-Wansharisi when he compiled the *Miyar.* The present case juxtaposes two legal norms: a father's obligation (imposed by the Quran and the Sunna) to provide for his children after his death; and an individual's right (sanctioned by the jurists) to dispose of his property during his lifetime in whatever manner he wishes. In his analysis al-Wansharisi expresses no overt interest in these norms or in the manner in which they relate to one another; his conspicuous silence was noted with regard to both the Quranic verses that establish the inheritance rights of children and the prophetic Sunna that establishes the underlying ethos of Islamic inheritance law.

Charged to ascertain the law (and not to judge the facts), al-Wansharisi devotes no overt attention to the human details of the case, specifically the plaintiffs' allegation that their father, Uthman b. al-Hasan, had colluded with al-Nasiri to deprive them of their lawful inheritance. Rather than consider the character of the buyer and seller, al-Wansharisi focuses his attention on formal, observable, and seemingly objective legal facts and legal relations:

> Did the transaction take place while the seller was sound of mind and body or while he was on his deathbed? Was the seller legally competent to undertake the transaction? Was he acting on his own behalf or on behalf of a third party? Was the sale price transferred to the seller, and did the seller immediately convey the property to the buyer? Is the plaintiffs' claim supported by the testimony of upright witnesses or, alternatively, by circumstantial evidence?

Al-Wansharisi's disregard for the specific human details of the case and for its normative, ethical, and Islamic dimensions may have conditioned his seemingly open and evenhanded juristic style, which focuses almost exclusively on one-dimensional legal considerations. As noted earlier, the principle figures in the case, with the exception of the plaintiffs, were members of a network of religio-legal authority that extended from the capital city of Fez to its surrounding countryside and beyond. Is it possible that al-Wansharisi's readiness to suspend judgment in this particular case was driven by his unwillingness to rebuke a fellow jurist, al-Nasiri, and a person who was known as the Mahdi al-Kaniksi? In support of this admittedly speculative hypothesis, we would like to draw attention to a subtle linguistic detail that bears on an important cultural assumption.

Although al-Wansharisi speaks for the most part in the formal language of the law, a revealing shift occurs at a key juncture in the argument, where he confronts the contention of two Andalusian jurists who maintained that eyewitnessing of a sale is required in the case of individuals who are reputed to have engaged in a "violation." Perhaps in an effort to avoid the implications of this argument, al-Wansharisi shifts from the level of formal legal language to that of everyday discourse, asserting it to be unimaginable, on the basis of his understanding of human nature, that a father would disinherit his child in favour of a stranger. In other words, the absence of a blood relationship between the buyer and the seller constitutes *prima facie* evidence that the sale was valid, irrespective of the children's claim that their father had engaged in fraudulent behaviour in order to disinherit them. This linguistic shift may be an indicator of juristic bias.

The fatwas preserved in the *Miyar* represent a meeting point of legal theory and social practice, a moment in the ongoing process whereby legal theory is actualised. The case that I have analysed points to the manner in which Muslim proprietors attempted to resist the perceived constraints of Islamic inheritance law and the manner in which the jurists assisted them in this endeavour. From the fatwa, we learn that different forms of *tawlij* were practised in eighth-century Medina, were "widespread" in twelfth-century al-Andalus, and were employed in fifteenth-century Morocco. It is my sense that practices similar to those embodied in the Maliki doctrine of *tawil*) have been common in Muslim societies at most times and in most places. Future research may qualify and refine this preliminary speculation.

Various Aspects of Law

Ifta under the Mamluks was an integral part of the judicial process and, as such, instrumental in the interpretation and application of legal doctrine. Fatwas made their way to court either directly at the request of a judge or via litigants. A valid fatwa by a qualified person constituted a strong legal argument in court and could be decisive to the outcome of disputes. Ifta was not restricted to occupants of public office, but rather was open to all those who had the requisite educational and personal credentials (Tyan 1955: 248). Muftis, however, sought to exercise effective control over their practice. Like many other Muslim professional groups, muftis enjoyed the benefit of specialised *adab* (rule) manuals.

The adab al-mufti works outlined the qualifications for ifta and the rules and ethical norms governing its practice. Moreover, they furnished muftis with precautionary measures to prevent abuse of ifta by unqualified individuals and unscrupulous petitioners. The fatwa examined here will serve as a concrete illustration of the practical relevance and applicability of the adab al-mufti discourse at the time of its issuance (see Masud 1984). This fatwa was issued by Taqi ud-Din al-Subki, father of the renowned Taj ud-Din al-Subki, the author of *Tabaqat ul-Shafiiyya.* Taqi ud-Din was himself an outstanding Shafii jurist and is credited with many novel contributions to his school's doctrine (al-Subki, Taj ud-Din, n.d., 6:186ff.). Born in Egypt in 1284, al-Subki enjoyed an illustrious career there as a teacher-scholar and mufti before being pressured by the

Mamluk Sultan to accept the Judgeship of Damascus, a position he held for sixteen years, until shortly before his death in 1355. In Damascus, he also held two teaching posts and, for a short while, was the preacher at the Umayyad mosque. Throughout his career, al-Subki was a prolific jurist; he issued fatwas regularly and composed some major works on law and jurisprudence, as well as numerous specialised treatises (al-Subki, Taj al-Din, n.d., 6:147ff.).

The source of this fatwa is *Fatwa ul-Subki,* an anthology of al-Subki's writings that was put together shortly after his death. Besides fatwas, this collection includes summaries of judicial decisions, several legal treatises, and miscellaneous exegetical notes, which are apparently excerpts of an unfinished book. Published years ago, *Fatwa ul-Subki* has been virtually neglected by scholars, although it offers a remarkably rich and reliable testimony about the different aspects of the career of a prominent Muslim jurist and the legal system in which he operated. Like many other texts in the collection, the fatwa singled out for discussion here represents the transcript of a document issued to a specific petitioner regarding an actual dispute. As an unedited copy of an original fatwa, this text faithfully preserves not only al-Subki's legal opinion about a particular point of law but also the mode in which he communicated his opinion. The latter feature proves to be of special significance in light of the circumstances that gave rise to the fatwa.

Masala: What do the master scholars, may God assist them, say regarding the case of a carpet maker to whom Zayd paid money to purchase whatever is needed for manufacturing carpets, and with whom Zayd determined the service fee. The artisan made the carpets, but delivered only some of them, claiming that the rest were stolen. Is he obliged to incur the loss for what he claims to have perished? Give us your fatwa, may you be rewarded (*aftuna majurin*) (P3).

He (al-Subki) answered, may God be content with him, by saying: This *futya* was presented to me last Friday in the Tayluni Mosque after the prayers, although it was worded differently. In fact, it pertained to a different case (*sura*), which is about a carpet maker to whom Zayd paid money to manufacture some carpets. The carpet maker delivered some of the carpets, but claimed that the rest had been destroyed. Is he obliged to incur the loss for what was destroyed (*hal yalzamuhu gharamata ma talifa*)? This was the wording of the fatwa or something to this effect (*aw ma hadha rıanahu*) (P_1). So I wrote on the petition sheet:

> This manufacturing contract (*al-istisna*) is invalid (*fasid*) and the carpet-maker is unconditionally liable for the money until he refunds his client. Moreover the damaged carpets are considered the property of the artisan. Therefore, he is the one liable for their loss (*min damanihi*). As for the carpets that are delivered, if the carpet maker and the client are able to reach a mutual agreement regarding them, the carpet maker may deduct their price from the money (already paid).

(This was my exact response) or something to this effect.

Then, on Saturday morning, as I was entering the class (*dars*) in al-Mansuriyya, a *futya* was presented to me (P_2), bearing the same question about which I had written a fatwa earlier.

Moreover, on the same sheet, there was also the writing (*khatt*) of someone stating that the carpet maker is not liable (*la yadman*) and that he is a fiduciary (*wa inna yadahu yad amana*), or something to this effect. So, I returned the sheet to the courier, knowing that the fatwa was unworthy of my consideration. Later, when I entered the classroom, some people asked me to read the fatwa, but I declined to do so because I do not like to malign or bad-mouth anyone.

We nevertheless discussed the case without specifying the author of the fatwa. I mentioned to those people that this was a famous issue (*masala*) that occurred frequently in cases of bookbinding and custom manufacturing of slippers, textiles, gowns, etc. According to al-Shafii's doctrine, the aforementioned contract is invalid, while it is valid according to the doctrines of Malik and Abu Hanifah. Al-Shafii states this explicitly in *al-Umm*, and our early colleagues (*al-ashab al-mutaqaddimun*) mention it in their books. Malik and Abu Hanifa justify their position on the basis of customary practice and necessity. Al-Shafii argues that this is an invalid contract of future sale (*salam*), and that it constitutes neither a sale of an object (*ayn*) nor employment for a service to be rendered upon an object. Thus the opinion that the money received (in payment for the carpets) is a deposit in trust (*amana*), that the payer is liable for its loss (*min daman al-dafi*), and that the recipient is not obliged to incur the loss is not upheld by anyone among the Muslims. Moreover, this opinion is not indicated by either the earlier or the later scholars, nor is it implied in their speech.

Indeed, it is contrary to the consensus of scholars. Because, according to us, this contract is invalid, and since the valid form of this contract entails an unconditional liability (upon the recipient), then so does its invalid form. Thus, the received money falls under the recipient's unconditional liability according to the terms of unconditional liability applicable to invalid contracts (*fa-huwa madmun alal-qabid daman al-uqud al-fasida*). Moreover, according to the principles of Malik and Abu Hanifa, the money is received in a valid (synallagmatic) contract. Thus it is legally equivalent to the price received in a valid sale, or the fee received in a valid contract of employment, both of which are subject to the recipient's unconditional liability by the intrinsic terms of (synallagmatic) contracts (*madmunan daman al-aqd*).

The opinion denying the applicability of the rules of unconditional liability to this case is not upheld by any group of jurists. It could have been maintained only by someone who does not possess even a smattering of knowledge. Indeed, such things are committed by someone combining two traits, one of which is laziness, a distracted mind, and ignorance about the shariah, its rules, the means of its attainment, and its sources. The second is a preoccupation with abridged books such as *al-Hawi al-saghir* and its likes. Such a person tires and exhausts his mind in unravelling the words of these books, although he does not comprehend real fiqh. Yet he mistakenly believes himself to have attained fiqh and commits such blunders. The aforementioned book, *al-Hawi,* and its like, are very good books that are useful for retrieving legal cases and indicating their rulings, although in a manner that yields cursory knowledge only. Such books are to serve as supplements for others. But it cannot be claimed that fiqh might be learned from them. The utmost that those who memorise such books may attain is some sort of virtue, but not fiqh. Virtue is of three kinds, one of which consists of knowing the detailed legal rules, learning them from the Book, the Sunnah, and the sayings of recognised leaders, and knowing their basis. This is *fiqh*, and those who possess it are the ones called the *'Ulema'* (*sic,* read *fuqaha*). The second kind of virtue consists of learning the religious sciences (*al-ulum ul-shariyya*) in an absolute sense, without attaining detailed legal understanding, as is the case in exegesis, hadith, and theology (*usul ul-din*). Those who possess this virtue are called *'Ulema'*. The third kind is different from the former two kinds. It is a science that is close to craftsmanship. Although we may call those who possess it learned people (*Fudala*), we may not call them either jurists or general scholars. Such people are often mistaken for jurists or general scholars, because others may fail to distinguish between the learned people, general scholars, and jurists. Those who occupy themselves with *al-Hawi,* especially, belong to the third kind of scholars (*fudala*).

It was subsequently reported to me that the fatwa (denying the carpet maker's liability) was reissued as a response to the case mentioned in this paper (i.e., in P3), and that other fatwas were solicited about it in the hope of finding someone who would endorse it. I do not know if anyone endorsed it. It was reported to me, and I am not sure whether it is true, that some people endorsed this fatwa, thinking that it involved the issue of the self-employed artisan (*masalat al-ajir al-mushtarak*). If this had indeed occurred, it would be indicative of a great deal of ignorance, and of remoteness from the essence of fiqh and from knowledge of peoples' conditions.

Then, this paper (*hadhihil-waraqa*) was presented to me together with another paper bearing the same question (P3), as well as a fatwa in the handwriting of the same person who had issued the fatwa denying the carpet-maker's liability. The courier asked me: "Is this that one (P_2) or a different one?" I said: "Indeed, it is a different one, for the question is different and the paper is different and does not even look like it (i.e., P_2)." I was surprised that someone would act in this manner, since it is the habit of knowledgeable people to admit their mistakes, and not to immerse themselves in error or to act deceptively. Moreover, I was told that my usage of the word *istisna* (manufacturing contract) was criticised. Oh God, what ignorance! This expression is used by al-Shafii in *al-Umm,* and by our early colleagues as well as other jurists, so how could this escape a jurist? It is more apt for someone like this to guard himself against falling into such things:

Not every man is qualified for battle and registries require good scribes and accountants.

Knowledge is difficult and not easily attained. Not all dispositions accept it. Indeed, some people spend their entire lives pursuing it without obtaining anything, while it is disclosed to others in a short time. It is a privilege that God bestows upon whomever He wills.

As for the question mentioned in this paper (P3), the aforementioned person had answered it by saying that the carpet maker is not liable (*la yalzamuhu al-daman*) unless he was negligent in maintaining the carpets, because he is a fiduciary (*li-anna yadahu yad amana*). This answer would still be wrong in this case, presuming that the actual case is identical to the case depicted in the question. For if the actual case did not involve other than what is mentioned here, it would constitute an invalid agency (*wakala*), since what is needed to produce carpets is unknown, and an agency regarding an unknown is invalid. Furthermore, if the agency is invalid, then everything the agent (*al-wakil*) buys, be it wool or anything else, is his property and not that of the principal (*al-muwakkil*). Thus, if the carpet maker manufactures carpets with the wool, and if these carpets are destroyed, they would be the carpet maker's loss. The carpet maker is not in a fiduciary position vis-a-vis the carpets, since a fiduciary position would arise only if the carpets were someone else's property, whereas they belong to the carpet maker. As for the money, it is in the hand of the agent, and the petitioner did not ask about it in any case.

Therefore, the answer that the carpet maker does not incur the loss for the carpets (*la yaghram ul-busut*) and that he is a fiduciary is wrong. However, even if we presume that this agency is valid, and that the wool is the property of the payer, workmanship is subsumed under objects (*al-sana mulhaqa bil-ayan*). The rule applicable to workmanship with respect to the issue of the fee is equivalent to the rule applicable to an object of sale with respect to the issue of the price; the artisan would be unconditionally responsible for it (the object of sale) and does not have a fiduciary capacity towards it (*yad ul-sani alayhi yad daman la yad amana*). Thus, to say that he has a fiduciary capacity is wrong. In order to determine the extent of the carpet-maker's liability, further specifications about the actual case are needed. The other mufti may have had a different case in mind. However, he does not mention this (in his response). Admittedly, the aforementioned answer may not be entirely wrong. Yet it is an unqualified statement where elaboration is due (*itlaq fi mawdi tafsil*). We have been asked to provide an answer to what is mentioned in this paper (P3), and have given an elaboration and a clarification of the ruling, may God exalted be willing (Al-Subki, Taqi al-Din, n.d., 1:447-449).

Before I analyse this case, it will be useful to summarise the main events al-Subki relates in his response. Shortly before receiving the petition leading to the text translated above (i.e., P_3; see note 7), al-Subki had received two other petitions (P_1 and P_2) pertaining to a slightly different version of the carpet-maker's case. In P_1 and P_2, it was indicated that the client paid the carpet-maker money to manufacture some carpets. But case P3 indicated that the client paid the carpet-maker money to purchase "whatever is needed" for making the carpets, and that he specified the carpet-maker's fee for this service. In responding to the first petition (P_1), al-Subki issued a written fatwa maintaining that the carpet-maker should bear the entire loss for the damaged carpets. One day after he had issued this fatwa, al-Subki received another petition (P2) about the same case. This time, however, the petitioner wished to obtain al-Subki's *written* opinion regarding another fatwa on the petition sheet, which would absolve the artisan of any liability for the stolen carpets. Al-Subki evidently was well acquainted with the author of this fatwa and deemed him unqualified to issue legal advice. Moreover, he considered the fatwa entirely inadmissible. In the end, he denied the petitioner's request, declining to write any comments on the submitted sheet. Some time later, the other mufti reissued his first fatwa as a response to the second version of the case (P3). This fatwa was approved by some of those who were consulted about it. Finally, al-Subki himself was consulted about the modified case, and about the fatwa denying the carpet-maker's liability as applied to this new version. The text translated here represents al-Subki's response to this last petition.

Notwithstanding the apparent anonymity of the petitioner, al-Subki must have inferred, as the events unfolded, that the fatwas about the carpet-maker's liability were being solicited on the carpet-maker's behalf. Moreover, he probably considered the "representation" of the case as an illegitimate attempt by the carpet-maker to use loopholes in the law to avoid having to compensate his client. Later on in this chapter I will examine how the carpet-maker's legal position in the second version of the case is improved. It will be shown how al-Subki's response to the last petition (P_3), especially in its final part, reflects his concern to expose and defeat the petitioner's legal scheme. But first I wish to analyse al-Subki's responses to the first two petitions submitted to him about the case. Al-Subki's response to P_1 highlights the problematic features of his response to P_3. Moreover, his response to P2 is a concrete illustration of the practical significance of some important instructions in the mufti manuals pertaining to the regulation of *ifta*.

Al-Subki must have perceived the first petition as an unsuspect and unproblematic request. The legal problem raised by the petitioner was familiar to him; it represented, as he explains, a type of problem that arose frequently between certain types of artisans and their clients in custom manufacturing contracts. Nothing in the formulation of the question warranted suspicion about the motives of the petitioner, whose identity was not disclosed. Thus al-Subki handled the case with no more than the conventional prudence required in issuing written fatwas.

From a legal point of view, the question was neither novel nor complex; it had a clear and uncontested solution in legal textbooks. Acting in conformity with the instructions in adab al-mufti works, al-Subki did not justify his opinion; the basis of his fatwa would have been quite apparent to the legal expert, and al-Subki was under no obligation to justify himself to the layperson (Ibn al-Salah ul-Shahrazuri 1986, 1:82; al-Nawawi 1990: 64).

Al-Subki's fatwa was a rigorous and straightforward application of Shafii doctrine. Its underlying reasoning may be explicated as follows. The contractual relationship between the carpet-maker and his client fits squarely under the definition of an *istisna*—a contract of custom manufacture—that is considered invalid in the Shafii school. Being invalid, the contract between the artisan and his client does not result in the transfer of ownership. Thus the manufactured carpets are the artisan's property, and since these carpets were damaged in the artisan's possession, he alone incurs their loss. Moreover, an invalid sale contract does not create mutual obligations of exchange between the contracting parties. Therefore, the client is not obligated to purchase the outstanding carpets.

As for the money received by the carpet-maker, it would have to be refunded because of the contract's invalidity (thus restoring things between contracting parties to their precontractual state). This is, however, only part of what al-Subki conveys in the terse statement about the money in his fatwa (*"al-darahim madmuna alal-akhdh"*). Al-Subki is also saying here that until the carpet-maker refunds the money, he will be unconditionally responsible for it. In other words, if this money were lost under any circumstances, the carpet-maker would incur the loss and would be obliged to compensate his client.

The carpet-maker's unconditional liability regarding the money is due to the fact that the money was received in a contract involving a bilateral exchange, a synallagmatic contract. Unconditional liability arises in this case, notwithstanding the invalidity of the contract, because according to a major Shafii legal principle (*qaida fiqhiyya*), the rules of liability applicable to assets that transfer hands in valid contracts are also applicable to the invalid counterparts of such contracts (*"kull aqd sahihuhu yaqtadi al-daman fa-fasiduhu kadhalika"*) (al-Suyuti n.d.:308).

Al-Subki's first fatwa is exhaustive insofar as it addresses all the implications of the case in question. He does not limit his answer strictly to the petitioner's specific question (should the carpet-maker incur the loss?). He also spells out the legal consequences of the invalid contract regarding the outstanding carpets and the money received. This is quite justifiable, since al-Subki must have considered, and rightly so, that providing this information was necessary to insure the proper resolution of the dispute at hand. However, al-Subki does not always volunteer legal information in this manner. Indeed, as shall be seen, in his fatwa about the second version of the carpet-maker's case (i.e., the last part of P3), he deliberately withholds from his petitioner significant legal information, which he feared the latter might misuse.

It will be recalled that al-Subki denied the petitioner's second request (P2), dismissing the courier without writing anything on the submitted sheet. Subsequently he explained to his students, by way of instruction, that the fatwa about which he was consulted in P2 was entirely inadmissible, as it ran against scholarly consensus. Yet this begs the question of why al-Subki declined to write his ready and effortless refutation on the petitioner's sheet.

Al-Subki states that he considered the fatwa on the petitioner's sheet unworthy of his consideration (*"laysat ahlan li-an araha"*). However, I would like to suggest here that al-Subki dismissed the petition about this fatwa not so much because the fatwa was wrong, but because of its author's poor credentials. In other words, al-Subki would have issued a written response about this fatwa, *on the petitioner's sheet,* if this fatwa had been issued by a qualified jurist. Because it was not, he refused to write on the same sheet as the other mufti, and would have done so even if the latter's fatwa had been admissible. The instructions in the adab al-mufti works highlight these significations in al-Subki's response.

The adab manuals instruct muftis not to write anything on a petition sheet that bears a fatwa by an unqualified person (*"man laysa ahlan lil-fatwa"*), regardless of the intrinsic merit of such a fatwa. Co-writing on a sheet with an unqualified person, it is explained, implicitly sanctions transgression on the domain of ifta. Unqualified muftis are to be ignored and systematically ostracised. At the same time, the manuals state that if a mufti discovers on a petition sheet a definite error in a fatwa by a qualified jurist, it is his duty to point this out, and to issue a valid fatwa on the same sheet, thereby forestalling a potential misapplication of the law. In fact, in such a case it is recommended that the mufti return the petition sheet to the author of the mistaken fatwa for revision. Muftis, however, are instructed not to comment on other fatwas by qualified jurists on the petition sheet, as these simply represent a different opinion and are otherwise admissible. (al-Nawawi 1990:60-62). Petition sheets are not intended to serve as a forum for juristic debate.

It is highly unlikely that the conformity between al-Subki's response to the second petition and the adab instructions is merely coincidental. *Fatwa al-Subki* includes two transcripts of petition sheets with fatwas by several jurists (al-Subki, Taqi al-Din, n.d., 1:467-472). These texts also indicate that al-Subki and his colleagues adhered in practice to the above described instructions. In both texts, divergent views are advanced by the muftis. Yet, with one justifiable exception, the muftis do not discuss other fatwas in their own response. definite error that, further down on the sheet, he retracts (*sahha-hahd*) explicitly, adopting another view. In between al-Sunbati's fatwas, there are fatwas by al-Subki and Badr al-Din ibn Jamaa, one of whom must have been responsible for discovering the error and rerouting the petition back to Al-Sunbati. Evidently, what accounts for the obvious disparity between the responses prompted by Al-Sunbati's error and the one committed by the mufti in the carpet-maker's case is al-Sunbati's qualification: according to *Tabaqat ul-Shafiiyya,* al-Sunbati was a well-known Shafii jurist who had adequate credentials to issue fatwas.

Finally, in the carpet-maker's case, it seems that the petitioner understood al-Subki's response to P2 in this context; he realised that al-Subki would refuse in principle to write a fatwa on the same sheet with the other mufti. Therefore, in P3, this technical obstacle was removed by providing al-Subki with a separate sheet on which to write his response.

Under the Mamluks, ifta was still largely an independent institution. Unlike judges, muftis did not have to be publicly appointed; fatwa giving was open to all those who were recognised by their fellow scholars as having the requisite intellectual and personal qualifications. The open character of this institution gave muftis their valued autonomy from the state, while allowing litigants and judges access to a larger pool of juristic resources. Notwithstanding its independence, ifta was closely regulated by its own practitioners.

Muftis adopted both moral and practical measures to curb unqualified incursions into their domain. The adab al-mufti manuals commence with a lengthy statement about the grave religious responsibility assumed in issuing fatwas and the dire eschatological consequences awaiting those who undertake the task without the requisite qualifications. Moreover, the manuals charge petitioners with the duty to consult only jurists with established credentials (Ibn al-Salah al-Shahrazuri 1986, 1:7ff, 85-86; al-Nawawi 1990:13ff., 71-72). Besides religious sanctions, though, muftis adopted practical measures such as the ones described here, which served to curb abuses of ifta while preserving the pluralism characteristic of this institution.

I stated earlier that al-Subki perceived the changes made to the case as an illegitimate attempt by the petitioner to avoid his liability. These changes recharacterised the contractual relationship in the case at hand, and in light of the relevant legal doctrine, the new contractual relationship could have improved the carpet-maker's position.

The second version of the case (P3), it will be recalled, indicates that the client paid the carpet-maker money to purchase "whatever is needed" for the production of the carpets, and that the client designated the carpet-maker's fee for this service. These added specifications transform the legal nature of the relationship between the carpet-maker and the client from a contract of future sale to a contract of employment.

On closer examination of the additional specifications, one observes that the carpet-maker in the new version of the case is required to perform two services: purchase the primary material and apply his expertise to change this material into carpets. In performing the first service, the carpet-maker is considered an agent, since he does not derive any gain from buying the material for his client. As an agent, he acts on behalf of, and to the benefit of, his client. Therefore, whatever he buys in his capacity as an agent belongs to the client—assuming the agency is valid. In performing the second service, the carpet-maker is an employee; he sells a skill rather than a finished product. He profits exclusively from selling this skill, not from the difference between the price of the carpets and the cost of the material. Thus one may conclude that the final aim of the added specifications was to establish that the carpet-maker was an employee hired to manufacture carpets from material provided by the client. Presenting the case in this manner, would allow the carpet-maker to take advantage of some lenient liability rules associated with the self-employed artisan.

The question of a self-employed artisan's liability towards objects he receives in conjunction with a contract of employment is a controversial one in Islamic law. Two main views were advocated regarding this issue:

(1) the employee bears a strict liability towards his client's object, and thus he incurs the loss unconditionally for any damage to that object (that is, he is *damin);*

(2) the employee bears a fiduciary liability vis-a-vis the object and therefore incurs the loss only for damages to the object due to negligence or transgression (that is, he is *amin*) (al-Dimashqi 1960: 179; al-Baghdadi 1308/1892:27-28).

How was this question treated in the Shafii legal school? In the *Kitab al-Umm,* al-Shafii admits both of the above-mentioned views, since, as he explains, there is no decisive textual evidence to favour either one (al-Shafii 1961, 3:261-262). Significantly, though, in later Shafii works, it is said that al-Shafii considered the employee a fiduciary but refrained from issuing fatwas to this effect because he feared that they might be abused. In light of this, Shafii jurists mention both opinions about the employee's liability but assert that treating the employee as a fiduciary represents the stronger doctrine (*"azhar ul-qawlayn"*) (al-Shirazi n.d., 2:408; al-Shirbini 1933, 2:351; al-Nawawi n.d., 5:228).

Shafii jurists, moreover, addressed separately the issue of the employee's liability when an object is damaged after he has performed his service. In *al-Muhadhab,* al-Shirazi (d. 1003) maintains that the employee in such a case incurs either the loss for the material or the fee, but not both. He justifies this opinion in terms of earlier Shafii doctrine, by linking the question of the fee to the employee's liability status (*amin* versus *damin*). The employee loses his claim to the fee, al-Shirazi argues, if he is considered a fiduciary and merits it if he is held liable (al-Shirazi n.d., 2:409). Al-Shirazi's argument rests on the assumption that an employee fulfils his contractual obligation and merits his fee only by delivering the manufactured product (*maa al-taslim*), and not merely by applying his expertise.

By contrast, Abu Zakariya al-Nawawi (d. 1277) dissociates the question regarding the employee's eligibility for the fee from that of his liability for the damaged object. In *Rawdat al-talibin,* he states that an artisan's workmanship may be conceived either as an effect (*athar*) or an object (*ayn*). If the workmanship is conceived as an effect, he maintains, the employee merits the fee, but otherwise he does not (al-Nawawi n.d., 5:231). The underlying rationale for Al-Nawawi's rule is made clear in a fifteenth-century Shii legal work. The *athar/ayn* distinction corresponds to two opinions about the nature of an artisan's obligation in a contract of employment; if workmanship is seen as an intangible effect, the employee fulfils his contractual obligation and merits the fee by applying his expertise. But if workmanship is treated as a tangible object, the employee fulfils his obligation only by delivering the product (al-Karaki 1410/1990, 7:274-276). By combining the latter two views about the nature of workmanship together with the two opinions about the employee's liability (that is, *damin* versus *amin*), al-Nawawi advances four solutions to the question of liability for a manufactured object. The following two may be singled out as more authoritative, in view of al-Shafii's preference to treat the employee as a fiduciary:

1. The employee is a fiduciary over the wool, but loses his claim to the fee (workmanship is *ayn*).
2. The employee is a fiduciary over the carpets and maintains his claim to the fee (workmanship is *athar*) (al-Nawawi n.d., 5:231).

The foregoing exposition clearly demonstrates that the carpet-maker's legal position in the second version of the case (P3) is significantly improved according to Shafii legal doctrine. In fact, the fatwa denying the carpet-maker's liability in the second version seems justifiable, since it corresponds exactly to one of the stronger solutions advanced by al-Nawawi; it grants the employee a fiduciary status over the manufactured carpets, thereby absolving him of any liability for the material. Moreover, it does not deny him the fee.

In P3, it will be recalled, the petitioner solicited al-Subki's opinion about the new version of the case and about the fatwa denying the carpet-maker's liability as applied to this version. Al-Subki addresses the petitioner's specific request only after providing detailed background information about his earlier encounters with the case, clearly in an attempt to expose the petitioner's questionable motives. Finally, in the last part of his response to P3, he turns to the legal question raised by the petitioner.

Al-Subki insists that the fatwa denying the carpet-maker's liability in the new version of the case is wrong, notwithstanding the added specification. He argues, first, that the case as described in the question involves an invalid agency, which precludes the possibility of ascribing a fiduciary status to the carpet-maker. Then he maintains that the fatwa would still be wrong even if the agency were presumed to be valid.

The first half of al-Subki's argument is unobjectionable. Al-Subki's rejection of the agency conforms to the general doctrine that invalidates contracts of agency with an indeterminate object (al-Shirazi n.d., 1:350); al-Subki must have construed the clause "whatever is needed" to constitute an invalidating factor on the ground of indeterminacy. Thereafter, his reasoning constitutes a straightforward application of the rules regarding invalid contracts. An invalid agency, al-Subki says, does not transfer ownership. Thus it is not possible to say that the artisan has a fiduciary status with regard to the carpets, for the compelling reason that the damaged carpets were the artisan's property.

The second half of al-Subki's fatwa proves to be less compelling. To begin with, this part of his fatwa is quite obscure; it is extremely difficult to identify its line of reasoning. The expository difficulties in the argument, though, may have been partly resolved by my translation. Al-Subki's argument may be explicated as follows. Granting the carpet-maker a fiduciary position over the carpets in toto, as the other mufti did, makes him a fiduciary over his own workmanship. However, the legal status of the employee's workmanship in a contract of employment, with regard to the issue of compensation and liability, is analogous to that of a concrete object in a contract of sale. An artisan would be liable for his workmanship until he delivers it to the client, just as a vendor would be liable for the object of sale until he delivers it to the buyer. Thus it is wrong to say that the carpet-maker is a fiduciary in relation to his workmanship.

This part of al-Subki's response is not as readily justifiable in terms of Shafii legal doctrine. Al-Subki is entitled to treat workmanship as an object and to issue a fatwa accordingly. However, he may not use such an inconclusive opinion to refute another fatwa based on a different but nonetheless admissible view of workmanship. Al-Subki must have been acquainted with the different opinions about workmanship expounded in al-Nawawi's *Rawdat ul-talibin.* He was, after all, an astute student of al-Nawawi and was already well acquainted with the latter's legal works at an early stage in his career (al-Subki, Taj al-Din, n.d., 6:156, 170). Why, then, does he overlook entirely this other view of workmanship in his fatwa?

It may be that the view of workmanship as an effect was considered admissible but weak by jurists after al-Nawawi. There is some evidence in the sources that points in this direction. If this was indeed the case, al-Subki's objection to the other fatwa would be justifiable; according to adab al-mufti manuals, a jurist is not at liberty to choose any one of the opinions in the school regarding a particular point of law. Rather he should base his fatwa on the weightiest and most plausible opinion in his school (*al-arjah, ul-asahh*) (Ibn al-Salah al-Shahrazuri 1986, 1:60-61; al-Nawawi 1990:42).

Yet, even if we grant al-Subki the benefit of the doubt on this point, his fatwa about the second version of the case would still be problematic. This becomes apparent if one takes into account not only what al-Subki says in his fatwa but also how he says it—and what he conspicuously chooses not to say. Al-Subki, it may be noted, focuses strictly on the mistaken segment of the other fatwa and stresses only the liability of the artisan. However, he avoids conceding the improvement in the carpet-maker's position in the new case. Thus when he entertains the possibility that the agency involved in the transaction might be valid, he does not spell out the implications of this possibility regarding the wool. He moves directly to assert that ascribing a fiduciary status to the carpet-maker in this case would also be wrong, because it involves ascribing to him a fiduciary status over his workmanship.

However, al-Subki does not state explicitly that if the agency were valid, the carpet-maker would not be liable for the wool—presuming no negligence on his part—since the wool in this case would be the property of his client. Al-Subki undoubtedly was aware of the implications of the new case regarding the wool. In fact, he indicates this at the end, when he concedes that the fatwa ascribing a fiduciary status to the carpet-maker may be valid in a qualified sense. However, he deliberately avoids explaining how this is so. Moreover, he defers providing a definite statement about the extent of the carpet-maker's liability on the unconvincing pretext of lacking specifications—presumably regarding the validity of the agency. The negative and evasive character of al-Subki's fatwa about the second version of the case is unmistakable.

Was al-Subki acting as a good mufti in issuing such a vague, incomplete, and biased fatwa about the second version of the case? From the narrow perspective of formal legal validity, the answer would not be in al-Subki's favour. However, if al-Subki's actions are interpreted in light of his concern to forestall an attempt to abuse the law, they would have solid justification in the norms of ifta at his time.

Muslim jurists were well aware of the existence of loopholes in the corpus of legal doctrine. In recognition of this fact, the adab manuals instruct muftis against assisting petitioners to avoid liabilities that are dictated by the intended meaning of the law (Ibn Al-Salah Al-Shahrazuri 1986, 1:82, 47; al-Nawawi 1990:38, 54-55). The mufti acting on the carpet-maker's behalf apparently furnished the latter with such objectionable legal advice, thereby violating a basic principle of ifta. Al-Subki reacted to this misconduct in conformity with his adab culture. In the manuals, it is stated that a mufti may issue a fatwa that does not conform to the apparent meaning of the law (*al-zahir*) if he suspects ill will on the petitioner's behalf.

The example provided in the manuals to illustrate this principle is not clearly relevant to this case (al-Nawawi 1990:56). However, we need not limit ourselves to the adab works, since these are necessarily an incomplete record of the larger discourse about fatwa giving that existed at al-Subki's time. Indeed, an excellent illustration of the principle at hand is provided by the anecdote, cited above, about al-Shafii's refusal to publicise his opinion about the employee's fiduciary status, for fear that it might be misused. The principle underlying this anecdote must have been an integral part of al-Subki's culture and education as a mufti, and was evidently the overriding consideration behind his actions in this case. Admittedly al-Subki did not go as far as misrepresenting the doctrine for the carpet-maker. However, he did not provide him with a full statement of the law, depriving him of written support for his attempt to evade his liability towards the client.

Moreover, al-Subki did not limit his response in P3 to the petitioner's question but also provided all the relevant background information about the carpet-maker's case. His decision to do so must have been informed by his professional training. Judging from the silence of the manuals on this issue, it seems that muftis were not expected to verify the facts of cases about which they were asked to issue fatwas. In general, they were only expected to provide a precise answer to the question posed by the petitioner; responsibility for verifying the applicability of a fatwa to the actual case fell to the judge. It was a different matter, however, if a mufti happened to know, or had reason to suspect, that the legal case as described by the petitioner (*surat-al-fatwa*) did not conform to the actual case (*surat al-hal*). In such an event, the manuals instruct the mufti not only to answer the petitioner's question but also to cite and provide the solution for what is suspected to be the actual case (Ibn al-Salah al-Shahrazuri 1986, 1:79). This is exactly the course al-Subki adopted.

The instructions in the manuals underscore the notion that a written fatwa was not to be treated merely as a medium for the mufti to communicate his opinion to the petitioner in a form that is preservable. A mufti had to keep in mind that a fatwa might be read by someone other than the petitioner. Thus muftis were advised to incorporate in their response all relevant information about the case. Moreover, they were to take all the precautionary measures to insure that their written fatwas would stand as autonomous and self-explanatory texts (Ibn al-Salah al-Shahrazuri 1986, 1:78; al-Nawawi 1990:45-46). In this case, al-Subki clearly did not compose his answer only for the benefit of the petitioner or the other mufti assisting him, since most of the information he provided was already well-known to those two readers. Rather, he also had in mind other potential readers who might be in a position to influence or decide the outcome of the case. The additional information al-Subki provided in his response would alert those readers to the petitioner's suspect motives. Moreover it placed his fatwa in its very particular context, thus justifying its problematic character.

Condemning Decrees

The "fatwas of condemnation" constitute an extraordinarily provocative genre of *responsa* in the annals of Islam. They provoked action; they aroused rebuke; and they served to banish from the fold of Islam the most troublesome elements, who threatened to unravel the fabric that bound one Muslim to another. Indeed, there is a long and rancorous tradition of condemnation that threads down to our own times. The list of those condemned reads like a Who's Who of Muslim militants—al-Hallaj; al-Ghazzali; Ibn al-Arabi; Muhammad Ahmad; Mirza Ghulam Ahmad—and, through the power of the poison (i.e., the fatwa), the wound to reputations was (in the case of many) judged almost incurable. Indeed, al-Hallaj (who endeavoured to bring dogma into harmony with Greek philosophy on the strength of mystic experience) was denounced by the Mutazila, excommunicated by the Imamiyya, and roundly condemned by a fatwa issued by authorities from the Zahiriyya. Later, he was arrested and imprisoned by the Abbasids of Baghdad. Following swiftly on another fatwa proclaimed by the Maliki qadi Abu Umar, he was exposed on a gibbet (in a kind of Muslim crucifixion), decapitated, and burned in 309/922 (Massignon 1961:127). Ibn ul-Arabi (d. 628/1240), whose manner and vision were also aligned with the mystics, was assailed as a dangerous innovator, and fatwas rushed from the pen of Ibn Taymiyya, Taqi ud-Din al-Subki, and Badr ud-Din b. Jamaa, among others (Ates 1971:710).

What these "militants" shared with countless others who cannot be mentioned here was a high individualism and an aversion to taqlid (following the opinion of another within a madhhab, or school of law)—an independence of approach that was to cast them in bad odour with the *'Ulema'* of their day. Muhammad b. Ali al-Sanusi (1202/1787-1859), the subject of this analysis (the so-called Grand Sanusi), achieved high rank on this infamous "honour roll" of *ghulat,* as he challenged some of the most deeply embedded practices in orthodox Islam. Like Ibn Taymiyya (d. 1328) and al-Ghazzali (d. 1111), to whom he displayed a natural and binding affinity, Muhammad al-Sanusi seems to have broken with taqlid from his earliest youth. One also senses in him an early disdain for the company of "kings" and an eager embrace of the leaders of the *turuq,* or religious brotherhoods.

Though learned in law and skilled in the reigning modes of scholarly expression, al-Sanusi's breadth of Sufistic sympathy extended to a constant quest for *baraka* (spiritual grace or charisma) and knowledge acquired from religious scholars, as exemplified by the number of associations he affected with leaders of religious brotherhoods. But, as he allowed his reputation to engulf that of his rivals and engrossed to himself an alarming number of partisans, these actions served only to further alienate him and anger his enemies.

In the late 1830s, we find al-Sanusi travelling in the Hijaz, the favoured disciple of Ahmad b. Idris al-Farsi (d. 1837), the celebrated founder of a popular brotherhood then thriving in the Muslim holy places. At the time of his death, the mantle of Ahmad b. Idris did no more than flutter over a host of aspirants before it descended in hot controversy on the figure of al-Sanusi.

The followers of the deceased split in acrimony, Muhammad al-Sanusi gathering to himself the bulk of adherents (Ziadeh 1958:45; Martin 1976:102-104). Even before this period, however, the teachings of al-Sanusi had stirred rumblings of concern among the leading *'Ulema'*. Of his abrupt departure from al-Azhar, Ziadeh (1958:39) has observed:

He had intended to stay for some time in Egypt, where he would pursue his learning at al-Azhar. But al-Sanusi decided to leave the place in much shorter time than he had intended. He seems to have been disappointed there. For one thing he did not find al-Azhar as congenial as he had expected, as the *Ulema* were courtiers of Muhammad Ali or else attached to the great Ottoman officials in Cairo. For another, al-Sanusi did not meet with the consideration he thought he should receive, for after all, when he arrived at Cairo he had already been recognised as an "*alim*" in his own right in North Africa. His views were not favourably received by the *Ulema*, and he was publicly denounced by Sheikh ul-Hanish as an innovator. Maybe the main disappointment he had there was the lack of spiritual activity and Sufi teachings at al-Azhar.

If Muhammad al-Sanusi failed in his attempts to obtain some recognition among the official clerisy of Egypt, he succeeded in securing their venomous opposition to his teachings. In 1843 (three years subsequent to his return to the Maghrib), a fatwa was issued at the instigation of Sheikh ul-Hanish ("the snake") accelerating the revulsion against the doctrinal positions assumed by the Sanusiyya. As we shall recognise, this message, replete with anathema and recrimination, signalled the early success of the Sanusiyya in Egypt and the Hijaz. And its tone of urgency suggests that the *'Ulema'* of these lands felt strongly that immediate action should be mounted against al-Sanusi and his partisans.

The Question: What do the people of learning (who separate from the pure shariah every element of deviation and falsehood) say regarding a man (i.e., Muhammad al-Sanusi) who has appeared in the land of the Hijaz (en route) to the Maghrib (who has with him) a party of people who alight on the fringe of the land and incite the people to exalt the greatness of their sheikh and enter his brotherhood? These servants make every effort to act upon his wishes in the same way that servants attend to kings, so much so that they do not enter upon religious service under him except after repeated requests to him during a special period. They are not permitted to visit him except during specific hours. They assert that their way is the path (*tariqa*) of the people. Those sent to him do not bear witness with him in the Friday prayer (i.e., he prays separately). Whenever he resides in a country for an extended period, the prayer service lasts a long time. He does not attend the community prayer, nor does he (attend) other prayers in the mosque. He commands the people to follow the precepts of the Quran and the Sunnah ("by word," but not by action). Whenever devoted servants come to him, he says to that group that they should direct themselves towards someone who will present to them the *wird* and write for them a special *dhikr,* and he delivers it to them saying, cleave to the one who ranks over you, even if he is a tax collector. Those appointed over (these initiates) do not deter them from any disapproved action. And they call themselves "Shadhiliyya," and they read loudly the *bismillah* (which is obligatory to all Muslims).

The imam breaks off speech after the greater part of the sacred pronouncement, and after the *fatiha* (first Sura of the Quran) there is a long interim. They make obligatory the reading on those who stand behind the imam which the substitute for the imam leads in a plain voice.

They prolong the time of prostration beyond the legal prescriptions, so as to allow strangers to join them in prayer. They display a god-fearing quality as they stand a long time in prayer lifting their voices strongly and raising their hands. They contend that breaking the fast of Ramadan during the journey is better than fasting during it. They gather for the prayer and they shorten the length of it in accordance with the duration of their stay in a land, even if they remain a long time there. They assert that they are Malikis, yet the common people have had aroused in them a suspicion of the Maliki *'Ulema'* owing to their (i.e., the Sanusis') lack of familiarity with the requirements of the madhhab.'

They assert that this *wird* (of theirs) is sunnah, and that he who disagrees with it is an innovator. Some of them, upon entering the prayer (*salat*), utter a shrill cry, and they do not rise up (and recover their senses) until the imam completes his prayer. Praying after a single *tayammum* is made obligatory among them. They contend that the action of *tayammum* is not broken until the *wudu* is broken, and they maintain that all the actions of the *wudu'* are obligatory. For the most part, his most eager followers are drawn from the ranks of the emirs and other important people and their servants. (The Sanusis) do not render hospitality to guests unless they are from the class of Arab sheikhs, and from those who obtain their wealth illegally, or by deception. They eat and supply themselves provisions from what (the aforementioned) possess. To him who refrains from that unlawful (situation), they say, "you will not reach what the sheikh has reached" (or, "subsist on what the sheikh and his followers subsist on").

O *'Ulema'* of Islam, Allah the Almighty has already made obligatory upon you that you should explain the truth and make clear the shariah, and respond to every falsehood emanating from the quarter of the deceived. Make clear to us what the Imam Malik (b. Anas (d. 795)) and the people of the brotherhood have obliged us to do. Do not guide us except by what is well known. By your (guidance) do not misdirect the leaders and the common people. Be concise in your reply, and perhaps Allah will be pleased with you and lead to the straight path he who returns to the Prophet (may Allah be pleased with him) in a state of penitence.

The Reply: Our learned sheikh (may Allah the Almighty have mercy on him and encompass with mercy his words), Mustafa al-Bulaqi (see Brockelmann 1943-1949, 356; 1937-1941, 705) replied (to the above queries): "Praise be to Allah. This closing off of the above-mentioned from the face of the aforementioned is an oppression of darkness. To assert that the path of the Sufis is like that is a lie upon them, since the perfect path of the people is clinging to the Messenger of Allah (may Allah bless him and grant him peace) and questing the moral temper of the noble descendants of the Messenger of Allah. The master of the humble people (may Allah bless him and grant him peace) indeed received in a friendly manner everyone who asked for a reception—even women and slaves—without reproach. He sat down with the poor and the homeless and others like them. Thus, to deny this tradition of common deliberation is to swerve from one's duty.

The way of the people is not to depart from the following of the Prophet (Pbuh). If they depart from this emulation, the following of such people cannot be sanctioned. What is Islam, if not the book of Allah and the Sunna of His messenger? Everyone who contradicts the Quran and the Sunnah is an apostate (and their acts are to no avail). Gathering for the public prayer is confirmed Sunnah, and its obligatory nature affirmed by the Imam Ahmad b. Hanbal (d. 855). This man's absence from the witness of the Friday prayer and the public prayer is a grievous affair and an indication that he does not in fact follow the way of the Sufis. His absence from the community gathering for prayer and other (obligatory) gatherings of the people is disobedience (of the commandments of Allah). What is to be gained from these wrongdoings (even) if he is present at these obligatory gatherings and held in contempt by Allah? For his people consider themselves in accordance with the law, whereas they are the purveyors of falsehood.

He commands the commoners among the people to follow the Quran and the Sunnah with words of truth (yet what he intends by this is falsehood and the abandoning of the obligatory legal rites (madhhabs), and the use of the laws from the Quran and the Sunnah without intermediaries). This constitutes a deviation from the straight path. His advice to others on the strength of these views is an indication of his own ignorance, when it is known to everyone that (certain) texts (from Quran and Sunnah) have been abrogated and other (texts) refuted owing to the opposition to those who related them, and still others abandoned due to strong opposition to them or to their replacement by stronger texts, or their confirmation by the four founding Imams (that is, the "founders" of the four madhhabs) in the face of opposition. What is held best is what is rendered accurate from the madhhabs of the founding Imams, because these legal rites contain people of high rank and long service—the people of truth and those concerned with the careful examination of it.

To abandon the accumulated opinion (taqlid) of these four canonical rites is to stray from the right path and to command by it the example of ignorance and rebellion. It is obligatory to follow the opinion of the learned from one of the four rites. These Sanusis deflect everyone from the true course of Sufism— the well-traced road verified by the religious texts. Initiates should possess in the first instance a clear knowledge of the religious tenets of Islam, then let those who wish to affiliate with a brotherhood (and who are entitled to that relationship)—let (them) do that, otherwise if (they) are unworthy of that relationship, it should be refused to (them).

It is obvious that the man (al-Sanusi) is ignorant of the obvious aspects of the shariah, and that he strays from the (true) path of the Sufis. From the vantage point of these circumstances, it is forbidden to enter into any agreement with him (along the lines discussed above), as it cannot be fulfiled legally, and it would be analogous to a sick man seeking a remedy from someone other than a physician. Alas! Perhaps man busies himself about that which would surely result in the loss of his carnal soul (*nafs*), and he enters into this folly without forewarning.

As to the words of the bestower of the *wird*, "stay in your condition, even if it is one of disobedience (to the laws of Islam)," and these words are uttered in the absence of any encouragement to repent and to become reconciled to the duties of Islam—these actions are *haram*—forbidden by every religious community (*milla*). Those who became non-believers from the Banu Israil (viz., the Jews) were cursed by the language of David and Isa b. Maryam (viz., Jesus, son of Mary) for the very reason that they rebelled against their community, displayed hostility towards it, and led others away from its prescriptions. And its leaders—how detestable are the actions of the Sanusis—their making loud the *bismillah* during the *salat* of the canonical prayers—their remaining silent before *fatiha* prayer and after it (are also to be condemned, for) the recitation of the *fatiha* is obligatory and in accordance (with the teachings) of the Imams. Again, their remaining long in the prostrations or their performance of the prostrations in a heedless manner, as well as their loud pronouncement of the *Qanut* (and the raising of the hands during the course of it)—all of that is contrary to what is in the Maliki books, which are under our obedience.

He who behaves thusly, and pretends to trace his beliefs back to our obedience, is (on the contrary) from the impostors. Breaking the fast (of Ramadan) during a journey—there is no need to emphasise that this is contrary to the text of the Holy Quran. It would seem that their doubt concerning this emanates from the hadith, "No good will come to those who fast during travel." The Imams have treated with forbearance those whom the fast truly damaged (during travel). These people, owing to their ignorance, are unable to unite the signs evident in the texts on these matters. They contravene the law that is upon the people in these matters. (As for) their shortening the *salat* while remaining four days in a single place—whether through custom or belief in the canonical propriety of the practice—their prayers during this period are of no value, and their actions are contrary to the texts of the Malikis. Their contention that they are Malikis, despite this (abominable) practice, is an action contrary to the texts of the madhhab of Malik, and gives the lie to the clear evidence against them, while not in any way depriving the explanation that guides the Maliki texts of its clarity. The *'Ulema'* of the madhhab do not conceal anything from the texts and indeed are not ignorant of them (or unlearned in regard to them).

He who forms this (contrary) opinion with (the Sanusis) has upon him the obligation of repenting of this view because such a conjecture is blameworthy and offensive to the *'Ulema'* of the Muslims. The further assertion of the (Sanusis) that their actions are Sunna, since (they are) in fact contrary to it, is itself an innovation (*bida*)—and denial of the shariah is falsehood. The Imam Malik (may Allah be pleased with him), instructed the people in the Sunna and the following of it to perfection. The people of his madhhab strove to strengthen the people in the following of the Sunna. (In contrast) the actions of the (Sanusis) are contrary to what is obligatory upon the

Malikiyya—and the books of the Malikiyya (praise be to Allah) are manifold, and their texts pure and unmingled concerning the replies which are appropriate to the actions of the Sanusis. He who wishes to demonstrate affection towards the Malikis, let him return to canonical texts (as interpreted by them).

The manner in which some of the Sanusis call out loudly at the commencement of prayer is a manifestation of mischief from Satan. (As for) their contention that performing prayers with a single ablution is legal, no Maliki has ever professed this—nor has any Maliki professed the belief that the Sanusis profess with regard to the constituent parts of the ablutions. For the most part, those who follow this man (al-Sanusi) are people of importance—worldly people, an indication that he is a dog from the dogs of this world (and a strike against his claims to be a Sufi (*tasawwuf*) because the majority of the people who follow the Prophets (PBUT) and the good people were from the poor and the weak among the populace).

Devouring impure wealth is a transgression of the law. The arguments adduced by those who seek the favours of this sheikh and by those who are attached to them (in) opposition (to the real teachings of the Prophets and the good people?) are an indication of their ignorance. (In any case,) adducing what is in the texts of the shariah does not turn on the action of this or that person nor on the sum (of the actions of many people) because the texts stand apart from the interpretation of them.

These people, owing to their pursuance of the aims of this world and their performance of contradictory acts as a result of their setting themselves and their knowledge apart in it—these people have abandoned the straight path. (Hence,) may the (good) people abandon them and busy themselves with their madhhab, and not be misled by their falsehood against the (obligatory) madhhabs, nor led from the straight path and made to deviate from it. There is the obligation upon everyone from the land of Peace (in his religion and in the matter of his salvation from the anger of Allah, the Almighty)—to move far away from these people (and may the running away be intense). It is well known to everyone that the rank of independent reasoning (*ijtihad*) has been cut short for some time, and that there is not in this time anyone who has reached the degree of *ijtihad*. He who fancies that (he has attained this rank) has already brought ridicule upon himself, and Satan has made sport with him.

Moreover according to the divine laws of existence, can any intelligent person believe that he is greater than his predecessors to the point that he is prepared to follow his own opinions and abandon what is obligatory from the principles (of Islam). The obligation on the custodians of Islamic customs (and on all those on whom Allah has extended His hands) is that they should keep away from these people and hinder them from harming the general populace and leading them astray and damaging the canonical madhhabs. If they do not leave, let us force them to leave the land, and send them far away from the pious people so that they might find relief from their evildoing and restore peace to their condition, if Allah wishes. And Allah is All-Knowing."

As we review the charges brought against Muhammad al-Sanusi and his followers, it will be noted that they fall into two principal categories: several of his teachings are denounced as dangerous innovations, and some of the ritual practices of the brotherhood are denounced further as having departed from the rigours of the Maliki convention and the pure path of the Islamic shariah. Still further, it will be noted that the tone of denunciation is unusually heated and personal—perhaps an indication of the haste with which this proclamation was conceived—surely a confirmation of the fact that the Grand Sanusi was not prepared to modify his voice to chime with that of the Maliki *'Ulema'*.

Moreover this fatwa must be understood within the genre of fatwas of condemnation and, indeed, of "fatwas that never were." This edict and others of the same classification seem to find their ancestry in the climate of uncertainty surrounding the weakness of Ottoman authority and the rapid rise of European activity in Africa, India, and the Middle East.

Europeans were quick to grasp in the fatwa an effective means of suppressing dissent, in emulation of Muslim authorities who employed these acrimonious censures as a lash against deviation and tendencies towards *ijtihad*. But here, as with the other fatwas of condemnation mentioned above, one is plagued by a suspicion that there is more in this malediction than meets the eye.

The Sanusiyya had begun to stress the view first put forth by Yahya b. Sharif al-Shafii (d. 1277/1860) that no Muslim should live under a non-Muslim power and that *hijra* from such lands was obligatory should they become part of the Abode of War (*dar ul-harb*). Though further research is necessary on this question, it is not far-fetched to suggest that Muhammad al-Sanusi's association with Abd ul-Qadir and the latter's advocation of *hijra* as a response to French activities in Algeria may well have had a role in the issuance of this censure of rebuke.

Clearly, what awakened the alarm of the *'Ulema'* of Egypt and the Hijaz was Muhammad al-Sanusi's thinly veiled claims to *ijtihad*—claims which, if upheld, would have elevated him far above the reach of his compeers in the madhhab and disturbed the settled climax of subordination. The Grand Sanusi was not the first to lay claim to this distinction, nor was the Sanusiyya the first *tariqa* to rival the authority of the traditional madhhabs. What compels our attention is that the Sanusiyya had begun to function as a madhhab and to claim for itself the distinction of a madhhab.

Again, Muhammad al-Sanusi's attempt to make *ijtihad* the common property of all Muslims of high learning caught the contempt of conservatives such as Sheikh ul-Hanish and Mustafa al-Bulaqi, who had fenced off *ijtihad* as a preserve of the Islamic past and cast down the Sanusiyya as a repository of shame and degradation. It had been argued that with the closing of the so-called *"bab* of *ijtihad"* (the gate of free inquiry) no Muslim retained the right to interpret freely the original sources (Quran and hadith). Still again, Muhammad al-Sanusi's rejection of the consensus of learned scholars (*ijma*) was seen as an arrogant effort to turn his sight from the accumulated wisdom of the ancients—the legal precedents that had become the touchstones of taqlid.

Of course, this is only one side of the controversy. It was the "Grand" Sanusi's belief that the official *'Ulema'* had forfeited their claims as inheritors of the Prophet and guarantors of his shariah. Over the minefield of their public scorn he treads deftly, isolating the truth as he perceived it, releasing its power against his detractors, depriving the objections of their force. The vanished prosperity—the low estate of the Muslim community (*umma*) across the map of nineteenth-century Islam—seemed a confirmation of this view. The Sanusiyya, he argued, was no more than a response to the despondency of the times.

Some of the ritual practices of the brotherhood are denounced further as having departed from the rigours of the Maliki code and the pure path of the Islamic shariah. The Sanusiyya stand accused of encouraging its followers to shorten certain prayers in the *salat* and dispensing with others altogether.

The fatwa also makes allusion to the raucous atmosphere that is said to have prevailed in their meetings and suggests that participants often passed into a feeling of stark detachment and took leave of their sensibilities. There is some evidence that serves to undermine this view. Several authors (though rather late in the chronology of this fatwa) have claimed that the Sanusiyya actually discouraged noisy *dhikrs* and indeed banned music, dancing, and extravagant movements of the extremities. If this view is to be sanctioned, however, it must be done so with the caution that practices condemned in this fatwa might well have been abandoned in a later period as the Sanusiyya sought to tone down activities that left it open to continued rebuke.

Through his use of *ijtihad*, Muhammad al-Sanusi had hoped to establish an entente between sufism and fiqh, but in this effort he was to meet with the same failure that beset his predecessors, as his talents went unvalued among the official *'Ulema'*. Again, though there may have been some effort to soften the more treasonable expressions, no real gesture of atonement was forthcoming from al-Sanusi, who seems to have done little to check the animosity of these feuds. Yet the Sanusiyya did not collapse under these objections, and the ambition of the Grand Sanusi found a footing in the numerous religious settlements (*zawiyas*) that began to rise up on the periphery of settled authority. It was in this sphere that the Sanusiyya were to effect some dramatic changes on the religious landscape until the revolution of Muammar Al-Qadhdhafi put a period to their influence in modern Libya.

How to Advice Legally?

Comparable in certain respects to an opinion issued by jurists in other societies, including our own, a fatwa is a discrete literary performance through which we may analyse the culture of the mufti, the rhetorical strategies that he employs, and his mode of reasoning (see White 1985, 1990). To illustrate the potential of a textual approach to fatwas that seeks to identify the juristic styles adopted by different muftis and the underlying cultural characteristics of fatwa giving in Muslim societies, An autograph fatwa of Ahmad al-Wansharisi (d. 1508) issued during the last quarter of the fifteenth century, characterise its juristic style, and attempt to break through the surface of the text to the interstices of the mufti's argument. This fatwa, which is preserved in the *Kitab ul-Miyar,* because it is of moderate length, includes a transcription of a legal document that facilitates the reconstruction of the dispute addressed by the mufti, and addresses a doctrinal issue that is of general interest—namely, the intergenerational transmission of property in pre-modern Muslim societies.

Inheritance in Islam

Islamic inheritance law, the *ilm al-faraid,* or "science of the shares," places substantial constraints on the freedom of a person to determine the devolution of his (or her) property: bequests may not exceed one-third of an estate and may not be made in favour of any person who qualifies as a legal heir.

The law's underlying ethos is reflected in a conversation that reportedly took place on the occasion of Muhammad's limiting bequests to one-third. When Sad b. Abi Waqqas asked the Prophet (Pbuh) if he might bequeath his estate to persons other than his heirs, he responded, "It is better for you to leave your heirs rich than to leave them destitute, begging from others. Any expense that you incur, seeking thereby the face of God, will be rewarded—even the morsel of food that you put into your wife's mouth" (Muslim 1930, 11:76).

Compulsory rules for the division of property have their basis in Quranic verses that traditionally have been understood as recognising two classes of heirs: "sharers," that is, those persons for whom the Quran specifies a fractional share of the estate (one or more daughters, a father, mother, or spouse—and, in the absence of children, one or more siblings), and agnates, who are arranged in a series of hierarchical classes.

The division of an estate proceeds as follows: the qualifying sharers take their Quranic entitlements, and the closest surviving male agnate inherits whatever remains. For example, if a man dies, leaving a wife, son, daughter, and brother, the wife and daughter inherit one-eighth and seven-twenty-fourths of the estate, respectively, as "sharers," and the son inherits the remaining seven-twelfths of the estate as the closest surviving agnate, totally excluding the brother from the inheritance. In theory, the person contemplating death is powerless to affect the relative entitlement of the heirs; he or she may not, for example, stipulate that the bulk of the estate will devolve on his or her son.

During the first centuries of Islamic history, Muslims throughout the Near East found themselves subject to these rules of partible inheritance, which, to the extent that they were applied in practice, resulted in the progressive fragmentation of wealth and capital. It is perhaps not surprising that Muslim proprietors found numerous ways to circumvent the inheritance rules and that they received important assistance in this regard from Muslim jurists. Working with and around the prophetic Sunnah cited above, the jurists taught that the inheritance rules take effect only on property owned by the deceased at the moment they enter their deathbed illness, and that proprietors are free to dispose of their property in any way they wish prior to that moment.

There are no restrictions on the amount of property that persons may alienate during their lifetime, whether in favour of their eventual heirs or anyone else, and Muslim proprietors may, therefore, shift assets to their desired heirs by means of a sale, gift, or acknowledgment of a debt—on the condition that these transactions conform to the requisite legal formalities. Frequently, however, a proprietor would pay lip service to these formalities while designing a transaction that created a merely nominal transfer of ownership.

A transaction of this type was designated by the Maliki jurists as *Tawlij* (alternatively, *Talij*), a relatively obscure term that was understood as referring specifically to transactions between parents and children; thus, a medieval lexicographer glosses the expression *wallaja malahu tawlijan* as "he gave (or transferred) his wealth to one of his children during his lifetime" (Ibn Manzur 1979, 2:400). By extension, the term *"tawlij)"* came to signify generally a "donation deguisee illegal "(Fagnan 1923:190 (emphasis mine)).

In fact, the Maliki jurists adopted an equivocal attitude towards *tawlij*). Although the practice technically was illegal, they would invalidate a transaction of this nature only if the plaintiff were able to establish its illegality on the basis of direct evidence (for example, if the witnesses to a transaction subsequently acknowledged its fraudulent nature) or if circumstantial evidence pointed unequivocally to its fraudulent nature.

In the absence of such evidence, the transaction was presumed to be valid, and the recipient of the property needed only to swear an oath attesting to its legitimacy. By placing no restrictions on inter vivos transactions and by adopting a benign attitude towards *tawlij*), the jurists accorded Muslim proprietors the freedom to dispose of their property as they saw fit.

A Dispute Rebuilt

The Document: Islamic legal doctrine encourages a qadi who is confronted with a difficult case to consult with a mufti before issuing a judicial decision (*hukm*). A *qadi* who requested a fatwa from a mufti customarily would attach to his question (istifta) copies of any documents relating to the case at hand; frequently, these transcriptions mentioned names of the people involved and were dated.

One of the virtues of al-Wansharisi is that he occasionally recorded not only a particular question and answer but also any transcriptions of legal instruments that may have been attached to the istifta", making it possible to follow the process whereby documented events were transformed into the abstract and impersonal language of the law. (Most fatwas in the *Miyar* that are formulated in abstract terms but not accompanied by such documents also have their source in real events and are not merely hypothetical cases constructed for scholastic purposes.) The fatwa to be examined here involves al-Wansharisi himself, who writes that he received a letter from the jurist Abu Zaid Abd ur-Rahman b. Muhammad Al-Ghasawi of Banu Burtal. The letter, al-Wansharisi adds, was written at the bottom of a legal document, which he reproduces as follows:

Praise be to God. (This is) a Copy of a Document that Reads, After "Praise be to God":

Uthman b. al-Hasan, who is known as (the) Mahdi al-Kaniksi, summoned (witnesses to hear him attest) with regard to himself, several years subsequent to (the sale's) date, being in a state of sound (mind and body,) voluntarily, and legally capable (of conducting his affairs,) that he had sold all his properties (*amlakahu kullaha*), that is, lands and gardens together with their contents, namely, fruit-bearing and non-fruit-bearing date palm trees and all of their material appurtenances and abstract rights, wherever they be, in the town of Banu Kanikas and in the town of Banu Budarmayn, and that which is in Jabal Arus and its jurisdictions, to the most pious scholar (*talib*), Abu al-Abbas Ahmad b. Ali b. Muhammad al-Nasiri.

The testimony included (the seller's acknowledgment) that he had been paid (*takhallasa min*) the entirety of the sale price for which he had sold (the properties) and that he had given the buyer a quittance with regard to the price for which it was sold, after receiving it (*bada qabdihi*). However, his witnesses did not know the amount of the price, because the acknowledger did not specify it at that time.

The attestation (was given), after its import was made known, while he was in the described state. They recorded their testimony therein, (as) requested of them, in the month of God, Al-Muharram, at the beginning of the year eight hundred and eighty (June 1475). (al-Wansharisi 1981-1983, 6:83)

This document refers to a sale transacted between Uthman b. al-Hasan and Abu al-Abbas Ahmad b. Ali b. Muhammad al-Nasiri. Of the former, we know only that he probably was a religious figure in the town of Banu Kanikas, where he was known as the "Mahdi al-Kaniksi," and that he was a man of wealth and means; of the latter, we know only that he was a jurist.

The document provides no indication of the nature of the relationship between the two men (nor does it indicate the number, gender, and age of any children that Uthman b. al-Hasan may have had at the time of the sale). From the document, we learn that at an unspecified date prior to 1475, Uthman b. al-Hasan sold to al-Nasiri "all his properties"—fields and date palm orchards in the towns of Banu Kanikas, Banu Budarmayn, and Jabal Arus and its environs.

For the sale to be valid, the buyer and seller needed only to have spoken certain prescribed formulas in the presence of two witnesses; no written documentation was required. Subsequently, in June 1475—while he was still sound of mind and body, and perhaps anticipating a challenge to the validity of the sale, Uthman had the terms of the sale certified by notary witnesses, in all likelihood in the presence of a *qadi*. The document that resulted from this procedure is known as an *ishhad*, or judicial certification (cf. Little 1984:224ff.).

The contents of the judicial certification point to the suspicious nature of the sale. The notary who drafted the *ishhad* specifies that the witnesses summoned by Uthman (who clearly were not the same individuals who had witnessed the sale itself) "did not know the amount of the price, because the acknowledger (Uthman) did not specify it at that time."

Further, the *ishhad* makes no reference to the conveyance (*hiyaza*) of the property from the seller to the buyer, generally an essential feature of a valid sale. It is, therefore, conceivable that Uthman b. al-Hasan designed the transaction to make it appear that he had sold his properties to al-Nasiri and that the properties no longer belonged to him, while in fact he continued to use the properties and any revenues that they generated, as he had done prior to the "sale" (This, of course, is speculation, for the real facts of the case cannot be known to us and may not have been known to al-Wansharisi).

8

Rights by Law

In an Islamic State, certain rights are conferred on the citizens, which are backed by law. In view of a great scholar, these rights are more extensive than the general human rights which have been described earlier, they need separate treatment.

Life, Safety and Property Rights

In the address which the Prophet delivered on the occasion of the Farewell *Hajj*, he said: "Your lives and properties are forbidden to one another till you meet your Lord on the Day of Resurrection". God Almighty has laid down in the Holy Quran: "Anyone who kills a believer deliberately will receive as his reward (a sentence) to live in Hell for ever. God will be angry with him and curse him, and prepare dreadful torment for him" (4:93). The Prophet has also said about the *dhimmis* (the non-Muslim citizens of the Muslim state): " One who kills a man under covenant (i.e. a *dhimmi*) will not even smell the fragrance of Paradise" (Bukhari and Abu Daud). Islam prohibits homicide but allows only one exception, that the killing is done in the due process of law which the Quran refers to as *bil-haqq* (with the truth).

Therefore a man can be killed only when the law demands it, and it is obvious that only a court of law can decide whether the execution is being carried out with justice or without justification. In case of war or insurrection a just and righteous government alone, which follows the *Shariah* or the Islamic law, can decide whether a war is just or unjust, whether taking of a life is justified or not; and whether a person is a rebel or not and who can be sentenced to death as a punishment. These weighty decisions cannot be left in the hands of a court which has become heedless to God and is under the influence of the administration. A judiciary like this may miscarry justice. Nor can the crimes of state be justified on the authority of the Holy Quran or

Traditions *(Hadith)* when the state murders its citizens openly and secretly without any hesitation or on the slightest pretext, because they are opposed to its unjust policies and actions or criticise it for its misdeed, and also provides protection to its hired assassins who have been guilty of the heinous crime of murder of an innocent person resulting in the fact, that neither the police take any action against such criminals nor can any proof or witnesses against these criminals be produced in the courts of law. The very existence of such a government is a crime and none of the killings carried out by them can be called "execution for the sake of justice" in the phraseology of the Holy Quran.

Along with security of life, Islam has with equal clarity and definiteness conferred the right of security of ownership of property, as mentioned earlier with reference to the address of the Farewell *Hajj.* On the other hand, the Holy Quran goes so far as to declare that the taking of people's possessions or property is completely prohibited unless they are acquired by lawful means as permitted in the laws of God. The law of God categorically declares "Do not devour one another's wealth by false and illegal means" (2:188).

Right of Personal Dignity

The second important right is the right of the citizens to the protection of their honour. In the address delivered on the occasion of the Farewell *Hajj,* the Prophet did not only prohibit the life and property of the Muslims to one another, but also any encroachment upon their honour, respect and chastity was forbidden to one another. The Holy Quran clearly lays down:

(a) "You who believe, do not let one (set of) people make fun of another set.

(b) Do not defame one another.

(c) Do not insult by using nicknames.

(d) And do not backbite or speak ill of one another". (49:11-12)

This is the law of Islam for the protection of honour which is indeed much superior to and better than the western Law of Defamation. According to the Islamic law if it is proved that someone has attacked the honour of another person, then irrespective of the fact whether or not the victim is able to prove himself a respectable and honourable person the culprit will in any case get his due punishment. But the interesting fact about the Western Law of Defamation is that the person who files suit for defamation has first to prove that he is a man of honour and public esteem and during the interrogation he is subjected to the scurrilous attacks, accusations and innuendoes of the defence council to such an extent that he earns more disgrace than the attack on his reputation against which he had knocked the door of the court of law. On top of it he has also to produce such witnesses as would testify in the court that due to the defamatory accusations of the culprit, the accused stands disgraced in their eyes. Good Gracious! what a subtle point of law, and what an adherence to the spirit of law! How can this unfair and unjust law be compared to the Divine law? Islam declares blasphemy as a crime irrespective of the fact whether the accused is a man of honour or not, and whether the words used for blasphemy have actually disgraced the victim and harmed his reputation in the eyes of the public or not. According to the Islamic law the mere proof of the fact that the accused said things which according to common sense could have damaged the reputation and honour of the plaintiff, is enough for the accused to be declared guilty of defamation.

Right to Maintain Privacy

Islam recognises the right of every citizen of its state that there should be no undue interference or encroachment on the privacy of his life. The Holy Quran has laid down the injunction: "Do not spy on one another" (49:12). "Do not enter any houses except your own homes unless you are sure of their occupants' consent" (24:27). The Prophet has gone to the extent of instructing his followers that a man should not enter even his own house suddenly or surreptitiously. He should somehow or other inform or indicate to the dwellers of the house that he is entering the house, so that he may not see his mother, sister or daughter in a condition in which they would not like to be seen, nor he would himself like to see them in that condition. Peering into the houses of other people has also been strictly prohibited, so much so that there is the saying of the Prophet that if a man finds another person secretly peering into his house, and he blinds his eye or eyes as a punishment then he cannot be called to question nor will he be liable to prosecution.

The Prophet has even prohibited people from reading the letters of others, so much so that if a man is reading his letter and another man casts sidelong glances at it and tries to read it, his conduct becomes reprehensible. This is the sanctity of privacy that Islam grants to individuals. On the other hand in the modern civilized world we find that not only the letters of other people are read and their correspondence censored, but even its photostat copies are retained for future use or blackmail. Even bugging devices are secretly fixed in the houses of the people so that one can hear and tape from a distance the conversation taking place behind closed doors. In other words it means that there is no such thing as privacy and to all practical purposes the private life of an individual does not exist.

This espionage on the life of the individual cannot be justified on moral grounds by the government saying that it is necessary to know the secrets of the dangerous persons. Though, to all intents and purposes, the basis of this policy is the fear and suspicion with which modern governments look at their citizens who are intelligent and dissatisfied with the official policies of the government. This is exactly what Islam has called the root cause of mischief in politics. The injunction of the Prophet is: "When the ruler begins to search for the causes of dissatisfaction amongst his people, he spoils them" (Abu Daud). The Amir Muawiya has said that he himself heard the Prophet saying: "If you try to find out the secrets of the people, then you will definitely spoil them or at least you will bring them to the verge of ruin". The meaning of the phrase 'spoil them' is that when spies (C.I.D. or F.B.I, agents) are spread all around the country to find out the affairs of men, then the people begin to look at one another with suspicion, so much so that people are afraid of talking freely in their houses lest some word should escape from the lips of their wives and children which may put them in embarrassing situations. In this manner it becomes difficult for a common citizen to speak freely, even in his own house and society begins to suffer from a state of general distrust and suspicion.

Personal Liberty

Islam has also laid down the principle that no citizen can be imprisoned unless his guilt has been proved in an open court. To arrest a man only on the basis of suspicion and to throw him into a prison without proper court proceedings and without providing him a reasonable opportunity to produce his defence is not permissible in Islam. It is related in the Hadith that once the Prophet was delivering a lecture in the Mosque, when a man rose during the lecture and said: " O Prophet of God, for what crime have my neighbours been arrested?" The Prophet heard the question and continued his speech. The man rose once again and repeated the same question.

The Prophet again did not answer and continued his speech. The man rose for a third time and repeated the same question. Then the Prophet ordered that the man's neighbours be released. The reason why the Prophet had kept quiet when the question was repeated twice earlier was that the police officer was present in the Mosque and if there were proper reasons for the arrest of the neighbours of this man, he would have got up to explain his position. Since the police officer gave no reasons for these arrests the Prophet ordered that the arrested persons should be released. The police officer was aware of the Islamic law and therefore he did not get up to say: "the administration is aware of the charges against the arrested men, but they cannot be disclosed in public. If the Prophet would inquire about their guilt *in camera* I would enlighten him". If the police officer had made such a statement, he would have been dismissed then and there.

The fact that the police officer did not give any reasons for the arrests in the open court was sufficient reason for the Prophet to give immediate orders for the release of the arrested men. The injunction of the Holy Quran is very clear on this point. "Whenever you judge between people, you should judge with (a sense of) justice" (4:58). And the Prophet has also been asked by God: "I have been ordered to dispense justice between you". This was the reason why the Caliph Umar said: "In Islam no one can be imprisoned except in pursuance of justice". The words used here clearly indicate that justice means due process of law. What has been prohibited and condemned is that a man be arrested and imprisoned without proof of his guilt in an open court and without providing him an opportunity to defend himself against those charges. If the Government suspects that a particular individual has committed a crime or he is likely to commit an offence in the near future then they should give reasons of their suspicion before a court of law and the culprit or the suspect should be allowed to produce his defence in an open court, so that the court may decide whether the suspicion against him is based on sound grounds or not and if there is good reason for suspicion, then he should be informed of how long he will be in preventive detention. This decision should be taken under all circumstances in an open court, so that the public may hear the charges brought by the government, as well as the defence made by the accused and see that the due process of law is being applied to him and he is not being victimised.

The correct method of dealing with such cases in Islam is exemplified in the famous decision of the Prophet which took place before he conquest of Mecca. The Prophet was making preparations for the attack on Mecca, when one of his Companions, Harib bin Abi Baltaa sent a letter through a woman to the authorities in Mecca informing them about the impending attack. The Prophet came to know of this through a divine inspiration. He ordered Ali and Zubayr: "Go quickly on the route to Mecca, at such and such a place you will find a woman carrying a letter. Recover the letter from her and bring it to me". So they went and found the woman exactly where the Prophet had said. They recovered the letter from her and brought it to the Prophet. This was indeed a clear case of treachery.

To inform the enemy about a secret of an army and that too at the time of a war is a very serious offence tantamount to treachery. In fact, one cannot think of a more serious crime during war than giving out a military secret to one's enemy. What could have been a more suitable case for a secret hearing; a military secret had been betrayed and common sense demanded that he should be tried *in camera.* But the Prophet summoned Hatib to the open court of the Mosque of the Prophet and in the presence of hundreds of people asked him to explain his position with regard to his letter addressed to the leaders of Quraish which had been intercepted on its way.

The accused said: " O God's Messenger (may God's blessings be on you) I have not revolted against Islam, nor have I done this with the intention of betraying a military secret. The truth of the matter is that my wife and children are living in Mecca and I do not have my tribe to protect them there. I had written this letter so that the leaders of Quraish may be indebted to me and may protect my wife and children out of gratitude". Umar rose and respectfully submitted: " O Prophet, please permit me to put this traitor to the sword". The Prophet replied: "He is one of those people who had participated in the battle of Badr, and the explanation he has advanced in his defence would seem to be correct".

Let us look at this decision of the Prophet in perspective. It was a clear case of treachery and betrayal of military secrets. But the Prophet acquitted Hatib on two counts. Firstly, that his past records were very clean and showed that he could not have betrayed the cause of Islam, since on the occasion of the battle of Badr when there were heavy odds against the Muslims, he had risked his life for them.

Secondly, his family was in fact in danger at Mecca. Therefore, if he had shown some human weakness for his children and written this letter, then this punishment was quite sufficient for him that his secret offence was divulged in public and he had been disgraced and humiliated in the eyes of the Believers. God has referred to this offence of Hatib in the Holy Quran but did not propose any punishment for him except rebuke and admonition.

The attitude and activities of the Kharjites in the days of the Caliph Ali are well known to the students of Muslim history. They used to abuse the Caliph openly, and threaten him with murder. But whenever they were arrested for these offences, Ali would set them free and tell his officers: "Asiong as they do not actually perpetrate offences against the state, the mere use of abusive Language or the threat of use of force are not such offences for which they can be imprisoned". The Imam Abu Hanifa has recorded the following saying of the Caliph Ali: "As long as they do not set out on armed rebellion, the Caliph of the Faithful will not interfere with them".

On another occasion Ali was delivering a lecture in the mosque when the Kharjites raised that special slogan there. Ali Said: "We will not deny you the right to come to the mosques to worship God, nor will we stop to give your share from the wealth of the state, as long as you are with us (and support us in our wars with the unbelievers) and we shall never take military action against you as long as you do not fight with us". One can visualise the opposition which Ali was facing: more violent and vituperative opposition cannot even be imagined in a present day democratic state; but the freedom that he had allowed to the opposition was such that no government has ever been able to give to its opposition. He did not arrest even those who threatened him with murder nor did he imprison them.

Right to Process

Amongst the rights that Islam has conferred on human beings is the right to protest against government's tyranny. Referring to it the Quran says: "God does not love evil talk in public unless it is by someone who has been injured thereby" (4:148). This means that God strongly disapproves of abusive language or strong words of condemnation, but the person who has been the victim of injustice or tyranny, God gives him the right to openly protest against the injury that has been done to him. This right is not limited only to individuals. The words of the verse are general. Therefore if an individual or a group of people or a party usurps power and after assuming the reins of authority begins to tyrannise individuals or groups of men or the entire population of the country then to raise the voice of protest against it openly is the God-given right of man and no one has the authority to usurp or deny this right. If anyone tries to usurp this right of citizens then he rebels against God. The talisman of Section 144 may protect such a tyrant in this world, but it cannot save him from the hell-fire in the Hereafter.

Liberty of Expression

Islam gives the right of freedom of thought and expression to all citizens of the Islamic state on the condition that it should be used for the propagation of virtue and truth and not for spreading evil and wickedness. This Islamic concept of freedom of expression is much superior to the concept prevalent in the West. Under no circumstances would Islam allow evil and wickedness to be propagated. It also does not give anybody the right to use abusive or offensive language in the name of criticism. The right to freedom of expression for the sake of propagating virtue and righteousness is not only a right in Islam but an obligation. One who tries to deny this right to his people is openly at war with God, the All-Powerful. And the same thing applies to the attempt to stop people from evil. Whether this evil is perpetrated by an individual or by a group of people or the government of one's own country, or the government of some other country; it is the right of a Muslim and it is also his obligation that he should warn and reprimand the evil-doer and try to stop him from doing it. Over and above, he should openly and publicly condemn it and show the course of righteousness which that individual, nation or government should adopt.

The Holy Quran has described this quality of the Faithful in the following words: "They enjoin what is proper and forbid what is improper" (9:71). In contrast, describing the qualities of a hypocrite, the Quran mentions: "They bid what is improper and forbid what is proper" (9:67). The main purpose of an Islamic government has been defined by God in the Quran as follows: "If We give authority to these men on earth they will keep up prayers, and offer welfare due, bid what is proper and forbid what is improper" (22:41). The Prophet has said: "If anyone of you comes across an evil, he should try to stop it with his hand (using force), if he is not in a position to stop it with his hand then he should try to stop it by means of his tongue (meaning he should speak against it). If he is not even able to use his tongue, then he should at least condemn it in his heart.

This is the weakest degree of faith" (Muslim). This obligation of inviting people to righteousness and forbidding them to adopt the paths of evil is incumbent on all true Muslims. If any government deprives its citizens of this right, and prevents them from performing this duty, then it is in direct conflict with the injunction of God. The government is not in conflict with its people, but is in conflict with God. In this way it is at war with God and is trying to usurp that right of its people which God has conferred not only as a right but as an obligation. As far as the government which itself propagates evil, wickedness and obscenity and interferes with those who are inviting people to virtue and righteousness is concerned, according to the Holy Quran it is the government of the hypocrites.

Liberty of Association

Islam has also given people the right to freedom of association and formation of parties or organisations. This right is also subject to certain general rules. It should be exercised for propagating virtue and righteousness and should never be used for spreading evil and mischief. We have not only been given this right for spreading righteousness and virtue, but have been ordered to exercise this right. Addressing the Muslims, the Holy Quran declares:

> "You are the best community which has been brought forth for mankind. You command what is proper and forbid what is improper and you believe in God."
>
> (3 : 110)

This means that it is the obligation and duty of the entire Muslim community that it should invite and enjoin people to righteousness and virtue and forbid them from doing evil. If the entire Muslim community is not able to perform this duty then "let there be a community among you who will invite (people) to (do) good, command what is proper and forbid what is improper, those will be prosperous" (3:104). This clearly indicates that if the entire Muslim people collectively begins to neglect its obligation to invite people to goodness and forbid them from doing evil then it is absolutely essential that it should contain at least a group of people which may perform this obligation.

As has been said before this is not only a right but an obligation and on the fulfilment of which depends success and prosperity here as well as in the Hereafter. It is an irony with the religion of God that in a Muslim country the assembly and association that is formed for the purposes of spreading evil and mischief should have the right to rule over the country and the association and party which has been formed for propagating righteousness and virtue should live in perpetual fear of harassment and of being declared illegal. Conditions here are just the reverse of what has been prescribed by God. The claim is that we are Muslims and this is an Islamic state but the work that is being done is directed to spreading evil, to corrupt and morally degrade and debase the people while there is an active and effective check on the work being carried out for reforming society and inviting people to righteousness. Moreover the life of those who are engaged in spreading righteousness and checking the spread of evil and wickedness is made intolerable and hard to bear.

Liberty of Conscience

Islam also gives the right to freedom of conscience and conviction to its citizens in an Islamic state. The Holy Quran has laid down the injunction: "There should be no coercion in the matter of faith" (2:256). Though there is no truth and virtue greater than the Religion of Truth—Islam, and Muslims are enjoined to invite people to embrace Islam and advance arguments in favour of it, they are not asked to enforce this faith on them. No force will be applied in order to compel them to accept Islam. Whoever accepts it he does so by his own choice. Muslims will welcome such a convert to Islam with open arms and admit him to their community with equal rights and privileges. But if somebody does not accept Islam, Muslims will have to recognise and respect his decision, and no moral, social or political pressure will be put on him to change his mind.

Freedom of Religion

Along with the freedom of conviction and freedom of conscience Islam has given the right to the individual that his religious sentiments will be given due respect and nothing will be said or done which may encroach upon this right. It has been ordained by God in the Holy Quran: "Do not abuse those they appeal to instead of God" (6:108). These instructions are not only limited to idols and deities, but they also apply to the leaders or national heroes of the people. If a group of people holds a conviction which according to you is wrong, and holds certain persons in high esteem which according to you is not deserved by them, then it will not be justified in Islam that you use abusive language for them and thus injure their feelings.

Islam does not prohibit people from holding debate and discussion on religious matters, but it wants that these discussions should be conducted in decency. "Do not argue with the people of the Book unless it is in the politest manner" (29:46)—says the Quran. This order is not merely limited to the People of the Scriptures, but applies with equal force to those following other faiths.

Protection from Arbitrary Imprisonment: Islam also recognises the right of the individual that he will not be arrested or imprisoned for the offences of others. The Holy Quran has laid down this principle clearly: "No bearer of burdens shall be made to bear the burden of another" (6:164). Islam believes in personal responsibility. We ourselves are responsible for our acts, and the consequence of our actions cannot be transferred to someone else.

In other words this means that every man is responsible for his actions. If another man has not shared this action then he cannot be held responsible for it, nor can he be arrested. It is a matter of great regret and shame that we are seeing this just and equitable principle which has not been framed by any human being, but by the Creator and Nourisher of the entire universe, being flouted and violated before our eyes. So much so that a man is guilty of a crime or he is a suspect, but his wife is being arrested for his crime.

Things have gone so far that innocent people are being punished for the crimes of others. To give a recent example, in Karachi (Pakistan), a man was suspected of being involved in a bomb throwing incident. In the course of police investigation he was subjected to horrible torture in order to extract a confession from him. When he insisted on his innocence, then the police arrested his mother, his wife, daughter and sister and brought them to the police station. They were all stripped naked in his presence, and he was stripped naked of all his clothes before their eyes so that a confession of the crime could be extracted from him.

It appears as if for the sake of investigation of crime it has become proper and legal in our country to strip the innocent women folk of the household in order to bring pressure on the suspect. This is indeed very outrageous and shameful. This is the height of meanness and depravity.

This is not a mere hearsay which we are repeating here, but we have full information about this case and can prove our allegations in any court of law. We would here like to ask what right such tyrants who perpetrate these crimes against mankind have to tell us that they are Muslims or that they are conducting the affairs of the state according to the teachings of Islam and their state is an Islamic state. They are breaching and flouting a clear law of the Holy Quran. They are stripping men and women naked which is strictly forbidden in Islam. They disgrace and humiliate humanity and then they claim that they are Muslims.

Right of Livelihood

Islam has recognised the right of the needy people that help and assistance will be provided to them. "And in their wealth there is acknowledged right for the needy and the destitute" (51:19). In this verse, the Quran has not only conferred a right to every man who asks for assistance in the wealth of the Muslims, but has also laid down that if a Muslim comes to know that a certain man is without the basic necessities of life, then irrespective of the fact whether he asks for assistance or not, it is his duty to reach him and give all the help that he can extend. For this purpose Islam has not depended only on the help and charity that is given voluntarily, but has made compulsory charity, *Zakat* as the third pillar of Islam, next only to profession of faith and worship of God through holding regular prayers. The Prophet has clearly instructed in this respect that: "It will be taken from their rich and given to those in the community in need" (Bukhari and Muslim).

In addition to this, it has also been declared that the Islamic state should support those who have nobody to support them. The Prophet has said: "The Head of state is the guardian of him who has nobody to support him" (Abu Daud, Tirmidhi). The word *wali* which has been used by the Prophet is a very comprehensive word and has a wide range of meanings. If there is an orphan or an aged man, if there is a crippled or unemployed person, if one is invalid or poor and has no one else to support him or help him, then it is the duty and the responsibility of the state to support him and assist. If a dead man has no guardian or heir, then it is the duty of the state to arrange for his proper burial. In short the state has been entrusted with the duty and responsibility of looking after all those who need help and assistance. A truly Islamic state is therefore a truly welfare state which will be the guardian and protector of all those in need.

Right of Equality

Islam gives its citizens the right to absolute and complete equality in the eyes of the law. As far as the Muslims are concerned, there are clear instructions in the Holy Quran and *Hadith* that in their rights and obligations they are all equal: "The believers are brothers (to each other)" (49:10). "If they (disbelievers) repent and keep up prayer and pay the welfare due they are your brothers in faith" (9:11). The Prophet has said that: "The life and blood of Muslims are equally precious" (Abu Daud; Ibn Maja). In another *Hadith* he has said: "The protection given by all Muslims are equal. Even an ordinary man of them can grant protection to any man" (Bukhari; Muslim; Abu Daud). In another more detailed Tradition of the Prophet, it has been said that those who accept the Oneness of God, believe in the Prophethood of his Messenger, give up primitive prejudices and join the Muslim community and brotherhood, "then they have the same rights and obligations as other Muslims have" (Bukhari; Nisai). Thus there is absolute equality between the new converts to Islam and the old followers of the faith.

This religious brotherhood and the uniformity of their rights and obligations is the foundation of equality in Islamic society, in which the rights and obligations of any person are neither greater nor lesser in any way than the rights and obligations of other people. As far as the non-Muslim citizens of the Islamic state are concerned, the rule of Islamic *Shariah* (law) about them has been very well expressed by the Caliph Ali in these words: "They have accepted our protection only because their lives may be like our lives and their properties like our properties" (Abu Daud). In other words, their (of the *(dhimmis)* lives and properties are as sacred as the lives and properties of the Muslims. Discrimination of people into different classes was one of the greatest crimes that, according to the Quran, Pharaoh used to indulge in: "He had divided his people into different classes, "... "And he suppressed one group of them (at the cost of others) (28:4).

Rule of Law

Islam clearly insists and demands that all officials of the Islamic state, whether' he be the head or an ordinary employee, are equal in the eyes of the law. None of them are above the law or can claim immunity. Even an ordinary citizen in Islam has the right to put forward a claim or file a legal complaint against the highest executive of the country. The Caliph Umar said, "I have myself seen the Prophet, may God's blessings be on him, taking revenge against himself (penalising himself for some shortcoming or failing)". On the occasion of the battle of Badr, when the Prophet was straightening the rows of the Muslim army he hit the belly of a soldier in an attempt to push him back in line. The soldier complained " O Prophet, you have hurt me with your stick". The Prophet immediately bared his belly and said "I am very sorry, you can revenge by doing the same to me. " The soldier came forward and kissed the abdomen of the Prophet and said that this was all that he wanted.

A woman belonging to a high and noble family was arrested in connection with a theft. The case was brought to the Prophet, and it was recommended that she may be spared the punishment of theft. The Prophet replied: "The nations that lived before you were destroyed by God because they punished the common man for their offences and let their dignitaries go unpunished for their crimes; I swear by Him (God) who holds my life in His hand that even if Fatima, the daughter of Muhammad, has committed this crime then I would have amputated her hand". During the Caliphate of Umar, Muhammad the son of Amr bin al-As the Governor of Egypt, whipped an Egyptian.

The Egyptian went to Medina and lodged his complaint with the Righteous Caliph, who immediately summoned the Governor and his son to Medina. When they appeared before him in Medina, the Caliph handed a whip to the Egyptian complainant and asked him to whip the son of the Governor in his presence. After taking his revenge when the Egyptian was about to hand over the whip to Umar, he said to the Egyptian: "Give one stroke of the whip to the Honourable Governor as well. His son would certainly have not beaten you were it not for the false pride that he had in his father's high office". The plaintiff submitted: "The person who had beaten me, I have already avenged myself on him". Umar said: "By God, if you had beaten him (the Governor) I would not have checked you from doing so. You have spared him of your own free will". Then he (Umar) angrily turned to Amr bin al-As and said: " O Amr, when did you start to enslave the people, though they were born free of their mothers?" When the Islamic state was flourishing in its pristine glory and splendour, the common people could equally lodge complaints against the Caliph of the time in the court and the Caliph had to appear before the *Qadi* to answer the charges. And if the Caliph had any complaint against any citizen, he could not use his administrative powers and authority to set the matter right, but had to refer the case to the court of law for proper judication.

Right against Evil

Islam also confers this right on every citizen that he will not be ordered to commit a sin, a crime or an offence; and if any government, or the administrator, or the head of department orders an individual to do a wrong, then he has the right to refuse to comply with the order. His refusal to carry out such a crime or unjust instructions would not be regarded as an offence in the eyes of the Islamic law. On the contrary giving orders to one's subordinates to commit a sin or do a wrong is itself an offence and such a serious offence that the officer who gives this sinful order whatever his rank and position may be, is liable to be summarily dismissed. These clear instructions of the Prophet are summarised in the following *Hadith:* "It is not permissible to disobey God in obedience to the orders of any human being" (*Musnad* of Ibn Hanbal).

In other words no one has the right to order his subordinates to do anything against the laws of God. If such an order is given, the subordinate has the right to ignore it or openly refuse to carry out such instructions. According to this rule no offender will be able to prove his innocence or escape punishment by saying that this offence was committed on the orders of the government or superior officers. If such a situation arises then the person who commits the offence and the person who orders that such an offence be committed, will both be liable to face criminal proceedings against them. And if an officer takes any improper and unjust measures against a subordinate who refuses to carry out illegal orders, then the subordinate has the right to go to the court of law for the protection of his rights, and he can demand that the officer be punished for his wrong or unjust orders.

Right of Political Participation

According to Islam, governments in this world are actually representatives *(Khalifa)* of the Creator of the universe, and this responsibility is not entrusted to any individual or family or a particular class or group of people but to the entire Muslim nation. The Holy Quran says: "God has promised to appoint those of you who believe and do good deeds as (His) representatives on earth" (24:55). This clearly indicates that *khalifa* is a collective gift of God in which the right of every individual Muslim is neither more nor less than the right of any other person. The correct method recommended by the Holy Quran for running the affairs of the state is as follows: "And their business is (conducted) through consultation among themselves" (42:38).

According to this principle it is the right of every Muslim that either he should have a direct say in the affairs of the state or a representative chosen by him and other Muslims should participate in the consultation of the state. Islam, under no circumstance, permits or tolerates that an individual or a group or party of individuals may deprive the common Muslims of their rights, and usurp powers of the state.

Similarly, Islam does not regard it right and proper that an individual may put up a false show of setting up a legislative assembly and by means of underhand tactics such as fraud, persecution, bribery, etc., gets himself and men of his choice elected in the assembly. This is not only a treachery against the people whose rights are usurped by illegal and unfair means, but against the Creator who has entrusted the Muslims to rule on this earth on His behalf, and has prescribed the procedure of an assembly for exercising these powers. The shura or the legislative assembly has no other meaning except that:

(1) The executive head of the government and the members of the assembly should be elected by free and independent choice of the people.

(2) The people and their representatives should have the right to criticise and freely express their opinions.

(3) The real conditions of the country should be brought before the people without suppressing any fact so that they may be able to form their opinion about whether the government is working properly or not.

(4) There should be adequate guarantee that only those people who have the support of the masses should rule over the country and those who fail to win this support should be removed from their position of authority.

Rights for Non-citizens

After dealing with the rights of the citizens of an Islamic state, we would like to briefly discuss the rights which Islam has conferred on its enemies. In the days when Islam came into focus the world was completely unaware of the concept of humane and decent rules of war. The West became conscious of this concept for the first time through the works of the seventeenth century thinker, Grotius. But the actual codification of the 'international law' in war began in the middle of the nineteenth century. Prior to this no concept of civilized behaviour in war was found in the West.

All forms of barbarity and savagery were perpetrated in war, and the rights of those at war were not even recognised, let alone respected. The laws which were framed in this field during the nineteenth century or over the following period up to the present day, cannot be called 'laws' in the real sense of the word. They are only in the nature of conventions and agreements and calling them 'international law' is actually a kind of misnomer, because no nation regards them binding when they are at war, unless, of course, when the adversaries also agree to abide by them. In other words, these civilized laws imply that if our enemies respect them then we shall also abide by them, and if they ignore these human conventions and take recourse to barbaric and cruel ways of waging war, then we shall also adopt the same or similar techniques. It is obvious that such a course which depends on mutual acceptance and agreement cannot be called 'law'. And this is the reason why the provisions of this so-called 'international law' have been flouted and ignored in every way, and every time they have been revised, additions or deletions have been made in them.

Law of War and Peace in Islam: The rules which have been framed by Islam to make war civilized and humane, are in the nature of law, because they are the injunctions of God and His Prophet which are followed by Muslims in all circumstances, irrespective of the behaviour of the enemy.

It is now for the scholars to find out how far the West has availed of the laws of war given by Islam thirteen hundred years ago; and even after the adaptation of some of the laws of Islam how far the West attained those heights of civilized and humane methods of warfare which Muslims reached through the blessings of Islam. Western writers have often asserted that the Prophet had borrowed everything in his teachings from the Jews and the Christians. Instead of saying anything in its refutation we will only recommend the reader to refer to the Bible so that he can see which methods of war are recommended by the sacred Book of these Western claimants to civilization and culture.

We have examined in some detail the basic human rights that Islam has conferred on man. Let us now find out what rights and obligations Islam recognises for an enemy.

The Rights of the Non-combatants: Islam has first drawn a clear line of distinction between the combatants and the non-combatants of the enemy country. As far as the non-combatant population is concerned such as women, children, the old and the infirm, etc., the instructions of the Prophet are as follows: "Do not kill any old person, any child or any woman" (Abu Daud). "Do not kill the monks in monasteries" or "Do not kill the people who are sitting in places of worship" (Musnad of Ibn Hanbal).

During a war, the Prophet saw the corpse of a woman lying on the ground and observed: "She was not fighting. How then she came to be killed?" From this statement of the Prophet the exegetists and jurists have drawn the principle that those who are non-combatants should not be killed during or after the war.

Rights during Battle

Now let us see what rights Islam has conferred on the combatants.

Torture with Fire: In the Hadith there is a saying of the Prophet that: "Punishment by fire does not behove anyone except the Master of the Fire" (Abu Daud). The injunction deduced from this saying is that the adversary should not be burnt alive.

Protection of the Wounded: "Do not attack a wounded person"—thus said the Prophet. This means that the wounded soldiers who are not fit to fight, nor actually fighting, should not be attacked.

The Prisoner of War Should not be Slain: "No prisoner should be put to the sword"—a very clear and unequivocal instruction given by the Prophet.

No one Should be Tied to be Killed: "The Prophet, has prohibited the killing of anyone who is tied or is in captivity".

No Looting and Destruction in the Enemy's Country: Muslims have also been instructed by the-Prophet that if they should enter the enemy's territory, they should not indulge in pillage or plunder nor destroy the residential areas, nor touch the property of anyone except those who are fighting with them.

It has been narrated in the Hadith: "The Prophet has prohibited the Believers from loot and plunder" (Bukhari; Abu Daud). His injunction is: "The loot is no more lawful than the carrion" (Abu Daud). Abu Bakr Siddiq used to instruct the soldiers while sending them to war, "Do not destroy the villages and towns, do not spoil the cultivated fields and gardens, and do not slaughter the cattle". The booty of war which is acquired from the battleground is altogether different from this. It consists of the wealth, provisions and equipment captured only from the camps and military headquarters of the combatant armies.

Sanctity of Property: The Muslims have also been prohibited from taking anything from the general public of a conquered country without paying for it. If in a war the Muslim army occupies an area of the Enemy country, and is encamped there it does not have the right to use the things belonging to the people without their consent. If they need anything, they should purchase it from the local population or should obtain permission from the owners. Abu Bakr Siddiq, while instructing the Muslim armies being despatched to the battle-front would go to the extent of saying that Muslim soldiers should not even use the milk of the milch cattle without the permission of their owners.

Sanctity of a Dead Body: Islam has categorically prohibited its followers from disgracing or mutilating the corpses of their enemies as was practised in Arabia before the advent of Islam. It has been said in the Hadith: "The Prophet has prohibited us from mutilating the corpses of the enemies" (Bukhari; Abu Daud).

The occasion on which this order was given is highly instructive. In the battle of Uhud the disbelievers mutilated the bodies of the Muslims who had fallen on the battlefield and sacrificed their lives for the sake of Islam, by cutting off their ears and noses, and threading them together to put round their necks as trophies of war. The abdomen of Hamzah, the uncle of the Prophet, was ripped open by Quraish, his liver was taken out and chewed by

Hinda, the wife of Abu Sufyan, the leader of the Meccan army. The Muslims were naturally enraged by this horrible sight. But the Prophet asked his followers not to mete out similar treatment to the dead bodies of the enemies.

This great example of forbearance and restraint is sufficient to convince any reasonable man who is not blinded by prejudice or bias, that Islam is really the religion sent down by the Creator of the universe., and that if human emotions had any admission in Islam, then this horrible sight on the battlefield of Uhud would have provoked the Prophet to order his followers to mutilate the bodies of their enemy in the same manner.

Return of Corpses: In the battle of Ahzab' a very renowned and redoubtable warrior of the enemy was killed and his body fell down in the trench which the Muslims had dug for the defence of Medina. The unbelievers presented ten thousand dinars to the Prophet and requested that the dead body of their fallen warrior may be handed over to them. The Prophet replied "I do not sell dead bodies. You can take away the corpse of your fallen comrade".

Prohibition of Breach of Treaties: Islam has strictly prohibited treachery. One of the instructions that the Prophet used to give to the Muslim warriors while sending them to the battlefront was: "Do not be guilty of breach of faith". This order has been repeated in the Holy Quran and the Hadith again and again, that if the enemy acts treacherously let him do so, you should never go back on your promise.

There is a famous incident in the peace treaty of Hudaybiya, when after the settlement of the terms of the treaty, Abu Jandal, the son of the emissary of the unbelievers who had negotiated this treaty with the Muslims, came, fettered and blood stained, rushing to the Muslim camp and crying for help. The Prophet told him, "Since the terms of the treaty have been settled, we are not in a position to help you out. You should go back with your father.

God will provide you with some other opportunity to escape this persecution". The entire Muslim army was deeply touched and grieved at the sad plight of Abu Jandal and many of them were moved to tears. But when the Prophet declared that "we cannot break the agreement," not even a single person came forward to help the unfortunate prisoner so the unbelievers forcibly dragged him back to Mecca. This is an unparalleled example of the observance of the terms of agreement by the Muslims, and Islamic history can show many examples of a similar nature.

Rules About Declaration of War: It has been laid down in the Holy Quran: "If you apprehend breach of treaty from a people, then openly throw the treaty at their faces" (8:58). In this verse, Muslims have been prohibited from opening hostilities against their enemies without properly declaring war against them, unless of course, the adversary has already started aggression against them. Otherwise the Quran has clearly given the injunction to Muslims that they should intimate to their enemies that no treaty exists between them, and they are at war with them.

The present day "international law" has also laid down that hostilities should not be started without declaration of war, but since it is a man-made rule, they are free to violate it whenever it is convenient. On the other hand, the laws for Muslims have been framed by God, hence they cannot be violated.

The Evaluation

This is a brief sketch of those rights which fourteen hundred years ago Islam gave to man, to those who were at war with each other and to the citizens of its state, which every Believer regards as sacred law. On the one hand, it refreshes and strengthens our faith in Islam when we realise that even in this modern age which makes such loud claims of progress and enlightenment, the world has not been able to produce more just and equitable laws than those given 1400 years ago.

On the other hand it hurts one's feelings that Muslims are in possession of such a splendid and comprehensive system of law and yet they look forward for guidance to those leaders of the West who could not have dreamed of attaining those heights of truth and justice which were achieved a long time ago. Even more painful than this is the realisation that throughout the world the rulers who claim to be Muslims have made disobedience to their God and the Prophet as the basis and foundation of their government. May God have mercy on them and give them the true guidance.

9

Protection by Law

The securities provided for the practical enforcement and to guarantee the fulfilment of the fundamental rights, have been discussed by refercnce in the foregoing chapters. But it will be in the fitness of things that they should not only be briefly repeated here, but putting together all other factors in this connection it should be examined how fundamental human rights were kept safely out of the reach of and constant meddling by the rulers in the Islamic State.

The important problem of humanity today is not the determination of these rights, preparation of their beautiful lists, their inclusion in the constitution of the country, issue of international charter and declarations of rights, and celebration of human rights day. The real problem, instead, is how to save the rights, that are being enumerated, displayed and recognised as human rights, from the usurpation and transplanting by the rulers of the day.

Islam has attached special importance to this practical aspect in its system of governance, and has provided such effective and firm safeguards to the fundamental rights, which on the one hand strike at the root of the possibilities of the development of the germs of dictatorship and Fascism in the rulers and the causes and motives that take them on to the path of oppression and tyranny and compulsion and violence; and on the other, ridding the common citizens of the fear and awe of human authority and their negative feelings of their own helplessness, arousing in them the spirit of self-reliance, magnanimity and fortitude and doubtlessness, create such a tremendous power of resistance in them that there is no room left for any body to thrust his sovereignty (absolute authority) over them.

The Quran in a short verse has revealed to us the truth about dictatorship, its causes and how it succeeds in getting sway over people. God has presented Pharaoh as the worst pattern of dictatorship before us, and out of the evil traits of his character that have been pointed out, one that was at the root of all of them was this:

> He took his people as facile and worthless. (Al Quran XLII: 54)

The Quran conveys to us in this verse that Pharaoh regarded his people as lowly, despised and weak as compared with himself, and it was this estimate of them that was at the root of declaring himself as their god and his dictatorship and Fascism. Immediately following this God says:

> And they obeyed him: truely were they a people rebellions (against God). (Al Quran XLII: 54)

This was the reason on which Pharaoh's dictatorship was based and flourishing. His own crime was that he took his people as facile and weak and ruled over them as a tyrant of the worst type. His egoism fed on their misery and suffering in debasement:

> Despressing a small group among them. (Al Quran XXVIII: 4)

But in the sight of God the people were no less blameworthy and contemptible since they were obeying him in abject subservience and were resigned to their fate of lowness and debasement. The Quran has declared them as a nation of transgressors—transgressing the limits set by God. The first and foremost limit set by God is that none save Him should be taken as their deity and Sovereign. The people guilty of such a heinous crime shall be meted out the fate of the people of Pharaoh, to save His servant from the torment of humiliation and debasement. God on the one hand made ample provision for putting checks on dictatorship in His code of conduct for human life and on the other made people extremely resistant to dictatorship and Fascism. The protections provided in the Islamic system of governance can be divided under four heads.

A. Purge of the concept of Sovereignty.

B. Purge of the leadership.

C. Limitation of powers.

D. Accountability of the emirate.

Let us now briefly examine each of them:

Power House

Islam has started its scheme of reform with a drastic change in the concept of sovereignty. The declaration of the Quran that God is not only your Creator, Master, Sustainer and Lord and Cherisher but your Sovereign and Ruler also, has struck at the root of the sovereignty of man. Taking God as the Sovereign means that the distinction of the ruler and the ruled between man and man has come to an end. From the common citizen to the highest, office bearer of the state stand at the same level, and man became free of the bondage of another man like himself. And those entrusted with the affairs of their slate, fearing the accountability before the Judge of judges and the punishment in the life Hereafter instead of compelling people to their own obedience, strictly stuck to the path (of righteousness) pointed out by the Quran and the Sunnahs. Under this concept of Sovereignty neither there is any possibility of taking to the dictatorship for any person, nor the necks of the citizens can be made so weak and pliable that they may bow down to any dictator in abject subservience. Neither an amir or Imam can imagine usurping the rights of the people, conferred on them by the Supreme Sovereign, nor can the people themselves be so docile as to permit them doing so.

This concept of Sovereignty drastically changes the attitude and behaviour of the government relating to the human rights. It was this concept of Sovereignty that manifested itself in the harangue of the first Caliph of the Prophet, Abu Bakr, the man of truth:

> To me your weakest individual is mighty, so long as I do not get him his dues (from the usurper) and your mighty ones are weak to me so long as I do not force them to yield what they have usurped from others.

This related to the human rights. And how much the responsibility of enforcing and respecting them, allowed him "to enjoy" the "pleasures and comforts" of authority during the two years and a quarter of his term of office of caliphate, he said a little before his death in a sad tone:

> If only I had transferred the burden of caliphate, that fell to me on the day of Saqifah Bani Saridah, to Umar or Abu Ubaidah; one of them would have been the Amir and I would have been his vizier. (advisor2)

Of the last instructions and advice that he gave before his death this was also one:

> Whatever I have taken from the Bait-al-mal, paid to me as subsistence allowance, be returned to it. And for this purpose such and such of my landed property be disposed off and the sale proceeds be deposited in the Bait-al-mal (public treasury).

So 'Umar, his successor, in compliance with his wishes sold the land in question and deposited the amount in the Bait-al-mal. Abu Bakr had left instructions in connection with his shroud and burial that he should be burried in the same two pieces of clothes that he usually put on during his life, since "a living person was more deserving of new cloth". (usually in vogue in enshrouding the dead bodies Tr).

Where such firm resolve and sense of responsibility exist and such (exemplary) spirit of sacrifice is at work where one'! own rights are concerned, is there the least little bit of possibility of dictatorship gaining front.

The second Caliph 'Umar, after being installed into the seat of the caliphate, said in his harangue:

> If I knew a person who could bear this burden with greater efficiency I would rather have been slain than undertaken this guardianship.

This much about the "aspiration to authority". And now something about his resolve relating to the enforcement of the rights:

> Listen, O people! I have been placed in charge of your (collective) affairs. But you must know that my sternness has given place to gentleness. However, those, who wrong others and usurp their rights, shall find me just as stern as ever. But for others, who are devout believers and God-fearing in their behaviour, I am extremely gentle. I will not allow any one to wrong any one else; I shall rub one of his cheek on the ground with my foot pressed against the other, until he bows down to justice. In spite of this sternness I rub my own cheek on the ground for the pious and the righteous soul.

And now the details of the benefits derived from the Highest Office of Authority. Before breathing his last as a result of the fatal wounds (inflicted by an assassin while he was leading congregational prayers Tr.), he had asked his son:

> O Abdullah bin-e-Umar! How much I owe to my creditors?
>
> On calculation it was found that it amounted to about eighty six thousand dirhams. (dirham was a small silver coin Tr.)

On learning that Umar said:

> If the family of Umar can pay it off with its assets, let them do so. If not, ask Bann 'Adi to extend their hand for help. And If even then you tail to meet the debt, ask the Qureshites to contribute their mite, but ask no other people for help. Abd-al-Rehman bin-e-'Auf said:
>
> Why not take a loan from the Bait-al-mal to repay your debts? Umar replied, "I seek refuge in God from such an approach. I don't want that you and your friends should say after my death that you relinquished your shares for the sake of Umar. In this way you shall put me under an obligation and in a hard fix from which God alone can deliver me.

What was the spirit behind this character? It was the same creed of the life Hereafter and accountability before the Sovereign; During the last moments of his life, he was in a state of great uneasiness and was trembling with fear. When Ibn-e-Abbas tried to console and calm him, he said:

> By God, If I had gold, the weight of the earth, I would have given it away in the way of God before being confronted with the torments provided by God (for the transgressors).

When Ibn-e-Abbas praised his period of caliphate, he said:

> Do you praise me and my purity of performance in the matter of caliphate and emirate? While I was with the Prophet of God, he was pleased with me. And as an

associate of Abu Bakr I remained loyal, obedient to him till the end of his days. But for myself I am mighty afraid of these affairs of your emirate and caliphate endangering my own safety in the accounability of the Hereafter".

This is that character which emerges on the basis of belief in the Sovereignty of God and making the rulers a blessing for humanity instead of being a scourge, a torment, completely closes the doors upon dictatorship.

The Concept of Trust: In the Islamic state the second powerful safeguard against usurpation of Human Rights is the concept that it is a Trust (from God) and its head is in the position of a trustee. After the covenant between God and His servant:

> Say: Truely my prayer and my service of sacrifice, my life and my death, are (all) for God, the cherisher of the world. (Al Quran VI:162)

> And God has purchased of the Believers their persons and their goods; for theirs, (in return) is the garden (of paradise) (Al Quran IX: 111)

Every thing that a Muslim has, becomes a sacred trust from God, and he is bound (by this covenant) not to use his right of exercise of his own free will and wish his unrestrained powers but strictly in accordance with the will of the real owner of the trust and His instructions. It is the result of this concept of Trust that when a person wrongs another, God accuses him of "Breach of Trust with his own inner self". So when Tamah bin-e-Ubairaq of the Bani Zafar tribe brought accusation of the theft of the steel armour against a Jew, God said to the Prophet in His revelation:

> Contend not on behalf of such as betray their own soul. (Al Quran IV: 107)

Meaning thereby that the servant of God who has sold his innerself to his Lord and cherishing he makes misuse of it, he is guilty of a breach of trust. Honouring the trust by him demands that the servant of God should take to the course of truth and honesty. Falsehood and treachery does more harm to their perpetrator than any one else, since as a betrayer of trust he degrades himself in the estimate of the real owner of the trust and makes himself liable to serve punishment at His court. Pointing to this fact about wrongfulness, it is said:

> And any who transgresses the limits of God does verily wrong his (own) soul.
> (Al Quran LXV I)

Which means the first target of the wronger's misdeed is his own self. His wrong may or may not do any harm to any one else but his own ruination and prediction are assured.

According to this concept of trust every body is burdened with accountability and responsibility according to the nature of the trust. Every one is accountable to his Lord for his deeds of omission and commission proportionate to the resources at his command and the powers, and authority with which he has been entrusted. The rightly guided Caliphs and other companions of the Prophet, in general, were fully conscious of this concept of trust. And that is why they tried to avoid being burdened with any post of responsibility. And once, under pressure from the people or under orders of the Amir, they were charged with any such post and accepted it, they did their utmost to do full justice to it. The fear of accountability pervaded their whole being to such an extent that there was not another man in the society more God-fearing than they.

Abu Bakr, the man of truth, says:

> Whoever is charged with the responsibility of governance, will have to render a heavy account, and will find himself liable to the severest penalty for his lapses. And he who escaped that burden reckoning with him will be easy, and he is not exposed to the danger of minute scrutiny. The rulers are most likely to oppress the Muslims. And one who wrongs and oppresses the Muslims betrays his trust with God.

Umar's fear of accountability before God is evidenced by the following statement of his on one occasion:

> If a kid gets lost somewhere along the river Euphrates, (Several thousand miles, from his seat of authority, the capital town of Medina!) I am mighty afraid of being called to account for it before God.

Whenever 'Umar was overwhelmed with the sense of responsibility of the burden of trust on his shoulder, he would pick up a handful of earth from the ground and clutching at it he used to say:

> If only I were dust, rather a non-entity! If only my mother bad not borne me!

Abu Bakr, Uthman and Ali were no less worried on this issue of accountability of the Hereafter. Umar bin-e-Abd-al-Aziz spent one whole night, after the late evening prayer, weeping. In the morning when asked by his wife, he gave the following reasons for his night-long wait:

> I (suddenly) found myself wholly responsible for the affairs of the entire Muslim Ummah. I came to think of the people away from their homes in strange lands, mendicants in miserable condition, indigents, the helpless oppressed prisoners and such other people. I realised that I will have to answer for all of them to God, and Muhammad (Sal' am) will stand against me in support of them. And 1 was mighty afraid that I would not be able to plead my case before God, and can never satisfy Muhammad (Sal' am) with any argument that I can offer. The idea made me shudder and I was mighty afraid about my own precarious position.

Strictly speaking, to a Muslim, his life and property and every thing over which he has power of utilisation, is a trust from God. But where caliphate and emirate are concerned the word "trust" has been used as a technical term. Abu Zar Ghifari once expressed a wish that he too should be appointed the Amir of some territory to which the Prophet said:

> You are weak and emirate is a trust and it will become a source of regrets and repentance to all save one who deserves it and taking charge of it squarely meets all the responsibilities of his post.

Similarly, he said on another occasion:

> Whoever appointed a person as a controller and ruler over something belonging to Muslims, when a better person and capable among Muslims was available, he would be guilty of breach of trust with God and His Apostle.

In another tradition he said:

> When you witness betrayal of trust, wait for the Dooms day. On being asked what is betrayal of trust, he said in reply that when rule governance and leadership are entrusted to an incapable person, they should wait for the Hour (Doomsday).
>
> (Bukhari, reported by Abu Hurayrah)

This concept of trust is an important means of safeguarding human rights and respect for them, and a great deterrent, in the way of usurpation of rights.

Priority of Duty: Islam in its system of thought and action has laid greater stress on the fulfillment of obligations than demanding and acquiring one's rights. The issue of demanding right is of secondary importance in comparison to the fulfillment of obligations. If the obligations are fulfilled faithfully and consciously the problem of rights simply does not arise. But as soon as the obligations are neglected or suspended, the question of rights raises its head. Whoever is under an obligation is in the position of a giver, and one to whom it is due is in the position of the recepient. Now in case the obligations are being fulfilled regularly in all sincerity, the recepient simply need not put forth his claim for them.

Since state is the Sovereign in the western secular political system, it enjoys the position of absolute authority. All the powers have become associated with it. In some countries, they have come to be concentrated in one place in the form of a communist state, and elsewhere under the theory of Division of Powers. In countries like the United States of America they have become divided into legislature, judiciary and the executive. But the final authority lies in the hands of the State.

The logical result of this state of affairs has been that the position of the citizens has become defensive. The anxiety for their safeguards has given the rights greater importance. And the obligations have not been stressed because there is no way of getting them fulfilled. Which is that superior (Irresistible. Tr.) power that can compel the state to fulfil its obligations? If the state usurps any rights, the affected individual with the greatest effort on his part, may get it recovered through the judiciary. But it is not certain that the judiciary can always extend that help to the aggrieved individual in the matter of restoration of the usurped rights. The state through curtailment of the powers of this institution, the judiciary, can deprive the individual of this facility.

Since rights in Islam are eternal and unchangeable, the state is shorn of the power of curtailing or limiting the powers of the judiciary, and is bound to exercise all its powers strictly in accordance with the injunctions of the Sovereign and the limits prescribed by Him. So all the stress here is on the fulfillment of the obligations.

The Quran, wherever it has addressed mankind, various Ummahs, the prophets individuals, the unbelievers and the polytheists, and the believers, has reminded them of their obligations, promising them honour and dignity in this world and in the next also, only on the basis of fulfilling their obligations.

The Quran in its entirety, from the beginning to the end, has no where addressed the deserving ones, prompting them to unite, form groups, organise themselves and snatch their due from the usurpers by force. This persuasion is not needed since the Sovereign has taken upon Himself to remove the defaulters in the fulfillment of obligations from the seat of authority, meting out to them chastisement in the form of ruination and perdition, bringing them to degradation and disgrace in the life of this world and effacing them totally and consigning them to the roaring flames of Hell-Fire.

Again, such persuasion is not needed also for the reason that the government of God through delegated authority (the Islamic State) is in fact a government for the guardianship of the recipients of rights its real mission is to ensure the fulfillment of the obligations through the powers of its (delegated) authority, and let the deserving ones have their dues in the smoothest possible manner.

The declaration of war against those withholding Zakah by Abu Bakr is a manifestation of this temperament and character of the Islamic State. He had neither been pressed by the recipients of Zakah for their rights, nor any individual or collective complaint in this behalf had been lodged with his government. He was actually appointed by God and His Apostle for this purpose of preventing the usurpation of the rights of people by forcze, if necessary.

Even today none of the eight groups deserving Zakah (under the Quranic injunction), enjoy the legal right of filing a suit in a court of law against any one who owes Zakah to the Bait-al-Mal, to realise his share. The deserving ones can only put up their claim for consideration of the government. Now it is the responsibility of the government to see if it can pay off their dues from the Zakah head of Bait-al-Mal or realise the requisite amount of Zakah due from the moneyed people to meet their needs.

In other words, the government is legally the supporter and guardian, and advocate and agent of the deserving lot. It is the factual plaintiff on behalf of the recipients of the right, and all the powers at its disposal are exercised for the fulfillment of the obligations or realisation of the rights from those at the paying end. Imam ibn-e-Taimiyah explaining the obligations of the government, says:

> The real objective of the governments and the emirates is to serve the servants of God and looking to their reform and moral rectitude. And when people shall abandon the faith they shall find themselves in great loss. And the bounties of the world conferred

> on them by God, shall not avail them in the least. And the spiritual gain from the temporal is of two kinds. One of them is to distribute the goods of this world among the deserving ones; and the other is to mete out due punishment to those indulging in excesses and oppression and also those trying to take what is not due to them or more than their due.

Just imagine what are the chances of the problem of human rights cropping up in a society in which devotional acts, teaching and preaching, education and training, the media of propagation and the various agencies and institutions of the government and all its power, put together and all the means at its command are together exerting pressure internally and externally on the, fulfillment of obligations.

Concordance of the Objective: The Quran points out the aim and objective of the existence of the Islamic State in the following verse:

> (They are) those who, if we establish them in the Land, establish regular prayer, and give zakat regularly, enjoin the right and forbid wrong: (Al Quran XXII: 41)

And identically, the same is the goal of the Muslim Ummah:

> Ye are the best of people evolved for mankind, enjoining what is right, forbidding what is wrong, and believing in God. (Al Quran 111:110)

In other words the objective of the individual and the collective life of the Muslims and that of their government and the state is identical—living a life of righteousness and rectitude and enjoining, what is right, on others, and abstaining from the path of evil themselves and forbidding 'others what is wrong. The unity of the objective in the individual and collective life is that be it a common Muslim citizen or the person in their highest seat of authority, they are the trodders of the same path and bound for the same goal. The direction of their journey is the same. All of them are engaged in the same activity, each one according to his position and capacity and in accordance with the resources and powers at his disposal. One entrusted with power and authority is exercising them to achieve that goal (in his privileged position of greater responsibility. Tr.), and the one with no other assets is striving towards that goal with his body, and soul only.

Where no such harmony exists, there is no longer any issue at stake, for contention between the individual and the state. Under the Islamic order the position of the amir of the state is not that of a ruler but that of a guardian and supervisor, and the relationship between the amir and the people instead of that of the usual ruler and the subjects is that of helpers of each other. God says:

> The Believers, men and women, are protectors, one of another: they enjoin what is just, and forbid what is evil: they observe regular prayers, practise regular charity (pay Zakat regularly Tr.) and obey God and His Apostle. (A1 Quran IX:71)

Now, even if the unlimited aspiration for power and authority of a ruler creates a situation of contention and confrontation, the citizens can always have recourse to the path illumined by the Quran for them:

> Help ye one another in righteousness and piety, but help ye not one another in sin and transgression: (Al Quran V: 2)

The amir, as soon as he digresses towards the path of sin and transgression furnishes the Ummah sufficient ground for withdrawing their cooperation, and he forfeits his right to their obedience.

This concord in the matter of the objective converts the concept of rulership into the concept of brotherhood, and the punishment of turning away from it resulting in loss of the right to loyalty and obedience, becomes a very effective means of the protection of the fundamental rights.

Importance of Man

The problem of the fundamental rights of man is in fact the problem of the dignity of humanity. Those coming to occupy seats so often lose mental balance, and by the spectacle of the wonders worked by their authority and the vast resources at their disposal create an illusion that they come to think of themselves as super human entities, and that they possess such high qualities which necessarily entitle them to sovereignty and rule, and the rest of the humanity (creatures of a much lower order than themselves) were only created to abjectly bow down to them.

This trend of thought has actually taken the form of theories and philosophical thought. It was this pattern of thought which gave birth to such a fabrication as the "Theory of Divine Origin", and the term "Divine Rights of Kings" was coined for the (unlimited) powers of the kings. Again, it was this misleading trend of thought which helped in coining such titles for kings as the "Protector of the World" and "Shadow of God" and presenting them as the ones specially sent by God to rule and thus degraded and put in disgrace the common people. These "Divine Rights and Divine Shadowness" became the cause of great distress for mankind and to save itself from the misery of it, the movement for the protection of fundamental rights had to be launched.

Islam has laid great emphasis on the dignity of man, and he is regarded as the most honoured and respectable entity, next only to God in the universe. In relating the incident of the creation of Adam, it has been said that God breathed into this Divine mould of clay of his own spirit and bowed down the angels to him. The Quran says:

> When I have fashioned him (in due proportion) and breathed into him of My spirit, fall ye down in obeisance unto him. (Al Quran XV: 29)

This verse also reveals that man, quite different from the rest of the creation that came into existence with the command of the Lord and Cherisher, "He", is a separate and special creation, and as compared with other creatures, he has been fashioned in the best possible mould. The Quran says:

> We have indeed created man in the best of moulds. (Al Quran XCV: 4)

Not only this but he was honoured and made superior to other creatures and all his bounties and forces at work in this universe were subdued for him to serve him. The Quran says:

> We have honoured the sons of Adam, provided them with transport on land and sea; given them for sustenance things good and pure; and conferred on them special favours above a great part of our creation. (Al Quran XVII: 70)

> Do ye not see that God has subjected to your (use) all things in the heavens and on earth. (Al Quran XXXI: 20)

This honour, superiority and greatness man came to have as a member of mankind, and there was no distinction of black and white, Arab and non-Arab, oriental and occidental and high and low, since they were born out of a single soul. The Prophet pointing to this greatness once said addressing the sanctum of Kaaba:

> How chaste art thou; and how wholesome thy atmosphere! How great art thou and how venerable thy status But by God, in whosc Hands lies the life of Muhammad, the honour and dignity of a Muslim's life and property and his blood in the sight of God is more important than thy sanctity. (Ibn-e-Majah, Tradition No.3932)

This was one aspect of man's status. Now let us see how has Quran, in order to tame the devil of pride and arrogance in man, and particularly to keep one in authority and in possession of resources, on the right track, brought home to him his own true position:

> Now let man but think from what he is created!. He is created from a drop emitted—proceeding from between the backbone and the ribs: (Al Quran LXXXVI:'S-7)

> (Consider) that We created you out of dust, then out of sperm, then out of a leech-like clot, then out of a morsel of flesh, partly formed, and partly unformed in order that We may manifest (Our power) to you. (Al Quran XXII: 5)

> O man! what has seduced thee from Thy Lord Most Beneficent ...Him who created thee, fashioned thee in due proportion, and gave Thee a just bias; in whatever Form He wills does He put thee together. (Al Quran LXXXII: 6-8)

Along with making this fact about his position evident to him, he was also told that:

> Every soul shall have a taste of death: In the end to Us shall ye be brought back. (Al Quran XXIX: 57)

> Wherever ye are, death will find you out, even if ye are in towers built up strong and high: (Al Quran IV:72)

When, with all his greatness and superiority, man has neither control over his life nor over death, where is any room for haughtiness.

In many verses of the Quran and the traditions of the Prophet, these two truths have been brought home to man in such a wise manner that he should be inclined to respect fellow men, fulfil his obligations in relations to them, should shun tyranny and excesses and should never be a victim of self-deceit or misunderstanding about himself.

These were the basic concepts which Islam brought home to man, and through them ridding him of the unhealthy trends of any aspiration to enslave any one or show willingness to be enslaved, showed him the way to pass his life honourably under the blessings of the universal sovereignty of God with the mutual relationship of equality and brotherhood.

Now we shall take stock of the Islamic injunctions regarding the practical problem of formation of the government.

Purge of the Leadership: To check completely dictatorship and fascism, in an Islamic state, the Muslims have been directed to be extremely careful in the very first stage of the formation of the government. And prescribing two regulations in connection with the election of the amir the wrong persons have been barred from finding their way to the (most important) post of emirate. The first of these regulations is that the person aspiring to a job, despite all his high qualifications and capabilities is unfit for it, since his aspiration for it is the greatest proof of the unsoundness of his intentions. God says:

> That Home of the Hereafter We shall give to those who intend not high-handedness or mischief on earth: (Al Quran XXVIII: 83)

The Prophet says:

> By God, we never appoint any one to any post to which he aspires or is avaricious. (Bukhari, Muslim)

> The worst betrayer of trust among you is one who is an aspirant to a post of responsibility. (Abu Daud)

He once said to Abu Bakr in connection with an inquiry relating to Emirate:

> O Abu Bakr! It is for him who is not at all interested in it, and not for him who is madly after it. It is for one who tries to run away from it, and not one who pounces on it. It is for one to whom it is said, 'This is thy due' and not one who himself asserts, 'This is my right.'

After this fist regulation of disqualification, the other instruction to the people was that they should elect the best person (most suitable) for the post of Amir, and norm for this quality, "best", was also elucidated, so that his character may be objectively scrutinised and tested, and personal like or dislike, kinship, territorial, group, lingual and racial prejudices or the outstanding apparent traits of personality, for example his facial beauty, the style of his dress, his style of hair, the fascination of his written word or speech and such other chorus may not recommend him in the election. It is this norm of election in view of which the Prophet said:

> Listen and obey, even if a Negro slave with a small scalp is appointed as your amir, so long as he rules according to the dictates of the Quran. Bukhari reported by Anas

The same norm 'Umar had before him when he was looking for his successor. Putting up the problem of the caliphate before the members of the Shura or the advisory body, he said:

> If Abu Huzaifa's slave, Salim, had been alive, I would have nominated him for the Emirate. If my Lord and cherisher questioned me about Salim, I would have said in reply. I had heard the Apostle saying that Salim loves Allah very much.

On this occasion when Mughira ibn-e-Sah'bah suggested to him that Abdullah ibn-e-Umar be nominated the next caliph, he said rather gruffly:

> God settle accounts with you! By God, I never for one moment thought of it. We are not interested in your affairs. Neither did I find, rulership something likeable that I may command it to my fainily. If it was something good I have had it. And in case it was bad to have it, it would be enough for one member of the Umar family that he be brought tc account for the well-being or otherwise of the Ummah of the Prophet Muhammad (P.B.U.H). I suffered much through self-abnegation, and totally deprived my family. I even with all this I am let off (on the Day of Reckoning) without any reward or punishment. I shall consider myself lucky enough.

The tradition of the Prophet and the saying of Umar make it evident that the best Amir is one who is well equipped with the knowledge, intellect and administrative capabilities to enforce the Quranic injunctions, whose character reflects love of God, and has all the traits liked by Him and His Apostle to the maximum degree.

In the election or nomination of those in command of the affairs of the Muslims, in addition to the general condition of his being a believing male, sane and rational and adult, the following qualifications have been regarded essential:

1. Taqwa or Piety

God says:

> The most honoured of you in the sight of God is (he who is) the most righteous of you. (Al Quran XLIX: 13)
>
> Shall We treat those who guard against evil the same as those who turn aside from the right? (Al Quran XXXVII: 28)

2. Capability

The person being elected must be fully capable of efficiently handling the job to be entrusted to his care.

> God doth command you to render back your Trusts to those to whom they are due;
>
> (Al Quran IV: 58)

Under this head, the traditions of the Prophet in which he has forbidden us to render trust to those incapable of holding them, and that to make an incapable person the superior and ruler where a better and most pious among the Muslims is available, is betrayal of trust with God and His Apostle, have already been quoted in the foregoing pages.

3. Justice and Equity

The first and foremost qualification of a ruler is justice. The following portion of the verse quoted above (IV: 28) mentions Justice as a requisite of a ruler:

> And when ye judge between man and man, that ye judge with justice.
>
> (Al Quran IV: 28)
>
> O David! We did indeed make thee a vicegerent on earth: so judge thou between men in truth (and justice): nor follow thou the lusts (of thy heart), for they will mislead thee from the Path of God: (Al Quran XXXVIII: 26)

The Prophet has said:

> On the Day of Reckoning the dearest and nearest to me will be the just ruler, and the most- detested person and one to be consigned to the worst torments in Hell will be the despot and the tyrant.

Umar, the second rightly guided caliph of the Prophet, when bidding farewell to the governors with fresh assignments used to give them the following instructions:

> I am not sending you out as tyrants but as the leaders and guides of people. Do not debase and disgrace Muslim with flogging. And don't put them in trial by praising them. Do not wrong them by depriving them of their dues. Do everything in your power to provide all possible facilities to the Muslims and go on working untiringly for their prosperity.

4. Wisdom and Administrative Capacity

Those at the helm of affairs of the Muslims must be the people who have the necessary qualifications of wisdom, administrative capability, and knowledge and understanding. The Quran says:

> Say: are those equal, those who know and those who do not know?
>
> (Al Quran XXXIX: 9)

> To those weak of understanding make not over your property which God hath made a means of support for you. (Al Quran IV: 5)

What those charged with authority among the Muslims, should be on the whole, is amply borne out by what Abu Bakr and Umar have said about them. Nominating Umar as his successor, Abu Bakr gave him sound advice:

> Umar! The first thing I warn you against is your own inner self. Every one's inner self has some cravings and some aspirations. And if you satiate one, the other must come up for satiation. And listen! Beware of those companions of the Prophet whose bellies have become distended. Their eyes show greed, and every one of them has his own interests foremost on his programme. If one of them stumbles due to a false step, the whole lot will be amazed. Beware! You are not the one that goes tumbling down. Get it well into your head so long as you fear God, they will be afraid of you. And as long as your own behaviour is good, the people will also behave in the right manner with you. This is my advice to you and I pray to God for your peace and well-being.

The will of 'Umar which he left for his successor comprises the following instructions:

> (1) Taqwa (Piety) (2) Favouring the righteous and forgiving the evil doers (3) Taxing only the surplus goods of the Zimmis and treating them kindly (4) To realise Zakat from the rich among the Bedouins and returning it to the poor (deserving) among them. (5) Justice for all that need it among the people and meeting their needs (6) Defence of the frontiers. (7) Abstaining from giving priority to the rich over the poor. (8) Strictness in the enforcement of the Commandments and limits prescribed by God and those showing no respect for the Divine injunctions to be disgraced publicly. (9) Keeping yourself at the same level with the people in dealing with them (no priorities, privileges and distinctions. Tr.). (10) In the realisation of the (peoples) dues no regard for the personality of the defaulter and heedlessness in the matter of reproach. (11) Equitable distribution of the spoils of war and self abnegation. (12) Neither oppressing the Zimmis nor allowing others to oppress them. (13) Giving thought to the Hereafter and making provision for it and disregard for the bounties of this world. (14) To guard against the cravings of the innerself getting the better of him. (15) To stand like a rock before the most violent storm for the sake of the Truth. (16) To be compassionate to the Muslim Ummah. (17) Respect for the elders giving dignity to the young and reverence for those learned in the religious lore. (18) Neither beating any one nor disgracing any one. (19) Not to deprive the believers of free gifts and grants. (20) Not to station the troops permanently guarding the frontiers lest the propagation of the race should come to an end. (21) Not to let the

> national wealth and resources keep confined to the rich people. (22) Not to close your door on the poor and the needy lest the mighty should devour the weak.

When Umar took over as the caliph. Ali gave him the following advice:

> If you want to follow your companion (Abu Bakr) and keep up to his level patch up your shirt, keep your trousers above your ankles, mend your shoes yourself, patch your leather socks, curtail your aspirations and never fill your stomach fully.

And Umar did live up to these counsels during the entire period of his caliphate. For the rest of his life since he died in harness a martyr's death.

This is the norm of the election and the essential qualifications of those charged with authority in Islam. If the Ummah elects its rulers according to this norm, and they too come up to it, there will be an atmosphere of mutual well-wishing and cooperation instead of confrontation between the individual and the state, and there will be no hindrance in the protection of the fundamental rights.

Limitation of Powers: After imposing stern conditions for the elections of those charged with authority, as soon as the Amir is installed into the seat of authority, Islam binds him with the limitations of powers in such a way that he can neither give himself the airs of the rulers nor can he put together the means of display of pomp and glory. These are some of the restrictions placed on the powers of the Amir:

1. Delegated Authority

The head of the Islamic state by virtue of, his office, discharges the duties of a two fold representation. He is on the one hand the vicegerent of the Sovereign on the basis of the responsibility of enforcing His commandments and instructions practically And on the other hand he is the deputy of the true vicegerents of the Sovereign being their elected representative.

Since the vicegerency has been conferred on every Muslim individually and they all delegate it to an individual of their choice, through manifestation of their free will in an election, thus devoting the responsibility of a duty to be discharged on the behalf. So he is the deputy (or representative) of them all. This dual deputation signifies that the head of the state is on the one hand accountable to God and on the other responsible to the people. This peculiar position of his, limits his own will and power to a very small sphere. This is the first and the greatest restriction placed by Islam on the powers of those charged with authority.

2. Eternal Constitution

The greatest safeguard of the fundamental rights in the Islamic State is that eternal constitution which is with us in the form of the Quran and the Sunnah and which has determined a code of conduct for man's life that can neither be amended nor cancelled. The Sovereign, determining the checks on the legislative powers of those charged with authority and the conditions of loyalty and obedience for the common people, has commanded:

> Follow (O man!) the revelation given unto you from your Lord, and follow not as friends and protectors, other than Him. (Al Quran VII: 3)

And those guilty of the slightest digression from this commandment have been given the divine verdict in very clear terms:

> If any do fail to judge by (the light of) what God hath revealed, they are (no better than) unbelievers...... they are (no better than) wrongdoers, they are (no better than) those who rebel. (Al Quran V: 44.47)

This law the following of which is being enjoined on the believers, since it does not change with the change of the government, is passed on to every new comer in authority, and so the rights conferred by it are never curtailed, suspended or cancelled. They are immutable and totally immune from the interference of the state.

3. Eternal Pattern of Sovereignty

This constitution has not only been preserved in the form of written word and the book comprising them, but also presents before us a permanent pattern to follow in its interpretation, elucidation and practical enforcement; and being embodied in the person, of the Prophet, makes such a solid and lucid manifestation of its sense that there is no chance of playing with words, to give them meaning suiting the lusts of the rulers and through desired interpretation, and even distortion and perversion, to chalk out new paths of digression (from the straight path). The Sovereign who has strictly forbidden following other than His own commandments, says about His Prophet:

> We sent not an Apostle, but to be obeyed, in accordance with the will of God. (Al Quran IV: 64)

And this obedience, too, should not be with any feeling of compulsion and revulsion but with perfect readiness of mind and willingness of the heart. The Quran continues in the same context:

> But no, by thy Lord, they can have no (real) Faith, until they make thee judge in all disputes between them, and find in their souls no resistance against thy decision, but accept them with the fullest conviction. (Al Quran IV: 65)

In the light of this commandment, from a common citizen to the head of the Islamic State, the real fountain-head of leadership, guidance, giving instructions and governance is the sacred person of the Prophet of God. In every thing pertaining to man's life their attitude shall be a demonstration of the following instruction of the Quran:

> So take what the Apostle assigns to you, and deny yourselves that which he withholds from you. And fear God; for God is strict in Punishment. Al Quran L1X: 7

And,

> Ye have indeed in the Apostle of God a beautiful pattern (of conduct).
> (Al Quran XXXIII: 21)

With the practical pattern of Sovereignty of the Prophet, no Islamic state any where in the world, can afford to overlook the word or deed of the Apostle of God in any matter pertaining to human life, and his interpretation and elucidation of any Quranic injunction. This eternal pattern of Sovereignty compels every head of the Islamic state to follow the Prophet. And this check on him putting an obstacle in the way of transgression or overstepping the limits of his powers puts an end to any oppression and excess.

4. Supremacy of the Judiciary

The eternal position of the Quran and the Sunnah means that the judiciary has supremacy over both the executive and the legislature. The executive cannot do any thing against the Quran and the Sunnah, and the legislature cannot legislate against the spirit of the Quran and the Sunnah. The judiciary is the protector of the citizen's rights. It can declare any laws violating these rights as null and void and can stop their enforcement, and making the orders issued by the executive ineffective, can provide strong protection to the citizens.

5. Limits of Obedience

Obedience of the Amir is conditional in Islam. And in this connection the Sovereign has Himself laid down a general rule:

> O ye who believe! Obey God and obey the Apostle, and those charged with authority among you. If ye differ anything, refer it to God and His Apostle.(Al Quran IV: 59)

The limits of obedience in an Islamic State determined by this Quranic verse are the following:

(1) Obedience is, in fact, due to Allah alone, and is binding upon the Muslims including the Apostle.

(2) Obedience in the second place is due to the Prophet of God, and is not different from that in the first item, but the only practical form of the obedience to God. Obedience to God for us (mortals) is nothing else but our obedience to the Prophet. That is why at another place it has been said in the Quran:

He who obeys the Apostle, obeys God: (Al Quran IV: 80)

Like the first, this obedience too is binding upon the Muslims, ordinary citizens and the rulers alike.

(3) Thirdly, obedience is due to one in authority. But like the first two, this is not unconditional. It is associated with the basic condition that the person in authority must be bowing with the rest in the first two items of obedience.

(4) If there is a contention between the person in authority and the believers on any issue, it will be decided on the authority of the Book of God and the Sunnah of the Prophet.

Along with this fundamental article of the constitution of the Islamic state, the Muslims have been given clear instruction that they should never obey any person who is a slave of his own innerself, mischief maker, tyrant and one violating the obligation of enjoining what is right and forbidding what is wrong. Certain Quranic verses in this context are noteworthy:

> Nor obey any whose heart We have permitted to neglect the remembrance of us, one who follows his own desires, whose case has gone beyond all bounds.
>
> (Al Quran XCII: 28)
>
> And follow not the bidding of those who are extragent,......who make mischief in the land and mend not (their ways). (Al Quran XXVI: 151-152)
>
> And hearten not to the sinner or the ingrate among them. (Al Quran LXXVI: 24)
>
> Heed not the despicable man,—ready with oaths, a slanderer going about with calumnies, (habitually), hindering (all) good, transgressing beyond bounds, deep in sin, violent, and cruel),...with all that, base- born.......because he possesses wealth and (numerous) sons, when to him are rehearsed our signs. "Tales of the Ancient," He cries! (Al Quran LXIIt: 10.15)

In this connection, the Traditions of the Holy Prophet further stating in detail the principle of obedience, have so much elucidated all its various aspects that there is no confusion left. He says:

> Listening and obedience is binding on Muslims whether it is pleasing or repugnant to him, so long as he is not ordered to do something sinful.' And when he is ordered to commit a sin, there is neither listening nor obedience. (Bukhari and Muslim)

That is to say, as soon as the Amir has made himself independent of the two items of obedience (God and His Prophet), he forfeits his rights to the obedience of the people, and the Muslims in that situation are bound to openly refuse to obey him. The Prophet has said very plainly:

> There is no obedience in transgression and sin. Obedience is only in what is right.
>
> (Bukhari and Muslim)
>
> There is no obedience for one who is a transgressor.
>
> (Bukhari and Muslim; Abu Daud and Nasai)
>
> No obedience for His creatures at the cost of disobedience to God.
>
> (Bukhari and Muslim)

His forfeiture of the right to the obedience of the people means in plain words that he is no more their Amir. He has been divested of his powers. No orders from him have any legal position, and the Muslims have now been entitled to have another Amir for themselves through fresh elections. If he goes so far in his transgression that the system of prayer is in disarray due to him, he has given a handle to the believers to take up arms against him.

There will come such people to rule over you whose programme in life manifests good and evil both mixed up. So those who showed disgust for their evil deeds, discharge their duty. And those who disapproved of them were also safe. But he who approved of their evil deeds and followed them, would be brought to back. The companions asked the Prophet, "Shall we not take up arms against such rulers?" The Prophet replied, "Not so long as they establish regular prayers". (Muslim)

When Abu Bakr took upon himself the responsibilities of the caliphate, recalling these limits of obedience, said:

> Obey me as long as I obey God and His Apostle, but if I am found guilty of something involving disobedience to God and His Apostle, you are no more under any obligation to obey me.

Umar, the second caliph, addressing a gathering, said:

> The greatest and most important duty of the ruler is to see whether the people are fulfilling the obligations enjoined on them by God. We shall enjoin upon you only that has been enjoined on you by God, and forbid you what God has forbidden you. All that we want is that the Divine injunctions be enforced far and wide.

And it was during the period of the caliphate of 'Umar that after the conquest of Iraq, many people had taken Christian women for wives in view of the permission granted for it in the Quran. 'Umar wrote to Huzaifah bin-al-Yamn that he did not approve of it. He wrote back to enquire whether it was his personal opinion or under an injunction of the Islamic Shariah, to which Umar replied that that was his personal dislike of it. Huzaifah wrote to him that they were under no obligation to follow his personal opinion.

Ali, the fourth caliph, said in one of his harangues:

> You are under obligation to obey me in what I order you, while I am myself obeying God, whether you like it or not. And what I enjoin on you, while transgressing the Divine Injunctions, there is no obedience" in transgression. Obedience is only in Maroof. Maroof:. Literally well known (to human nature) and having an affinity for it. As a technical term of the Islamic Shariah, it comprises the acts, attitudes, and the behaviour, that the normal people with an unsullied nature have approved in every age. Truth, keeping of one's plighted word, justice, equity and kindness, to name a few, have always been regarded as desirable and laudable. Obedience is only in Maroof. This conditional obedience of those in authority left no room for their high handedness in the matter of people's rights conferred on them by God. They are entitled to

people's obedience only so long as they respect these rights and do not take any step detrimental to them. If they contravene this principle the people need not obey them. And as a reaction against this they will be justified in their striving to depose him from the emirate. These limits and conditions of obedience provide the citizens, a guarantee for the protection of their fundamental rights against the onslaughts on them by the rulers.

6. The Obligation of Consultation

There is yet another obligation, for the person those in authority, that cannot take any step without first consulting those persons of the Ummah who can give sober advice. The way he is elected by the mutual consultation and concurrence of the opinions of the Muslims, he is also under obligation to manage the affairs of the state by consultation under the following injunction of the Quran:

> Who (conduct) their affairs by mutual consultation; (Al Quran XLII: 38)

Even the Prophet of God was no exception to it. He is being instructed:

> And consult them in affairs (of moment): (Al Quran III: 159)

The Prophet of God was himself in authority (by virtue of being commissioned by God). He was directly guided by God. So he was not so much in need of consultation. But since he had to leave a pattern after him for those succeeding in the office of authority to manage the affairs of the Islamic state, he was made to establish a tradition of mutual consultation. He often consulted his companions on various major and minor issues. This tradition (of consultation) was so much liked by God that in some matters before giving him instructions be waited for the companions of the Prophet to opine on those issues, and when one of such opinions was approved by Him, by authorisation and approval of it through revelation, the person offering the opinion was encouraged. So we find that the revelation approved the opinion of 'Umar on the issue of the prisoners of war of Badr, the death service of the hypocrites. Burdah, prohibition of alcohol, taking the station of Ibrahim as the place of prayer, and entering the house unannounced during the time people usually rest in bed. The Prophet once addressed Abu Bakr and 'Umar, the most eminent among his companions, saying that if they come to a consensus on any issue he would not oppose them (Musnad Ahmad).

Ali is reported to have said:

> Once I asked the Prophet if a certain problem confronted them after his passing away which was neither mentioned in the Quran nor he (the Prophet) himself had opined on it, what should be our course of action. The Prophet said in reply that they should bring together the most devout among the believers of his Ummah and put the puzzling issue for their mutual consultation, but never take a decision on a solitary opinion.

About its importance and real spirit the Prophet had said:

> Whoever suggested to his brother something about which he was certain was not the right course, betrayed the trust reposed in him by his brother. (Abu Daud)

After the definite Quranic injunction and the Sunnah of the Prophet, no Amir of the believers can take any action (in important matters) without consultation. This obligation of consultation impedes the course of dictatorship and inspires the political life with spirit of democracy. It is worthwhile to note here the basic point that the principle of consultation in Islam depends not on the majority of opinions but their soundness. In other words, only the opinion that is nearest to the spirit of the Quran and the Sunnah will be acceptable, and it will be put into practice after Ijma. The consensus of the Mujtahids of the Ummah on a certain issue during a certain period. The consensus of the learned ones raises the status of Ijma for above the personal opinions of individuals however great in learning and piety, when the majority of the erudite in the religious love has conceded to it. Without the support of the Quran and the Sunnah the majority of opinion carries no weight and is to be given no importance.

Abu Bakr consulted the eminent companions on the issue of those withholding Zakat. The majority of the companions were not in favour of declaring war against them. But he did not concede to their opinion, since according to his understanding of the Quran Jihad was the right course to take in their case. Later on all the dissentients agreed that Abu Bakr's decision was based on sound reasoning and participated in the Jihad. Similarly, 'Umar dissented from the majority of consultants on the issue of distributing the arable lands of the conquered Iraq and Syria. Companions of the stature of Bilal and Abdur-Rahman bin-e-Auf were insisting that the lands be distributed among the conquering armies. A general meeting of the advisory body was called and after long deliberations extending over several days, 'Umar succeeded in convincing them of the soundness of his own opinion. He had come upon a verse of the Quran (LIX:7) which he brought powered in support of his stand on this controversial issue and they came to a consensus.

These precedents also make it evident that the Amir, with all his, superiors in sight, cannot take any decisive action on the basis of his own personal information and satisfaction on any issue, unless and until he has had a consensus on the satisfaction of the majority on the soundness of his own opinion.

The relationship of the Amir and the advisory body had been brought out by 'Umar in the meeting called by him on the issue of the distribution of lands in these words:

> Gentlemen, I have given you the trouble to come here because I wanted that you should take off some of the heavy load of your affairs on my shoulders, since I am also a weak mortal like you. Today you are called upon to determine the right. Some of you have differed from me, and some have concurred. It is not my desire that you should come to my way of looking at the problem. You have the Book of God with

> you that tells you only the truth. By God! I have said any thing on which I want to act, I had no other intention but following the truth.

It was also Umar who had said:

> No (office of the) caliphate without consultation.

Emphasizing the importance of consultation he goes so far as to say:

> The person who invites you to the emirate for himself or any body else without seeking the opinion of Muslims it does not become you not to kill him.

After Uthman died a martyr's death, and people wanted to install Ali in the seat of authority—thus vacated he said:

> You people are not authorised to do it. It is the business of the Shura or the advisory body and the companions of (the battle of) Badr. The person whom they elect for this purpose shall be the caliph So we shall get together and deliberate over it.

Abu Musa Ashari regarded this consultation as the difference between caliphate and monarchy:

> Emirate (caliphate) is that instruction which comes into existence as a result of consultations (sort of referendum Tr.). And monarchy is that established with the might of the sword.

This principle of consultation has fully guaranteed the expression of opinion to all those whose rights are under consideration. This consultation is not limited to the members of the Shura. A common citizen can change the opinion of the entire Shura and the Amir if he can bring the authority of the Quran and the Sunnah in support of his contention. An old lady was exercising this right on others when she made 'Umar, the second caliph, realise the error of his decision of living the quantum of women's dower, and he took back his order immediately.

7. The Obligation of the Objectives and the Priorities

Yet another restriction on the person in authority is that he cannot make any amendments in the objectives and the priorities of the state, since such alterations will go against the concept of the Trust. He can utilise the monetary resources of the state (Bait-al-Mal) only under those heads that have been determined by the Islamic Shariah, or by the decision of the Shura. And how much he (the Amir) is himself entitled to from the Bait-al-Mal (as subsistence allowance) is also for the Shura to determine. After the election of the first caliph (Abu Bakr) when the question of his subsistence arose, 'Umar took him to Abu 'Ubaidah, the Nazim of the Bait-al-Mal (Treasury Officer), from the market place where he (Abu Bakr) was standing with cloth for sale. The Nazim, elucidated the principle of determining the allowance to him saying:

> We are fixing an allowance for you equivalent to the income of an average person among the migrants (from Maklesh), which is neither equal to that of the richest, nor that of the poorest among them.

This subsistence allowance was fixed at four thousand dirhams: an old oriental weight and silver coin, originally two thirds of an Attic drachma. It is about 3.071 gms annually. But through a testament of his before his death he had got returned to the Bait-al-Mal, all that he had received (during the twenty seven months of his term as caliph. Tr.).

Umar, elucidating the principle of the share of the caliph from the Bait-al-Mal, had said:

> For me nothing more from the bounties of Allah is allowance than a pair of clothes for the summer season and another for the winter, and subsistence for my family equivalent to that of an average person among the Quraish, for, I am a common man among the believers.

He determines the following basic principles regarding the responsibility of the Bait-al-Mal:

> With regard to this goods (the resources of the Bait-aI-Mal) I do not consider right save these three things—taking justly, giving away justly and withholding it from (serving the cause of) falsehood. My relationship with you is that of the guardian of the orphan with his (the orphan's) goods. If 1 am not in need, I shall not take any thing from it. And, if in want, I shall take according to the barest minimum of my needs.

Ali, the fourth caliph, also kept his subsistence allowance at the level of Shaiklain (Abu Bakr and Umar), and passed a life of great austerity.

We have already thrown ample light on the aims and objectives of the Islamic state. Its only objective is to proclaim the religion of God over all others:

> Establish the Faith Or the way of life and make no divisions therein.
>
> (Al Quran XLll: 13)

The goal of the collective power of the Islamic state and each and every one of its citizens is this:

> And religion is all for Allah. (Al Quran VIII: 39)

The person in authority cannot afford to keep any other objective in vein. The Prophet has severely warned his successor and all the believers:

> The person who introduces something into our faith which is to be rejected.
>
> (Mishkat, chapter on Adherence to the Book of God and the Sunnah)
>
> Whoever honoured an innovator, helped in the demolition of the Faith.
>
> (Mishkat, chapter of Adherence to the Book of God and the Sunnah)

These are the restrictions placed on the powers of the person in authority. The ruler, tightly bound by the delegated authority and along with that fully observing the limits prescribed by the Quran and the Sunnah, obligation of consultation, conditional obedience, and obligation of the objectives and priorities of the Islamic state, can hardly dream of usurping the fundamental rights.

Along with the concept of the government, purge of the leadership and limitation of the powers, Islam has made extraordinary arrangements for keeping an eye over the activities of the Amir and calling him to account. In the foregoing pages we have discussed the way and means of vigilance. In this connection it would be better to recall the sequence of the means of vigilance to have an idea how Islam has established the superiority of the people over the government, making it a democracy in the true sense of the world.

1. Reckoning of the Hereafter

The first and foremost agent of vigilance is the fear of the (reckoning of the) Hereafter, which has always a tight grip over his mind and nerve. The omniscient and well-acquainted and omnipresent Entity, (God), Who is going to call him to account for each and every deed of his, and here in this life, is closer to him than his own jugular vein, has forewarded him, that:

> Whosover follows My guidance, on them shall be no fear, nor shall they grieve. But those who reject Faith and believe Our Signs, they shall be companions of the Fire; they shall abide therein. (Quran II: 38-39)
>
> Not one of the beings in the heavens and the earth but must come to (God), Most Gracious, as a servant. (Al Quran XIX: 93)

The Prophet has said:

> Every one of you is an overseer and protector, and will be asked to account with regard to those entrusted to his charge. So the Amir (of the believers) will be called to account in connection with the people. And the house wife is an overseer over her husband's household and his offspring, and she will be asked to render account on that score. (Bukhari and Muslim, reported by Abdullah bin-e-Umar)
>
> One who has been entrusted with the collective affairs of the Muslims and he betrays that trust, Allah shall bar his entry to heaven. (Unanimous)
>
> When somebody has accepted the responsibility of the collective affairs of the believers, and he did not strive for their well-being and did not tire himself as he would in the management of his own affairs, Allah would throw him into Hell-Fire face-down. (Tabrani, Kitab-al-Khiraj)

Accountability of the Hereafter is an internal vigilance that never leaves man alone, in company or in solitude, and continues the process of self-reckoning all the time. In the presence of this internal system of watch and ward, even if there is no external vigilance, there is hardly any likelihood of his going astray and taking to the path of oppression and evil. It was the result of this acute sense of accountability that during the caliphate of Abu Bakr, 'Umar as the Qadi of the Islamic state for two years had not a single case brought to his court. That was because every individual of the Society, including their Amir, were discharging their duties so efficiently that no question of (usurpation of) any rights ever cropped up.

2. Accountability Through the Courts

The head of the Islamic state enjoys no immunity against the citizens. And any citizen can bring a suit against him.

The caliph of the believers, 'Umar had a contention with Ubai bin-e-Kab on some matter. The latter filed a suit against him in the court of Zaid bin Thabit, the then Qadi of Medina. The Qadi issued someone to 'Umar to present himself in his court. He came to attend the court but neither he nor the plaintiff had any witness to testify in their case. According to rules, 'Umar had to make his statement on oath. When Ubai discerned that 'Umar was ready to take an oath, he withdrew his case.

'Ali, the fourth caliph, saw a Christian selling his (Ali's) armour in the market, and claimed it as his. On his refusal to oblige, the case was brought to the court of Qadi Shariah, who asked 'Ali to produce a witness which he failed to do. So the case was decided in favour of the Christian, and 'Ali accepting that decision of the court said, "Shariah, you have pronounced the right judgment in this case". The Christian was amazed at this decision and said, "Such justice could come only from the Prophets of God, that the Amir of the believers is dragged to the court and has to put up with the decision against himself. To tell the truth the armour belongs to the Amir of the believers. It had dropped down from his camel's back and I had picked it up".

This status of the judiciary was maintained even during the period of the Umayyid caliphate. Utaiba says:

> "I was sitting with bin e-Imran, the Qadi of Medina, when the head of the bodyguard of the caliph Hisham bin Abdul Malik came to him with Ibrahim, bin-e-Muhammad, and said, 'In a contention between the Amir and Ibrahim, the former has sent me as his agent or attorney to your court.' The Qadi asked him to produce his credentials. He said in reply, "Do you mean to say I have told a lie?" The Qadi said to him mildly, 'Not that 1 doubt your statement, but it involves a point of law, and until you produce evidence to this effect no decision on your case can be pronounced.' He went back and acquainted the caliph Hisham with the situation. Hisham personally attended the court and after hearing the case the Qadi pronounced judgement against the caliph".

And it was from the court of this same Qadi Muhammad bin-e-Imran in another case that caliph Mansoor was summoned. The complaint was lodged by some owners of camels in connection with certain rights of their's. The Qadi wrote to him "Give them their due or present yourself at the court". The caliph presented him at the open air court in the Prophet's mosque, and the Qadi decided the case against him and in favour of the camel drivers.

These precedents make it evident that in an Islamic state a common citizen can file a case against the highest office bearer and bring him to the dock and can get his right restored. The power of the state that it can summon the greatest man to the court, makes its grip on the executive so firm that fear of facing the court alone becomes an effective vigilance and people's rights' are not jeopardised.

3. Accountability Through Shura

The importance and function of Shura has come for mention earlier. Here we shall take up only its aspect of calling the ruler to account. The function of the members of the Shura is not just to express their opinion when the Amir calls them to opine on a certain issue. Their real job is to keep an eye on the activities of the government. They are the brain of the Ummah as well as its eyes. Their vigilant eye keeps back the person in authority from overstepping the limits of their powers and misappropriation of the public lands or the Bait-al-Mal. As a matter of fact every citizen of Islamic state Muslims in particular, have a right rather it is an injunction to them from God, that they speak the truth, enjoy what is good and spread it as far as they can, and put checks upon evils and do every thing in their power to keep their society on the path of justice and equity. But this duty devotes on the members of Shura most, who are elected only for this function in an Islamic state. In connection with management of the collective affairs of the believers they are the select addressees of the following instructions of God and His Prophet:

> Help ye one another in righteousness and peity, but help ye not one another in sin and transgression. (Al Quran V: 2)
>
> O ye who believe! fear God and always say a word directed to the Right. (Al Quran XXXIII: 70)
>
> The Believers, men and women, are protectors of one another: they enjoin what is just, and forbid what is evil. (Al Quran IX: 71)

The Prophet says:

> Whoever of you witnesses on evil should change it with the might of his arm. If he cannot do that, he should try to stop it by word of his mouth. And if even that is not possible, he should have a disgust for it and an urge to remove it. And this is the lowest degree of belief. Muslim, Tirmidi, and Abu Daud The most superior type of Jihad (striving in the way of Allah) is to say what is right before a despotic ruler. Abu Daud, Tirmidi, Nasai

There will be rulers coming after me. Whoever supports them in their falsehood and helps them in their tyranny is not from me and I am not from him (such a man has nothing to do with Islam and its teachings).

Shura in a way has ascendancy over the ruler. The latter is under obligation to consult the Shura, but the members of the Shura are not bound to express their opinion only when they are called by him for consultation. They can opine on the activities of the person in authority, give him useful suggestions and can call him to account publicity whenever they feel it is necessary to do so. Under these conditions it is not possible for the person in authority to do as he is pleased, to usurp somebody's right, or take coercive measures against the deserving.

4. Accountability Through the People

Islam does not allow the Ummah, after they have elected the Amir and the members of the Shura, to leave all the business of the state to them for their appointed term and remain unconcerned themselves and leaving them alone to do what they like until the next elections. Since the government is the most important and most effective and the riches in resources to achieve the objective for with each and every individual of the Ummah is striving with his life and resources, they can never afford to shirk the responsibility of vigilance, and from time to time taking stock of their performance with regard to achieving that objective. For them it is not just the problem of bread and butter, clothing and shelter.

Much above that is the establishing of the Religion of God. Neither any individual of the Muslim Society can afford to squander the limited resources at his disposal and be guilty of betrayal of trust, nor allow others to go on recklessly washing the collective resources of the believers, entrusted to their charge. It was the demonstration of this sense of responsibility that prompted Salman Farsi to object to 'Umar having two sheets of garments instead of one that everybody had received as his share, and publicly interrupting him and refusing to listen to his harangue, even knowing well enough how much 'Umar was given to sacrifice, public service and austere piety, and agreed to listen to him only when 'Umar had explained his possession of an additional sheet as a gift from his son, who also testified to it on the spot.

Similarly, the old woman had publicly opposed 'Umar in his declared intention of delimiting the power of women, asking him to remain within the limits of his powers and not to meddle with a right conferred on women by Allah.

The rightly guided caliph never tried to crush this sense of calling their rulers to account. Rather, they encouraged it. Abu Bakr in his inaugural public address, on taking, over as the first caliph of the Prophet, had said, "If I keep on to the right path in my conduct (of managing your affairs) cooperate with me. But if I fail in that, do correct me (with force)". Similarly, 'Umar, his immediate successor, just to test the sense and the power of the people of holding to account their rulers, once said to a gathering: "What will you do if I slacken in my vigilance, and adopt a policy of drift in the management of your affairs?" Bishr bin-e-Sad stood up and drawing his sword from its scabbord said:

> "We shall behead you?" 'Umar feigned to get angry and said to him rebukingly. "Does thou say that about me regardless of my high position?" He said with emphasis," "Yes you, you and none else". Umar was very much pleased with this bold reply and said, "Thank God, there are men among my people who will drag me to the right path were I ever to digress from it.

The same was the course adopted by. 'Uthman and 'Ali. Uthman was the target of criticism but he never tried to stop the wagging tongues through bribe or coercion. The Khazrites went to the extent of virtuperation in case of 'Ali, and even threatened to kill him but he took no notice of it and said, "Verbal demonstration of antagonism was not enough to justify any action against them".

Along with all these means of the accountability of those in authority, it should also be borne in mind that Islam has not limited its sphere of vigilance to Public Affairs alone, but the Private Affairs too are encompassed by it. In the matter of Maroof and Munkar: Literally means alien to human nature. In the Islamic terminology it includes acts, attitudes and behaviours for which men of wholesome nature in every age and under any order, true or false and corrupt, have, had abhorrance. Barring the few perverts, nobody ever approved and acclaimed falsehood, breach of trust, tyranny and injustice and other evils.

The fundamental rule of Islam is that whatever is determined for the collection is equally bad for the individual. A crime committed secretly is no less an evil than one committed openly. If drinking and gambling in public are cognizable offences, they are just as much cognizable in the privacy of a hotel, a club or one's own home. Since the law of the Islamic Shariah does not divide life into two compartments of individual and collective (public and private. Tr) associating itself with only one of them but encompasses the whole of it, and does not allow the private life of an individual to be ruined through pursuit of lusts by excluding it from its sphere of vigilance. It was in keeping with this principle that the lives of the Prophet, the rightly guided caliphs and other companions were exposed to public view.

After this review of the fundamental concepts of the status of the person in authority, the conditions of his election, the limitation of his powers, the limits of obedience to him and all the measures of holding him to account one can have an idea how powerful and effective are the safeguards against usurpation of the fundamental rights in the Islamic society. And the great wealth of peace and security, prosperity and satisfaction of those groups of people and the territory to which these protections are afforded, can only be imagined. Did the Islamic order last only thirty years?

While studying the safeguards provided for the fundamental rights in Islam a pertinent question can arise in the mind of the reader that with all these powerful and all-pervading protective measures, how Islam came by this tragedy that its unparalleled order of Justice and Equality could not survive the brief span of thirty years' of the rule of the rightly guided caliphate. The spirit of democracy came to an end during this short period. Monarchy came to have full sway over the democratic order. The Ummah had no say in the election of the caliph. Inherited monarchy usurped the place of elected caliphate. Bait-al-Mal was no more a public trust controlled by the believers, but became the personal property of the rulers. The order of the Shura, freedom of self expression, and the freedom of the judiciary also ended with the other institutions. The tribal and territorial prejudices raised their heads and murders, plunder, bloodshed and tyranny and oppression made their appearance here in the Islamic order in all those forms in which it would have existed in any other un-Islamic system of government. During the dynasties of Banu Umayyah and Banu Abbas and the following period such incidents came to be of common occurrence which could not be called by any other name but tyranny. What explanation can be offered for this remarkable change? And does this change not prove that the Islamic order could survive only thirty years after the Prophet's death, and failed after that period?

This question appears very pertinent and weighty enough in the light of the historical facts. But in fact it is based on a misunderstanding. Such questions come to the minds of those who regard Islam and the behaviour of the Muslims as one and the same thing, when it is a fact that Islam has an entity of its own quite independent of its votaries. Its principles and rules and regulation are themselves arguments in its favour. The behaviour of the Muslims is not a criterion to judge Islam. Rather, the opposite is the case. The behaviour of the Muslims shall be judged on the criteria provided by Islam to see to which category of the votaries of Islam they belong, and how far they are sincere in their assertions of devotion to Islam. It would not be proper to take Muslims for other peoples and nations of the world. If their true position is properly understood there would be no justification for posting their misdeeds to the ledge of the Islamic order.

The other states of the world are themselves sovereigns in their states. So the royal farmans issued by their kings, the laws framed by their parliaments and other legislatures, the orders promulgated by their rulers and the decisions pronounced by their courts have the position of an authority and arguments in their favour. And as we have already explained under the discussion of constitution in these states law is another name for the will of the rulers. The law has no independent entity of its own beyond the state and its manipulations. Rather, it is bound by their wishes. If the law in vogue obstructs their path in taking any step, they clear it through amending that law or replacing it by another serving their purpose. And then this amended or new law becomes an authority. The former law becomes cancelled since it is no more effective, and has no legal position in the courts. Now reference is made to the new or the amended law, and it remains in force so long as afresh one does not come to take its place. This process of legislation only keeps the entire legal system involved in regular amendments, cancellation, limitations and suspensions, but also serves as an authority to make any law effective or ineffective. And in this entire process at no stage the legislator is considered law-breakers. The courts go on discarding the laws cancelled by the legislators and decide the legal cases on the basis of the latest legislation.

As against this, in Islam, neither any rulers of the Muslims nor the Ummah as a whole enjoys the position of legislator. Their power of legislation is conditioned by due regard for the spirit of the Quran and the Sunnah. Those of their rulers who turned away from the Quran and the Sunnah, promulgated laws contrary to Islam or adopted an attitude in direct conflict with the injunctions of God on His Prophet, their position is that of rebels, traitors and law-breakers.

They have been much more despicable to the Muslims themselves than to others, and the Muslims have in fact adopted this very attitude towards them. The orders and laws promulgated by them could never become a part of the Islamic legal code. They could never attain the position of authority and argument. Their authority could not bring about the slightest change in the law of the Shariah, which has a separate entity of its own independent of and beyond the powers of the state. The Muslims recognised and accepted the decisions of only those Muslim rulers as precedents who strictly followed the law of the Shariah. They recognised as authority the orders and decisions of only 'Umar bin-e-Abdul-Aziz among the rulers of Banu Umayyah.

Among the Banu Abbas no ruler was considered worthly of consideration in this respect. And only the collection of edicts that Aurangazeb among the Mughal emperors of India got compiled under his own supervision found its way into the books on Muslim jurisprudence. But his grandfather, Akbar's Din-e-Elahi was despised and rejected in his own period. In the Islamic history extending every fourteen centuries, the laws framed by the monarchs and dictators were never considered worthy of notice even. And as against this the laws framed by the lowly and ascetic legists like Imam Abu Hanifa, Imam Malik, Imam Hanbal and Imam Shafii which had been derived from the Quran and Sunnah attained the position of Law, and today Muslims all over the world follows these four schools of the Islamic jurisprudence.

In the subcontinent upto the middle of the nineteenth century this Fiqh (jurisprudence) was the law in the courts, and even during the British period justice was dispensed in the courts according to this law where the personal matters of the Muslims were concerned. In short, the law of the Islamic Shariah has never been cancelled or suspended during any period of history. Even the kings abided by its laws. Their person could not become the fountain-head of law. Few of them like Akbar tried to invent Din-e-Elahi in opposition to the law of the Shariah, and tried to thrust it on people but could not succeed in his attempt. The law framed by him also got buried with him. The Muslim millat (community) never allowed that it should be absorbed in the law of the Shariah.

Undoubtedly, there were remarkable changes in the system of governance. The concept of vicegerancy and trust that was the guiding spirit of the Islamic state disappeared. The delegated authority got converted into personal authority, and then commenced that long drawn series of tyranny and mischief with which every student of history is well acquainted. But how can any one infer from the historical facts that Islam failed them? The historical record is the record of the failure of the Muslims and not that of Islam. How can the objectionable or disgraceful behaviour of any Muslim ruler or a Muslim group be regarded as the failure of Islam? And how does it prove that the measures provided by Islam for the protection of the fundamental rights became ineffective after thirty years?

Every creed, ideology, school of thought, principle or tradition really depends for its efficacy or inefficacy on the firmness of the belief and faith and living upto it. This is the first and foremost condition to bring into play the effects and fruits of any system or ideology. Without fulfilling this basic condition of the firmness of creed and obligation of living upto it, no system or ideological way of life can bear fruit. Truth is admittedly the best principle of life. But can we be benefited by its blessings without taking to truth of speech in practical life. If it is not so, would it be proper to decide in face of the abundance of falsehood and the majority turning away from the truth, that the principle of truth has become ineffective, since it has failed to make itself binding on a large number of people. And would we be justified in advising people to give up truth on the plea that the majority of people do not practise it? Or will those banishing it from their lives be deemed despicable and guilty, and every sensible and conscious person will advise this defaulting majority to give up the apparently very effective falsehood and talking to truth, make it effective?

In fact, it is man's own belief and conscious resolve and effort which give their effectiveness to principles and ideologies. Without this spirit of belief and exercise, every principle and every ideology is no more than a collection of words. The British unwritten constitution is considered as the ideally democratic constitution. But do mere abstract words of the constitution have all the effectiveness and force to make them as practicable, useful if enforced in any Asian or African country as they have proved in Britain? If not, who will be held responsible for failure of the constitution or the nation that made it a failure through its own behaviour.

The failure of a way of life and the failure in giving effect to it are two different things, which should not be mixed up. We can declare any system a failure only when the answer to any one of the following questions is in the affirmative.

1. Has experience proved it defective and useless?
2. Has the advanced knowledge and discernment of man proved wrong the principles presented by it, in the light of intellect and reasoning?
3. Has man discovered better and more practicable principles than these?
4. Has the long journey of history made them outdated and impracticable?
5. Has it become so much deformed and perverted that it is no more possible to sort out the right from the wrong elements?

None of these questions can be answered in the positive where Islam is concerned. Islam in practice has proved itself superior to all other systems of life in the world. Which is that ideological way of life, ancient or modern which has, in comparison to Islam, during the thirty years of its enforcement might have brought about such a magnificent revolution of justice and equality and prosperity and goodness? Islam alone has the distinction of not only remaining in force for thirty years with its true spirit and teachings but attained its ideal form. No other system could be enforced in its ideal form on this earth even for a second. Thirty years is not a brief period for the practical experiment with any ideology. Which of the Islamic principles or regulations were proved wrong during this period of trial? Which are those defects, if at all any, have been discovered? Again, has man really discovered any system superior to it? We have earlier in this book, taking stock of Islam and other systems of life, seen that the utmost that human intellect has been able to present does stand no where in comparison with Islam. There are no valid reasons to declare Islam outdated and impracticable. Historical facts provide ample evidence that whenever Islam was into practice strictly in accordance with the conditions imposed by it, the Muslim society came to enjoy all the blessings of the rightly guided caliphate, and Islam once again appeared in its true form and full glory. The evils that had crept into the political system of Islam after the rightly guided caliphate, have been mentioned earlier. But with all the corruption and perversion about sixty years after the rightly guided caliphate, when 'Umar Abd-ul-Aziz was installed into the seat of authority, and removing all the traces of monarchy, resolved to enforce once again the Islamic order with its original spirit, the entire society was revolutionised.

The Islamic revolution was brought about anew in all its full former glory, and it appeared that the period of the rightly guided caliphate had returned. This proves that Islam had not failed them, but the Muslims, and particularly their rulers had become victims of inaction and negligence in the matter of living upto it. When after sixty years, he made a firm resolve to reform the practice of Islam, and tried it all over again, he found the system just as true, dynamic and fruitful as regards the results, as it had proved during its first trial by the rightly guided caliphate. And after thirteen centuries, when Syed Ahmad Shaheed wanted to enforce it in his short-lived Islamic state in Peshawar it came into action with all its comprehensiveness and perfection, and not one of its principles proved—impracticable.

It is neither the case with Islam that its teachings have become so much perverted that sorting out the sound from the unsound is no more possible. The Quran has been preserved for us without the change of an iota in it. Each and every incident of the life of the Prophet, every deed and word of his have been so carefully preserved of which there is no other example in the world. The period of the rightly guided caliphate history has preserved in its pages like the true image in a mirror. The work done in the field of the Islamic Fiqh (jurisprudence) by the (most capable men of the) Ummah is there in its original form.

Moreover, detailed literature for guidance exists concerning every walk of life and on all the problems of the modern age. Any person wanting to know what are the Islamic teachings on a particular issue, would find difficulty in access to them? The fundamental teachings of Islam and its principles and laws are before us in a very clear and definite form. No part of them has been perverted and none became ambiguous. In other words, the thing known as Islam, has been with us on the highway of history continually for the last fourteen hundred years without any defects. During this long journey Muslims at times remained very close to Islam and at others too far from it. But it was never their sad experience that the Muslims intended to come close to Islam but finding it non-existent or buried in the pages of history. They had failed to do so.

Under these circumstances the objection levelled at Islam that it lasted only thirty years aims at creating misunderstanding and nothing more. The fact is only this much that the Muslims lived up to the dictates of Islam with their heart and soul in it, for thirty years only. Later on their political system got corrupted and corruptions formed in the society. But the question may be asked how did it effect the soundness of Islam. On what basis was it regarded impracticable? Does the presence of certain kings and dictators in the Islamic history prevent us from putting true Islam into practice? Shall we be justified in putting up the excuse that since people like Hajjaji b. Yusuf and Hassan b. Sabab have stood between us and the rightly guided caliphate, it will not be possible to rehearse the order of that period once again? After all, what is the relevance of the activities of the rulers and monarchs in the context of the mutual relations between Islam and the Muslims?

The Muslims never established any relation with them for guidance. The common man among the Muslims does not remember their names even. Their orders and edicts were never considered worth mentioning even or making reference to them in any matter. As against this, even the Muslim children are acquainted with the names of the rightly guided caliphs, the eminent companions, and the four Imams of the most popular schools of jurisprudence, Abu Hanifah, Malik, Shafii, and Ahmad b. Hanbal, as also Imam Bukhari, Ibn-e-Taimiyah, Ghazzali, Shah Wali-Ullah and such other Muslim elite in the religious sphere, since these personages, right from the time of the Prophet, have relevance in the matter of transferring to the Muslims their religious legacy and in maintaining continuity of their attachment to Islam. It was due to them that the Muslims never lost contact with the contemporary world and Islam never evaded contemporary problems. It has been advancing in every age with the times and offering guidance to the Muslims in every age.

Now let us take stock of the objection that the Islamic order lasted only thirty years, from another angle. This objection is applicable to the political system of Islam and that too only partially. But the individual and collective life of the Muslims in general has always been subservient to Islam. The Islamic law has been at work in their moral, social, educational, private, cultural and judicial aspects of life. Their political life, too has not been altogether cut off from Islam. Under the Islamic order the religion and politics never parted ways as they did in the Christian Church and the state in Europe, When the ascendancy of the Church ended in Europe, the state totally banished religion from the collective life and limited it to the individual life.

The legislative powers of the state were no more governed by the religious injunctions and rules and regulations. The philosophy of secularism freed it from the hold of religion on it. As against this, in the entire history of the Muslims before the period of colonialism, there is not one example where a Muslim monarch or any ruler completely suspending the law of the Shariah might have enforced the law framed by himself. The Muslim monarch did violate the law of the Shariah, but consigning it to the care of the mosque and the *Madrasa* (religious bodies and institutions), they never became totally unconcerned with the law of the Shariah. The law of their states was the law of the Shariah, and all the affairs of the life of the people were decided by the courts according to the law. All the Muslim monarchs were not tyrant, oppressor, and given to a life of ease and luxury, voluptuousness and de bauchery. There have been among them many who are famous for their piety, righteousness and austerity. There have been kings like Nasiruddin Mahmood and Aurangzeb who had imposed upon themselves austere piety and never touched the public treasury where their own upkeep was concerned. They prepared caps and made copies of the holy Quran for their own and their families, subsistence.

A majority of them we find just Godfearing and mindful of their people. Their characters bore a deep imprint of Islam. Undoubtedly they were far superior to the contemporary monarchs of the non-Muslim world. Since we judge them on the norm of the rightly guided caliphate, they appear low in our estimate, but compared with the contemporary rulers and their systems of governance with the contemporary systems of governance in the world, their position becomes entirely changed.

These facts amply reveal the truth that the objection levelled at Islam that it lasted only thirty years, is incorrect. It would, however, be correct to say that the Muslim Ummah could not maintain it at the level of the rightly guided caliphate in the sphere of practice. But we would like to repeat our question to these fault-finding people that if a firm resolve is made today to enforce Islam in it pristine purity what is there that stands in our way. Is it the fault of Islam or the evil intentions of those drunk with the lust for power and intoxication of ruling over fellowmen as their god?

Another objection raised in connection with the "failure" of Islam by the orientalists and their camp followers among the Muslims, is this that in the Islamic society of the early period after the Prophet, political, economic, judicial and social institutions could not come into existence or at least could take no definite mould on whose basis a definite structure of the Islamic system of governance could emerge.

The Islamic society according to its structure was a rather advanced type of the tribal society in which the central position of the tribal chief had been taken by the caliph. In this type of personal rule, the reigns of the state were in the hands of an individual who managed all the affairs of the state from his seat of authority in the mosque. He distributed the spoils of war, issued orders and instructions to the governors and the military commanders, received their reports of their performance, dictated replies to their queries, supplied them with the necessary resources, gave a hearing to their complaints, helped the common people in distress, settled their disputes and furnished guidance in matters relating to jurisprudence. Since every body had access to the caliph, they approached him directly with their major and even minor problems.

In this way, the caliph came to have a central position and centralisation of powers instead of decentralisation obstructed the path of the autonomous and semi-autonomous institutions coming into existence. Since the rightly guided caliphs were extremely pious, righteous and selfless and with God-fearing heads of the state, every thing was in its proper place and the affairs of the state ran smoothly. But, when the rulers who were shorn of that selflessness excellence and the magnanimity and purity of character of their predecessors, came into power, this system which had not been based on firmly established institutions rapidly deteriorated and so many evils found their way into it.

This objection is based more on prejudice than on ignorance of facts. And the real motive behind it is this aspiration of the west that all the credit of the concept of human rights, the movement launched for their attainment, and like the philosophy of democracy credit for the political, economic and social institutions should be added to this account alone. Otherwise the fact is that during the period of the rightly guided caliphate, particularly during the period of Umar, the foundations of the Islamic state had been firmly established on well-founded institutions, and during the period of Banu Umayyah and Banu Abbas these institutions became much more expanded and much better organised.

Law is Supreme

After taking stock of the rights in the democratic and socialist countries we shall now see how far have the protections provided for the practical enforcement of the fundamental rights by these countries been effective and have succeeded in protecting the individual against the oppression and tyranny of the State.

In the western system of law and politics, constitution is regarded as the greatest protector of these rights, and the effective form of their practical enforcement suggested is the inclusion of these rights in the constitution and making them enforceable through the judiciary. On the surface it appears very effective and in some Western countries, particularly Britain, America and France, it is in fact so in a big way.

Nearly all the countries of the world act on the constitutional method of rule, and the people regard the most sacred legal document of the constitution as their great source of strength. But when we analyse the constitutions of various countries and study the course of events in these countries, the fact is revealed that the constitution which is considered the greatest protector of the fundamental rights is itself not immune from the usurpatory and plundering action of the government.

Barring America and Britain, whose written and unwritten constitutions we shall discuss later on a look at the constitution of any country of the world, will show that there is a whole chapter of "Constitutional amendments", through which the ruling party with the requisite majority and the appropriate modus operandi gets a free hand in amending the constitution and moulding it according to its own wishes and requirements. In this way these constitutions, which usually get framed by the majority party or under its aegis arm this party with unbridled and unlimited powers to rule in a dictatorial fashion. And usually they see to it that in the early stages of constitution making the firmness and definiteness of the constitution are badly damaged so that what remains is a rickety business. Dorothy Pickles analysing this state of affairs writes:

> Constitutions are made by politicians who are bound by their loyalty to their own party doctrines and attitudes, and sometimes in addition by the requirements of coalition governments.

The basic philosophy of a constitutional government is that the sphere of the powers of the rulers may be delimited and they must be made to abide by it. And if they overstep their well-defined powers, the judiciary should prevent them from doing it. But we find that the practical shape of things is just the opposite. The judiciary which is entrusted with the responsibility of keeping over-bearing rulers in their place, itself comes to work under the constitution framed by these same rulers and politicians and the powers conferred by them. What is, after all, the fountain-head of the powers of the judiciary?

That same constitution in framing which it has had no say, and which is constantly tampered with by the rulers in the form of amendments, and abrogations, pruning and suspension; which serves no other purpose except to nationally limit the powers, which after all they manipulate to suit to their wishes and motives. More so by amending some clauses or by including some others and deleting yet another or by declaring a state of emergency and exercising the powers acquired under it, they suspend the concerned sections and then in case of the enforcement of new laws, effective with retrospective effect, they find a way for every desired move at their own sweet will. The judiciary, whose powers are constantly changing due to frequent amendments and deletions in the constitution, can never stand in the way of the rulers, since the legislature has ascendency over it, and this legislature is overridden by the ruling party by virtue of its brute majority. The Supreme Court of Pakistan, in the case State versus Zia-ur Rahman, elucidating the sphere of the power of the judiciary has remarked in its judgement:

> While it is true that judicial power cannot be taken away, the jurisdiction of the functionaries entrusted with the administration of justice can legitimately be defined by the Constitution. Thus it is for the Constitution to say what jurisdiction the High Court will exercise and what the Supreme Court. Similarly, the Constitution itself may even prescribe that certain categories of classes of cases shall be decided by Tribunals other than the High Court or the Supreme Court. No objection can be taken to this kind of demarcation of functions. Indeed, if such demarcation is not done, there would be chaos, for, no one would know what are the precise limits of their own respective jurisdictions.

Now, it is evident that the determination of these powers is in the hands of the legislators, or in other words, the rulers. Therefore the courts are bound to conduct their business of dispensation of justice with these limited powers, which the rulers are pleased to confer on them. It is the result of this bitter truth that even such measures of the rulers which totally pervert the spirit of the constitution, are regarded as perfectly in keeping with the constitution since they can always find legal justification for amending it, and in this way a step that was prohibited and illegal till yesterday, would become justifiable and legal the next day only because of an amendment in the constitution. No moral principle or any well known code of justice and equity comes in the way of effecting such changes. The court is simply bound by the codified law and not by any moral code. So we find that the Supreme Court while pronouncing its verdict in the case of Brigadier (retd.) F.B.Ali and Colonel (retd.) Abdul Aleem Afridi, has written:

> It is first sought to be contended that the Ordinances were not law at all, because, they purported to unreasonably deprive a citizen of even the norms of a judicial trial. But this generalisation cannot be accepted. Law has not been defined in the Constitution of 1962 and, therefore, in its generally accepted connotation, it means positive law, that is to say, a formal pronouncement of the will of a competent law-giver. There is no such condition that a law must, in order to qualify as a law, also be based on reason or morality. The Courts cannot strike down a law on any such higher ethical notion nor can Courts act on the basis of philosophical concept of law as pointed by me in the case of Asma Jilani.

In the circumstances, I too find myself unable to say that the impugned Ordinances are not law, and, therefore, violative of Fundamental Right No. I.

Now, where the codified law enjoys such supremacy, and the law itself is the formal declaration of the Law-givers, will and 'pleasure, the courts can provide the citizen with only that much of protection as has been permitted to them by the limits of the powers approved by the constitution in force for the time being and the ordinance issued by the rulers. How shall these laws be deemed legal or illegal? Expounding this point; the Chief Justice of the Supreme Court, Justice Hamid-ur-Rahman says in the case of Asma Jilani.

So far as a Judge is concerned, a definition is necessary, all that he has to see is that the law which he is called upon to administer is made by a person or authority legally competent to make laws and the law is capable of being enforced by the legal machinery. This, in my view, brings in the notion both of legitimacy and efficacy.

The supremacy of the rulers in the matter of framing the constitution or in sphere of the legislation, and the determination of the powers and jurisdiction of the judiciary also being in their hands, makes it clear how helpless in fact the judiciary is before the framers of the constitution and law. The raw deal received by the provisions of the constitution relating to the fundamental rights in Bangaldesh, India and Pakistan in the later half of 1975 is clear proof of the helplessness of the judiciary in the matter of protecting these rights. In Bangaldesh, Mujib established the dictatorship of a single party, put a ban on other opposition parties and incarcerated their leaders, gagged the press, made the legislative assembly a non-entity and by depriving the judiciary of the powers of enforcing the fundamental rights, made it wholly ineffective, but all this was held as perfectly constitutional. In India, when Mrs. Indira Gandhi, in order to save herself from the penalty of winning the election through malpractices, tried to render ineffective the decision of the court against her, the majority of the ruling party in the parliament amended the constitution and thus provided her protection.

The powers of the judiciary were curtailed, the opposition parties were banned, Indira's opponent in the elections Raj Narain, who had won the case against her in the High Court and his supporters in the political field were all put behind the bars, declaring a state of emergency all the fundamental rights were held suspended and the newspapers raising voice against all this were throttled to death. When all this was over, Indira's advocate, Mr.A.K. Sen stood in the highest court of the country, but shorn of powers, and said:

> "The concept of free and fair elections is notional and it cannot be treated as a basic feature of the constitution. The courts are not competent to sit in judgement whether the elections were conducted fairly and in a free atmosphere or not.

And this entire game, too, was played under the constitution and the powers conferred by it. Therefore the supreme court, which was bound by the amended constitution for its decisions had to exhonerate Mrs. Gandhi of all the malpractices the High Court had held her guilty of and penalised under the unamended constitution.

In our own country, Pakistan, where the fourth constitution is now in force, simultaneously with its enforcement, the fundamental rights were suspended under a state of emergency. Later on, through an ordinance and by means of the fourth and fifth amendments they were curtailed. As the declaration of the state of emergency, issue promulgation of ordinance and the series of amendments in the constitution were also under the powers conferred by the constitution, all this was regarded as constitutional. And by virtue of this constitutionality the rulers cannot be charged with the commission of any offence by the law court.

The same state of affairs exists in other countries of Asia, Africa and South America where the constitution, instead of acting as the protector of fundamental rights, has become the protector of the dictatorial authority of the rulers, supporter of their tyrannical measures and a means of unlimited powers for them. Commenting on this state of affairs CD. Kernig says:

> In the 20th century, however, the representatives of the people have themselves often proved to be unreliable where the safeguarding of fundamental rights was concerned. Not infrequently majorities have modified the fundamental rights laid down in the constitutions, and with them often the entire constitution itself.

Every constitution in the world along with giving a free hand to the rulers to amend the constitution, under a "state of emergency" confers such powers on them in a state of emergency which enables them to do away with what little remains of the fundamental rights. And then for a state of emergency the existence of objective conditions is not necessary. The rulers can declare it at their discretion whenever they feel like doing so. And immediately after such declaration, the constitution frees them of all the limits imposed by it under normal condition. They can impose martial law under the constitution, can deprive the judiciary of all its powers and the people of all their fundamental rights. Neither the constitution nor the law of the land can stop them from doing such things.

In addition to these shortcomings of the constitution and its helplessness before the rulers, there is the problem of its very existence and survival which is a much more complicated one. It is a commonplace phenomenon, and we have a very bitter experience of it here in Pakistan, that the change of government, internal revolutions, rebellion of the army, external aggression, and the irreconciliable differences between the political parties, all give the constitution the sack.

With every outgoing ruling party or person the constitution enforced by it also departs, and every newcomer appears on the stage of power with the draft of a new constitution, and the powers of political authority which he wields, confer the same legal position on this new constitution, which in its predecessor's time was occupied by the earlier constitution In the Asma Jilani case, referring to the international law the learned Chief Justice of the Supreme Court observed:

> According to the international law a victorious revolution or a successful coup detat is an internationally recognised legal method of changing a Constitution.

Factual evidence and this elucidation of international Law can give us an idea how frail, uncertain and unstable the legal document called the constitution is, notwithstanding it distinguished position of supremacy. When its own existence is not guaranteed, how much trust can be reposed in it for the protection of the fundamental rights, which are part and parcel of it? How can the constitution, which is itself constantly mutatory, become a protector of immutable and inalienable human rights?

This also makes it evident that the claim of the inalienability of the fundamental rights is not correct. The only means of determining and enforcing these rights is the constitution. Without constitution these rights have no legal basis left for their existence. And the constitution is a puppet whose strings are in the hands of the government.

At times it is amended at others something is added to it, at yet other times some portions of it are curtailed or suspended and so often it departs alongwith the outgoing rulers. Under these changing conditions, the fundamental rights at times find a place in the constitution, at others they get abridged, at yet other times they are suspended and now and then alongwith the abrogated constitution they themselves get eliminated. If the inhabitants of a country are lucky in having them intact, the traps of the varying interpretations given to them make them ineffective. In principle they are much above that common law, but their enforcement is always "in keeping with the law", and within the limits of the constitution the are made lawful with the addition of prefixes and suffixes like 'if, but', 'provided', 'unless' etc. And this law is put into practice according to the will of the rulers, C. D. Kernig writes in this context:

> That fundamental rights are rooted in the texts of modern constitutions and yet have always been subject to interpretation "according to law" (although in essence they are considered to be inviolable).

It is the result of this accord with the law that the fundamental rights regarded as inalienable and inviolable can be suspended merely by enforcing section 144 of the criminal procedure code by a Deputy Commissioner (or Collector) of a district and the constitution is unable to come to the rescue of the affected citizens.

This helplessness and inconsistency of the constitution clearly indicates that it is not a reliable protector of the fundamental rights. Nor is there any ground to regard these fundamental rights as inviolable on the basis of guarantees provided in the constitution.

After this general survey of the position regarding the enforcement of the constitution in the world, let us now have a look at the British and American constitutions also, which are deemed the best model of democracy, and at the first sight the form of their enforcement also appears fairly satisfactory.

In Britain no written constitution exists at all. Therefore these fundamental rights there are not guaranteed constitutionally. The British parliament is a sovereign body. Its legislative powers suffer no limitations whatsoever. No court in England can strike down the laws enacted by the British parliament, nor can it stop their enforcement. There, the fundamental rights are protected by the common law of the land, and for their enforcement one has to go only to the common law courts. But in spite of having no written constitution, in the matter of fundamental rights, the British citizens are much better placed than the citizens of other countries of the world. That is why Jennings says with great pride:

> In Britain we have no Bill of Rights; we merely have liberty according to law: and we think—truly, I believe—that we do the job better than any country which has a Bill of Rights or a Declaration of the Rights of Man.

But this satisfaction is gradually declining, and the legal experts in Britain are stressing the need of a written constitution for the protection of fundamental rights. Thomas Paine was the first person to realise this need, who had written in a very sarcastic manner, in 1971, in his book *Human Rights*:

> The boasted English constitution is a fraud: it does not really exist at all:
>
> One member says this is constitution, and another says that is constitution, it is one thing, tomorrow it is something else while maintaining the debate proves there is none.

A prestigious British journal *The Economist* in its issue of November 8, 1975 had written in its latest survey report on fundamental rights:

> Twenty years earlier, the assertion that "Britain had the best position in regard to the fundamental rights", appeared very strong. The supporters of this claim can bring in their support to the argument that during the passage of the reformative bills on abortion, divorce and racial discrimination, the parliament has established a commendable record in the matter of its regard for the civic rights. But now the conservatives will put forth the examples of delimiting the rights of property and restrictions on membership of the unions. And the supporters of the labour party in the same vein shall out forth the law of the migrants passed by the conservatives with retrospective effect and the restrictions imposed by their Industrial Relations Act on the right to strike work.

"Moreover, there are some other aspects in which the law of land is opposed to the general principles of the international law rather the European convention for the Human Rights. One such example is the power of preventive detention of the suspected people under the law of Prevention of Terrorism. This law has been passed by the parliament in November 1947.

According to this report the liberal member of the parliament Alien Beith introduced a bill in the parliament to invite attention to the distressing fact that the document of European Convention for Human Rights which Britain had signed twenty years ago, had not till then been brought on Britain's statute book.

A protracted struggle between the parliament and the king in Britain has resulted in the king getting divested of all powers and being replaced by the parliament as a dictatorial body since there are no limits of any sort on its powers of legislation, whereas the constitution's only purpose is to keep the rulers's powers within proper limits. And today this aspect is the cause of greatest anxiety. *The Economist*, analysing the problem of the fundamental rights in Britain writes: "A law relating to rights can be passed and for its protection a constitutional Court can also be established with powers to declare certain law against the fundamental rights, but the real difficulty is that if in spite of these powers of the court, the parliament enacts a law that is unconstitutional, what can the helpless court do to remedy the ill. Can it enforce its verdict against the parliament? At the most it can declare a certain law unconstitutional. But to kill the powerful giant of the strong tradition of the parliament's supremacy is not so easy". The analyst arrives finally at the following conclusion: (p. 25)

A satisfactory Bill of Rights depends on the change in the political system and particularly the system of holding elections, the effects of the rival partisanship arising from this system and the effects on the mutual relations between the government and the Parliament. In other words before any Bill of Rights a constitutional document will be needed. (p. 25)

Throwing light on the general trend of the public opinion, this report tells us that in the decade beginning from 1970, the campaign for the demand of the Fundamental Rights has been gathering momentum and from 1974 onward, it has become intensive. The Ministry of Interior is now having consultations with other government departments whether such a law is going to be practicable and will receive general appreciation. Since Britain is regarded as the cradle of democracy, and most countries of the world including Pakistan, where parliamentary system of government is in vogue, follow the British pattern. Therefore, it will be in the fitness of things that we have a look at the opinions of those demanding the Bill of Rights, so that we may have an idea of what the Britishers themselves think of their Constitution.

The well-known legal expert, D.W. Hanson commenting on the supremacy of the Parliament with reference to the greatest charter of human rights, the "Magna Carta", says:

> From a legal point of view, the most important event is this that the Barons did not allow their antagonistic political role to follow the path of the principle of the common law. As against this they adopted a course, as a result of which, a political compromise was arrived at between the Lords and the common members of the Parliament. That is why to solve the problem of Double Majesty, which had arisen powerfully in the seventeenth century, instead of the supremacy of the law, the idea of the supremacy of the Parliament was adopted. This supremacy of the parliament has deprived the fundamental rights of the protection of the constitution and has left them entirely at the mercy of conventions.

The well known legal expert, a former judge and dean of the Faculty of Law in Birmingham University, Professor Hood Phillips, writes:

> "The British constitution contains 'Fundamental' rights in the strict sense. The principles relating to individual's liberty can be altered by ordinary act of Parliament, and there is no legal limit to the extent to which Parliament can abridge or abolish rights which in many constitutions are regarded as fundamental".

In this connection, citing the examples of the performances of the parliament, he tells us that the parliament passing the Defence of the Realm Act, during the first world war and during the second world war the Emergency powers Defence Act, conferred on the government such extensive powers encompassing all aspects of the national defence and economy which are unparalleled in the history of parliaments. Later, in 1940, another act was passed which passed through all the stages of discussions and readings in the Houses and the royal sanction in just one day. Through this act the citizens were bound to surrender their lives, properties and services to His Majesty. In 1920 under conditions of peace, to arm the government with the emergency powers, an Act was brought into existence under which civic liberties could be suspended by declaring a state of emergency during internal turmoil and chaotic conditions. This law has been pressed into service several times in cases of strikes by the labour at the ports and the employees of transport department and power houses. Professor Phillips explaining the real cause of insistence on the supremacy of parliament and denial of a written constitution to the nation, says:

> It has invited the leaders of both sides in the political 'game' giving inordinate power to the Prime Minister of the day, which will be inherited by the leader of the opposition in due course, while the general public are apathetic or unaware.

After taking stock of the British constitution in detail, he arrives at the following conclusion:

> A written Constitution with judicial review is desirable for this country. We have seen that there are no legal limits to what Parliament can do by ordinary legislation, that the Government virtually controls the activities of Parliament, that the maximum "duration of a Parliament is too long, that the existence of a (reformed) Second Chamber with some power of rejection or delay is essential, that important areas of law and practice are uncertain, that the Parliament Act 1949 is of doubtful force, that too much power is concentrated in the hands of the Prime Minister, that the dissolution of Parliament needs to be regulated, that the law relating to judicial tenure should be improved, and that there is a call for a new Bill of Rights

A judge of Britain, Sir Leslie Scarman, exposing the respect for the fundamental rights, observes:

> Do you think that the deeply disturbing practices of interrogation to which rest was had in Northern Ireland would have occurred had Birtish law possessed at the time fully developed code of human rights.

Making a demand for the Bill of Rights he says:

> If human rights are to be protected in a manner consistent with our international obligations, some means other than the common law must be found. Legally at the mercy of a legislature, which is itself, save in a minority situation, at the mercy of the executive, is no sure guarantee of human right.

Without a Bill of Right protected from repeals, amendment or suspension by the ordinary process of a bare Parliamentary majority controlled by the government of the day, human rights will be at risk.

J.J.Craik Henderson, exposing the sovereignty of the parliament says:

> Perhaps instead of referring to a supreme Parliament it might be more correct to say that the Cabinet is supreme in the exercise of Executive power and of law making through its control of the majority Party in the House of Commons.

Expressing his dissatisfaction over the present protections in connection with the fundamental rights, he goes on to say:

> If one could be sure that Ministers could be relied on to observe the niceties and conventions of the constitution and always to act wisely, then a strong Executive and

a flexible constitution giving all power to the Cabinet would be best, but unfortunately nobody can be sure of this and accordingly some safeguards ought to be provided.

The campaign now going on in Britain for the constitutional safeguards to the fundamental rights. Professor Charles' Howard MacIlwain of the Harward University, had foretold in 1947. He says:

> As the restraining influence of tradition grows weaker, the danger of a tyranny of the majority comes nearer and the time may arrive when convention must give way to law if the rights of minorities are to be respected and safeguarded as they have been in the past. A popular despotism must result if the omnipotence of parliament ever becomes in practice what it now is in law.

And today the Britons are witnessing emergence of that dictatorship. And it is for this reason that they are carrying on a campaign for a written constitution and a Bill of Rights so that dictatorship may be checked and it may be brought and kept under the judiciary. It is really strange, but a fact, that not only in Britain, but even in its colonies like Canada, New Zealand and Australia no where the fundamental rights have constitutional safeguards.

In Canada a Bill of Rights was passed in 1960, but it does not restrict the parliament's power of legislation. It has been made clear in it that even if a law is in contravention of it, the courts cannot stop its enforcement. Justice Borar Laskin of Canada, has elucidated it, in the following words:

> "The Bill of Rights is only meant for the guidance of the Ministry of Law so that it may be before it when it comes to legislation".

Its main importance may lie in the direction to the Minister of Justice to examine all proposed legislations for consistency with the purposes and provisions of the Bill of Rights and to report any inconsistency to the House of Commons.

The Canadian Prime Minister, Lester Pearson tried, to have the Bill of Rights incorporated in the constitution but failed. Prime Minister, Trudeau somehow got it passed in 1969, but its status remained the same as in 1960. In 1963, the Prime Minister of New Zealand, J.R. Hanan tried to get the Bill of Rights passed but the parliament rejected it. More or less the same is the situation in Australia. The citizens of Britain and its colonies are at the mercy of the parliament in respect of the fundamental rights. Their only support lies in the respect for traditions and customs. Undoubtedly the roots of respect for these traditions are deep enough and no government dare deny them. But due to the ascendency of the parliament and helplessness of the judiciary there is no firm guarantee of constitutional protection of the fundamental rights. According to Justice William O. Douglas of the Supreme Court of America:

> "British constitution is really the tradition of 'self-control' practised by the members of parliament and the British rulers.

But the judges, legal experts and citizens of Britain do not believe in this tradition of self control alone as the reliable protector of the fundamental rights, since this tradition cannot stand in the way of the suspension, abrogation and curtailment of these rights. The parliament can put an end to them whenever it is pleased to do so, and there can be no appeal against its action.

After Britain, let us have a look at the American constitution. It is regarded as the ideal democratic constitution in as much as it entrusts the judiciary with the task of protecting the fundamental rights, and it enjoys supremacy over the legislature. It can strike down the laws framed by the Congress if it finds them contrary to the Constitution and can stop their enforcement. But notwithstanding the supremacy of the judiciary, in the event of internal turmoil, upsurge or external aggression, the executive and the Congress acquire unlimited powers. Under Article I, Section 9 and Clause 2, martial law can be clamped on the country, the fundamental rights can be suspended and the courts shorn of the powers of entertaining writ petitions.

Explaining this clause Willoughby writes:

> In time of war, or of domestic insurrection or disorder when so called martial law has been declared the privilege of the writ of habeas corpus, together with all the other civil guarantees may for the time being, be suspended.

In 1954 the Congress passed the Immunity Act under which under certain conditions any body could be deprived of the right of not being compelled to bear witness against himself, which has been unconditionally recognised in the fifth amendment of the Constitution. In the same year in spite of the freedoms of assembly, and forming organisations, guaranteed by the constitution, the communist party was banned and the supremacy of the judiciary could not help by declaring the step unconstitutional and getting the ban on the party lifted.Professor Macllwain commenting on the protection of the fundamental rights in the American constitution says:

> There is a constant threat to all the rights of personality we hold dearest—such rights as freedom of thought and expression and immunity for accused persons from arbitrary detention and from cruel and abusive treatment. These have always been endangered when -reasons of state have been thought to require it. At times it seems to me that just now we are in special danger of forgetting these rights and these dangers.

These facts amply reveal that the fundamental rights are not wholly inviolable even in America and Britain. As for the real reasons behind the somewhat seemingly satisfactory conditions in Britain and America, Dorothy Pickles says:

> The only ultimate safeguard of constitutionality would seem to be the practice of it over a long period of time, and circumstances do not always permit this. Invasion, defeat in war, deep-seated and irreconciliable political division within a country-these can make the normal development of constitutional government very difficult, and even impossible. The United State and Great Britain have both been fortunate in

> that they have enjoyed long periods of comparative invulnerability from external aggression and have been relatively free from the internal instability.

This would mean that the protection of fundamental rights in America depends much more on the favourable conditions prevalent in these countries than on the strength of their constitutions and traditions. If these conditions change and these counties too are exposed to foreign aggression or internal disturbances, their constitutions and traditions would not be able to help their citizens. The strength of the constitutions of these countries is based on the peculiar conditions prevailing there and the continuity of their history. Therefore the countries that borrowed from their constitutions overlooking their historical background, instead of coming by any advantages or blessings got involved in difficulties. Confessing it Lord Amery says:

> The rise of dictatorships and of one party government has been the almost inevitable consequence of the ineffectiveness of constitutions which reproduced the outward force of the British Constitution without that spirit of strong and stable government which is of its essence.

Burke, in a letter of his to a member of French Assembly, advising him to abstain from imitating the British constitution, writes:

> When I praised the British Constitution and wished it to be well studied, I did not mean that its exterior form and positive arrangement should become a model for you or for any people servilely to copy.

From this discussion we arrive at the conclusion that the British and American constitutions too do not guarantee the irrevocability of the fundamental rights. And even if the people of these countries are being benefited by their constitutions, it is limited to them alone. If any other country tries them, the result will soon be apparent in the form of dictatorship.

About the socialist countries we have already said that barring "economic rights" there are no other rights in existence there. And the other rights that have been mentioned in the constitution are not realizable through the judiciary. That is why there is no problem of the protection of the fundamental rights there in any form. A socialist state itself decides all the rights, and also prescribes the limits of their enforcement. It is, so to say, all in all—(to quote a Persian saying, the cup, the cup maker and the clay of the cup, all rolled into one,) —beyond that (the party) there is neither any right nor any authority to enforce a right. This examination of the constitution of the democratic and socialist countries reveals the fact that the constitution itself provides no certain guarantee of the protection of the fundamental rights. Our own observation and experience bear testimony to the fact that we cannot rely on just the document of the constitution for the determination and practical enforcement of the fundamental rights. The greatest fault of these constitutions is that there is no sanction power behind them that can compel the rulers to abide by the limitation placed in the exercise of their powers and which may thus provide eternal protection to the fundamental rights.

10

Personal Freedom

Theory of the Universe

Social foundation of Islamic justice does not treat the matter as a question of pure theory, nor as a counsel of perfection. For by its own nature, Islam is a faith of achievement, of work in the sphere of practical life; it is not a religion of mere words, or idle theory existing only in a world of shadows.

As we have already seen, Islam has a basic theory of the universe, of life, and of man. We have seen also that the thought of 'social justice' has its roots in that basic theory, and enters into its general scheme. We have discovered that the nature of Islamic belief about human life makes social justice essentially an all-embracing justice which does not take account merely of material and economic factors.

Islam does not divide the individual into body and soul, into differing intellectual and spiritual sides. It holds that the values of this life are material and spiritual at one and the same time, and that no division is possible in such a unity. It holds also that mankind is essentially one body, its members mutually responsible and interdependent, a body in which there are no isolated and outcast societies.

Many times, it has seemed that the reality of history falsifies this fundamental Islamic theory. So first we must discover what is this reality of history. The reality which Islam regards as ultimately true is not the state of affairs of any one individual, or in any group or nation; rather it is that limited, definite, and fixed reality on which the faculties of frail human individuals are set, when they turn away from the pursuit of immense and fix their thoughts on the larger and more comprehensive things in human life, the things which endure from eternity to eternity. For Islam scans all standards, and reckons with all kinds of interests; its aim is the achievement of a purpose which includes all humanity from beginning to end.

It may appear to be an inconsistency when we take the comprehensive view, which embraces all men, rather than merely one individual, one group, or one nation. The comprehensive view of social justice with its far reaching aims will serve later on to explain the regulations which Islam lays down. These cannot be correctly understood when they are taken individually; nor when they are understood only of the individual in relation to society, of society only in relation to the group; nor when they are understood only of the group in relation to the nation, or of the nation only in relation to other nations.

This comprehensive view will serve to explain the regulations on individual possession, on the poor-tax, on the law of inheritance, on the rules for estates, on politics, in commercial transaction, in a word, it will explain all the regulations prescribed by Islam for individuals, societies, nations, and races. At this point, we have no intention of dealing with all this; we shall, then content ourselves to deal with the general foundations on which Islam established its regulations for social justice, within the limits of its universal theory. And from the nature of these we will see that Islam believes in the unity of body and soul in the individual, and in the unity of the spiritual and the material in life.

Similarly, it believes in an identity of aim in the individual and in society, in the identity of interests of the various societies within a race, and in an identity of purpose among all the races of mankind. And this despite the apparent divergence of their more immediate and limited interests. The following are the foundations on which Islam establishes justice:

1. Absolute freedom of conscience.
2. The complete equality of all men.
3. The permanent mutual responsibility of society. With each of these foundations we shall deal in turn, explaining its nature and its objective.

Freedom of the Individual

Complete social justice cannot be assured, nor can its efficiency and permanence be guaranteed, unless it arises from an inner conviction of the spirit. It must be claimed by the individual, it must be needed by society. There must be a belief that it will serve the highest purposes of mankind. It must arise also from some material circumstances which prompts the individual to demand justice, as being required by the situation, yet unobtainable. No man can claim justice by law unless he first claimed it by instinct and by the practical methods which accompany instinct. Similarly., society will not proceed with such legislation, even when it is started, unless there is a belief which demands it from within, and practical threats which demand it from without. It is these facts which Islam has in mind in all its ordinances and laws.

It is the Christian view that freedom of conscience is one of the luxuries of life; and that to turn towards the Lord's Kingdom of Heaven and to spurn the life of this world is true way of guaranteeing to man his freedom and to the soul its happiness. Now this is true; but it is not the whole truth. The needs of life are not paramount under all circumstances, nor do material necessities always outweigh man's final destiny; but at most times man must submit to their demands.

So to ignore the material needs of life, or to refuse them, is not always the better way. It was Allah who created life, and He did not create it for man, to neglect it and to check its growth. Certainly it is desirable that man should rise superior to material needs and above his bodily appetites. But it is not desirable that because of these aims he should neglect life altogether.

That is one way to achieve the realisation of the powers latent in human nature together with the elevation of that nature above submission to the demands of material necessity; it is even the soundest and the safest way. But what Islam aims to do is this—to integrate the needs of the body and the desires of the spirit in one unity, and to satisfy by a freedom of conscience the inner instinct which is borne of practical reality. So, it is not unmindful of either side of the question.

On the other hand, the communist view is that economic freedom alone satisfies the need for freedom of conscience, and that it is purely economic pressure on the individual which prompts him to overstep his legal rights of justice and equality. This too is true; but it is not the whole truth. For economic freedom of itself has no guarantee of permanence in society, unless there is also freedom of conscience within the mind. For alone it produces only another from of tyranny—the repression of individual gifts and abilities and inclinations; and these are things which cannot be satisfactorily dealt with by legal methods alone.

It produces also a repression of the individual, inasmuch as his natural abilities are unable to find an outlet and have no opportunity of growing in competition with others. Thus, inevitably the individual is cheated in his desire for that equity which the law has promised him, because he has the inner conviction that he is getting less than he deserves. And similarly on the other hand, laziness and pride are encouraged.

The man who has the greatest abilities and who can produce the most will always overcome the law of absolute equality. If he cannot do that, he will hate and resent it; in which case, either he will rebel, or the divine spark will be extinguished, his abilities will atrophy, and his power of production will be lessened.

But where equality has its roots in a profound freedom of the conscience as well as in civil and religious law, and if the instinct for it is powerful among the strong and the weak alike, then it will be accepted as a rise in status for the weak, and for the strong, a fall. It will answer the need of the soul for a belief in Allah, and in the unity and mutual responsibility of the community.

It will inculcate a belief in the unity of human nature and its attributes. Such is the aim of Islam when it grants complete and absolute freedom to the human conscience; but at the same time it stipulates that first the needs of the body and the material necessities of life must be guaranteed alike by the authority of the law and by the authority of the conscience.

Worship of One Allah

Islam began by freeing the human conscience from servitude to any one except Allah and from submission to any save Him. There is no supreme authority anywhere except in Allah, nor can any other have power for evil or good. None save He can supply provision of anything on Earth or Heaven, nor can there be any mediator or intermediary between man and Him. Allah is the only possessor of power, and all others are but underlings, without control either over themselves or over others.

> "Say; He is Allah the One, Allah the Undivided. He brought not forth, nor was He brought forth, there has never been any equal to Him".

Since, Allah is One, His worship is also one, and to Him alone must all men turn. There is no object of worship except Allah, nor can men take one another as Lords apart from Him. No man among them can excel any other except by Allah's doing and through His grace.

> "Say, O people of the Book, come to a word which is fair between us and you; namely that we worship none but Allah, that we associate nothing with Him, and that we do not take one another as Lords apart from Allah.

Islam has an intense interest in this belief, and the Quran emphasises it in various passages. The Prophets in their day imagined that their people would turn to them with some sort of worship, or with a reverence of some kind or another; but Islam strove to free the human conscience completely from this belief. So, Allah says of His Messenger, Muhammad:

> "And Muhammad is only a messenger; messengers have passed away before him. So, if he dies or if he is killed, will you then turn back upon your heels?"

And He addresses the Prophet himself with a great sincerity, saying:

> "Thou hast nothing to do with this matter, either He may relent towards them, or He may punish them".

In the same way, he addresses to Muhammad in another place something like a threat:

"If we had not made thee stand firm, thou hast almost leaned towards them a little. In that case We would have made thee, taste the double of life and the double of death; then thou couldst not have found a helper against Us". So too He commands him to proclaim openly his true position:

> "Say, I call only upon my Lord, and with Him I associate nothing, Say: Verily I wield no power over you, either to harm you or to set you right. Say: No one can protect me from Allah, nor can I find a shelter from Him".

And He speaks of those who deify Jesus, the son of Mary, charging them with unbelief and folly:

> "They are unbelievers who say that Allah is the Messiah, the son of Mary. Say: Who, then, will control Allah in the least if He wishes to destroy the Messiah, the son of Mary, together with his mother and all those who are on the Earth". Or in another passage He says of the Messiah:
>
> "He is only a servant whom we have favoured, and whom We have made a parable for the Children of Israel".

He takes him as one of the witnesses of the Resurrection, and in the Quran, Jesus the son of Mary, himself answers the assertion which some people make about his divine nature; he establishes his own innocence of this assertion in which he had no part, answering it in a strong, forceful, and impressive manner. When Allah said:

> "O Jesus! Son of Mary, was it thou who didst say to the people, Take me and my mother as Gods apart from Allah. He replied:
>
> "Glory be to Thee, it is for me to say what to me is not the truth. If I did say it, then You knowest it. Thou knowest what is within me, but I know not what is within Thee. Verily, Thou art He who knoweth secret things. I said nothing to them save what Thou didst command me; Serve Allah, my Lord and your Lord. I was a witness to them as long as I was among them; but when Thou didst take me away, then Thou Thyself was a watcher over them. Thou art a witness over all things. If thou dost punish them they are The servants; if Thou dost forgive them—Thou art the Glorious, the Wise."

And other passages are similar. The Quran places insistent emphasis on this belief, on its proof and on its clarity, in order to ensure freedom of the human conscience from any form of association with Allah as regards His divinity and His holiness. For such association would oppress the conscience, and would make it worship some created thing among the servants of Allah.

Jesus and Allah

If Jesus was a prophet or a messenger, he was still only one of His servants. And if it is held that he was not a servant in His, then all mediation between Allah and His servants is denied; there can be no priesthood and no mediator.

So, every individual can make his own practical relationship with his creator and can strengthen his own weak and frail nature with the power which is from eternity to eternity. So he can draw from that power, strength, glory and courage, can know His mercy and care and sympathy, can strengthen his faith and empower his spirit.

Islam insists most strongly upon the reality of this experience, and upon the individual realizing that he has the ability to call upon that great Power day and night.

> "Allah is gentle with His servants".
>
> "And when My servants ask thee about Me, verily, I am near to answer the prayer of him who prays, when he prays to Me. So, let them ask an answer from Me, let them believe in Me, and perhaps they may be guided all right".
>
> "And despair not of the comfort of Allah; verily, none despair of the comfort of Allah except the unbelieving people".
>
> "Say: O My servants who have squandered your own resources, do not despair of the mercy of Allah; verily Allah forgives all faults".

Islam has prescribed five times of prayer, in which every day the worshipper stands before this Lord in which the creature draws near to his Creator. These are at stated times, and not merely when it occurs to anyone to stand before his God, and to draw near in adoration and prayer. The purpose of these prayers is not only words or movements; rather their aim is to direct the whole man, heart, mind, and body at the same time, towards Allah. This is in line with general theory of Islam on the unity of human nature in its creatureliness, and of the unity of the Creator in His divinity.

> "So woe to those who pray, and of their prayers are careless".

When the conscience is freed from the instinct of servitude to and worship of any of the servants of Allah; when it is filled with the knowledge that it can of itself gain complete access to Allah; then it cannot be disturbed by any feeling of fear of its livelihood or fear for its station. This fear is an ignoble instinct which lowers the individual's estimation of himself, which often makes him accept submission, or abdicate much of his natural honour of many of his rights.

But Islam insists strongly that glory and honour are the rights of man, and that to be proud of his rights and to persevere in the search for justice is deep-seated in the human soul. By reason of all this—over and above its religious law—it insists on the guarantee of an absolute social justice, under which man shall not suffer from neglect.

Therefore, it is particularly anxious to oppose the instinct of fear, whether of life or of livelihood, or of station. For life is in the hand of Allah, and no creature has the power to shorten that life by one hour or by one minute. No creature has the right to cut off from life one single soul, nor has any creature the right to inflict the slightest mark or the least injury on any single living being.

> "But it is not given to any soul to die, except by the permission of Allah, a permission written and dated". "Say: Nothing will come upon us save what Allah has prescribed for us; He is our Master". "Each community has its appointed time, and when their time comes they will not be an hour behind, nor will they go before their time".

In which case there can be no cowardice and no cowards; for life and destiny, good and evil are in the hand of Allah, and of no other.

> "Say: Shall I choose as a patron any other than Allah, the Maker of Heaven and Earth? He, it is who giveth food, and who needeth not to be fed".
>
> "Allah maketh wide provisions for whom He will, or He is sparing". "And how may beasts do not carry their own provision. Allah maketh provision for them and for you".
>
> "Say: Who giveth you your provision from Heaven and Earth? Or who hath power over hearing and sight? Who bringeth forth the living from the dead, and bringeth forth the dead from the living? And who settleth the affair in order? They will say, Allah".
>
> "O ye people, remember the favour of Allah towards you. Is there any Creator save Allah, who giveth you from Heaven and Earth your provision? There is no god save He how, then, are ye kept from him?"
>
> "And do not kill your children because of poverty; We shall provide for you and for them".
>
> "And if you fear poverty; Allah will enrich you from His bounty if He wills".

The Quran lays it down that the fear of poverty is inspired only by the Evil One, in order to weaken and impede the soul in its trust in Allah and in its own nature.

> "The Evil One promises you only poverty, and bids you to indecency; but Allah promises you pardon from Himself, and bounty; Allah is bountiful, wise".

In that case, there is no reason for any man to be oppressed by anxiety about his livelihood, for his provision is in the hand of Allah, and in His hand alone; and not one of His created servants has the power to cut off any man's provision, or to withhold from him any part of that provision.

This belief certainly does not rule out trade and commerce, but it does strengthen the human heart and empower the human conscience. It sets the poor man who is anxious over his livelihood on a level with the man who thinks that his provision is in his own hand, to be won with all his own strength and resource.

The instinct of fear does not then keep the poor man from seeking what is his due, or from taking pride in himself, it means that does not have to give up any of his rights or compromise his honour in order to ensure his provision. This is the meaning of the Quranic teaching, as it is the objective of Islam; this is the true application of the general Islamic philosophy in hortatory and legal form.

Fear for one's position or station in life often runs back to the fear of death or injury, or to the fear of poverty or destitution; and Islam is insistent that the individual be freed from this fear also, for no creature can have any power over another creature in this matter,

> "Say O Allah, wielder of the kingly power, thou givest that power to whom Thou wiliest. Thou wilt; in Thy hand is the good. Verily, Thou over all things art powerful".
>
> "Allah hath not chosen any son, nor is there any Gog along with Him; else would each God have assuredly championed that which is created, some of them would assuredly have overcome others. Glorified be Allah above that they allege".
>
> "Say: In whose hand the rule over all things? Who giveth protection and seeketh none? If you have any knowledge, you will say: when Allah help you, then none can defeat you; but if He abandon you, then who will help you after Him?"

The Quran lays it down that the fear of poverty is inspired only by the Evil One, in order to weaken and impede the soul in its trust in Allah and in its own nature.

> "The Evil One promises you only poverty, and bids you to indecency; but Allah promises you pardon from Himself, and bounty; Allah is bountiful, wise".

In that case, there is no reason for any man to be oppressed by anxiety about his livelihood, for his provision is in the hand of Allah, and in His hand alone; and not one of His created servants has the power to cut off any man's provision, or to withhold from him any part of that provision. This belief certainly does not rule out trade and commerce, but it does strengthen the human heart and empower the human conscience. It sets the poor man who is anxious over his livelihood on a level with the man who thinks that his provision is in his own hand, to be won with all his own strength and resource.

The instinct of fear does not then keep the poor man from seeking what is his due, or from taking pride in himself, it means that does not have to give up any of his rights or compromise his honour in order to ensure his provision. This is the meaning of the Quranic teaching, as it is the objective of Islam; this is the true application of the general Islamic philosophy in hortatory and legal form.

Fear for one's position or station in life often runs back to the fear of death or injury, or to the fear of poverty or destitution; and Islam is insistent that the individual be freed from this fear also, for no creature can have any power over another creature in this matter,

> "Say: O Allah, wielder of the kingly power, thou givest that power to whom Thou wiliest. Thou wilt; in Thy hand is the good. Verily, Thou over all things art powerful".
>
> "Allah hath not chosen any son, nor is there any Gog along with Him; else would each God have assuredly championed that which is created, some of them would assuredly have overcome others. Glorified be Allah above that they allege".

"Say: In whose hand the rule over all things? Who giveth protection and seeketh none? If you have any knowledge, you will say: when Allah help you, then none can defeat you; but if He abandon you, then who will help you after Him?"

"Whosoever there be who desires honour, to Allah belongs all honour".

"To Allah belongs all honour, and to His Messenger, and to the Believers".

So here again there can be no fear, for all power belongs to Allah alone, and all honour, is Allah's: "And He is supreme above His servants; He is the Wise, the Informed".

But sometimes the human spirit is freed from servitude to priestly things, and from subservience to a fear for its life or its livelihood or its station, only to fall a prey to social values. Even though it derives from them neither profit nor loss, it still may be under the influence of such values as money, power, rank or lineage. When the conscience recognises its practical allegiance to any of these values, its very observance of them renders it incapable of true freedom, so that it cannot feel any real equality with its fellows.

Worth of Spirituality

So here Islam applies itself to all these values, and puts them in their proper place; it pays them neither too little attention nor too much, and thus it restores the true values to their proper and essential status, the true values which are either latent in a man's spirit or given expression in his acts. Thus it minimises the effect of the material values, and checks their impact on the human spirit. So it makes this matter also—so far as Islam can undertake to give practical and legal guarantees—a means towards the complete freedom of the conscience.

"Verily, the noblest of you in Allah's eyes is the most pious of you". And the noble man in Allah's eyes is he who is really and truly noble.

"The Arab has no eminence over the foreigner except his piety". "And then said:

"We are the greater in wealth and in children, so we shall not be punished. Say: Verily my Lord maketh wideth provision for whom He will, or He is sparing. But the majority of people will not understand. Neither your wealth nor your children are things which bring you near to Us; but only he who believes and who acts righteously will be near to Us. For such men there is a double recompense for what they have done, and they shall be safe in Upper Chambers".

So let them have their greatness in wealth and children, this is no value which will bring them any discrimination or any fame, but only he who believes and acts righteously. For faith is the permanent value apparent in life; these are the two real values which can command respect. At the same time Islam does not depreciate the value of wealth or of family:

"Wealth and sons are an ornament for life in this world". An ornament. But it does emphasise that such things are not such as to elevate or lower a man's true status, "the things which endure, the works of righteousness, are better in the Lord's sight-better for reward, and better for hope".

The Quran deals with material values and spiritual values by coining a parable about them in the souls of two men; it lays down no formal preference for one of them over the other, but at the same time it paints a clear and appealing picture of the believing soul, and of the reality of its values. Coin for them a parable. There were two men, to one of whom gave two gardens of vines which We surrounded with palm trees. And between them, we set a patch of arable land. Each of the gardens produced its fruit without failing in any way, and between the two of them, we caused a stream of flow. So this man had his fruit, and in dispute with his neighbour he said to him:

> 'I have more wealth than you, and my family is mightier.' So he went into his garden, sinning against his own soul, and saying:
>
> "I do not think that this will ever pass away, nor do I believe that The Hour will come. But even if I am taken back to my Lord, I will surely find something better than this in exchange". But his neighbour said to him in dispute:
>
> Have you no belief than Him who created you out of dust, then out of semen, and then formed you as a man? Nay, Allah is my Lord, and I will not associate any other than my Lord. Why did you not say when you entered you garden:
>
> "As Allah will; there is no power save in Allah".

If you thought me inferior to yourself in wealth and children, it may be that my Lord will give me something better than your garden; and that He will send down on this a thunderbolt from Heaven, so that next morning it will be only smooth, bare soil. Or the next morning the water may have sunk so deep in the ground that you cannot find it.

> "Then his fruit was encompassed, and the next morning he was turning down the palms of his hands in dismay at what he had spent on it, for it had fallen down upon the trellises; and he was saying. Would that I had not associated another with my Lord. He had no party to help him except Allah, and so he was helpless".

In this there is apparent, both the pride of the believer in his faith, and his contempt for those values of which his neighbour boasted, when he disputed with him. What confuses the issue is that his neighbour, who is so proud of his garden, does not appear to associate any other with Allah. But the Quran accounts him as one who does so, and makes him finally admit such an act of association. That is to say, he associated with Allah a purely material value, and gave to it a high mental regard; while by contrast the true believer would not associate anything with Allah.

So too in the story of Qorah the Quran portrays two characters in face of the temptation of wealth and property. There is a portrait of the character which is made conceited by such values, the character which is weakened and made mean, and which is seen to be small in contrast with the great. And on the other hand there is the portrait of believing souls which are mighty and strong, and which never stoop to smallness or weakness.

Now Korah was one of the people of Moses, and had authority over them. We gave him so much of the treasures that the keys of it weighed down a band, strong though they were". Then his people said to him:

> "Do not exult; for Allah loveth not those who exult. But rather, through what Allah has given you, seek the future above, without forgetting your part in this world. Do good, as Allah has done good for you, and do not seek to cause corruption on the Earth; for Allah loveth not those who cause corruption.' He said:
>
> "This has been given to me solely on account of the knowledge which I possess".

Did he not, then, know that before his time Allah had already destroyed generations which were stronger than him in power, and which had gathered more wealth? The sinners will not be asked about their crimes.

"So Korah went out among his people in his pomp, and those who were eager for the life of this world said: 'Would that we had something the same as has been given to Korah. Indeed he is a very fortunate man". But those who had been given knowledge said:

> 'Woe to you. The reward of Allah is better for him who believes and acts righteously; but only those attain it who have had endurance".

Then we craft the Earth for him and for his house, and he had no party to help him except Allah, nor was he one of those who could help themselves. So in the morning those who the previous day had envied his station were saying:

> "Ah, How wide a provision does Allah make for His servants as He wills, or how sparing He is. If Allah had not been gracious to us, He would have cleft the Earth for us. Ah, how the unbelievers fail to prosper".

Islam is organised around its view of these teachings; and so Allah forbids His Prophet, Muhammad, to attach any value to those things in which some men find a deceitful enjoyment.

> "Do not cast your eyes longingly at those things which We have given for the enjoyment of some classes of men, things which are the followers of the life of the world. For We gave them in order to test these men; the provision of your Lord is better and more enduring".

Some authorities interpret this verse and its implications as meaning merely that the rich should be left to enjoy their riches, while the poor should be content with their poverty. But this is a false exegesis which is inconsistent with the general spirit of Islam. This explanation is typical of those crafty Churchmen of despotic ages who use it to quieter the public conscience and to divert it from the quest for social justice. Such men must bear the responsibility themselves, for Islam cannot countenance such an exegesis.

In point of fact, this verse and others similar to it refer rather to the rehabilitation of the true human values, and to the necessity of rescuing the poor from their state of weakness and helplessness under the purely material values of wealth and possessions.

Corroboration of this exegesis is to be found in the fact that Allah commands his Prophet not to attach importance to these values, and not to encourage the people to respect them.

> "Content yourself with those who pray to their Lord in the morning and in the evening, as they seek His presence. Do not let yourself wander from them, seeking the adornment of the life of this world. Do not obey anyone whose heart We have made careless of Our remembrance, who follows his own desires, and who lives in excess". "Do not let their wealth astonish you, nor their children; Allah intends only to punish them in the life of this world, intends that they may themselves perish while they are yet unbelievers".

The Prophet and the Blind Beggar

In this connection we must also remember the story of Muhammad with the blind beggar, Ibn-Umm-e Maktum, and with Al-Walid ibn al-Kughira, the chief of the people. It is a story in which Allah delivers a sharp rebuke to His Prophet.

> "He came forward and turned away because the blind man came to him. That will teach you whether perhaps he will purify himself?"
>
> "Or whether he might let himself be reminded, and the reminder profit him? The man who is rich to him you have given your attention caring nothing that he has not purified himself. But the man who comes to you earnestly inquiring and in fear-him you neglect".

A moment of human weakness had assailed Muhammad in his desire that Allah might bring Al-Walid over to Islam, and he was intent upon this matter when Ibn-Umm Maktum came to him, seeking some knowledge of the Quran, calling to him again and again while he was still occupied with Al-Walid. The Prophet was annoyed with the beggar, and forward upon him; but his Lord rebuked him sharply for it in these words which are almost the strongest possible rebuke. Therein He endorses the values for which Islam stands, he points out what must be its true path and its constant endeavour namely, to free the conscience.

So finally the human soul is freed from its bondage to holy things, is freed from its fear of death and injury, of death and humiliation save for what Allah ordains, it is freed from all regard for outward appearances, and for the values of society; yet after all this it still remains in subjugation to its own nature, swayed by its pleasures and its appetites, by its desires and its longings. Thus an inner tyranny replaces the outer which the soul has escaped, and the complete freedom of conscience which Islam desires is nor achieved; nor can there be any realisation of that supreme human aim, social justice.

Islam is not unaware of this hidden weakness in the freedom of the conscience, and it bestows upon it a profound attention. This is evidenced by its care for the innermost depths of the soul, and again by its preoccupation with all the abilities and endowments of the individual. And here Islam comes to the same point as Christianity makes its supreme objective:

> "Say, there are your fathers and your sons, your brothers and your wives; there are your tribes, and the money you have earned, the commerce which you fear may suffer, and the dwellings in which you take pleasure. If these things are dearer to you than Allah and his Messenger, if they are dearer than a holy war in His cause, then wait in idleness till Allah starts on His work. Verily Allah does not guide people who are impious".

Here, in one verse are gathered up all the attractions, the longings, and the desires—all the weak points of the Human soul; and they are placed on one side of the balance.

On the other side are placed the love of Allah and of His messenger, and the love for holy war in his cause. It is a striking contrast, and it provides a complete escape from strangling desires. The soul which it thus completely freed is the soul which Islam seeks, and which it summons to its true destiny. Thus man can rise superior to humiliating necessities, can control the direction of his own course, and can seek after things which are greater and farther reaching than his own little ephemeral pleasures. Again he says:

> "The love of desires is made to appeal to men in their wives and their children, in hoarded hoards of gold and silver, in excellent horses, and cattle, and land; these things are the treasures of the life of this world. But of a better thing than these? For those who are pious there are gardens in the presence of their Lord, through which rivers flow; and long shall they dwell there. There are pure wives for them, and there is favour from Allah; Allah is observant of His servants".

This is not an attempt to drug the mind, nor yet is it a summon to austerity or to a neglect of the good things of life, although in this way some have seen fit to interpret the Quran, and in this way others have understood Islam. This is simply a summon to freedom, and to an independence of the weakness of desires and passions.

Accordingly, there can be no harm in the enjoyment of the good things of life, so long as man can control them, rather than they him.

> "Say who has forgotten the adornments of life which Allah has made for his servants; or who has forbidden the good things of his provision". "And do not forget your part in this world".

To this same line of thought belongs the ordinance of fasting; for its purpose is to raise the soul for a space of time above the necessities of all-powerful human nature. By fasting; the will is strengthened and elevated, making man superior to his nature, because he has risen above his necessities.

To this end, the Quran recommends various methods, among them being the inspired warning about the temptation of wealth and children, which occurs in the phrase:

> "Your wealth and your children are only a temptation". In this there is a stern warning which is sorely needed by human weakness in the face of wealth and children.

This is particularly shown in the covetousness which assails a man where his possessions or his family are concerned; he accepts what he would not otherwise accept, submits to what he would otherwise not submit to, and commits sins that he would not otherwise commit. So that "a child is an inducement to avarice, a cause of cowardice," as said by the Messenger of Allah.

Yet even after this, when a man is freed from all things which would deprive him of his full spiritual status, he may still be in need. He is in need of food, and so he is humiliated; for there is no need which is more humiliating. The empty belly cannot appreciate high-sounding phrases. Or else he is compelled to ask for charity, and all his self-esteem leaves him lost forever. This is met in Islam by the religious law which aims at preventing the causes of such need, and at putting an end to them where they can be found.

Accordingly it makes the claim of the individual to a competence, a responsibility of the state, and of the rich member of the community; it is a responsibility whose neglect will be punished in the world to come, as it is punishable by death in the present world. A full discussion of this will follow when we come to elaborate the economic theory in Islam. For this reason Islam forbids begging, and envisages a community of Muslims who have suffered loss by fighting in the cause of Allah, and who cannot travel the Earth for wealth; it describes their nobility on the grounds that:

> "They do not beg importunately from the people". So too, the Prophet gives a coin to a beggar, and then says:
>
> "Verily the better that one of you should get a rope and collect a bundle of firewood on his back and sell it, even if Allah does not give prosperity; better this than that you should beg from the people that they may give to you or refuse you".

And again He says:

> "A generous hand is better than a stingy hand". And he exhorts men to avoid all shameful means of getting money other than begging; for begging is regarded by Islam as a necessary evil. As for the proceeds of the poor-tax, this is the law. It is to be taken as a right, and is not to be given as a charity.
>
> "And of their wealth there was a settled share for the beggar and the outcast".

Welfare of Muslims

Thus share is taken by the state, and is spent on the welfare of Muslims, to supply their bodily needs, to preserve their self-esteem, and to retain to them their power of conscience. If this is not sufficient, provision is made to take sufficient from wages and salaries from the wealth of men of means and the richer classes to meet the needs of the poor and the humble.

Thus Islam approaches the question of freedom from every angle and from all points of view; it undertakes a complete emancipation of the conscience. It does not deal only with spiritual values, or only with economic values, but with both together. It recognises the practical reality of life, and equally the spiritual power of the soul; it attempts to awaken in human nature the highest desires, and to evoke the loftiest abilities, thus bringing that nature to complete freedom of conscience.

Without such complete freedom human nature cannot prevail against the force of humiliation and submissiveness and servility, nor can it lay claim to its rightful share in social justice; nor can it state the responsibilities of such a justice when it has attained it.

This freedom is therefore one of the corner stones for the building of social justice in Islam. More so it is principal corner stone on which all the others must rest.

Human Equality: Suppose, then, that the human mind has come to know all this freedom of conscience; it is free from the least shadow of servility, be it to death or injury, to poverty or weakness, unless what comes by Allah's permission. It is released from the tyranny of the values of social standing and wealth; it is saved from the humiliation of need and beggary, and it can rise superior to its desires and its bodily appetites.

It can turn towards its one sole Creator, to whom all things must turn without exception and without fail; and so it can find a complete independence of the material necessities of life. When the human conscience has come to know all this, it will have no need of anyone to preach equality to it in words, for it will already have experienced the full meaning of equality. It will also not endure the distinctions which arise from worldly values at all. It will seek equality as its right, and will strive to ensure that right; it will guard it carefully when it is gained and it will accept no substitute for it. It will bear the responsibility of guarding and defending its equality, whatever it may cost in effort and labour.

When the establishment of equality is rooted in the conscience, when it is safeguarded by religious law, and when it is guaranteed by its own adequacy, the poor and the humble will not be the only persons to desire it. Even the rich and the powerful will support it, because their conscience acknowledges those values which Islam is intent on establishing and confirming, as we have already outlined them. This is what actually happened in Islamic society fourteen centuries ago, as will be shown in the course of this book.

But despite this, Islam is not content with the acknowledgment, assured and profitable results of freedom of conscience; rather it emphasises the principle of equality in word and precept, so that everything may be clear and firm and definite. There was an age when some men asserted their claim to be of the progeny of the Gods, while others asserted that the blood which flowed in their veins was not of the nature of common blood, but was blue blood—royal or noble blood. It was an age when there were faiths and religions which divided the nations into classes; some were created by the head of a God, and hence they were holy, while others, having been created by the feet of a God, were despised.

A dispute centrad around woman; had woman a soul, or had she not? It was age in which a master was permitted to kill his slave, or to punish him in any way, because slaves belonged to a different class of humanity from that of their masters. In this age Islam was born; it taught the unity of the human race in origin and in history, in life and in death, in privileges and in responsibilities, before the law and no nobility except in piety. That formed a revolution in human thinking, and it has continued to this day; it was an achievement to which humanity had not till then aspired. That is to say, what was theoretically established by human laws during and after the French Revolution was established as a matter of practice by Islam more than fourteen centuries ago. No God can possibly have progeny:

> "Say, He is Allah the One, Allah the Undivided. Fie brought not forth, nor was He brought forth; there has never been any equal to Him?"

"And they said, 'The Merciful has taken a son.' You have committed a terrible thing, at which the very heavens almost are torn apart, and the earth cleft as under, and the mountains fallen down in pieces. For they attribute a son to the Merciful, But the Merciful has no need to take a son. There is nothing in Heaven or in Earth which does not approach the Merciful as a servant; He has counted them and given to them an exact number, and all of them must come before Him singly on the Day of Resurrection". Or again, there can be no such thing as blue or noble blood; and as for one being created by the head and another by the foot of a God:

> "Did We not create you out of mere water which We stored in a secure place until a decreed time? We set the time, and good was Our setting".
>
> So let man consider from what was he created? He was created from the dropping water, from water issuing from between the lions and the ribs.
>
> "It was Allah who created you from dust, from the seed and who then set you in pairs. No female conceives or gives birth without His knowing it; none is given long life and none is given short life, unless it be in a Book. Verily that is easy for Allah".
>
> "We have created man out of an extract of clay; when We made him a seed lodged in a secure place; We made the seed a clot of blood, and We created the clot into a morsel. We created the morsel bones, and We clothed the bones with flesh. We made him grow as a new creation; blessed be Allah, the best of Creators".

The Quran goes on to repeat this teaching in many passages, to impress on the mind of man the oneness of his origin and his growth. The human race, as a whole, is made from dust, and the individual—every individual—from mere water. And the Prophet repeats this truth in the Traditions:

> "Each of you is man; and man is of dust". Thus he increases man's reliance in his sense and his intelligence.

When it is thus denied that one individual can be intrinsically superior to another, it follows that there can be no race and no class which is superior by reason of its origin or its nature. Yet there are some races which to the present day insist that there does exist such a superiority. There cannot be:

> "O, ye people, revere your Lord who created you from one soul, creating from it his mate; and He spread abroad from these two many men and women".

There was originally only one soul; from it came its mate; and from the two of them there spread abroad both men and women. So all are of one origin, all are brothers in descent, all are equal in origin and nature. The noble Prophet of Islam said:

> "O ye people, We created you male and female, and We made you race and tribe. That you might know one another. Verily the noblest among you is the most pious".

These races and tribes were not made for the purpose of rivalry or enmity, but for mutual knowledge and friendliness; all of them in the eyes of Allah are equal, and there can be no superiority except in piety. But this is another question, unconnected with origin and nature; in these respects:

> "People are all equal as the teeth of a comb" as said by the noble Prophet of Islam.

This equality extends its compass over all mankind, and transcends both patriotism and religion; for since the Messenger said, "All Muslims are of one blood," Islam grants to men of other faiths rights of blood equivalent to those enjoyed by Believers—so long as there is a compact between them and the Muslims.

> "Whoever kills a Believer by mistake, the penalty is to set free one Believing slave, and to deliver the blood—money to the dead man's family—unless they give it as alms. If the killer is of a people who are at enmity with you, but is himself a Believer, then he must set free a Believing slave. If he is of a people with whom you have a compact, then he must deliver the blood-money, and set free a Believing slave".

Thus, the atonement to be made by a non-Muslim killer whose people have a compact with the Muslims is exactly the same as that to be made by a Muslim killer. The same tendency to equality is shown by the fact that Islam fixes the atonement for an accidental killing as the liberation of a slave; this indicates that it regards freeing a slave as a means of giving life to a soul.

Thus, this new life is given in exchange for the life which has been taken by the accidental killing; for in the eyes of Islam slavery is akin to death, while freedom is akin to life.

As for deliberate murder, in vengeance or in hatred, the principle in "A life for a life;" and there is no difference between a prince and pauper, a signore and a slave, the Messenger said:

> "Him who killed his slave We have killed; him who mutilated his slave We have mutilated; him who gelded his slave We have gelded".

Thus Islam has freedom from the conflict of tribal and racial and religious loyalties, and thus it achieved an equality which civilization in the West has not gained to this day. It is a civilization which permits the American conscience to acquiesce in the disappearance of the Red Indian race, a disappearance which is being organised in the sight and hearing of the government. It permits also Field Marshal Smuts in South Africa to introduce racial laws which discriminate against coloured Indians.

Islam follows up any suspicion of discrimination between men, or of superiority of one over another; no matter what its form or guise, nor matter what its cause, Islam condemns it. Even in the cause of the Prophet Muhammad, the Quran constantly reminds his people that he is human like the remainder of mankind; and Muhammad himself reiterates the same fact that he was a Prophet, loved and respected by his people, yet always afraid that the love and respect might lead to make him preeminent or superior to others. So here he is, telling his people:

> "Do not venerate me, as the Christians venerate Jesus, son of Mary; I am only a servant of Allah, and His Messenger,"

Or again, when he comes into a meeting in which all present rise to their feet out of respect for him, he says:

> "Whoever wishes that men may stand to greet him, let him take his seat in hell-fire".

And when Muhammad's family thought that as a Messenger he would raise their status or their rank, and would confer on them a form of aristocracy above the ordinary, Muhammad refused them everything of that kind save the nobility of good works and he said to them plainly:

> "If my people cannot approach me through their good works, shall you, then, approach me through your genealogies? Verily the noblest of you in the sight of Allah is the most pious".

If Muhammad's family enjoyed no superiority except that of good works to raise them above the level of the people, no one ever can enjoy such a superiority. And again, when Muhammad was accosted by the blind man, when he turned away from the poor man, Ibn Umm Maktum, to pay attention to Al-Walid ibn al-Mughira, who was the chief of his people, there came swiftly upon him a stern reproof which was almost a condemnation; thus he was brought back to recognise the absolute equality and complete parity of all men, or when some of the rich nobles looked with contempt on marriage for themselves or for their families with poor men or women, there came the command of Allah:

> "Settle the unwed among you in marriage, and those who are upright among your male and female slaves. If they are poor, Allah will enrich them of His bounty; Allah is generous and wise".

Relation between Male and Female: As for the relation between the sexes, Islam has guaranteed to women complete equality with men with regard to their sex; it has permitted no discrimination except in incidental matters connected with physical nature, with customary procedure, or with responsibility, in all of which are customary procedures, or with responsibility, in all of which the privileges of the two sexes are not in question. Wherever the physical endowments, the customs, and the responsibilities are identical, the sexes are equal; and wherever there is some difference in these respects, the discrimination follow that difference. In the spiritual and religious sphere, men and women are equal.

> "Whoever does goods works, man or woman, and is a Believer such shall enter into Paradise and shall not be wronged one jot".
>
> "Whoever does good works, man or woman, and is a Believer—We shall make their life a good life, and We shall give them their reward for the best that they have done".
>
> Then their Lord answered them:
>
> "I shall not waste the work of any one of you who works, male or female; you belong to one another".

Or again in the sphere of possessing and administering money they are equal.

> "Men shall have a portion of what their parents and their near relatives leave; and women shall have a portion of what their parents and their near relatives leave".
>
> "Men shall have a portion of what they have gained; and women shall have a portion of what they have gained".

In the law about a man getting double the share of a woman in an inheritance, the reason is to be found in the responsibility which a man carries in life. He marries a woman, and he undertakes to maintain her and their children; he has to bear the responsibility of the whole structure of the family. So it is no more than his right that for this reason, if for no other, he should have the share of two women. The women, on the other hand, if she is married, has the responsibility of providing for herself from what her husband gives her; if she remains unmarried or if she is widowed, she must provide for herself out of what she inherits. So the question here is one of difference in responsibility, which involves a similar difference in the law of inheritance. Or there is the case of men being overseers over women.

> "Men are overseers over women because of what Allah has bestowed of His bounty on one more than another, and because of what they have contributed in the way of wealth".

The reason for this discrimination lies in physical endowment, and in use and not in the matter of oversight. Because a man is free from the cares of the family, he can attend to the affairs of society over considerable periods, and can apply to these affairs all his intellectual powers. On the other hand a women is restricted most of her life to these family cares. The result is that these responsibilities promote in women in the direction of reflection and thought. So when man is made to oversee woman, it is by reason of physical nature and custom that this ordinance stands.

Besides which, the man has the financial responsibility, and the economic sphere is closely linked with that of oversight, which is essentially the acceptance of responsibility. Ultimately the fundamental point here is one of the balance of privileges and responsibilities in the sphere of the sexes, and in that of life as a whole.

"The same is due to women as is due from them; but men have a precedence over them". This Precedence is the oversight, the reason which we have demonstrated. Again there appears to be an instance of discrimination in the question of the giving of evidence.

> "Call two of your men as witnesses; or if there are not women, then call one man and two women from those on whom you agree among the people who are present. So if one of the women goes astray, the other may remind her".

In this verse itself the explanation is made clear; by the nature of her family duties the growth of the woman's spirit is towards emotions and passions, just as well as in man it is towards contemplation and thought, as we have already said. So when she is forgetful, or when she is carried away by her feelings, the other will be there to remind her. Thus the question in this case is one of the practical considerations of life rather than one of the inherent superiority of one sex to the other, or of a lack of equality.

Bibliography

Abou El Fadl, Khaled: *Speaking in God's Name: Islamic Law, Authority and Women,* Oneworld, England, 2001.

Abun-Nasr, Jamil M.: *The Tijaniyya: A Sufi Order in the Modern World,* Oxford University Press, London, 1965.

Adam, Lebor: *A Heart Turned East: Among the Muslims of Europe and America,* St. Martin's Press, New York, 2001.

Afary, Janet: *The Iranian Constitutional Revolution, 1906-1911: Grassroots Democracy Social Democracy and the Origins of Feminism,* Columbia University Press, New York, 1996.

Ahmed, Rashid: *Jihad: The Rise of Militant Islam in Central Asia,* Yale University Press, New Haven, 2002.

Ahmet, T. K.: *God's Unruly Friends: Dervish Groups in the Islamic Later Middle Period, 1200-1550,* University of Utah Press, Salt Lake City, 1994.

Alexander, D.: *Ibn 'Arabi and the Later Islamic Tradition: The Making of a Polemical Image in Medieval Islam,* State University of New York Press, Albany, 1998.

Algar, Hamid: *Religion and State in Iran 1785-1906: The Role of the Ulama in the Qajar Period,* University of California Press, California, 1969.

Al-Ghazali: *Al-Ghazali on the Manners Relating to Eating: Book XI of the Revival of the Religious Sciences,* The Islamic Texts Society, Cambridge, 2000.

Ali, Wijdan: *Modern Islamic Art: Development and Continuity,* University Press of Florida, Gainesville, 1997.

Alisa, Rubin: *Debating Islam in the Jewish State: The Development of Policy toward Islamic Institutions in Israel,* State University of New York Press, Albany, 2001.

Allievi, Stefano: *Muslim Networks and Transnational Communities in and across Europe,* E.J. Brill, Leiden, 2003.

Amir, A. S.: *Authority and Political Culture in Shi'ism,* State University of New York Press, Albany, 1988.

Andrew, S. and Ann Arbor: *Monetary Change and Economic History in the Medieval Islamic World,* Ashgate/Variorum, Aldershot, 1992.

Anoushiravan, Ehteshami: *Islamic Fundamentalism,* Westview Press, Boulder, 1996.

Arberry, Arthur J.: *Revelation and Reason in Islam*, George Allen & Unwin, London, 1977.

Arjomand, Said Amir: *The Shadow of God and the Hidden Imam,* University of Chicago Press, Chicago, 1984.

Armstrong, Karen: *Islam: A Short History,* Modern Library, New York, 2002.

Arthur, John: *A Sufi Martyr: The Apologia of 'Ain al-Qudat al-Hamadhani,* George Allen & Unwin, London, 1969.

Ashk, D.: *Islamic Law, Epistemology and Modernity*, Routledge, New York, 2003.

Atil, Esin: *Levni and the Surname: The Story of an Eighteenth Century Ottoman Festival,* University of Washington Press, Seattle, 2000.

Augustus, Richard: *Civil Society and the Middle East,* E.J. Brill, Leiden, 1997.

Aziz, A.: *Studies in Islamic Culture in the Indian Environment,* Oxford University Press, Oxford, 1999.

Badran, Margot: *Feminists, Islam and Nation: Gender and the Making of Modern Egypt,* Princeton University Press, Princeton, 1994.

Banani, Amin: *Poetry and Mysticism in Islam: The Heritage of Rumi,* Cambridge University Press, New York, 1994.

Barlas, Asma: *Believing Women in Islam: Unreading Patriarchal Interpretations of the Quran,* University of Texas Press, Austin, 2002.

Baron, Beth: *The Women's Awakening in Egypt: Culture, Society and the Press,* Yale University Press, New Haven, 1997.

Bennigsen, Alexandre: *Mystics and Commissars: Sufism in the Soviet Union,* University of California Press, Berkeley, 1986.

Bibars, Iman: *Victims and Heroines: Women, Welfare and the Egyptian State,* Zed Books, London, 2001.

Binder, Leonard: *Islamic Liberalism: A Critique of Development Ideologies,* University of Chicago Press, Chicago, 1988.

Bisharat, S.: *Contemporary Art from the Islamic World,* Interlink Publ. Northampton, 1990.

Blair, Sheila S.: *Images of Paradise in Islamic Art,* University of Texas Press, Austin, 1991.

Bloom, Jonathan M.: *Paper before Print: The History and Impact of Paper in the Islamic World,* Yale University Press, New Haven, 2001.

Bruce, B. L.: *Nizam ad-din Awliya: Morals for the Heart,* Paulist Press, New York, 1992.

Buehler, Arthur F.: *Sufi Heirs of the Prophet: The Indian Naqshbandiyya and the Rise of the Mediating Sufi Shaykh,* University of South Carolina Press, Columbia, 1998.

Camille, H.: *The Book of Nature: An Anthology of Spiritual Perspectives on Nature,* Independent Publishers Group,Chicago, 2006.

Chittick, William C.: *The Heart of Islamic Philosophy: The Quest for Self Knowledge in the Teachings of Afdal al-Din Kashani,* Oxford University Press, Oxford, 2001.

Clifford, G.: *Islam Observed: Religious Development in Morocco and Indonesia,* University of Chicago Press, Chicago, 1971.

Cole, Juan R.I. and Nikki Keddie R.: *Shi'ism and Social Protest,* Yale University Press, New Haven, 1986.

Combs-Schilling, M.E.: *Sacred Performances: Islam, Sexuality and Sacrifice,* Columbia University Press, New York, 1989.

Craig, William L.: *The Kalam Cosmological Argument,* Harper and Row, New York, 1979.

Crystal, Jill: *Oil and Politics in the Gulf: Rulers and Merchants in Kuwait and Qatar,* Cambridge University Press, Cambridge, 1995.

Daftary, Farhad: *The Ismailis: Their History and Doctrines,* Cambridge University Press, Cambridge, 1990.

Daniel, Norman: *Islam and the West: The Making of an Image,* Oneworld, Oxford, 2000.

David, Nicolle: *Warriors and their Weapons around the Time of the Crusades: Relationships between Byzantium, the West and the Islamic World,* Ashgate/Variorum, Aldershot, 2003.

Denys Johnson-Davies: *Forty Hadith Qudsi,* The Islamic Texts Society, Cambridge, 1997.

Deweese, Devin: *Islamization and Native Religion in the Golden Horde: Baba Tukles and Conversion to Islam in Historical and Epic Tradition,* Pennsylvania State University Press, Pennsylvania, 1994.

Dhanani, Alnoor: *The Physical Theory of Kalam: Atoms, Space and Void in Basrian Mu'tazili Cosmology,* E.J. Brill, Leiden, 1994.

Donald, Hill R.: *Islamic Technology: An Illustrated History,* Cambridge University Press, Cambridge, 1986.

Donald, Little P.: *Islamic Studies Presented to Charles J. Adams,* E.J. Brill, Leiden, 1991.

Douglas, Ramage E.: *Politics in Indonesia: Democracy, Islam and the Ideology of Tolerance,* Routledge, New York, 1995.

Dunn, Ross E.: *The Adventures of Ibn Battuta: A Muslim Traveler of the Fourteenth Century,* University of California Press, Berkeley, 1990.

Echevarria, Ana: *The Fortress of Faith: The Attitude Toward Muslims in Fifteenth Century Spain,* E.J. Brill, Leiden, 1999.

Edmund Ghareeb: *War in the Gulf, 1990-91: The Iraq-Kuwait Conflict and its Implications,* Oxford University Press, Oxford, 2001.

Eickelman, Dale: *Knowledge and Power in Morocco,* Princeton University Press, Princeton, 1985.

Elizabeth, A. M.: *Islam and Human Rights: Tradition and Politics,* Westview Press, Colorado, 1999.

Elizabeth, Warnock and Basima Qattan Bezirgan: *Middle Eastern Muslim Women Speak,* University of Texas Press, Austin, 1978.

Ernst, J. and Eleanor Sims G.: *Islamic Art: A Biennial Dedicated to the Art and Culture of the Muslim World, 1990-1991,* Oxford University Press, Oxford, 1997.

Ervand, A.: *Iran between two Revolutions,* Princeton University Press, Princeton, 1982.

Esack, Farid: *The Quran: A Short Introduction,* Oneworld, Oxford, 2002.

Esfandiari, Haleh: *Reconstructed Lives: Women & Iran's Islamic Revolution,* Johns Hopkins University Press, Baltimore, 1997.

Ezzedin, Ibrahim: *An-Nawawi's Forty Hadith,* The Islamic Texts Society, Cambridge, 1997.

Fakhry, Majid: *Islamic Occasionalism and its Critique by Averroes and Aquinas,* George Allen & Unwin, London, 1958.

Fakhry, Majid: *Philosophy, Dogma and the Impact of Greek Thought in Islam,* Ashgate/Variorum, Aldershot, 1994.

Farhad, D.: *The Assassin Legends: Myth of the Ismailis,* I.B. Tauris, London, 1994.

Fatemeh, K.: *Reading Mystical Lyric: The Case of Jalal al-Din Rumi,* University of South Carolina Press, Columbia, 1998.

Fauzan, Saleh: *Modern Trends in Islamic Theological Discourse in 20th Century Indonesia: A Critical Study,* E.J. Brill, Leiden, 2001.

Fawaz, A.: *America and Political Islam: Clash of Cultures or Clash of Interests?,* Cambridge University Press, Cambridge, 1999.

Firestone, Reuven: *Journeys in Holy Lands: The Evolution of the Abraham Ishmael Legends in Islamic Exegesis,* State University of New York Press, Albany, 1990.

Galina, Yemelianova M.: *Islam in Post-Soviet Russia,* RoutledgeCurzon, New York, 2002.

Gaudefroy-Demombynes, Maurice: *Muslim Institutions,* Greenwood Press, Westport, 1984.

George, F.: *Essays on Islamic Philosophy and Science,* State University of New York Press, Albany, 1975.

Ghassan, S.: *Democracy without Democrats?: The Renewal of Politics in the Muslim World,* I.B. Tauris, London, 1994.

Gilles, Kepel,: *Jihad: The Trail of Political Islam,* Harvard University Press, Cambridge, 2002.

Godfrey, G.: *A History of Ottoman Architecture,* Thames & Hudson, New York, 2003.

Goitein, S.D.: *Studies in Islamic History and Institutions,* E.J. Brill, Leiden, 1966.

Goodwin, Jason: *Lords of the Horizons: A History of the Ottoman Empire,* Henry Holt and Co, New York, 1999.

Grabar, Oleg: *Muqarnas: An Annual on Islamic Art and Architecture,* E.J. Brill, Leiden, 1988.

Grabar, Oleg: *The Formation of Islamic Art,* Yale University Press, New Haven, 1987.

Graham, William A.: *Divine Word and Prophetic Word in Early Islam,* The Hague, Mouton, 1977.

Hafeez, Malik: *Iqbal: Poet-philosopher of Pakistan,* Columbia University Press, New York, 1971. Haleem, Harfiya Abdel: *Islam and the Environment,* Ta-Ha Publishers, London, 1998.

Hallaq, W. B.: *Authority, Continuity and Change in Islamic Law,* Cambridge University Press, Cambridge, 2001.

Hamid, Rez: *The Sacred Law of Islam: A Case Study of Women's Treatment in the Islamic Republic of Iran's Criminal Justice System,* Ashgate, Aldershot, 2003.

Hamilton, A. R.: *Modern Trends in Islam,* Octagon Books, New York, 1972.

Henry, C.: *Spiritual Body and Celestial Earth: From Mazdean Iran to Shi'ite Iran,* Princeton University Press, Princeton, 1977.

Hillebrand, Carole: *The Sultan's Turret: Studies in Persian and Turkish Culture,* E.J. Brill, Leiden, 1999.

Hinds, Martin: *Studies in Early Islamic History,* Darwin Press, Princeton, 1997.

Holt, P.M.: *Cambridge History of Islam,* Cambridge University Press, Cambridge, 1970.

Homerin: *From Arab Poet to Muslim Saint: Ibn al-Farid, his Verse and his Shrine,* University of South Carolina Press, Columbia, 1994.

Hooglund, Eric: *Twenty Years of Islamic Revolution: Political and Social Transition in Iran since 1979,* Syracuse University Press, Syracuse, 2002.

Hourani, Albert H.: *Arabic Thought in the Liberal Age, 1798-1939,* Cambridge University Press, Cambridge, 1983.

Huband, Mark: *Warriors of the Prophet: The Struggle for Islam,* Westview Press, Colorado, 1998.

Hugh, Kennedy: *Muslim Spain and Portugal: A Political History of al-Andalus,* Addison-Wesley, Boston, 1997.

Hunter, Shireen T.: *Islam, Europe's Second Religion: The New Social, Cultural and Political Landscape,* Praeger, Westport, 2002.

Husain, M.: *The Origins and Early Development of Shi'a Islam,* Oxford University Press, Oxford, 002.

Ibn Khaldun: *The Muqaddimah: An Introduction to History,* Princeton University Press, Princeton, 1969.

Ibrahim, Ozdemir: *The Ethical Dimension of Human Attitude Toward Nature,* Ministry of Environment, Ankara, 1997.

Iftikhar, Haider M.: *Islam, Nationalism and the West: Issues of Identity in Pakistan,* MacMillan, New York, 1999.

Ikhwan, al-Safa: *The Case of the Animals Versus Man before the King of the Jinn,* Twayne Publishers, Boston, 1978.

Inalcik, Halil: *An Economic and Social History of the Ottoman Empire, 1300-1914,* Cambridge University Press, Cambridge, 1994.

Irwin, Robert: *The Middle East in the Middle Ages: The Early Mamluk Sultanate, 1250-1382,* Croom Helm, London, 1986.

Israeli, Raphael: *Islam in China: Religion, Ethnicity, Culture and Politics,* Lexington Books, Lanham, 2002.

Izz al-Din, Muil Yusuf: *The Environmental Dimensions of Islam,* Lutterworth, Cambridge, 2000.

Jacob, C.: *The Middle East and North Africa in World Politics: A Documentary Record,* Yale University Press, New Haven, 1979.

Jahanbakhsh, Forough: *Islam, Democracy and Modernism in Iran, 1953-2000: From Bazargan to Soroush,* E.J. Brill, Leiden, 2001.

James, Kritzeck: *Modern Islamic Literature from 1800 to the Present,* Holt, Rinehart and Winston, New York, 1970.

Jamil, M.: *A History of the Maghrib in the Islamic Period,* Cambridge University Press, Cambridge, 1987.

Jan, Knappert: *Textual Sources for the Study of Islam,* University of Chicago Press, Chicago, 1986.

Jane, Dammen M.: *The Encyclopedia of the Quran,* E.J. Brill, Leiden, 2001.

Javad, Nurbakhsh : *Spiritual Poverty in Sufism,* Khaniqahi Nimatullahi Publication, London, 1984.

Jawad, Haifaa A.: *The Rights of Women in Islam: An Authentic Approach,* St. Martin's Press, New York, 1998.

Jawed, Nasim A.: *Islam's Political Culture: Religion and Politics in Pre-divided Pakistan,* University of Texas Press, Austin, 1999.

Johannes, J.G.: *The Neglected Duty: The Creed of Sadat's Assassins and Islamic Resurgence in the Middle East,* MacMillan, New York, 1996.

Johannes, K.: *The Arts and Crafts of Turkestan,* Thames & Hudson, New York, 1985.

John, L. and John Voll O.: *Islam and Democracy,* Oxford University Press, Oxford, 1996.

John, Renard: *Seven Doors to Islam: Spirituality and the Religious Life of Muslims,* University of California Press, Berkeley, 1996.

John, Robert: *An Introduction to Religious Foundations in the Ottoman Empire,* E.J. Brill, Leiden, 1986.

John, Talbott E.: *The War without a Name: France in Algeria, 1954-1962,* Alfred A. Knopf, New York, 1980.

Jonathan, B.: *Islam: A Thousand Years of Faith and Power,* Yale University Press, New Haven, 2002.

Judith, Tucker E.: *A Social History of Women and Gender in the Modern Middle East,* Westview Press, Boulder, 1999.

Juynboll, G.H.A.: *Muslim Tradition: Studies in Chronology, Provenance and Authorship of Early Hadith,* Cambridge University Press, Cambridge, 1983.

Kaegi, Walter E.: *Byzantium and the Early Islamic Conquests,* Cambridge University Press, Cambridge, 1992.

Kamali, Mohammad Hashim: *Principles of Islamic Jurisprudence*, The Islamic Texts Society, Cambridge, 2000.

Kanan, Makiya: *Republic of Fear: The Politics of Modern Iraq,* University of California Press, Berkeley, 1998.

Kaplan, Jeffrey: *Review of Mawil Izzi Dien's The Environmental Dimensions of Islam,* Environment, Culture, Religion, Worldviews, 2001.

Karpat, Kemal H.: *The Politicization of Islam: Reconstructing Identity, State, Faith and Community in the Late Ottoman State,* Oxford University Press, Oxford, 2002.

Kasaba, Reat: *The Ottoman Empire and the World Economy: The Nineteenth Century,* State University of New York Press, Albany, 1988.

Kayali, Hasan: *Arabs and Young Turks: Ottomanism, Arabism and Islamism in the Ottoman Empire, 1908-1918,* University of California Press, Berkeley, 1997.

Keddie, Nikki R.: *Religion and Politics in Iran: Shi'ism from Quietism to Revolution,* Yale University Press, New Haven, 1983.

Keller, Shoshana: *To Moscow, not Mecca: The Soviet Campaign Against Islam in Central Asia, 1917- 1941,* Praeger, Westport, 2001.

Kelly, J.B.: *Sultanate and Imamate in Oman,* Chatham House, London, 1959.

Kemal, Salim: *The Philosophical Poetics of Alfarabi, Avicenna and Averroes: The Aristotelian Reception,* Routledge Curzon, New York, 2003.

Khadduri, Majid: *War and Peace in the Law of Islam,* Johns Hopkins University Press, Baltimore, 1955.

Khalid, B. S.: *Western Dominance and Political Islam,* State University of New York Press, Albany, 1995.

Khare, R.S.: *Perspectives on Islamic Law, Justice and Society,* Rowman & Littlefield, Lanham, 1999.

Khuri, Fuad I.: *Imams and Emirs: State Religion and Sects in Islam*, Saqui Books, London, 1990.

Koch, Ebba: *Mughal Art and Imperial Ideology: Collected Essays,* Oxford University Press, Oxford, 2001.

Kohlberg, Etan: *A Medieval Muslim Scholar at Work: Ibn Tawus and his Library,* E.J. Brill, Leiden, 1992.

Kristina, Nelson: *The Art of Reciting the Qur'an,* University of Texas Press, Austin, 1986.

Kurzman, Charles: *Liberal Islam: A Sourcebook,* Oxford University Press, Oxford, 1998.

Laleh, B.: *Encyclopedia of Islamic Law: A Compendium of the Major Schools,* Kazi Publ., Chicago, 1996.

Lane, E.W.: *Arabic-English Lexicon,* The Islamic Texts Society, Cambridge, 1984.

Lapidus, Ira M.: *A History of Islamic Societies,* Cambridge University Press, Cambridge, 1988.

Lawrence, Bruce B.: *Shattering the Myth: Islam Beyond Violence*, Princeton University Press, Princeton, 1998.

Leaman, Oliver: *An Introduction to Medieval Islamic Philosophy,* Cambridge University Press, Cambridge, 1985.

Lelyveld, David: *Aligarh's First Generation: Muslim Solidarity in British India,* Princeton University Press, Princeton, 1978.

Lewis, Bernard: *Islam from the Prophet Muhammad to the Capture of Constantinople: Politics and War,* Oxford University Press, Oxford, 1987.

Lobban, Carolyn: *Islamic Law and Society in the Sudan,* Frank Cass & Co., London, 1987.

Madelung, Wilferd: *Religious Schools and Sects in Medieval Islam,* Variorum, London, 1985.

Mahdi, Muhsin: *Alfarabi and the Foundation of Islamic Political Philosophy,* University of Chicago Press, Chicago, 2001.

Majid, Khadduri: *Al-Shafi'i's Risala: Treatise on the Foundations of Islamic Jurisprudence,* Islamic Texts Society, Cambridge, 1999.

Mannan, M.A.: *Islamic Economics: Theory and Practice,* Westview Press, Colorado, 1987.

Mannheim, R.: *Spirit and Nature: Papers from the Eranos Yearbooks,* Pantheon, New York, 1954.

Marie, Broxup: *The Islamic Threat to the Soviet State,* St. Martin's Press, New York, 1983.

Marsot, Afaf Lutfi al-Sayyid: *Egypt in the Reign of Muhammad Ali,* Cambridge University Press, Cambridge, 1984.

Martin, Richard C.: *Approaches to Islam in Religious Studies,* Oneworld, Oxford, 2001.

Mason, Herbert: *The Death of al-Hallaj: A Dramatic Narrative,* University of Notre Dame Press, Notre Dame, 1991.

Massignon, Louis: *Essay on the Origins of the Technical Language of Islamic Mysticism,* University of Notre Dame Press, Notre Dame, 1997.

Matinuddin, Kamal: *The Taliban Phenomenon: Afghanistan, 1994-1997,* Oxford Oxford University Press, Karachi, 1999.

McAmis, Robert Day: *Malay Muslims: The History and Challenge of Resurgent Islam in Southeast Asia,* William B. Eerdmans Publ., Grand Rapids, 2002.

McChesney, R. D.: *Waqf in Central Asia: Four Hundred Years in the History of a Muslim Shrine, 1480-1889,* Princeton University Press, Princeton, 1991.

Menashri, David: *Post-Revolutionary Politics in Iran: Religion, Society and Power,* Frank Cass & Co., London, 2001.

Messick, Brinkley: *The Calligraphic State: Textual Domination and History in a Muslim Society,* University of California Press, California, 1993.

Metcalf, Barbara Daly: *Making Muslim Space in North America and Europe,* University of California Press, California, 1996.

Michael, Frassetto: *Western Views of Islam in Medieval and Early Modern Europe,* MacMillan, New York, 1999.

Michael, H.: *Arab Politics: The Search for Legitimacy,* Yale University Press, New Haven, 1977.

Milo, Cleveland Beach: *Art of the Persian Courts: Selections from the Art and History Trust Collection,* Rizzoli, New York, 1993.

Minault, Gail: *Secluded Scholars: Women's Education and Muslim Social Reform in Colonial India,* Oxford University Press, Oxford, 1998.

Mohamed, Alam: *Islam,* Pinter, London, 1994.

Moojan, Momen: *An Introduction to Shi'i Islam: The History and Doctrines of Twelver Shi'ism,* Yale University Press, New Haven, 1985.

Mottahedeh, Roy P.: *Loyalty and Leadership in an Early Islamic Society,* Princeton University Press, Princeton, 1980.

Murata, Sachiko: *The Tao of Islam: A Sourcebook on Gender Relationships in Islamic Thought,* State University of New York Press, Albany, 1992.

Musallam, Basim: *Sex and Society in Islam: Birth Control before the Nineteenth Century,* Cambridge University Press, Cambridge, 1983.

Nasr, Seyyed Hossein: *The Need for a Sacred Science,* State University of New York Press, Albany, 1993.

Nawal, H.: *Islam and the Environment: A Legalistic and Textual View,* State University of New York Press, Albany, 1995.

Nayereh, Tohidi: *Women in Muslim Societies: Diversity within Unity,* Lynne Rienner, Boulder, 1998.

Necipoglu, Gulru: *Architecture, Ceremonial and Power: The Topkapi Palace in the Fifteenth and Sixteenth Centuries,* MIT Press, Cambridge, 1992.

Nicholas, Rescher: *Studies in Arabic Philosophy,* University of Pittsburgh Press, Pittsburgh, 1967.

Nicholson, R.A.: *The Idea of Personality in Sufism,* Cambridge University Press, Cambridge, 1923.

Nielsen, Jorgen S.: *Towards a European Islam,* MacMillan, New York, 1999.

Nikki, Keddie: *Women in the Muslim World,* Harvard University Press, Cambridge, 1978.

Nurbakhsh, Javad: *Dogs from a Sufi Point of View,* Khaniqahi Nimatullahi Publ., London, 1989.

O'Kane, J.: *The Concept of Sainthood in Early Islamic Mysticism,* Curzon Press, Surrey, 1996.

Ormsby, Eric L.: *Theodicy in Islamic Thought: The Dispute Over Al-Ghazali's Best of All Possible Worlds,* Princeton University Press, Princeton, 1984.

Ouyang, Wen-Chin: *Literary Criticism in Medieval Arabic-Islamic Culture: The Making of a Tradition,* Edinburgh University Press, Edinburgh, 1997.

Parviz, Manzoor S.: *Environment and Values: An Islamic Perspective,* Manchester University Press, Manchester, 1984.

Patricia, Horvatich: *Islam in an Era of Nation-States: Politics and Religious Renewal in Muslim Southeast Asia,* University of Hawaii Press, Honolulu, 1997.

Paul, Noble: *Political Liberalization and Democratization in the Arab World,* Lynne Rienner, Colorado, 1998.

Paul, W. E.: *Abu Ya'qub al-Sijistani: Intellectual Missionary,* I.B. Tauris, London, 1998.

Peck, Malcolm C.: *The United Arab Emirates: A Venture in Unity,* Westview Press, Boulder, 1986.

Pedersen, Lars: *Newer Islamic Movements in Western Europe,* Ashgate, Aldershot, 1999.

Peirce, Lelie P.: *The Imperial Harem: Women and Sovereignty in the Ottoman Empire,* Oxford University Press, Oxford, 1997.

Perez, H.: *Islam and Science: Religious Orthodoxy and the Battle for Rationality,* Zed Books, London, 1991.

Peter G. R.: *Islam and the Malay-Indonesian World: Transmission and Responses,* University of Hawaii Press, Honolulu, 2001.

Peter, G. and Anthony Johns H.: *Islam: Essays on Scripture, Thought and Society—A Festschrift in Honour of Anthony H. Johns,* E.J. Brill, Leiden, 1997.

Peters, F.E.: *Aristotle and the Arabs: The Aristotelian Tradition in Islam,* New York University Press, Washington Square, 1968.

Pipes, Daniel: *Slave Soldiers and Islam: The Genesis of a Military System,* Yale University Press, New Haven, 1981.

Price, Daniel E.: *Islamic Political Culture, Democracy and Human Rights: A Comparative Study,* Praeger, Westport, 1999.

Pusch, Barbara: *The Ecology Debate Among Muslim Intellectuals in Turkey,* Les Annales de l'Autre Islam, 1999.

Quinn, Frederick and Quinn, Charlotte A.: *Pride, Faith and Fear: Islam in Sub-Saharan Africa,* Oxford University Press, Oxford, 2003,

Qureshi, Naeem M.: *Pan-Islam in British Indian Politics: A Study of the Khilafat Movement, 1918- 1924,* E.J. Brill, Leiden, 1999.

Rahnema, Ali: *Pioneers of Islamic Revival,* Zed Books, London, 1994.

Rai, Milan: *War Plan—Iraq: Ten Reasons against War on Iraq,* Verso, London, 2002.

Ralph, H. M. and Eden Naby: *Afghanistan: Mullah, Marx and Mujahid,* Westview Press, Colorado, 2002.

Ramakrishna, Lajwanti: *Panjabi Sufi Poets,* Oxford University Press, London, 1938.

Randall, Pouwels L.: *The History of Islam in Africa,* Ohio University, Athens, 2000.

Raphael, Israeli: *Islam in China: A Critical Bibliography,* Greenwood Publication, Westport, 1994.

Rashid, Ismail K.: *Palestinian Identity: The Construction of Modern National Consciousness,* Columbia University Press, New York, 1997.

Raymond, L.: *The Dervish Lodge: Architecture, Art and Sufism in Ottoman Turkey,* University of California Press, Berkeley, 1992.

Renard, John S.J.: *Ibn 'Abbad of Ronda: Letters on the Sufi Path,* Paulist Press, New York, 1988.

Reuven, E.: *Jihad: The Origin of Holy War in Islam,* Oxford University Press, Oxford, 2002.

Ricardo, Rene: *Islam and the Politics of Resistance in Algeria, 1783-1992,* Africa World Press, Lawrenceville, 1999.

Richard, Antoun: *Muslim Preacher in the Modern World: A Jordanian Case Study in Comparative Perspective,* Princeton University Press, Princeton, 1989.

Richard, C. and Mark R.: *Defenders of Reason in Islam: Mu'tazilism from Medieval School to Modern Symbol,* Oneworld, Oxford, 1997.

Robert, Brenton: *The Druze,* Yale University Press, New Haven, 1988.

Robert, H.: *Islamic Art and Architecture,* Thames & Hudson, London, 1998.

Robert, Irwin: *Islamic Art in Context: Art, Architecture and the Literary World,* Harry N. Abrams, New York, 1997.

Robert, W.: *Civil Islam: Muslims and Democratization in Indonesia,* Princeton University Press, Princeton, 2000.

Robinson, Francis: *The Cambridge Illustrated History of the Islamic World,* Cambridge University Press, Cambridge, 1999.

Robinson, Neal: *Discovering the Quran: A Contemporary Approach to a Veiled Text,* SCM Press, London, 1996.

Rodinson, Maxime: *Europe and the Mystique of Islam,* I.B. Tauris, London, 2002.

Rosamond, E. M.: *Bazaar to Piazza: Islamic Trade and Italian Art, 1300-1600,* University of California Press, Berkeley, 2001.

Roy, Olivier: *Islam and Resistance in Afghanistan,* Cambridge University Press, Cambridge, 1990.

Saeed, Abdullah: *Islamic Banking and Interest: A Study of the Prohibition of Riba and its Contemporary Interpretation,* E.J. Brill, Leiden, 1997.

Salameh, Khader: *The Qur'an Manuscripts in the Al-Haram Al-Sharif Islamic Museum, Jerusalem,* United Nations Education, Paris, 2001.

Seyyed Hossein N.: *The Philosophy of Mulla Sadra,* State University of New York Press, New York, 1975.

Shaham, Ron: *Family and the Courts in Modern Egypt: A Study Based on Decisions by the Sharia Courts, 1900-1955,* E.J. Brill, Leiden, 1997.

Shaheen, Jack G.: *Reel Bad Arabs: How Hollywood Vilifies a People,* Olive Branch Press, New York, 2001.

Shaikh, Farzana: *Community and Consensus in Islam: Muslim Representation in Colonial India, 1860-1947,* Cambridge University Press, Cambridge, 1989.

Sivan, Emmanuel: *Radical Islam: Medieval Theology and Modern Politics,* Yale University Press, New Haven, 1990.

Soucek, P.P.: *Content and Context of Visual Arts in the Islamic World,* Pennsylvania State University Press, Pennsylvania, 1988.

Spellberg, Denise A.: *Politics, Gender and the Islamic Past: The Legacy of 'A'isha bint Abi Bakr,* Columbia University Press, New York, 1996.

Tazeen, M. M.: *The Sacred and the Secular: Bengal Muslim Discourses, 1871-1977,* Oxford University Press, Calcutta, 1995.

Tessler, Mark: *A History of the Israeli-Palestinian Conflict,* Indiana University Press, Bloomington, 1994.

Tibi, Bassam: *Arab Nationalism: Between Islam and the Nation-State,* Macmillan, New York, 1997.

Toby, E. H.: *The Rise of Early Modern Science: Islam, China and the West,* Cambridge University Press, Cambridge, 1995.

Trimingham, J.S.: *Islam in West Africa,* Clarendon Press, Oxford, 1959.

Trimingham, Spencer, J.: *The Sufi Orders in Islam,* Clarendon Press, Oxford, 1971.

Tucker, Judith E.: *Women in Nineteenth Century Egypt,* Cambridge University Press, Cambridge, 2002.

Uslu, I.: *The Environmental Problems: From Transformation in the Conception of Cosmos to the Ecological Catastrophe,* Insan Press, Istanbul, 1995.

Uwaysi, Abd al-Fattah Muhammad: *The Muslim Brothers and the Palestine Question, 1928-1947,* Tauris Academic Studies, London, 1998.

Vassiliev, Alexei: *The History of Saudi Arabia,* New York University Press, New York, 2000.

Vatikiotis, P.J.: *Islam and the State,* Croom Helm, London, 1987.

Victoria, Finlay: *Faith in Conservation: New Approaches to Religions and the Environment,* World Bank Publications, Washington, 2003.

Villalón, Leonardo A.: *Islamic Society and State Power in Senegal,* Cambridge Cambridge University Press, Cambridge, 1995.

Viorst, Milton: *In the Shadow of the Prophet: The Struggle for the Soul of Islam,* Anchor Books, New York, 1998.

Von Grunebaum, G.E.: *Classical Islam: A History, 600-1258,* George Allen & Unwin, London, 1970.

Waines, David: *An Introduction to Islam,* Cambridge University Press, Cambridge, 1995.

Wansbrough, John: *Quranic Studies: Sources and Methods of Scriptural Interpretation,* Cambridge University Press, Cambridge, 1977.

Ward, Rachel: *Islamic Metalwork,* Thames & Hudson, London, 1993.

Watt, William Montgomery: *Muhammad at Mecca,* Clarendon Press, Oxford, 1953.

William, Montgomery: *Islamic Philosophy and Theology: An Extended Survey,* Edinburgh University Press, Edinburgh, 1985.

Yamani, Mai: *Feminism and Islam: Legal and Literary Perspectives,* New York University Press, New York, 1996.

Yasser, T.: *The Transformation of Islamic Art during the Sunni Revival,* University of Washington Press, Seattle, 2002.

Yemelianova, Galina M.: *Russia and Islam: A Historical Survey*, MacMillan, New York, 2002.

Zafrulla, Muhammad: *Muhammad, Seal of the Prophets,* Viking Press, New York, 1981.

Zaheer, Hasan: *The Separation of East Pakistan: The Rise and Realization of Bengali Muslim Nationalism,* Oxford University Press, Karachi, 1994.

Zaman, Muhammad Qasim: *The Ulama in Contemporary Islam: Custodians of Change,* Princeton University Press, Princeton, 2002.

Index

J

❑❑❑